# BRITISH POLITICAL THOUGHT IN HISTORY, LITERATURE AND THEORY, 1500–1800

The history of British political thought has been one of the most fertile fields of Anglo-American historical writing in the last half-century. David Armitage brings together an interdisciplinary and international team of authors to consider the impact of this scholarship on the study of early modern British history, English literature and political theory. Leading historians survey the impact of the history of political thought on the 'new' histories of Britain and Ireland; eminent literary scholars offer novel critical methods attentive to literary form, genre and language; and distinguished political theorists treat the conceptual and material relationships between history and theory. The outstanding examples of critical practice collected here will encourage the emergence of new research on the historical, critical and theoretical study of the English-speaking world in the period *c.* 1500–1800. This volume celebrates the contribution of the Folger Institute to British studies over many years.

DAVID ARMITAGE is Professor of History at Harvard University. He is the author of *The Ideological Origins of the British Empire* (2000), *Greater Britain, 1516–1776: Essays in Atlantic History* (2004), and *The Declaration of Independence: A Global History* (2006), and editor of *Bolingbroke: Political Writings* for Cambridge Texts in the History of Political Thought (1997), *Theories of Empire, 1450–1800* (1998), and *Hugo Grotius: The Free Sea* (2004). He is also co-editor of *Milton and Republicanism* (with Armand Himy and Quentin Skinner, 1995) and *The British Atlantic World, 1500–1800* (with Michael J. Braddick, 2002).

T0384811

# BRITISH POLITICAL THOUGHT IN HISTORY, LITERATURE AND THEORY, 1500—1800

EDITED BY

## DAVID ARMITAGE

*Department of History, Harvard University*

Published in association with the
Folger Institute, Washington, DC

 CAMBRIDGE
UNIVERSITY PRESS

CAMBRIDGE UNIVERSITY PRESS
Cambridge, New York, Melbourne, Madrid, Cape Town, Singapore,
São Paulo, Delhi, Dubai, Tokyo

Cambridge University Press
The Edinburgh Building, Cambridge CB2 8RU, UK

Published in the United States of America by Cambridge University Press, New York

www.cambridge.org
Information on this title: www.cambridge.org/9780521130851

First published 2006
This digitally printed version 2010

*A catalogue record for this publication is available from the British Library*

*Library of Congress Cataloguing in Publication data*

British political thought in history, literature and theory, 1500-1800 / edited by
David Armitage.
p. cm.
Includes bibliographical references and index.
ISBN-13: 978-0-521-87041-2 (hardback)
ISBN-10: 0-521-87041-0 (hardback)
1. Political science–Great Britain–History. 2. Great Britain–Politics and government.
3. Politics in literature. I. Armitage, David, 1965- II. Title.

JN175.B75 2006
320.0941´0903–dc22
2006020043

ISBN 978-0-521-87041-2 Hardback
ISBN 978-0-521-13085-1 Paperback

# Contents

# Acknowledgements

Earlier versions of most of the papers collected in this volume were presented at the conference 'British Political Thought in History, Literature and Theory', held at the Folger Shakespeare Library in Washington, DC, in April 2005. The conference was planned by the Steering Committee of the Center for the History of British Political Thought: John Pocock, Kathleen Lynch, Linda Levy Peck, Gordon Schochet and myself. The event would not have been possible without the support of the Folger Institute or the invaluable work of Kathleen Lynch, Owen Williams, Virginia Millington and Carol Brobeck. That a volume of chapters has emerged so quickly is in large part due to the help and encouragement offered by the Steering Committee, not least by its long-serving former member, Lois Schwoerer, but especially by its chair, John Pocock. It is also thanks to the exceptional research assistance of Paul B. Davis and to the support of the Humanities Research Centre at the Australian National University. The confidence and enthusiasm of Richard Fisher on behalf of Cambridge University Press have been invaluable throughout. Finally, I am particularly grateful to the contributors for the efficiency and cheerfulness with which they undertook revisions under tight deadlines: they have amply proved that the history of British political thought is among the most cooperative and collegial of all fields of study.

# Notes on Contributors

DAVID ARMITAGE is Professor of History at Harvard University. Among his publications are *Milton and Republicanism* (co-editor, 1995), *The Ideological Origins of the British Empire* (2000) and *The Declaration of Independence: A Global History* (2006). He is now working on a study of the foundations of modern international thought and editing John Locke's colonial writings.

NICHOLAS CANNY, MRIA, FBA, is Professor of History and Director of the Research Institute in the Humanities and Social Studies at the National University of Ireland, Galway. Among his publications are *The Elizabethan Conquest of Ireland: A Pattern Established, 1565–1576* (1976), *The Oxford History of the British Empire*, volume 1: *The Origins of Empire* (editor, 1998) and *Making Ireland British, 1580–1650* (2001). He is currently working on a study of Europe and its expanding world, 1450–1700, and editing Edmund Spenser's *View of the Present State of Ireland*.

RICHARD E. FLATHMAN is George Armstrong Kelly Professor of Political Science at The Johns Hopkins University. Among his publications are *Thomas Hobbes: Skepticism, Individuality, and Chastened Politics* (2nd edition, 2003), *Reflections of a Would-be Anarchist* (1998) and *Pluralism and Liberal Democracy* (2005).

ANDREW HADFIELD is Professor of English at the University of Sussex. Among his publications are *Shakespeare, Spenser and the Matter of Britain* (2003), *Shakespeare and Republicanism* (2005) and *The Oxford History of the Irish Book*, Vol. 3: *The Irish Book in English, 1550–1800* (co-editor, 2005). He is now working on a biography of Edmund Spenser.

TIM HARRIS is Monro–Goodwin–Wilkinson Professor in European History at Brown University. Among his publications are *Politics under the Later Stuarts* (1993), *Restoration: Charles II and His Kingdoms, 1660–1685* (2005) and *Revolution: The Great Crisis of the British Monarchy, 1685–1720* (2006). He is now working on a 'prequel' to *Restoration* and *Revolution* and on a study of prejudice in early-modern England.

JEAN E. HOWARD is William B. Ransford Professor of English and Comparative Literature at Columbia University. Among her publications are *Shakespeare's Art of Orchestration* (1984), *The Stage and Social Struggle in Early Modern England* (1994) and *Engendering a Nation: A Feminist Account of Shakespeare's English Histories* (co-author, 1997). Her next book will be a study of the relationship of London comedies to the changing nature of the city, 1598–1642.

DUNCAN IVISON is Associate Professor of Political Science at the University of Toronto and of Philosophy at the University of Sydney. Among his publications are *The Self at Liberty: Political Argument and the Arts of Government* (1997), *Political Theory and the Rights of Indigenous Peoples* (co-editor, 2000) and *Postcolonial Liberalism* (2002).

COLIN KIDD is Professor of Modern History at the University of Glasgow and Fellow of All Souls College, Oxford. He is the author of *Subverting Scotland's Past* (1993), *British Identities before Nationalism* (1999) and *The Forging of Races: Race and Scripture in the Protestant Atlantic World, 1600–2000* (2006).

KIRSTIE M. MCCLURE is Associate Professor of Political Science and English at the University of California Los Angeles. Among her publications are *Judging Rights: Lockean Politics and the Limits of Consent* (1996) and *Feminist Perspectives on John Locke* (co-editor, forthcoming).

JOHN MORRILL, FBA, is Professor of British and Irish History at the University of Cambridge. Among his publications are *The Nature of the English Revolution* (1993), *The British Problem, c. 1534–1707* (co-editor, 1996) and *'Uneasy Lies the Head that Wears a Crown': Dynastic Crises in Tudor and Stewart Britain and Ireland, 1504–1746* (2005). He is now working on a study to be entitled *Living with Revolution in Seventeenth-century Britain and Ireland.*

KAREN O'BRIEN is Professor of English Literature at the University of Warwick. Among her publications are *Narratives of Enlightenment: Cosmopolitan History from Voltaire to Gibbon* (1997), 'Poetry against

Empire: Milton to Shelley', in *Proceedings of the British Academy* (2002) and *Feminist Debate in Eighteenth-Century Britain* (forthcoming).

J. G. A. POCOCK is Harry C. Black Professor of History Emeritus at The Johns Hopkins University. Among his publications are *The Varieties of British Political Thought, 1500–1800* (co-editor, 1993), *The Discovery of Islands: Essays in British History* (2005) and *Barbarism and Religion*, 4 volumes to date (1999–2006).

GORDON SCHOCHET is Professor of Political Science at Rutgers University. Among his publications are *Patriarchalism in Political Thought* (1975), *Proceedings of the Folger Institute Center for the History British Political Thought*, 6 volumes (co-editor, 1999–2003) and *Rights in Context* (forthcoming). He is now working on political Hebraism in early-modern Europe.

LOIS G. SCHWOERER is Elmer Louis Kayser Professor of History Emeritus at The George Washington University. Among her publications are *The Declaration of Rights, 1689* (1981), *The Revolution of 1688–1689: Changing Perspectives* (editor, 1992) and *The Ingenious Mr. Henry Care: Restoration Publicist* (2002). She is now working on a study of guns and civilians in Tudor-Stuart England.

QUENTIN SKINNER, FBA, is the Regius Professor of Modern History at the University of Cambridge and a Fellow of Christ's College, Cambridge. Among his publications are *The Foundations of Modern Political Thought*, 2 volumes (1978), *Reason and Rhetoric in the Philosophy of Hobbes* (1996) and *Visions of Politics*, 3 volumes (2002).

JOANNE H. WRIGHT is Assistant Professor of Political Science at the University of New Brunswick. She is the author of *Origin Stories in Political Thought: Discourses on Gender, Power and Citizenship* (2004). She is now working on a study of John Locke's midwifery notes.

STEVEN N. ZWICKER is Stanley Elkin Professor in the Humanities at Washington University. Among his publications are *Lines of Authority: Politics and English Literary Culture, 1649–1689* (1993), *Reading, Society and Politics in Early Modern England* (co-editor, 2003) and *The Cambridge Companion to John Dryden* (editor, 2004).

# Introduction

## David Armitage

The field of research and teaching known as the history of British political thought has been one of the most fertile areas in anglophone historical scholarship of the last half-century. Its practitioners can be found in universities across the English-speaking world and increasingly beyond it as well. Their writings have provided prescriptions of method as well as models of practice for students of political thought working in other languages and on other political traditions, even those which were founded on different philosophical principles and which have developed along quite distinct historical trajectories.[1] Over the past fifty years, students of British political thought have mapped its contours from the late fifteenth century to the early nineteenth century.[2] In this enterprise, the term 'British' has been construed ever more broadly, to encompass the political reflections of any of the inhabitants of Britain and Ireland, of the migrants who left those islands, and of their descendants who settled around the globe. The history of British political thought is therefore becoming an enterprise almost as expansive in its subject-matter as it has been in its international impact.

For the last twenty years, the study of this history has been associated particularly with the Center for the History of British Political Thought at the Folger Shakespeare Library in Washington, DC. The Center was founded by J. G. A. Pocock and Gordon Schochet in 1985. In that year, Pocock laid out a vision for its work in a manifesto that was generous geographically, generically and methodologically: 'The "great texts" of English, Scottish, and American political thought are secure in their places within our program, but at the same time the "history of political thought" we seek is a history of language, literature, publication,

---

[1] Castiglione and Hampsher-Monk 2001.  [2] Pocock, Schochet and Schwoerer 1993.

and audience. It embraces the ephemeral tracts and pamphlets as well as the great texts.'[3] Since 1985, the Center has pursued this vision through over thirty seminars and conferences out of which more than fifteen books as well as numerous articles and essays have emerged.[4] The Center's twentieth anniversary in 2005 offered an occasion to review the field's achievements and its prospects from the perspective of the three disciplines where its work has so far had its greatest uptake: history, English literature and political theory. The chapters in this volume arose from that occasion but all aim to transcend a specific moment to reflect more broadly on the disciplinary dialogues that have so far shaped the history of British political thought and that will continue to inform it in future.

The last two decades have witnessed changes in the arguments within academic fields as great as the shifts in the relations among them. For example, at the moment of the Center's founding, the 'linguistic turn' was still a relatively novel (and, for some, anxiety-provoking) move for historians to undertake.[5] Twenty years later, most historians, especially those who term their interests cultural, social or intellectual history, have absorbed its lessons and can wield its tools without undue anxiety in their search for the meanings of past utterances, acts and events. Similarly, literary scholars who were taking up embattled positions during the so-called 'Theory Wars' of the mid-1980s have now moved on to calmer debates in a period self-consciously described as 'after Theory'.[6] The so-called 'New' Historicism is no longer quite so new and has become a familiar resource for scholars across a wide range of literatures.[7] Moreover, in the same period, the social sciences have become more hospitable to interpretive and hermeneutic approaches which complement, but more often counter, positivist models of research.[8] Historians have thus become more alert to questions of language and meaning at a time when scholars of literature have been more eager to write historically and when at least some social scientists have returned to history and to hermeneutics. Such a moment of convergences across

---

[3] Pocock 1985a, p. 284.
[4] Schochet, Tatspaugh and Brobeck 1990–93; Peck 1991; Schwoerer 1992; Pocock, Schochet and Schwoerer 1993; Mason 1994a; Robertson 1995a; Burgess 1996; Smith 1998a; Morgan 1999a; Connolly 2000; Ohlmeyer 2000; Mendle 2001.
[5] Jay 1982; Toews 1987; Pagden 1987b.
[6] Kastan 1999.
[7] Gallagher and Greenblatt 2000.
[8] Skinner 1985; Winch 1990; Scott and Keates 2001.

disciplinary boundaries bodes well for the future of collaborative work in interdisciplinary fields such as the history of British political thought.

Many of the individual chapters in the volume engage directly with these broad disciplinary developments; taken together, they offer an array of models and methods for the future history of British political thought. Though they are collected in sections that acknowledge the primary disciplinary affiliations of their authors, they all address matters of common concern to students of British political thought. As J. G. A. Pocock, Gordon Schochet and Lois Schwoerer point out in their opening overview, the history of British political thought as it has been practised at the Folger Center and elsewhere arose originally from the concerns of historians but over the past half-century it has been in constant (if not always mutually comprehending) conversation with political theory and it has drawn increasingly on the methods of literary scholarship. It has done so within a broad but bounded chronology running from the decades before the Reformation to the generations after the French Revolution. That both these sets of events were pan-European in scope indicates the ample geography within which the field has developed. A series of exploratory workshops held at the Center in recent years on the networks of political exchange between Britain and Ireland on the one hand and continental Europe on the other has traced that geography; future efforts in this direction may expand the geography yet further. Studies will soon appear of British political thought in predominantly non-anglophone areas (such as South Asia).[9] Students of British political thought are thus testing the manifold possibilities for globalizing their subject, just as other intellectual historians are beginning to do.[10]

For the moment, though, historians of British political thought continue to pursue their work mostly within the lines set by the historiographies of early-modern Britain and Ireland. The four chapters by John Morrill, Colin Kidd, Nicholas Canny and Tim Harris each test the limits of historiographical models for understanding the thought and actions of historical agents, especially those in the sixteenth and seventeenth centuries. Morrill's survey of recent developments in what was once called the 'New' British history offers an array of possible

[9] For example, Travers forthcoming.
[10] Bayly 2004, chs. 3, 6, 8; compare Schneewind 2005; Megill 2005; Armitage 2006; and Ivison, in this volume.

approaches, most of which he sees as 'reproduc[ing] distinctive frameworks of reference that can be found in the history itself', such as those
he terms 'incorporative', 'federal' and 'perfect', according to the differing
conceptions of political union debated during the seventeenth century.
If Morrill is somewhat sceptical about much of the history that has
been written within such frameworks, Colin Kidd has another solution
to offer from within the period itself. He avoids the twin dangers
of retrospection and teleology by focusing on what contemporaries
themselves would have described as *British* political thought: that is,
the so-called 'matter of Britain', 'a distinctive and long-running genre
of political argument which debated the location of authority within
the island of Britain, or sometimes the British Isles'. Kidd argues that
attention to the matter of Britain demands interdisciplinary work but
not necessarily the kind that arises when current disciplines adopt one
another's questions and procedures. Serious students of early-modern
conceptions of the matter of Britain may need to be equipped with
a working knowledge of ecclesiology, feudal jurisprudence and heraldry
but will be ill-furnished if they borrow tools too readily from toilers in
other fields such as political theory.

The place of Ireland and Scotland within the matter of Britain was as
vexed a question for contemporaries as it has proved to be for those who
study their history. Nicholas Canny's chapter makes this point especially
clearly. If *British* political thought is taken as the norm, political thinking conducted within (and about) Ireland comes to seem increasingly
anomalous between the mid-sixteenth and the mid-seventeenth centuries:
in the earlier period, 'political discourse in Ireland . . . was but a provincial
echo of political culture in Britain' but 'that which flourished there
a century later was radically different from British norms both in form
and in ambition'. However, if placed in the broader context of pan-
European political and religious thought, the course of Irish political
thinking becomes more comprehensible, not least because Irish political
actors were consciously engaged in cosmopolitan conversations that
were not confined to Britain and Ireland alone.

As the example of Ireland shows, historians of political thought
must accommodate the scope of their inquiries to the scale at which their
subjects conducted their arguments, whether that was local, regional,
national or transnational. This question of scale is also the problem
Tim Harris confronts in his chapter through an examination of political
thinking in Britain and Ireland between the Exclusion Crisis of the late
1670s and the immediate aftermath of the Glorious Revolution in the

early 1690s. Like Kidd, he argues that the questions asked of the past largely determine the answers that come back in return. The 'Britannic turn' in early-modern historiography will only provide adequate answers to questions contemporaries themselves viewed in the terms of the Three Kingdoms of Britain and Ireland; such a perspective can reveal patterns otherwise hidden to historians who frame their inquiries nationally but, equally, in many cases the national scale may be a more appropriate level at which to work. 'Depending on the questions we ask,' Harris concludes, 'sometimes the Three-Kingdoms perspective is going to come into sharp focus, at other times the national (or local, or continental) will.'

Scholars of early-modern literature have not confronted such matters of the appropriate geographical scale for their research, at least until recently.[11] For many purposes, they have not needed to, because nationally-defined canons of literature have been investigated and interpreted within frameworks of genre, trope, technique and form that have rarely been circumscribed by specific national contexts. Andrew Hadfield's study of republicanism in early-modern English (meaning 'English-language') literature illustrates this point well. He firmly reminds those historians and political theorists who have been interested in recovering the heritage of republicanism that, for most English writers of the sixteenth and seventeenth centuries, republicanism was neither an autonomous political language nor a practical political programme but rather 'a literary phenomenon ... because it consisted of a series of stories', such as the rape of Lucretia, the assassination of Julius Caesar and the rise of Augustus.

All these republican narratives found their way into the work of William Shakespeare, of course, but that does not mean that we should therefore deem him a 'republican writer'. As Jean Howard shows in her chapter, the dramas which made up the bulk of Shakespeare's oeuvre did not 'elaborate a consistent political position'. Indeed, the very fact that many of the techniques of early-modern English drama used dramaturgical principles inherited from the morality plays and were also closely akin to the widely-shared Renaissance rhetorical procedure of arguing *in utramque partem* (on both sides of a question) meant that Shakespeare's plays could only be vehicles for testing political thinking through what Howard calls 'embodied representation'. Embodying ideas

---

[11] E.g., Baker and Maley 2002.

in this way could also have radical implications, as when persons who may generally have lacked political agency within their own society were represented on stage as taking political initiatives, as in *The First Part of the Contention* (2 *Henry VI*). However, such representations do not allow us to call Shakespeare a 'democratic' writer, any more than *Henry V* made him an aggressive monarchist, for example.

Historians who study British political thought may also need to be reminded that texts not usually canonized as literary may nonetheless deploy literary techniques. That is the central message of Steven Zwicker's chapter on the overlapping literary strategies of irony, disguise and deceit found in a wide array of texts including the pungent histories of Tacitus, the elusive poetry of Dryden and the comic drama of Congreve. He argues that historians, interested as they mostly are in discursive and argumentative works, have tended to study the 'horizontal dimension' at the expense of the 'vertical dimension of political languages, their performance at specific moments and under particular strain'. One might restate this by saying that historians of all kinds, and not just historians of political thought, are generally more concerned with the diachronic than with the synchronic dimensions of their subjects. Zwicker argues that greater patience with the seeming instability of literary language and genre can reveal that vertical, synchronic, dimension usually hidden to history.

Conversely, it might seem, Karen O'Brien argues in her study of ideas of imperial liberty and benevolence in the poetry of the long eighteenth century, the diachronic study of literary texts (particularly poetry) may itself uncover not just forms of political thinking but even novel political thoughts that conventional materials of historical research do not contain. She proposes that such ideas emerged from an 'inter-generic conversation' in which poets sometimes took the lead. In particular, she shows that conceptions of imperial trusteeship and benevolence, especially as directed towards indigenous peoples around the globe, can be found earlier in the poetry than in the formal prose or much of the political practice of the period. In light of this, historians may need to follow her advice to seek new archives (such as those comprising poetry), while also heeding Zwicker's counsel to be more aware of – and even to revel in – the very literariness of the materials that make up the richest of those archives.

As we have seen, the diachronic and the synchronic dimensions of political thinking have parallels in differing geographical scales (local or national, national or transnational) on which the history of British political thought might be conducted. At the risk of inducing intellectual vertigo, we might add to these intersecting dimensions those of political thought as past action and political theory as a present resource. Here we enter the domain of our third and last suite of chapters, those by students of political theory. Duncan Ivison's experiment in globalizing the history of political thought picks up where Karen O'Brien's study of imperial benevolence leaves off, by implicitly treating the question why such benevolence might have been necessary at all, and what part a seemingly benign language, such as that of subjective (or individual) rights, played in the malevolent spread of empire around the globe. By placing one specifically British manifestation of that language – John Locke's – into histories at once local to the early-modern period and global in extent, Ivison shows that 'history provides a critical resource for surveying the uses of various concepts and theories over time, and especially the conflicts and choices that were made around the concepts and values we now take for granted', such as rights themselves.

A similar concept that can likewise be taken for granted is the separation between public and private on which our conception of rights largely depends. Joanne Wright's chapter shows how misleading it would be – both historically and conceptually – to read back contemporary distinctions between public and private into the past. As Wright acknowledges, the impetus behind inquiries into historical conceptions of the public and the private arose initially from late twentieth-century feminist theory: without present pressures, then, we would not be animated by study past problems. However, as many other chapters in the volume illustrate, the shape and scale of current concerns can only be imposed on the past at the cost of misunderstanding, at best, and conceptual violence, at worst. Yet the gulf between past and present is not unbridgeable. In the case of a writer as acute as Margaret Cavendish, Duchess of Newcastle, the distance between her concerns and ours can in fact be theoretically salutary: 'we neither share her precise concerns, nor see public and private from her perspective, but her language is not so different from our own that we cannot gain some insight from her analysis'. The fact that Wright's prime example of this is drawn from a literary work – Cavendish's closet-drama, *The Convent of Pleasure* – only affirms the interdisciplinary implications of such an insight.

The gulf between past and present is spanned historically by the transmission of texts and hermeneutically by the analysis of those texts: or, so our last two chapters, by Kirstie McClure and Richard Flathman, lead us to conclude. McClure consciously draws methodological inspiration from literary theory (in particular, the work of Mikhail Bakhtin on 'speech-genres') and from cultural historians who have investigated the material transmission of texts to investigate the manifold meanings accumulated, and sometimes shed, by texts as they travel through many hands across time and space. Meaning, she argues, cannot be divorced from form, especially the material form in which ideas are transmitted. Every reader selects and recombines the apparent (and not so apparent) meanings within a specific text; however, some readers have more power to affect meaning by virtue of their roles as editors, annotators, excerpters or anthologists. The works that make up pillars of the canon, among intellectual historians and political theorists (and, we should add, among literary scholars), are not quite as solid and imposing as they might seem, at least if our aim is to comprehend the full range of meanings they have acquired over time. Examples like the *Vindiciae Contra Tyrannos*, John Locke's *Two Treatises* and Edmund Burke's *Vindication of Natural Society* amply affirm a point that could be made with a host of other works: 'To the extent that political theorizing consists in offering not simply a perspective on the political world but also an orientation to action within it, its containment within conventional genre distinctions looks more like a matter of academic convenience than a characteristic of historical expressions'.

The question of what might count within political theory as either 'orientation[s] to action' or 'historical expressions', and what might be the relation between the two, is the subject of Richard Flathman's concluding chapter. Just as the volume begins with an historian's scepticism about historical categories, in John Morrill's chapter, so it ends with a political theorist's doubts concerning history's relevance for the manifold possibilities for studying and writing political thought. Precisely because past utterances were so varied in their forms, and also because present concerns will differ from theorist to theorist and from context to context, Flathman does not find it possible — let alone necessary — to choose between what he calls 'the canonical and conceptual conceptions of the study/writing of political thought'. Either will have its value, but only depending upon the question at hand to be studied or the problem to be resolved. Often we may not need to make the choice because more than one possibility will have to be in play simultaneously. In such cases we will find ourselves, in the teasing words of Ludwig Wittgenstein, 'between the games' of different disciplines.

Quentin Skinner reminds us in his Afterword that the study of past thought never ceases to reveal aspects of our own ways of thinking that might otherwise remain obscure to us: 'As our world revolves, it catches light from the past in ever-changing ways'. Conversely, we might recall that because the objects from the past that we study are themselves multifaceted we may only be able to examine one of their faces while simultaneously obscuring others from our view. To comprehend all the features of complex forms, like those of political thought, demands that we adopt multiple perspectives upon them. But we can only do this in collaboration with others who view those same objects in rather different lights. The chapters in this volume have been written in just such a spirit, to open up new perspectives on the multiple histories that might yet be written of British political thought.

# CHAPTER I

# The History of British Political Thought: A Field and its Futures

*J. G. A. Pocock, Gordon Schochet and Lois G. Schwoerer*

The 'history of British political thought' as a field of research has its own history which is now more than half a century old. Two impulses drove its early development. The first, British in origin, arose from the work of scholars active at Cambridge University since about 1950: among them Peter Laslett, J. G. A. Pocock, J. H. M. Salmon, Quentin Skinner, John Dunn, Gordon Schochet and others too numerous to list, to whom the term 'Cambridge School' has been applied. The other, American in origin, arose from the work of Caroline Robbins, Douglass Adair, Bernard Bailyn and their associates who explored English and British political thought in the late-seventeenth and eighteenth centuries – notably the 'commonwealth' critique of the Hanoverian regime – so as to lead towards American rebellion and independence, republicanism and federalism.[1] These two impulses have continued to operate within the history of British political thought and have served largely to shape the problems it has encountered and discovered.

'The Cambridge method', as it has become known, consists in the assignment of texts to their contexts. These 'contexts' are of many kinds and need to be carefully defined, but if one is the context of historical and political circumstances, another is the context of political language. In early-modern England, Britain and Europe, 'political thought' was expressed (a) in Latin and in a number of vernaculars; (b) in a diversity of specialized discourses constructed by distinct if intersecting clerisies, among whom ecclesiastics, jurists and humanists may serve as an initial classification; and (c), in England at least, in an imperfectly controlled print culture, where 'broadsides', which are ephemeral and usually directed to the less learned, contributed significantly to the context of political language. Since the beginning of the Cambridge enterprise,

---

[1] Robbins 1959; Bailyn 1967; Adair 1974.

it has been important to determine not only in what circumstances and with what intentions a given author wrote, but also in terms of what 'language' he (if male) chose to conduct his argument; cases are on record where authors were offered a choice of languages and knew what choices they were taking.

The work of historians of British political thought has therefore consisted largely in discovering the 'languages' in which that thought was from time to time conducted and in tracing their histories, particularly within the period from roughly 1500 to 1800 which might be defined as early-modern.[2] There has been a consequence. The 'thought' of a given author, whether he were polemicist or philosopher, has been increasingly presented as a series of speech acts performed in linguistic and circumstantial contexts, which revealed his intentions and set limits to his ability to perform them, but which may also be used by a historian to recover what they were.

However, this tendency to contextualize may have widened the gap which has long been opening between 'the history of political thought' and 'political theory'. The historian is interested in what the author meant to say, succeeded in saying, and was understood to have said, in a succession of historical contexts now distant in time. The theorist wishes to use the author's text in contexts set by the theorist's own enterprise of enquiry, which has no guaranteed identity with the enterprise the author was pursuing. Though the theorist is not a historian, the activity in which he or she is engaged has been going on a long time and has a history which the theorist may need to reconstitute, but will do so in terms set by the theoretical enterprise. These terms will not be those the historian of political thought will use in reconstituting a history of language and discourse. Of the three authors of this chapter, one has been both political scientist and historian in his day, one continues to teach political theory in a department of political science and the third has spent her whole working life as an historian. None expects to see a time when the two disciplines will not find it easy to fall into misunderstandings.

There are signs that the old canon-based 'history of political thought' — formed by selecting great texts and drawing lines to connect them — may be coming back into fashion. However, the canon constructed by political theorists will never look quite the same as the canon

---

[2] Schochet, Tatspaugh and Brobeck 1990–93; Pocock, Schochet and Schwoerer 1993.

recognized by historians of political thought. There are reasons at once generic, chronological and even geographical for this failure to converge. Historians of political thought will insist that the work of political theorists said to be of canonical importance looks somewhat different when read in the context of more popular and vernacular literature, as in the case of Milton's prose works and poetry and the ephemera that poured from the presses in the 1640s.[3] Or Hobbes's *Leviathan* may be juxtaposed with the literature of the controversies over *de facto* authority and allegiance.[4] Comparisons of the languages of these two genres hold their own fascination and illumination, both historical and (we should insist) theoretical, but such studies of genre continue to be largely the work of historians rather than of political theorists.

As the examples of Milton and Hobbes indicate, what we have here called 'Cambridge' scholarship has tended to focus on the period of Renaissance, Reformation and English civil wars. It may be at some risk of becoming a research project limited to the cultural conditions then obtaining. Closer to the concerns of the early-modern historian and scholar, it has not proved easy to advance beyond the age of Hobbes and Locke into the huge changes that came over English, Scottish and American political thought between the revolutions of 1688–1689 and 1776, despite the inspirational part (already noted) that studies of the latter crisis played in the field half a century ago. We might still ask what would happen if it were carried beyond the age of the early-modern clerisies and their print culture, into the nineteenth century or the twentieth. Illuminating findings would surely emerge, but even they would only partly close the gap between the historians of political thought and their neighbours, the political theorists, whose canon extends from Plato (though rarely before) to Rawls (and occasionally after).

There have also been geographical boundaries to much of the history of British political thought as it has been generally practised. Its work has been largely coincident with the ambit of the field once called the 'new' British history – that is, the Three Kingdoms of England, Scotland and Ireland and their extensions into the Atlantic world – whose own history of research and teaching now extends back over thirty years.[5] A central problem raised by the coincidence of these fields is the

---

[3] Armitage, Himy and Skinner 1995.    [4] Wallace 1968; Skinner 2002c, pp. 287–307.
[5] Pocock 1974; Pocock 2005.

question: In what sense is it possible to speak of '*British* political thought'? Is this simply a portmanteau term, denoting whatever political literature may have taken shape in any of the cultures contained by 'British history'? Does it denote their aggregate or rather their inter-actions? Is there a time — probably modern rather than early-modern — when there is the political thought of a self-aware and self-perpetuating 'British' community, or does it remain a conversation as to how and how far such a community does or should exist? These are questions only a programme of enquiry extended beyond the late eighteenth century can hope to resolve. They are also questions few political theorists are likely to attempt to answer, or even to be impelled to ask, even when studying the canonical texts of early-modern British political thought. There is little sign that Thomas Hobbes knew Leviathan had three kingdoms to deal with, though James Harrington clearly did. English political thought thus goes on being about England and English history, even when it is about Britain. This Anglocentricity cannot be eliminated; it is part of the history we are seeking to understand.

The history of British political thought has perhaps diverged farthest from the concerns of the canonical political theorists in its investi-gations to date of the political thought of Scotland and Ireland. Yet it is also here that the field has achieved some of its most notable advances. It has established that there is a canon of major Scottish political thinkers, at least from John Mair to James VI, and that a 'history of Scottish political thought' can be perhaps written through the centuries of early-modern history.[6] Questions about the existence of 'British' political thought become vastly more complicated when asked of the kingdom of Ireland during the sixteenth to eighteenth centuries.[7] Here one has to deal with three languages (Gaelic as well as Latin and English), four ethnic groups (after the arrival of Scottish as well as English settlers in Ulster), and above all three churches (those of Rome, England and Scotland). For reasons of which the continued existence of a Catholic majority would appear to be chief, the attempt to organize Ireland as a third kingdom on the Tudor-Stuart model was unsuccessful,[8] and the presence of Ireland within British history is the presence of an antithesis

---

[6] Mason 1994a; Robertson 1995a; Burns 1996; Mason 1998.
[7] Morgan 1999b; Ohlmeyer 2000; Connolly 2000.
[8] Canny 2001.

and paradox: its role in British history is precisely that it refuses to be part of British history. Irish historians rightly look for an Irish history that lies outside British history, and point out that Ireland's Catholicism made it part of the debate within the Catholic world in ways in which the British kingdoms refused to be. All this is true; nevertheless, it can still be said that Irish history cannot be understood without British history or British history without Irish history; and there is besides, especially in the eighteenth century, a Protestant Ireland (perhaps two) whose debates with England and itself are debates over its place in a British world, to the point where settler and indigenous nationalisms begin to converge or merge. There are respects in which eighteenth-century Ireland and America are cases of the same order.

One way to recognize such similarities is to situate England, and the British kingdom after it, in a series of contexts each composed of a society of states – the multiple monarchy of the Three Kingdoms itself, Atlantic and Indian empire, or the European republic of the *ius gentium*, for examples. Richard Tuck and David Armitage are developing a new historical narrative,[9] with Grotius rather than Hobbes as its pivotal figure, which studies thought and discourse less about the internal structure and problems of the political community than about its relations with other states and communities – some of them, in an age of empire, not organized as states at all. This approach is not ideologically neutral; it has to beware of a market-driven post-modernism which denies human autonomy by rendering it contingent, but it is historiographically valuable and promising.

We now need to examine, with reference to different periods, with what centres of cultural production writers in the British Kingdoms exchanged texts and ideas about church, state and history; of what other European political societies they were aware and what they knew about them; of what writers in these societies knew in their turn about them. This is to ask that the idea of 'Europe' be rendered specific instead of being used to deny specificity. It also opens up the field of a European *respublica litterarum* in which political discourse was conducted both nationally and transnationally. It invites attention to how literati responded to war, which was endemic and persistent throughout the period; not surprisingly, Suàrez, Grotius, Pufendorf, and Vattel wrote variously on war and peace, just war theory, the law of nations, the right

---

[9] Tuck 1978; Tuck 1993; Tuck 1999; Armitage 2000; Armitage 2004a.

of self defence, the conduct of war, and what came to be called international law. The idea of 'Europe', like that of 'empire', changed greatly during the eighteenth century. The ways in which it changed will be the source of a valuable inquiry, but one to be conducted both within and well beyond the conventional boundaries assigned to the history of 'British' political thought.[10]

Those boundaries are being further expanded, in rather different directions, by the increasing recognition of a problem of general importance to the historian: that of the literary genres in which the activities termed 'political thought' have been conducted, and of the disciplines by which their history is to be studied. In the last two decades, the study of English literature has been increasingly historicized and has become increasingly aware of its subject's political character and context. The approach assumes no chasm between literature, conventionally understood as poetry, plays and, later, novels, and the 'literature' of political thought. Still, the assumptions and objectives of the two disciplines have not (and should not) become identical, and perhaps this is why the methodologies of the 'Cambridge school' and 'the new historicism' (if this terminology may still be used) have yet to be brought into close confrontation or collaboration. The problem might be approached by stating it as one of genre. The literary forms in which 'political thought' was conducted were typically — or so we have chosen to suppose — the pamphlet, the tract and the treatise, to which documents of a more public character, such as statutes, proclamations, confessions, sermons and articles, must on occasion be added. We enlarge this category by taking account of a print culture in which 'pamphlet' literature at times exploded uncontrollably; the radicalism of the unlicensed press in George Thomason's London is currently out of fashion,[11] but will surely not long remain so.

What may be said of all these literary forms is that they are intensely and immediately disputatious; they rebut the positions of others and expect rebuttal in their turn (even when the anticipation takes the form of censorship and prohibition). If we now turn to the classic categories of 'literature' as an art form — the poem, the play and later the novel — we may find that these are no less political. For example, the plays of Shakespeare are particularly rich explorations of the nature of political

---

[10] Cf. Hay 1968; Pagden 2002.    [11] Reasons for this are explored in Mendle 2001.

power, resistance, counsel and republican thought. Also drenched with political ideas is the poetry of Donne, Milton, Marvell and Dryden. Such literature may even employ the same political languages as the pamphlet, tract and treatise, but the patterns of disputation are not so obvious. It is not impossible to write a poem or play in response to another — are there instances here of counter-rebuttal? — but the patterns of response will be, in every sense, less immediate. It may be that at this point the literary scholar focuses on the 'literary' techniques — irony, narrative, dramatization — to be found in the tract or treatise no less than in the poem or play, and the two disciplines begin to merge in a study of rhetoric. This is a field of methodological enquiry in which a great deal of progress has been made but in which a great deal yet remains to be done.

As we understand that language is conscious art as well as political message, found equally in the tract, the poem and the play, there appears the possibility of material arts conveying such messages by means that are not verbal at all, though they may be converted into discourse. This approach assumes that the object, whatever it may be, is a 'text' situated in a 'context' which is to be read, in ways different from a verbal text, to be sure, but to the same end of discovering meaning. That meaning often includes political ideas and messages, which may be conveyed by tapestry, portrait, sculpture, painting, or architecture. For example, the emblem-panels of Mary Stuart, Queen of Scots, are deeply imbued with political ideas. The portraits of such sixteenth-century figures as Robert Dudley, Earl of Leicester, are also saturated with political meaning. In these cases, however, there remains (as it did in that of poetry) the question of where the conversation initiated by the message is to be found, and how we are to validate the statements we make about it. It would seem that we need to retain the presence of highly organized speech, writing and typography, capable of both criticism and disputation, if we are to have histories of intellectual activity at all. It is at this point that historians of British political thought may use the perspective and methodology of cultural historians to enhance understanding of intellectual history, and vice versa.

Law, both as a means of maintaining social and political order and as a vehicle that carries political values and represents the polity, was a hallmark of politics in the early-modern period. England and then Britain was transformed from a polity in which the humanistic perspective of counsellors was gradually replaced by the more specifically lawyerly understandings of politics that went back at least to Fortescue in the fifteenth century. The growing domination of politics by lawyers led to an increasing tendency to look to the law and its principles to solve political problems. That was the peculiarly English common law, an historically rooted, evolving, and unmodified mixture of legislation, practice, and judicial interpretation. This common law, as the embodiment of the historical wisdom and constitutional practice of England, with the natural rights of liberty and property that were already part of the English constitution, was asserted time and again as the nation's primary defence against what were seen as governmental and especially monarchical excesses. Once an issue between the crown and the nobility, by the late sixteenth century, conflicts about the proper reach of political power were between the crown and its supporters and parliament, the latter increasingly seeing itself as the representative of the 'people'. 'The law' and its history thus run unbroken through the history of early-modern British political thought; but as important as it was, the law alone was incapable of resolving constitutional conflicts about the nature of political power, for those conflicts often called in question the very possession of the law and the legitimate ability to interpret it.

Study of the law as central to early-modernity long preceded (and in part inspired) the history of British political thought as a field. Other major fields of inquiry have grown up alongside and in tandem with this field, perhaps most fruitful among them the history of women and gender. An enormous amount of work has been done in the last decade by feminist historians and literature specialists in identifying early-modern European and English women political thinkers, uncovering their writings (much of it still in manuscript form), presenting their views and assessing their significance. At a level of theory, we have begun looking beyond what women had to say about the distinction between private and public, which is central to the political theory of gender throughout most of its history. In fact women wrote in sophisticated and complex terms about the political issues that pervaded the early-modern era, such as the separation of church and state, toleration, different constitutional forms and the contract theory of government.[12] In the historical narrative, a sequence of phenomena seems to be emerging throughout the era. One rich and well-documented debate is about queenship, imposed upon the English and Scottish monarchies during the half-century when the reigns of a series of female sovereigns gave

[12] Smith 1998a.

rise to the derogatory phrase 'the monstrous regiment of women'. Elizabeth's reign is evaluated, as it was by contemporaries, in these terms, and it can be asked whether the restoration of masculine rule by James VI and I returned either monarchy to what it had previously been.[13]

There were, moreover, the women prophets of the English Interregnum, whose history carries on into that of Quakerism,[14] and after them the remarkable group of philosophers — Anne Conway, Mary Astell, Damaris Cudworth Masham — whose Platonism and anti-Platonism bear on the changing relations of church and state at the end of the seventeenth century.[15] As we move into the politeness and sociability of the eighteenth century, it may be that 'the rise of the social' offered women a new level of visibility, no longer rigidly domestic if it was not yet political;[16] but at the end of the age stands the figure of Mary Wollstonecraft, warning in post-Rousseauean terms that this was not going to be enough.[17] It will be increasingly important to see what happens to the history of political thought when we deepen our attention to what such women had to say within and about it.

The 'Cambridge method' as applied to the various fields we have described does not always lead to the construction of sequential narratives but rather to the recovery of past contexts in which texts are situated and their character or intention and performance reconstructed; to this extent its procedure has been archaeological. Much of the work of historians of British political thought could not unfairly be summarized as the unending pursuit of contexts and texts to place in them, to which no theoretical limit is discerned. This is to enrich the past in its diversity, and to enhance our understanding of an activity, 'political thought', by revealing in how many ways it has been conducted and how many things it has been. But the synchronic needs to point the way into the diachronic, and we should continue to pursue the afterlife of texts: their reception, interpretation, and passage from expressing the intentions of their authors — which they may perpetuate — to articulating the understandings of their readers. It is here that have been built up the more or less mythic histories of 'great texts' and their 'influence' that the 'Cambridge method' came into being to replace; but the creation and persistence of those myths are part of the history we are studying.

The possibility of narrative increases as the history under study becomes less one of acts and more one of 'languages'. The existence

---

[13] McLaren 2000.    [14] Mack 1992.    [15] Broad 2002; Springborg 2005.
[16] Taylor and Knott 2005.    [17] Taylor 2003.

of a 'language of political thought', changing as it is used by authors over time, can in principle be validated, and there comes into view the possibility of a history — going on in how many concurrent contexts? — in which languages change and affect one another, come into use and pass out of it, and it is possible to look through them to the political experience that at least claims to justify them. There should in principle be a subjective history of English or British politics consisting less of what the historian holds to have happened than of what contemporaries thought was happening and how they organized their articulation of experience at various discursive and theoretic levels. Such a history might be followed across the whole early-modern period: what narrative sequence it contained might prove to be a narrative of historical change. The possibility of long-term processes, taking place in a *moyenne durée*, is currently unfashionable but should not be dismissed.

There remains the dwindling but probably not vanishing band of political theorists who make use of historically surviving or reconstituted materials — texts, languages, philosophical positions — in pursuit of investigations of their own, by definition not those of the history but of the 'theorist'. They act in history and should be conscious of doing so; like most actors in history they do not act as historians, but change history by acting upon it in other ways. Since they are aware of history, the investigations of theory they construct will generate histories of their own activity, and will also lead to new reassessments of the history they share with others. Though they will never write histories in the 'Cambridge' manner, it is possible to suppose a philosopher — an Arendt or a Foucault, for example — who changes our perception of history by pointing to changes which 'philosophy' has brought to light, but historians now perceive to be validatable. After some decades practising the history of British political thought, we can report that while this description has become increasingly independent of political theory and philosophy, its relation with these modes of enquiry has been greatly changed and questioned, but has not disappeared.

# PART I

# British Political Thought and History

# CHAPTER 2

# Thinking about the New British History

## John Morrill

I

Almost every historian believes but struggles to prove that knowledge of the past helps us to understand the present. It is so much easier to see how experience of the present helps us to understand the past. It is therefore no surprise that interest in the *British* past as against the *English, Welsh, Scottish* and *Irish* pasts has grown exponentially over the past 25 years. In part this recovery of a sense of the integrity of the 'British', 'British and Irish', 'archipelagic' past (the instability of nomenclature is itself revealing of the contended nature both of the process of recovery and of what is recovered) is the result of the debate that is raging about the *future* shape of the United Kingdom, in the face of devolutionary (and separatist) political and cultural movements in Scotland and Wales (even England), and in the face of uncertainty about the future relationship between the North of Ireland and (a) Britain (b) the Republic of Ireland. In part it is also a result of the soul-searching that has been going on across Britain and Ireland about whether their future destiny lies primarily as part of 'Europe' or in relation to the Anglophone diaspora, not only (or not particularly) the British Commonwealth but in a special relationship with the United States. In part it also results from the natural desire of historians to move on from worked-out seams to open up new ones: for example, from theories of historical causation rooted in the dynamics of class dialectic and conflict to ones based on ethnic and cultural conflict (itself connected with the previous points). And partly it is a result of specific scholars laying down challenges and proposing new conceptual frameworks.

II

The new British history is a growth industry, but it is important to start by noting that the form and content of this history is far from

agreed. Historians, however, merely fall into camps that reproduce
distinctive frameworks of reference that can be found in the history
itself. For the purposes of clarity, I will call these camps the 'incorporative', the 'confederal', the 'perfect', and the 'pontoon-building'
modes of British history.

When James VI of Scotland became King of England and Ireland
in 1603, a great debate broke out about how, how far (and whether) this
union of crowns should be accompanied by a union of the kingdoms.
Elizabeth had successfully banned any public discussion of the nature
of a Scottish succession to the English (and its dependent Irish) titles;
and James had muted public discussion amongst the Scots out of fear
of alienating Elizabeth and endangering his claim.[1] And so we get the
intense debate of the years 1603–1608 about the 'union project'. When
lawyers and clerics came to put their minds to the issue, they could see
there were at least three ways forward.[2]

The first was an incorporative union, such as the Anglo-Welsh Union
of 1536–1543, in which Welsh political, legal, religious and social
institutions were assimilated to English ones. This is the kind of union
that Cromwell achieved by his conquests of Ireland and Scotland,
and which was enshrined in the Protectoral constitution: an enlarged
English Parliament, a London-based policy-making executive, and the
gradual assertion of English legal process and English substantive law
throughout the archipelago.

The second was a federal union, in which each kingdom kept its own
political, legal, religious and social institutions but with a new layer of
'federal' institutions overlaying them. This is what Scottish Covenanters
and (for the most part) Irish Confederates (and Irish royalists) strove
for in the 1640s – legislative and judicial autonomy and mechanisms
(in the case of the Covenanters) for ensuring a British perspective in
foreign policy; and what the Scots achieved in a very different and risky
way in 1707 (legislative incorporation but full protection for the
autonomy of Scottish legal and ecclesiastical institutions).

And the third was a 'perfect union', in which existing institutions were
integrated or superseded by a new purpose-built set designed by James

---

[1] I am grateful to Susan Doran and Alexander Courtney for their discussions of how fragile
James felt his hold on the succession to be in the last ten years of Elizabeth's reign. Their papers
on the subject will hopefully be published in the near future; for now see e.g. Doran and
Richardson 2005.

[2] For these distinctions, see Galloway 1986; Galloway and Levack 1985.

(not so much a new Solomon as a new Solon).[3] This was never again attempted or even envisioned. In broad terms, in 1603—1608 the English wanted the first, the Scots wanted the second and James VI and I wanted the third.

Naturally there were also some intellectually unexciting people who preferred to muddle through; who did not see any reason why a union of the crowns should imply any change in the relations of the kingdoms. This tended to be the English approach to state-building across the century, an unconsidered assertion of their own superiority. It produced some extraordinarily muddled thinking that cost lives. For example, Connor Maguire, second lord Enniskillen, was tried in England for treasons committed in Ireland, but denied trial by his peers, or execution by the axe, because his title was not recognized in England. The story has a gruesome end: 'while he was hanging, an officer cut the rope, letting Maguire drop alive, and commanded the executioner to open him. A struggle between condemned and executioner ensued, and, to spare him, the executioner cut the peer's throat'.[4] More generally, the failure of the English Commonwealth in 1649 or of the Williamite government of 1688—1690 to make any provision for the legitimation of their seizures of power through Irish constitutional forms is striking. At most, these improvised settlements represent an intellectual equivalent to the military expedient of building pontoons when obstacles got in the way of progress.

As it is in history, so it is in historiography. There are incorporative, confederal, perfect and pontoon-building approaches. The incorporative approach is best represented by historians, almost all of them English, who use British history to address problems of English history, producing a form of enriched English history. We need to understand what English relations with Scotland and Ireland contributed to the breakdown of the Stuart polity in 1642 or 1649, for example, but the unit of study remains principally England. Conrad Russell's *The Causes of the English Civil War* (1990) and the more disguised *The Fall of the British Monarchies* (1991) are fully alert to the inter-connectedness of political systems, political cultures and political and religious histories, but for

---

[3] In the fourth of his Trevelyan Lectures in Cambridge in 1994, Conrad Russell argued that in his speech to Parliament on 21 March 1610, this is exactly what James had in mind and that he did speak of himself as a new Solon. It would be a tragedy if these lectures on James and his Parliaments, which Russell had prepared for publication, did not see the light of day.

[4] Mac Cuarta 2004. For the wider significance of this tale, see Orr 2000, pp. 389—421.

the purpose of explaining events in England.[5] And in a less brazen way, the same can be said of Austin Woolrych's *Britain in Revolution* (2002) or even of David Scott's richly textured *Politics and War in the Three Stuart Kingdoms* (2004).[6] This kind of history has appealed to those principally concerned with political conflict and the history of ideas – with any aspect of state formation or the patterning of Reformation thought or politics. It has not been favoured by those concerned with political culture, social and economic development or identity formation.

This has produced as an interesting counter in an enriched Scottish history of the kind recently and spectacularly demonstrated by Allan Macinnes in his *The British Revolution* (2004).[7] This is a challenging and constantly startling account of the War of the Three Kingdoms from a Scottish hub, with the involvement of all the European states evaluated from an Edinburgh and not a London perspective. Whether everyone will find persuasive Macinnes's attempted dialectic between 'Britannic imperial monarchy' (the drive to incorporative union) and 'gothic constitutionalism' (ancient constitutionalism and little-Englanderism) remains to be seen. In the meantime, this attempt to see the failure of the one and the accommodation of the other startles and unsettles; and it certainly derails the Britannic historicism also known as 'enriched' English history.

Then there are advocates of confederal history, in the form of those who demonstrate the case for separate histories but overlay it with a concern with how the histories influence one another. A good example of this is the more recent work of Nicholas Canny (in his editorial conceptualization and participation in the first volume of *The Oxford History of the British Empire* (1998); but also in a range of essays including 'Irish, Scottish and Welsh Responses to Colonization *c.* 1530–*c.* 1640',[8] included in a collection of essays which itself exemplifies this approach). It is here that David Stevenson was a pioneer in his work locating Scottish-Irish history in a British context with his studies of the Scots, English and Irish armies in Ireland and of Montrose's campaigns with Irish troops in the mid 1640s. These are studies that illuminate the history of each kingdom by transcending them; but the aim is to illustrate each not some 'greater' history.[9] A particularly fine example of this is

[5] Russell 1990; Russell 1991.     [6] Woolrych 2002; D. Scott 2004.
[7] Macinnes 2004.     [8] Canny 1998; Canny 1995.
[9] Stevenson 1980; Stevenson 1981.

Jane Dawson's *The Politics of Religion in the Age of Mary Queen of Scots: The Earl of Argyll and the Struggle for Britain and Ireland* (2002).[10] This is first and foremost a masterly study of the politics and political culture of mid sixteenth-century Scotland. It is also a study of international and above all English intervention in the high politics of Scotland and how the fifth Earl of Argyll accommodated himself to the skilful and effective politicking of William Cecil and the unskilful and disruptive politicking of Elizabeth I. Central to the thesis is how Cecil's management helped to stabilize *English* interests in Ulster (and Elizabeth's to destabilize them), given that the 'highland' side of the Campbells straddled the channel between Antrim and the Western Isles. Three histories are illuminated; no new history is created.

A more characteristic example would now be the volume edited by Allan Macinnes and Jane Ohlmeyer that began life as a conference entitled 'The Awkward Neighbour' and which now has a subtitle of 'Awkward Neighbours'.[11] Essays in that book illustrate the way that confederal British history is best suited to cultural history: 'Sense of Identity in the Armies of the English Republic'; 'Britain, Race and the Iberian World Empire'; 'The Formation of Cultural Attitudes: The Example of the Three Kingdoms in the 1650s'. When it turns to political and intellectual history, anxieties about the approach mount: as one essay asks, 'Is British History International History?'.[12]

If we are looking for 'perfect' British history, we mainly have to look thus far at biography. For it is perfectly clear that there are important individuals who see their worlds as one. They might have multiple identities as they have multiple titles (Duke of Lennox *and* of Richmond; Marquis of Hamilton *and* Earl of Cambridge; Earl of Clanrickarde *and* of St Albans), but they thought and acted in a way that transcended the limitations of single-nation or single-kingdom history. They resided at a court at which the nobility of three kingdoms mingled; their land-ownership, marriage and entrepreneurial strategies were archipelagic; when civil war broke out they thought about how to utilize and safeguard their interests by an archipelagic plan. We are beginning to get a generation of political and intellectual biographies that demonstrate this new dimension: for example, Jane Ohlmeyer's *Civil War and Restoration in the Three Stuart Kingdoms: The Career of Randal Macdonnell, Marquis*

---

[10] Dawson 2002.    [11] Macinnes and Ohlmeyer 2002.
[12] These essays are, in turn, by James Scott Wheeler, Arthur Williamson, Sarah Barber and Conrad Russell in Macinnes and Ohlmeyer 2002.

*of Antrim, 1609—1683* (1993), the life of a man married to the widow of the great Duke of Buckingham, heir to the Lordship of the Isles and the last great Catholic landowner of Ulster; or Patrick Little's *Lord Broghill and the Cromwellian Union with Ireland and Scotland* (2004), the study of a scion of an English settler in Ireland and a strong voice in all parts of the Cromwellian *imperium*.[13] Studies of the first Duke of Ormonde and the second Marquis of Hamilton are hot on their heels.[14]

As for the pontoon-builders, I will simply point out that much intellectual history remains breathtakingly blinkered. Look at the extensive literature on monarchical republicanism 1540—1640. None of the discussion of how to regulate and make accountable queens and kings of England — and how to make disputed succession subject to positive and not to natural and divine law — notices the much greater dilemmas and the more radical solutions that were proposed by the Presbyterian Scots and the Catholic Irish in the century and a half after the accession of Elizabeth and specifically the century beginning around 1580.[15] Thus the thought of both the English and the Old English in Ireland about the constitution appropriate to a kingdom from which the King's person was perpetually absent had its own impact on English thought about English monarchy; just as the political thought of the supporters of the Irish rebels during the Nine Years War (itself deeply influenced by debates amongst the *Leaguers* in France, where many of the Irish bishops studied or lived) challenged many of the assumptions of the English about the applicability of humanist models across a federated *monarchia*.[16]

In 1649, the English beheaded the King of Britain and Ireland, but only abolished monarchy in England and Ireland. The Scots were told to resume their historic identity as a freestanding monarchy to the North of the English Commonwealth. They refused to accept independence and committed themselves to restore the Stuarts to all their kingdoms — but within as perfectly formed a monarchical republic as it was

---

[13] Ohlmeyer 1993; Little 2004.

[14] *The Oxford Dictionary of National Biography* also shows the way forward: compare the lives of the following in the *ODNB* with those in the original late Victorian/Edwardian *Dictionary of National Biography*: James, 1st Duke of Hamilton (by John Scally), Archibald Campbell, 5th Earl of Argyll (by Jane Dawson), Alexander Henderson (by John Coffey).

[15] Armitage 2000; Armitage, Himy and Skinner 1995; Burns and Goldie 1991; Norbrook 1999; van Gelderen and Skinner 2002, chs. 2, 5, 15; Skinner 2002b, chs. 1, 2; Wootton 1996.

[16] See the forthcoming studies of Irish constitutionalism by Alan Orr and Catholic political thinking by David Finnegan.

possible to imagine: as covenanted trustees with strictly circumscribed powers. This dramatic development has gone essentially unnoticed and its significance unevaluated.[17] Jonathan Scott is one of the historians who have consistently refused to examine the internal dilemmas of the British and Irish kingdoms and peoples in his remarkable books on English state formation. This is in part because he wants to examine the dynamic and dialectical intellectual and geopolitical interactions between England and continental Europe. So his references to Scotland and Ireland are pontoon-building. As we will see, I do not see these as alternative, but as integrated parts of the process.[18]

We have thus moved a long way in the past thirty years of fevered activity. There are at least twenty collections of essays that arose from conferences about the early-modern British problem. These include the Anglo-American Conference of Historians in the Institute of Historical Research in London, the first ever Trevelyan Fund Conference in Cambridge and the first meeting of leading historians from all the territories of the would-be British state system in Galway. Journals including the *American Historical Review* have devoted special numbers to the issue or to its ancillary, Atlantic history. Major universities including Cambridge and then Oxford have created courses devoted to the self-conscious activity of thinking about the relationship. And the PhDs and the monographs have followed.

III

It is important to stress how much of a revival or recovery this is. In the decades before the 1970s there was virtually no historical exploration of the links between the polities ruled by the Tudors and Stewarts, no '*British* history' of the kind just discussed. If there were more space than I am permitted here, we could fruitfully explore how concern with 'the matter of Britain' waxes whenever there is a threatened and actual shifting of the tectonic plates which lie beneath 'Britain'. In the years around 1921, around 1800, around 1707, around 1603 and around 1541 the relationship between the peoples and polities within the archipelago shifted. At each moment there is a surge of interest in the history

[17] See the third of my Ford's Lectures in British History, 'Inextricable Labyrinths: Presbyterian Dilemmas, 1648–1650', delivered in the University of Oxford, February 2006.
[18] See the indexes in J. Scott 2000; J. Scott 2004.

of their relationships. Then interest ebbs away until the next quake approaches.

Within the early-modern period itself, we find the same discussion amongst historians as in the 1980s and 1990s. Whether it was the long assault by Renaissance and Reformation Scottish historians on, and the increasingly half-hearted defence by English historians of, Geoffrey of Monmouth's account of the Trojan origins of the British kingdoms and the natural subordination Wales and Scotland to Brutus's kingdom;[19] whether it is the way that the Union of the Crowns in 1603 caused historians like John Clapham to republish his *Historie of England* (1602), suitably amended, as *The Historie of Great Britannie* in 1606, or Edward Ayscough to focus on the relations between the kingdoms in his *Historie Contayning the Warres, Treaties, Marriages and Other Occurrents betweene England and Scotland* (1607), thus making clear the indelible mark each had made on the other;[20] whether it was the way Irish-born scholars (Protestant and Catholic) sought to define the historic autonomy of the peoples (*sic*) of Ireland from Britain,[21] the relationship between the peoples and/or the kingdoms was at the centre of historical debate. Even the chronicles which preceded the emergence of the new empirical historicism could become deeply involved in the geopolitics of Britishness. Thus both editions of Raphael Holinshed's *Chronicles of England, Scotlande, and Irelande* (published in 1577 and 1587, respectively) offered separate histories of the Three Kingdoms, but it was precisely their attempt to show the connections between them that led them to be censored by the Privy Council.[22]

At the end of the process by which there developed a British state system if not quite a British state, eighteenth-century historians had certainly developed a sense of British identity and practised British history. Perhaps the classic example is David Hume, whose discussion of seventeenth century *integrates* English and Scottish (if not Irish) history into a self-aware plaid. Close scrutiny reveals separate strands but the effect is a tight weave. Let us take his discussion in Volume 3 of

---

[19] Most graphically brought out in a succession of works by Roger Mason: Mason 1991; Mason 1994a; Mason 1994b; Mason 2004. See also Kidd, in this volume.

[20] Clapham 1602; Clapham 1606; Ayscough 1607; for a brief review of this literature, see Woolf 1990, esp. pp. 55–65.

[21] Ford and McCafferty 2005, chs. 4, 5, 11.

[22] Holinshed 1577; Holinshed 1587. There is an admirable short account in the life of Holinshed in *The Oxford Dictionary of National Biography*: Clegg 2004.

his *History of England* (*sic*) of the winter of 1644–1645.[23] Hume's account of the terms discussed between royalist and parliamentarian negotiators is the only one before the twenty-first century to give full consideration to the Irish and Scottish articles; the trial of Laud is set in the context of Scottish insistence on destroying him; and there follows a linking paragraph that tells us that '[w]hile the king's affairs declined in England, some events happened in Scotland which seemed to promise him a more prosperous issue of the quarrel' (throughout his kingdoms). The next page explores how Montrose's freedom of action was transformed by the downfall of Hamilton at Court which gave Montrose far more influence; and great care is taken to show how that in turn limited the freedom of movement of Covenanting armies and commissioners in England. The role of Irish troops in these Scottish campaigns is fully explored. This may have been history with a moral purpose – to demonstrate the illegitimacy of rebellion and the perils of priestcraft and of enthusiasm – but it is unselfconscious British History. From then on, there was a steady decline throughout the nineteenth century, and a very low trough for most of the twentieth century.[24]

IV

Whig historiography focused on constitutional documents, and especially on parliamentary Acts. Whether these Acts were passed by, or these debates held in, the English, the British or the United Kingdom Parliament the result was the same – an assumption of Anglo-centricity. Scotland and Ireland were marginalized in every sense. The supreme demonstration of this is the assertion of 1688 as the Glorious (and bloodless) Revolution.[25] Glencoe and Killiecrankie, the Boyne and the walls of Derry were disagreeable offstage noises, the death-rattle of traditions of violence that England had put behind it and would radiate out to the outlying regions in the decades that followed. Scots and Irish were allowed to take part in civilizing those parts of the world fortunate enough to be incorporated into the British Empire. But they were Britons carrying a British Englishness with them.[26]

---

[23] Hume 1983, v, pp. 455–65.    [24] Morrill 1999, pp. 67–78.

[25] Trevelyan 1939 encapsulates the view; as does the term 'Glorious Revolution' recreated in the 1930s and found in the title of 117 books and essays since 1936 listed in the Royal Historical Society Bibliography online (www.rhs.ac.uk/bibl, accessed 20th January 2005).

[26] See Claydon 1999, pp. 115–21.

From not later than the 1920s, however, this view was to give ground to new and less patronizing historical traditions. First, historians became preoccupied with analysing the underlying economic and social structures within which people operated, on the social-science assumption that people's behaviour is determined, or at the very least shaped, by those structures. Since the economic and social structures of Scotland and Ireland were little studied, or so far as they were studied believed to represent a pattern of sharp contrast from the patterns thought to prevail in England (and Wales), the story of how glacial change in English society created fissures in the political and institutional structures that eventuated in civil war in the 1640s became an exclusively *English* story.[27] This is most obviously seen in the work of Christopher Hill and the 'Oxford School' of the 1950s to 1980s – scholars like David Underdown, Brian Manning and Gerald Aylmer. All had some concern about what the English did in Ireland, but none saw it as more than a dire epiphenomenon of the social conflict boiling over in England.[28]

Second, and related to this, there was a growing fascination – which reached its peak in the late 1960s and early 1970s – with the 'radical' movements spawned by the war and with the print culture associated with these movements. Since these were essentially English movements, there was a resulting de-emphasis on the popular cultural responses to the collapse of royal and noble power in Scotland and Ireland. Neither the 'Whiggamores' of Scotland nor the 'Tories' or 'wood-kerne' of Ireland wrote pamphlets and thus they remained outside the concern of monoglot-English scholars who failed to recognize the potential of these 'brigands' to produce the kind of progressive ideas with which they yearned to identify.[29]

Third, there was a strong tendency – driven as much as anything by the PhD industry – towards atomization, with fewer and fewer broad research monographs and more and more tightly-drawn studies.

[27] Stone 1965, in which the views of Professors Tawney, Stone, Trevor-Roper and many more are extracted and summarized. The whole book is a testament to how imposing historical castles built on sand can sometimes appear at the time.

[28] Hill 1961; Hill 1972; Hill 1985; Hill 1998; Underdown 1985; Underdown 1996; Manning 1976; Aylmer 1986.

[29] For some fascinating preliminary thoughts on these groups, see O'Ciardha 1997, pp. 164–84. For the same kind of reason, historians before the 1970s lavished interest and space on the Levellers and not on the much more numerous and widespread Clubmen: see the comments of David Underdown in Eley and Hunt 1988, pp. 338–9.

This created a series of discrete debates, with textbooks and survey books acting as guides to particular debates rather than whole fields. The proliferation of studies of pre-civil war and civil war counties and county towns is one obvious example of this. Since Scottish and Irish politics remained clan- or name-driven, with counties that lacked the institutional and cultural strength of early-modern English counties, there was no scope for the development of a comparative approach here.

Fourth, this in turn reinforced the tendency for historians in and of Scotland and Ireland to write within their own separate historiographical tradition,[30] and not to participate in — or especially to take note of — the blinkered English historiographical discourse.[31] Furthermore, in the universities of Scotland, Scottish history, and in the universities of Ireland, Irish history, were hermetically sealed off from other branches of history, and ne'er were the twain ('Modern' and 'Scottish' history, 'British' and 'Irish' history) encouraged to meet.[32] Few of the major figures in Scottish and Irish history specialized in early-modern history, most of the Professors being medievalists (or, in the case of Ireland, of recent history), and many of those employed to teach early-modern history were medievalists by training whose concern to look for continuities in Scottish or Irish history rather than contiguities within British history.

I have to be more speculative when I talk about the development of research and teaching in British (as against English, Irish and Scottish) history outside Britain. The situation no doubt differs from place to place. There were many reasons why doctoral students from the Commonwealth or the USA would spend any research time they had in London or else at Oxford and Cambridge. English public records, and even more English private records, were much more systematically calendared than Scottish or Irish ones; and this was reinforced in the era of microfilm when English records, including books published in England (the Thomason Tracts, for example) were far more extensively commercially filmed and disseminated.[33] In fact, it is an important

---

[30] See the traditions reflected in the Moody, Martin, and Byrne 1976; and in Lynch 1991.
[31] For some especially interesting recent comments on this, see Canny 2003b, pp. 723–48.
[32] As late as the mid 1980s external examiners to the Modern History Department of more than one Scottish University were not invited to moderate the scripts for special subjects in Scottish History at the heart of their own specialism, the task instead being entrusted to external examiners in Scottish History whose expertise was remote from the subjects in question.
[33] For John Pocock's own acute observations on the differences in record-making and record survival in the different territories, see Pocock 1975b, pp. 611–13.

aspect of British state formation, that there was never a centralization
of archives — the Victorians established separate Record Offices in
London, Edinburgh and Dublin (later Belfast) but not in Cardiff
(but, interestingly national libraries were established over a more ragged
timescale in all four territories).[34] US and Old Commonwealth
Universities would typically have two or three specialists in British
history, and there would be a tendency to take scholars in 'mainstream'
areas, which would reinforce Anglo-centricity. There would be little
opportunity or incentive for the handful of specialists in non-English
British history to collaborate with English 'British' historians.

The result of all this can be seen in the textbooks used in higher
education across the twentieth century. As I have argued elsewhere,
there was an inexorable separation out of national histories from the
late nineteenth century and from the establishment of the Whig
paradigms in G. M. Trevelyan's *England Under the Stuarts* (1904) and of
the Marxist paradigms, as represented by Christopher Hill's *The Century
of Revolution, 1603–1714* (1961) — which misses England out of its title,
but misses Britain out too, and even manages to miss Scotland and
Ireland out of its maps.[35] For me (at least in retrospect) a low point
was reached when Lawrence Stone published *The Causes of the English
Revolution* (1972), an over-triumphalist summation of forty years'
debate and argument on that subject precisely defined. It contains
no index entry at all for 'Scotland' or 'Scottish', and just one entry
to 'Ireland' under the heading 'Irish Rebellion' which leads the reader to
seventeen lines of text unpromisingly prefaced by the words 'tension
was enormously increased by two *chance* events, of which the first was
the death of the Earl of Bedford . . . [and] the second . . . was the outbreak
of the Irish Rebellion'. British history had reached a very low ebb
indeed.[36]

V

One historian above all others was the prophet of the new history:
John Pocock. He has wrestled with the need for, and with the hazards of,

---

[34] On another occasion, it would be interesting (in terms of elite notions of Britishness) to discuss
why there is a British Academy (and a Royal Society and a Royal Academy of the Arts)
which covers the whole of the UK, and a Royal Irish Academy (which ignores borders in the
island of Ireland) and a Royal Society of Edinburgh for scholars based in Scotland. But there
is no Academy for scholars based in England only.
[35] Trevelyan 1904; Hill 1961; Morrill 1999, pp. 68–78.
[36] Stone 1972, pp. 137–8 (my emphasis).

a history that embraces several peoples in three kingdoms. He has had more that is pertinent to say than anyone else, especially in exploring the dynamics of state formation and national identity as an aspect of intellectual history. In 1973, Pocock returned to New Zealand to deliver the first J. C. Beaglehole Memorial Lecture, named after a historian who had pioneered the raising of historical consciousness and a self-aware historiography of the South Pacific region. Two years later, Pocock published an adjusted version of that lecture under the title 'British History: a Plea for a New Subject'.[37] It began by scolding A. J. P. Taylor for his purposeful indifference to the nomenclature of English and British history, and he explored the ambiguities and carelessness of usages over time, and the reality that there was no real 'British history' as against English, Scottish, Irish, Welsh and 'colonial American' history. Pocock's first attempted definition of this new subject was 'the plural history of a group of cultures situated along an Anglo-Celtic frontier and marked by increasing English political and cultural domination'. This captures well one of the treacherous essences of the subject as it has emerged — that it is both about state formation and how processes of state formation were conceptualized and explained and acted out; *and* that it was also about the way national identities within this partially achieved state system evolved and changed as a result of the interactions between the peoples in the context of English military, institutional and cultural aggression: as Pocock has put it, 'the fact of hegemony does not alter the fact of a plurality, any more than the history of a frontier amounts to denial that there is a history beyond the advancing frontier'.[38]

The central section of that first article is a bravura attempt to see how this definition applies to the main periods of 'British' History since the establishment of the Anglo-Norman realms in southern England, southern Scotland and eastern Ireland. For example, he suggests that, for the thirteenth to the fifteenth centuries, it is 'the history of contacts and penetrations between three *loci* of Anglo-Norman power';[39] or for the seventeenth century, he suggests it is the recovery and exploration

---

[37] First published in New Zealand (Pocock 1974) and then lightly revised as Pocock 1975a.

[38] Pocock 1975b, pp. 605–6.

[39] Pocock 1975b, pp. 608–9 It is surprising how little use early-modern historians have made of the 'British History' developed so brilliantly for medieval history by Rees Davies, Robin Frame and others. For Davies, see his four presidential addresses to the Royal Historical Society under the collective title 'The Peoples of Britain and Ireland': Davies 1994; Davies 1995; Davies 1996a; Davies 1997; also, see Frame 1990; Davies 1988; Davies 2000.

of the notion of the crisis of the mid seventeenth century not as
'the English Revolution', 'the Irish Rebellion' and 'the wars of the
Covenanters' but 'the war of the Three Kingdoms'.[40] This is, Pocock
insisted, a pluralist history. And this makes it an addition to four
'national' histories, not a substitute for them; and in the remainder of
the essay, he explores some of the lineaments of continuing English,
Scottish and Irish historiographies.

This is not to acknowledge the possibility of a historiography of
little England, little Ireland or little Scotland: as Pocock points out, 'Irish
history is to an inordinate degree the history of responses to England,
while English historians writing of Ireland maintain...the traditional
tone of mild wonder that some things should be going on in their
otherwise orderly universe'.[41] More provocatively, he argues that 'Scottish
national and historical consciousness remains one in which the choices of
identity are open, probably because they cannot be resolved...Scottish
history has been, and may remain, a mere matter of choice, in which the
acceptance of anglicization, the insistence on the concept of Britain,
Lowland localism and Gaelic romanticism, remain equally viable
options and the problem is to reconcile one's sense of identity with
one's awareness of so open-ended a structure of choice'.[42] So 'national'
histories can and should take account of the interactions between them;
but the explanatory thrust and purpose is to make sense of the history
of one nation/territory. In each case the 'national' historian is interested
in how the 'other' affects the particular, not about the two-way (or indeed
three-way/four-or-more-way) pattern of cause and effect. We will see
later how and why this matters.

When he came to reconsider the case for a new British history in 1983
(in an article sub-titled 'in search for the unknown subject' although
I would preferred 'in search of a forgotten subject'), John Pocock used
the concepts of *verità effettuale* and *verità quasi-effettuale* as a way into
the darkness. As English historiography engorges the territories to the
North and West, 'there is no caesura, no change or key or structure,
no sense that the history of England has become part of something
else',[43] a point illustrated in relation to the Acts of Union of 1707
or 1801. This is because English historiography is constructed around

---

[40] A term Pocock derived from Beckett 1966, ch. 4, 'The War of the Three Kingdoms'.
[41] Pocock 1975b, p. 614.      [42] Pocock 1975b, p. 615.      [43] Pocock 1982, p. 312.

the assumption of 'the interaction of governing institutions with a continuous social fabric'.[44] (I would gloss this by saying that this notion of a continuous social fabric was discussed in terms of slowly evolving sets of vertical social relations – this in itself is responsible for the absence of 'British history' for much of the twentieth century.) This can be contrasted with a Scottish or Irish (or colonial American) historiography constructed as a *verità quasi-effettuale* – 'the history of a people intelligible within the parameters they have constructed for themselves but overlaid, repressed and distorted by the imposition of a "British" structure, which is English and irrelevant'.[45] Whereas the earlier essay looked mainly at the incomplete and messy processes of state formation, this second essay examines the non-national aspects of the British non-nation non-state:

the premises must be that the various peoples and nations, ethnic cultures, social structures and locally defined communities, which have from time to time existed in the area known as 'Great Britain and Ireland', have not only acted so as to create the conditions of their several existencies, but have also interacted so as to modify the conditions on one another's existence and that there are processes here that can, and should, be studied.[46]

'British history' is thus the study of 'the formation and disruption of state structures' and of the transoceanic expansion of the peoples caught up in that process, as the transatlantic seaboard 'acquired inhabitants with modes of consciousness corresponding to this experience'.[47] British history is about the connection between the fumbled military and political expansion of England and Englishness and of the resistance and adaptation of non-English peoples to that fumbled expansion.[48]

VI

So far, it seems, so straightforward. But there are complications. One more essay by Pocock leads into deeper waters. The Center for the History of British Political Thought at the Folger Library has systematically explored the theme of 'Britishness', and in the 1990s explored Anglo-Scottish and Anglo-Irish political exchange across the period

---

[44] Pocock 1982, p. 312.  [45] Pocock 1982, p. 313.
[46] Pocock 1982, p. 317.  [47] Pocock 1982, p. 318.
[48] Much of the remainder of that article is a demonstration of this model in relation to key aspects of each time-period from the eleventh to the twentieth centuries: Pocock 1982, pp. 321–36. Important for Pocock's exegesis of the early-modern period is his encounter with Webb 1979: Pocock 1982, pp. 326–8.

1560—1800. To the first of the resulting volumes, focusing on 1603, Pocock contributed an essay entitled 'Two Kingdoms and Three Histories? Political Thought in British Contexts'.[49] In it, he speaks of British political thought as 'a discourse directed at the "matter of Britain"',[50] that is at the problematics of conceiving and realizing a political entity to be known by that name. This proves to be no simple matter. The political entity was, in the early-modern period (and certainly to 1707) only in a limited sense a political entity: the same ruler *acted* as king according to very different sets of rules and conventions in each of his kingdoms, one telling example being the way that James VI had a spiritual identity in England by virtue of the English Reformation by Act of State (Crown and Parliament) and in Scotland by virtue of an act of noble and popular rebellion in defiance of the Crown.[51] At one level, then, a history of British political thought (strictly construed) is the act of recovering how men (for the most part) in the past reflected on what to do when there existed two (or more) political bodies (and persons) defined by two apparently incommensurable systems of royal and national law. And in the British case, 'the union of head and body, which constituted a political kingdom . . . formed by laws that were nationally and culturally specific [which meant that] the more "absolute" (and less relative and contingent) each kingdom's laws and customs, the harder it was to merge its personality with another's'.[52]

But what the essay also makes clear is that British history is absolutely non-teleological in the strong sense[53] — in the sense that it is 'the self-authenticated history of a self-perpetuating polity or culture'.[54] It is the history of Britain as it might-have-been (or better, as it might-become: that is, it is the history of an aspiration)[55] and it is a history of those who sought to subvert that might-become, of that aspiration. Since what is imagined as might-becoming changes over time, so does that history mutate. French history is the history of what became France; Spanish history of what Spain became (without Portugal, but with the Basques), British history, however, is something different.

---

[49] Pocock's essay begins with a frank confession: 'A Center for the History of British Political Thought must sooner or later pay attention to its own title', Pocock 1994, p. 293.
[50] Pocock 1994, p. 312, on which, see now Kidd, in this volume.
[51] Pocock 1994, pp. 300—2.       [52] Pocock 1994, p. 306.
[53] See Burgess 1990, pp. 614—16.       [54] Pocock 1994, p. 311.
[55] Unless one considers 1800—1922 as being the multi-national state that the subject yearns to find — a period with one head of state, one sovereign legislature, one imperial system, but more than one legal system, several religious systems, several self-consciously separate nations.

And this history of might-becomes is brilliantly caught by Roger Mason in the introductory essay to the volume he edited on the Union of 1603. He defends the period covered by his volume (1560–1650) as breaking down a chronology derived from English dynastic caesuras and making clear that Scotland's destiny was set much more from the events of 1558–1563 than from the events of 1603.[56] In 1558 Mary Tudor died and Mary Stewart married Francis II of France. It seemed entirely likely that England (and Ireland) would be a Protestant Caesaro-papalist *monarchia*; and that Scotland would be to France what Ireland was to England or The Netherlands were to the Spanish (or hispanicized) Habsburgs – an outlying colonial dependency. And any son of Francis and Mary would have been seen as the rightful Catholic ruler of England ahead of the heretic bastard Elizabeth. It was thus also possible that the dynastic rivalries involved in this dynastic ménage-à-trois would have led to Habsburg/Valois(/Tudor) rivalries being fought on British soil rather than continental soil. Whatever the outcome, English liberties and monarchical republicanism are unlikely to have prospered. What prevented this was the defining event in early-modern Scottish history, the noble/popular rebellion that overthrew the French protectorate of Mary of Guise and established the Scottish Reformation; and the most important contingency of all the dynastic contingencies that shaped the geopolitics of sixteenth-century history, the ear infection that carried off Francis II in 1560 before he could impregnate Mary Queen of Scots.

As both Pocock and Mason point out, any canon of Scottish political texts 'arrestingly begins with an affirmation that Scottish history can only be written within the context of a *Historia Maioris Britanniae*'.[57] Or, as Mason puts it in the introduction (and as he explores it in another essay in the volume) 'the idea of Britain as a single geopolitical entity . . . [had] distinguished medieval antecedents, but more pertinently it had been strongly touted in the 1540s . . . [This] "Edwardian moment" was loaded with connotations of English hegemony . . .'.[58] How so many Scots came to terms with the advantages as against the disadvantages of this is the theme of the rest of the book, and of the succeeding volume

---

[56] Mason 1994a, pp. 3–6. The following paragraph is my additional gloss to the points he makes – for a fuller discussion, see Morrill 2005.

[57] Pocock 1994, p. 293, alluding to Major 1892.

[58] Mason 1994a, p. 7; compare Mason 1994b.

on the Union of 1707 edited by John Robertson.[59] The fact is, that
(with the massacres of the nobility at Flodden and Solway Moss all too
fresh in the minds of the survivors and of the children of the dead) many
(even most) Scots recognized the necessity of accommodation with this
over-mighty and awkward neighbour. By 1560, long term independence
was an unreality; and a majority had come to prefer accommodation
with Protestant England to colonial dependency on Catholic France.[60]
The civil wars of 1567–1574 confirmed that polarization; 1603 showed
'the English had it'; the refusal in 1649 to accept the English offer
to regain their independence is the most telling demonstration of all;
and the war of the two dynasties of 1689–1746 which had nothing to
do with the break-up of the British polity, but the internal arrangements
within it, put the seal on it. In all this, 1560 not 1603 is the point at which
'the awkward neighbour' became the necessary bedfellow.

## VII

While the Folger Center volumes on Scotland fitfully explore the
internal dynamics of nationhood – as in Edward Cowan's essay on what
the political thought of the Covenanting eighth Earl of Argyll owed to
the discourses of the *Gaedhealtachd*[61]– this is an issue that could not be
ducked when attention was turned to a Britain-Ireland dialectic. It is
a startling (and largely unexplored) fact that few if any Englishmen
acquired property in Scotland by purchase or marriage in the century
between the Union of the Crowns and of the Kingdoms, although many
Scots acquired property especially by marriage in England. This is just
one of the many asymmetries between Scotland's relations with England
and Ireland's relations with England. A history that thinks of Anglo-
British imperialism in Ireland starts from a very different base. An Irish
Parliament dominated by the descendants of twelfth- and thirteenth-
centuries colonists erected a kingdom in Ireland, but did not create an
Irish Crown. There was a military occupation of large parts of Ireland
by new waves of English and (after 1603) Scottish settlers. Gaelic
landowners who had not been consulted about the creation of the Irish
kingdom were expropriated for resisting its claims to sovereignty, itself
a concept of little resonance to their way of viewing the world. All this
needed justifying; and all this needed to be challenged and resisted

---

[59] Robertson 1995a.    [60] I have argued this vigorously in Morrill 1994.    [61] Cowan 1994.

intellectually as well as militarily and in languages understood by and acceptable to the international Catholic community whose support would be critical to any sustained resistance. Those who erected the kingdom became increasingly unhappy with the Caesaro-papalist pretensions of an Anglo-British Empress and Emperors, and with the pressure to subordinate the peoples of Ireland not only with an English kingdom but to the English Parliament.

And yet almost all those who saw themselves as the older communities of Ireland – the 'Irish' and the 'English of Ireland' – there was no question of separating themselves from loyalty to the House of Stuart. Those who fought the bitter battles of the 1640s and (although this is now more contentious) those who fought the bitter battles of the 1590s, struggled to redefine themselves and the kingdom of Ireland within a confederated triple monarchy; not to break away from it into an unworkable independence or a new dependency on the Kings of Spain or France. No wonder John Pocock could say that ' "Irish" history is not part of "British History" for the very reason that it is largely the history of a largely successful resistance to being included in it; yet it is part of "British History" for precisely the same reason'.[62] We are back to the 'might-becomes' or in this case the 'might-not-becomes' – the history of what is not rather than the history of what is.

If 1560 turns out to be the underestimated date in Scottish-British history, 1580 turns out to be the turning point in Irish-British history. In Hiram Morgan's edited collection *Political Ideology in Ireland, 1541–1641* (1999), the real starting point is with the translation of Gerald of Wales's *Expugnatio Hibernica* added to the second edition of Holinshed,[63] with its Norman contempt for Gaelic culture and sense of effortless superiority for the institutions of the English in the second edition of his *Chronicles* (1587) and with the historical and historiographical furores released by the publication of Edmund Spenser's *View of the Present State of Ireland*. Morgan's volume is very much a history of the way that England's relationship to Ireland was contested in the period 1580–1640, the strident voices of the incorporators (Spenser, Sidney, Beacon, Davis) clashing with the voices of Richard Stanihurst, David Rothe, Philip O'Sullivan Beare and the bards in Latin and in Irish defending King, Faith and Fatherland.[64] It is striking for the way it

---

[62] Pocock 1995, p. 295.
[63] Added in the second edition (Holinshed 1587).
[64] Morgan 1999b.

integrates (so comfortably in comparison with the volumes on Scottish responses to Anglo-British imperialism) chapters about English writers on 'the proto-Irish problem' and Irish writers on the same. This can also be said with equal conviction of Jane Ohlmeyer's volume, staidly entitled *Political Thought in Seventeenth-Century Ireland: Kingdom or Colony* (2000).[65] But something else is noteworthy: Morgan's authors show awareness of the ways in which particular traditions of ancient, biblical and continental humanist thought were conscripted by participants in the debates, but it shies away from a re-examination of the 'Quinn-Canny' thesis of Ireland as a stepping stone to English colonization in the Americas.

## VIII

British History is thus a story of not what is, or even what was, but what was in the process of becoming.[66] We have become used to the idea of a nation as an 'imagined community'; perhaps we need to become used to the idea of a state as an imagined community too. That process of a state that was imagined existed from the years 1541–1543, from the Act of the English Parliament for Union with Wales, from the Act of the Irish Parliament for the creation of the Irish Kingdom, and from the marriage treaty made by Henry VIII as the feudal suzerain of Scotland for the marriage of his ward Mary of Scotland to his son Edward and the prospect of a union of Crowns, complicated by the claims of that Scottish Queen to the English throne from the moment that the husband intended by that treaty died. The process was accelerated by the regal union of 1603 and was fully realized for the only time between 1653 and 1660. With the Union of the British Parliaments in 1707 and of the British and Irish Parliaments in 1800, there was legislative unity; but the churches and legal systems of Scotland and England remained and remain distinct, and the confessional state failed in Ireland in ways that had implications for political practice in Britain. From 1603 and most certainly from 1707 there was a state system in and for Britain and Ireland as complete and as ineffectually challenged as any state system. And yet this process reinforced the sense of separate identity in the existing peoples of Ireland and perhaps in Scotland and Wales (in these latter two alongside a sense of shared British identity). In short, a British state

---

[65] Ohlmeyer 2000.    [66] Morgan 1999b, p. 19.

system may have developed across the early-modern period; a nation-state emphatically did not. At root modern Scottish and Irish resistance to the new British history stems from an English concern with state formation and not national identity; English resistance to it stems from a concern not to get bogged down in the complexities of the nationhood part of the nation state.

Thus a major problem with the new British history has been in striving to create a trans-*national* history *in addition* to the four national histories. What it has done is to raise awareness of how much of the new British history was in danger of becoming little more than that 'enriched English History' which I have accused Conrad Russell of practising,[67] and against which Nicholas Canny has warned us.[68] There are those – at one time mainly in Ireland but now much more in Scotland – who write a nationalist history in terms of heroic resistance to English military might and cultural barbarism.[69] There are those who stress the comparative and interactive nature of the histories of the kingdoms, the way events in the one affect – both immediately and indirectly – events in the others; events can change the way people behave or how they think about themselves and their priorities for action. This is something Scottish and Irish historians had long practised in relation to England, but interestingly, not in relation to one another.[70] And there were those – John Pocock included, I think – who have called for a new and perfect British history, something that reconceptualized the unit of study, something that created new agendas for research, but importantly over and above rather than against the local histories of the kingdoms of England, Ireland and Scotland.

IX

This leads us on to the other massive destabilizing element in the new British history: its lack of self-sufficiency as a unit of study. It has been often enough said that most inhabitants in England did not know or

---

[67] Morrill 1993, p. 260.
[68] Canny 1993, pp. 49–82; Canny 1995, pp. 147–69; and most explicitly Canny 1992. See also Burgess 1999, pp. 11–18.
[69] Excellent examples of this would be the splenetic Ferguson 1977; or Patrick Riley's studies of the Union of 1707 as a 'political job', e.g. Riley 1978.
[70] There was some pioneering work by Stevenson (see Stevenson 1980; 1981), but it is really only with the creation of the AHRB Research Centre for Scottish-Irish Studies at the University of Aberdeen in 1999 that this exploration has taken off. One early triumph of this collaboration is Macinnes 2004.

recognize the difference between being English and being British, that most inhabitants of Wales and Scotland knew the difference and were willing to use both as befitted their happenstance, and that very few residents of Ireland (the main exceptions are to be found amongst the Scots of Ulster after 1641) ever recognized themselves as British. All these points became clearer as the early-modern period progressed. Although nothing I have just said is particularly contentious, the development of an explanatory framework in which each people's sense of itself is profoundly influenced by the interactions among peoples is much more contentious. In part this is because there are disturbing asymmetries in the contexts of complex interactions. If we focus on the seventeenth century,[71] we find intense Scottish migration to and economic, military, cultural interaction and exchange with northern Europe (The Netherlands and the whole of the Baltic rim) for which there is no English or Irish alternative. Similarly we find intense Irish migration to and economic, military, cultural interaction and exchange with southern (and especially Habsburg) Europe for which there is no English or Irish alternative. And we find intense English migration to and economic, military, cultural interaction and exchange with *all* of Europe and new worlds across the oceans for which there is no Irish or Scottish alternative.[72] In other words, there are strongly exogenous factors shaping national identities and Scottish and Irish historians are keen to emphasize, as John Pocock was to emphasize, the importance of how the various 'peoples and nations [of Great Britain and Ireland] have not only acted so as to create the conditions of their several existences, but have also interacted so as to modify the conditions on one another's existence and that there are processes here that can, and should, be studied'.[73] Much more work clearly needs to be done on this.

Perhaps more obvious is the way a European context helps explain the development of what historians have tended to call 'multiple' or 'composite' monarchy, a term I find unhelpful and for which I have proposed an alternative — the concept of a dynastic conglomerate or (perhaps better) agglomerate. The notion of composite monarchy

---

[71] Simply for reasons of time and space; comparable but different arguments could be made for the sixteenth and eighteenth centuries.

[72] Once again the Welsh get short-changed. But in the seventeenth century, the Welsh had no independent access to the Continent, and they shared in the same range of extra-British contacts with the English.

[73] Pocock 1982, p. 317.

conveys all too settled and institutional a feel – in the British case, how the Three Kingdoms of England, Scotland and Ireland came naturally together and how the political, religious, economic and cultural integration and resistance to integration played itself out within a given 'triple monarchy'. My suggestion is that we should consider the process as the development of a *dynastic agglomerate* rather than a composite monarchy. Dynastic agglomerate is an awkward, uncomfortable phrase for an awkward, uncomfortable entity. It helps us to keep at the front of our minds how unstable the evolving composite was. We have seriously undercalculated the acute dynastic instabilities of medieval and early-modern Britain and Ireland – the uncertain succession law and the rights of heirs male and heirs general, the way that the habit of Scottish monarchs to die or lose the throne while their heirs were in their swaddling clothes kept evergreen the English Crown's rights to feudal suzerainty over Scotland. The relations of the kingdoms and people could easily have taken a different path – what if Henry VIII had died before Mary Tudor was born; if the King of France had accepted the offer from the Duke of Northumberland of the kingdom of Ireland in return for troops to make good the succession of Jane Grey; or if Mary Stewart had had a son by Francis II before the latter succumbed to an ear infection? A number of scenarios were supported in the mid-seventeenth century and during the war of the two dynasties (1689–1746) for radically different configurations of the kingdoms. 'Dynastic roulette' created the dynastic agglomerates of Charles V, of the Vasas and of the Austrian Habsburgs and it also caused them to transmute.[74]

But of course European history can be made to British history what British history is to the separate histories of its own constituent territories – a contested set of relationships through which definition and redefinition take place. It can hardly be absurd to locate all those constituent histories against a European context in the period of Saxon, Norse and Norman invasion and settlement; or to locate Norman expansion within the archipelago within the context of an *imperium* that straddled *la Manche* and sought to unite Lowland England with large parts of France; or to locate the early-modern period except against the backdrop of European Renaissance and Reformation and two-way exchanges with Europe: British intellectual history is not only a story of the thinkers and texts seeping across from the continent to be absorbed

---

[74] Morrill 2005.

and sent forth in English utterance with British settlers but a two-way
dialogue or dialectic with both Catholic or Protestant Europe. It can
hardly be absurd to examine eighteenth-century Britain in the context not
only of the Atlantic world but in terms of a war of two dynasties and in
terms of an Anglo-Hanoverian/German *monarchia*. More generally, as we
have just seen one of the unfulfilled dimensions of the new British history
is to examine the way different parts of Britain draw differentially on
parts of Europe. To simplify by speaking of just one century: the Scottish
people, at all kinds of levels and in all kinds of ways, were linked into an
economic, cultural and geopolitical system that was northern European
(Dutch as well as Scandinavian). The Irish people were linked into an
economic, cultural and geopolitical system that was southern European
(including Habsburg Spain and Austria). The English (and Welsh) people
were linked in a more profoundly eclectic way with all of Europe. As we
study the evolution of a state system and the refashioning of national
identities, this dimension needs far more careful calibration. There are
those historians, most militantly Jonathan Scott, and more carefully
Jane Ohlmeyer or Allan Macinnes, who would invert John Pocock's
privileging of the Atlantic over the English Channel as the sea of change
in modern historiography. Jane Ohlmeyer's argument that the best way
to understand the dynamics of the War of the Three Kingdoms in the
mid century is as part of a War of the Five Kingdoms (France and Spain
as well as the British monarchies) has been persuasive.[75] At the very least,
British historiography gains from a comparative European approach.
What was happening within the British Isles is perhaps best understood
by close comparison with what is happening as the kingdoms of Iberia
come together or (as in the case of Portugal) fail to come together; as
'France' emerges from the congeries of territories that had little or no
shared identity before the sixteenth century (Brittany, Burgundy,
Languedoc, Lorraine, etc.); as the Baltic agglomerates form and
unform; or as the territories of the Austrian Habsburgs change in shape
and identity like a constantly reworked lump of clay.

[75] Ohlmeyer 1993.

# CHAPTER 3

# The Matter of Britain and the Contours of British Political Thought

## Colin Kidd

As a proclaimed field of study 'The History of British Political Thought' provides cover for a certain degree of ambiguity. Traditionally, of course, within the field of history, 'British' has served as a polite synonym for 'English'. For some English historians, unfortunately, 'British history' is no different in substance from English history, the label a politically correct formulation aimed at assuaging the sensitivities of the non-English peoples of the British Isles. In this light, the contours and agenda of British political thought remain largely English, or at best Anglo-British. Elsewhere, especially among pre-modern historians, there has been a more profound attempt to reconceptualize British history. Awoken from their profound anglocentric slumbers by the meta-historical promptings of John Pocock,[1] many medievalists and early-modernists have begun to perceive that Whig historiography was not only teleological, but also limited in its perspectives and interpretations by a narrow, if unconscious, English nationalism. These revisionist historians now recognize that the conventional narrative of English state formation makes little sense without some understanding of the relationships between England and the 'satellite' nations of the British world. Their counterparts among the inward-looking and – as often as not – doctrinally nationalist historians of Ireland, Scotland and Wales have also become aware of the intellectual impossibility of autarkic, self-enclosed histories of these countries divorced from the history of Greater England (or from some other supra-national context such as the Atlantic or North Sea world).

In this way the common grazing which we now know as 'the new British history' has been carved out of the existing fields of English, Scottish, Irish and Welsh history. Its existence depends on a somewhat uneasy accommodation between the revulsion anglocentricity provokes in

---

[1] Pocock 1975a; Pocock 1982.

non-English historians and the instrumental needs of English historians seeking more compelling explanations of English state formation. Nor do these approaches to the subject exhaust the possible meanings of the history of British political thought. British political thought amounts to something other than the sum of English, Scottish, Irish and Welsh contributions to political argument, or even to a pan-British conversation over British state formation. British political thought might also be understood, quite specifically, as political thought about the entity or entities which comprise the British Isles.

Isolated case studies apart, and with the stunning exceptions of Rees Davies's *The First English Empire: Power and Identities in the British Isles, 1093–1343* (2000) and David Armitage's *The Ideological Origins of the British Empire* (2000),[2] historians have tended to overlook the existence of a distinctive and long-running genre of political argument which debated the location of authority within the island of Britain, or sometimes the British Isles. For the sake of convenience we might term this genre 'the matter of Britain'.[3] Although our focus in what follows is on the Anglo-Scottish relationship, the matter of Britain is not meant to exclude Ireland, and a parallel story could be told of a contested Anglo-Irish matter of Britain, to which we shall occasionally allude.

Ironically, as we shall see, attention to the 'matter of Britain' reverses the recent trend towards a decentred history of British political thought, serving, instead, as a reminder of the pronounced asymmetries in the relations of England with its less powerful British neighbours. Indeed, the central preoccupation of the matter of Britain lay in the pan-Britannic pretensions of England and its institutions, pretensions which were underpinned by the historic and confusing conflation of 'England' and 'Britain'. Not only did the dominant position of England in the British Isles from the middle ages onwards produce an enduring and decisive imbalance in the interactions of its constituent nations; but there is also a deeper problem, what Krishan Kumar has described as the 'synecdochical' relationship of England, the island of Britain and the whole archipelago.[4] This imagined congruence of the English and the British has haunted British history over the past millennium; more particularly, it constitutes a central, if unexplored, feature of political thought about Britain and the British Isles.

---

[2] Davies 2000; Armitage 2000; compare Ferguson 1974.
[3] Compare Davies 1996b. See also Hay 1968.
[4] Kumar 2003, p. 7.

Early-modern British political culture inherited a well-defined but vigorously contested 'matter of Britain' from the clerks, churchmen and chroniclers of the middle ages. 'The matter of Britain' is, of course, a term familiar to students of medieval literature. The formulation appeared in late twelfth-century romance as a description of the Arthurian tales popularized by Geoffrey of Monmouth's early twelfth-century *Historia Regum Britanniae*, of which, as Julia Crick reminds us, a remarkable two hundred and fifteen manuscript copies survive.[5] Although Geoffrey's *Historia* is now best known as a fictive concoction of legend and romance, in the medieval period it also enjoyed a potent ideological significance. The Anglo-Norman exploitation of Galfridian history blurred the ethnic distinction between the English (Saxon or Norman) and the pre-Saxon peoples of Britain. Instead it became – and long remained – common to trace the origins of English institutions back to ancient British origins.[6] This appropriation of the ancient Britons as the founders of English institutions contributed to the distorting elision of England and Britain which has since bedevilled British history. Further, Galfridian accounts of a pan-Britannic kingship exercised by Brut, first king of the ancient Britons, who awarded England to his eldest son Locrinus, and Scotland and Wales to his younger sons, and of a later high kingship enjoyed by King Arthur, the conqueror of Ireland, over the whole of the British Isles, became the canonical justification of English monarchical claims to a suzerainty over the rest of Britain or the British Isles.[7]

However, the matter of Britain had become a matter of political controversy long before it assumed canonical expression in Geoffrey's *Historia*. The vaunt of English monarchs that they were overlords of the other peoples of Britain resounds, as the late Sir Rees Davies reminded us, from at least the early tenth century, when the coinage of Athelstan described him as *rex totius Britanniae*. According to Davies, this British overkingship should not be confused with formal rule or direct kingship. The high-kingship conferred prestige rather than power, and it did not preclude the existence of other power centres or legitimate political authorities, with the single proviso that these acknowledged the suzerainty of their Britannic overlord. According to Davies, 'a fairly relaxed *superioritas*' had prevailed – at least until the era of Edward I. Not that the pretensions of Edward I's predecessors on the English throne were complacently accepted by the rulers of tributary polities. Rather it is

---

[5] Crick 1989; Crick 1991.  [6] Kidd 1999, chs. 4, 5.  [7] Monmouth 1966, pp. 75, 221–22.

in the claim to English overlordship and the ideological resistance which it provoked that one finds the origins — however rudimentary — of British political thought.[8]

The kings of Scotland proved reluctant — and ambiguous — vassals of their English overlords. In 1095 Edgar of Scotland conceded that he held the Lothians in the south-east of Scotland — though not his crown itself — from the King of England. From 1124 the fact that Scottish kings possessed estates in England conveniently confused the terms of Scottish vassalage to the Plantagenet monarchy. Scottish kings from David I to Alexander III were happy enough to pay homage for their lands in England, obfuscating the issue of whether they were vassals to the crown of England in respect of their Scottish territories. There was, however, an unfortunate exception, when William the Lion found himself the prisoner of Henry II and won his freedom only by way of an unambiguous acceptance of English overlordship in the Treaty of Falaise (1174). This treaty was explicit about Scotland's subordination to the high kingship of England. The Treaty pointedly did not describe Scotland as a kingdom (*regnum*), but merely as a land (*terra*). Moreover, this land was ruled, according to the Treaty, by William the Lion as *rex Scottorum*, while Henry II of England was its suzerain king (*dominus rex*). However, by the Quitclaim of Canterbury in 1189 William was able to buy back these concessions (or some of them at least) at a steep price from the impoverished crusader-king, Richard I.[9]

Although the matter of Britain focused on the vexed question of where suzerainty (if any) resided within the island of Britain or the British Isles, this issue did not only take the form of debates about the location of temporal power. There was also the closely related — perhaps, indeed, indicative — issue of the locus of ecclesiastical jurisdiction in Britain or the British Isles. According to the Council of Windsor in 1072 the remit of the archbishopric of York encompassed Scotland as well as England north of the Humber. At this stage the papacy backed the metropolitan claims of York over the Scottish church, but these were resisted by the Scottish bishops and by the Scottish crown, which recognized such ecclesiastical pretensions as a spiritual front for temporal designs. Naturally, Henry II took the opportunity offered by the enforced Treaty of Falaise to confirm the rights of the English church over the church in Scotland. Nevertheless, the Scottish lobby at the papal curia

[8] Davies 2000, pp. 9–10, 20, 37.      [9] Stones 1970, pp. 2–17; Davies 2000, pp. 12–14.

was indefatigable, and in 1192 by Pope Celestine III's bull *Cum Universi* the church in Scotland was recognized as a *filia specialis* ('special daughter') of the Papacy.[10]

The reign of Edward I witnessed both the emergence of a more determined policy to realize a pan-Britannic sovereignty and also the appearance of a recognizable body of British political thought, in the pleadings of English and Scottish delegations at the papal curia. Edward exerted his right as *dominus superior* of Britain to judge the disputed succession to the Scottish crown; and then when his choice, King John Balliol, began to resist the demands of his paramount lord, invaded Scotland, removed Balliol, and attempted to incorporate the vassal-kingdom of Scotland within his own dominion. The crisis in Anglo-Scottish relations raised questions of ecclesiastical as well as political autonomy. In 1299 Pope Boniface VIII wrote to Edward I and to the archbishop of Canterbury enquiring why the king of England had invaded the papal fief of Scotland. Edward I's response to Boniface VIII resurrected Geoffrey of Monmouth's version of the origins of the British state under Brutus and the later history of Scotland's feudal subjection to the superior crown of England. The Scottish submissions at the papal curia in 1301, handled by the canon lawyer Baldred Bisset, punctured the Galfridian interpretation of British history, insisting instead on a long and separate history of Scottish national autonomy. The arguments of Bisset's *processus* resurfaced in a later letter to the papacy, the Scottish Barons' letter to Pope John XXII in 1320, better known as the Declaration of Arbroath, which remains today the foundational text and canonical manifesto of Scottish nationalism.[11]

This anti-Galfridian counter-historiography of Britain was consolidated and rendered more systematic in the *Scotichronicon* of John of Fordun and his continuator Walter Bower. Fordun's account of the establishment of an independent, sovereign political community in Scotland under its first king, Fergus MacFerquhard in 330 BCE involved an explicit rejection of Geoffrey's Brut legend, and remained the standard version of Scottish origins – in Scotland at any rate – until the second quarter of the eighteenth century. For over three centuries the independent origins of the Scottish monarchy in 330 BCE was

---

[10] Broun 2002; Barrell 1995; Davies 2000, pp. 11–12, 38; Ferguson 1977, p. 21.
[11] Barrow 1988, esp. pp. 116–18, 185, 241, 306–11; Goldstein 1993, chs. 2, 3; Reynolds 1990, pp. 273–6.

the crucial element in Scottish political thought, a body of argument which not only defined the nature of the Scottish kingdom, but also advanced its own reading of political relationships on the island of Britain.[12]

Early-modern debate about the nature of Britain and the British Isles was an extension and amplification of this well-defined conversation in medieval British political argument. Too much ideological capital had been invested in the matter of Britain for it to be lightly abandoned. The Scottish philosopher and historian John Mair, or Major (1467–1550) criticized both the origin legends of the Scots and the English in his *Britanniae Majoris Historia* (1521) in an attempt to reconcile England and Scotland in a peaceful and cooperative British future founded upon mutual respect.[13] Nevertheless, Mair's *Historia* — its deconstructive sophistication notwithstanding — was to be of marginal influence in the shaping of early-modern Scottish political thought, its message of Anglo-Scottish reconciliation almost immediately eclipsed by newer versions of the familiar Scottish origin myths.[14] Nor did sixteenth-century English propagandists drop the Galfridian interpretation of British history. Henry VIII's *Declaration, Conteyning the Just Causes and Consyderations of This Present Warre with the Scottis* (1542) justified his invasion of Scotland on the basis of a Galfridian imperialism and the grounds of the English crown's claim to a feudal superiority over Scotland.[15] A sceptical critique of ancient Scottish history by the Welsh antiquary Humphrey Lhwyd in his *Breviary of Britayne* (Latin edition 1568; English translation 1572) provoked the Scots humanist polymath George Buchanan into a vigorous defence of the Scottish myth of sovereignty in his mammoth *Rerum Scoticarum Historia* (1582).[16]

Another round of debate was instigated by Raphael Holinshed who devoted a chapter of his *Description of Britaine* to the crown of England's 'sovereignty' over the whole island of Britain. Under the influence of Geoffrey, Holinshed traced this authority back to the succession of Brutus's eldest son, Locrinus, to the imperial crown of England, when 'seignorie over Albania [Scotland] consisted in Locrinus'. This 'seignorie' or 'sovereignty' had been confirmed by the later homages performed

[12] Fordun 1871–1872; Ferguson 1998, pp. 43–53; Goldstein 1993, ch. 4.
[13] Major 1892, pp. 1–2, 50–52.
[14] Boece 1574; Bellenden 1821.
[15] Armitage 2000, pp. 37–8.
[16] Mason 1987, p. 74; Buchanan 1690.

by the subordinate kings of Scotland to their English overlords.[17] Holinshed's assertion of English claims over Scotland provoked an outraged, but highly sophisticated, response from the eminent Scottish feudal jurist, Thomas Craig of Riccarton (1538?–1608) in his Latin manuscript treatise, *De hominio*, which was ready for publication by 1602, but not published until 1695 when, as we shall see, it appeared in an English translation. Craig not only denounced the imperial delusions of the British History, but, as the author of another distinguished manuscript treatise, the *Ius Feudale*, eventually published to European acclaim in 1655, also went on to expose the absurdity of a domestic feudalist parsing of the Anglo-Scottish relationship. Craig pointed out the anachronism on which the ancient English claim to feudal superiority rested. The terminology of superiority, fee and homage belonged to the tenth century, at the earliest, and had not been imported into Britain till the Norman Conquest. Anglo-Scottish history did not conform to feudal precepts. Kings of England had not exercised feudal rights of wardship over the kingdom of Scotland when the latter experienced a royal minority, nor had the consent of the king of England been required at the inauguration of Scottish kings (with the exception of King John Balliol), as it would have been had Scotland been a fief, whereby the vassal was required to seek renovation of the fee within the year whenever the person of the lord or vassal changed. Craig insisted upon the rights of 'majesty' belonging to the Scottish crown, evidence for which was clear in the international recognition Scotland enjoyed within the affairs of Europe. The kingdom of Scotland, Craig insisted, had participated freely, unconstrained by England's pretended pan-Britannic suzerainty, in the sphere of inter-regnal conflict, treaties and alliances. Although writing in a pre-Grotian context, Craig was making the point that Scotland did not belong to the *ius feudale*, but was an independent actor in international affairs.[18]

The Union of the Crowns in 1603 did nothing to resolve the matter of Britain. Rather, by bringing Scotland within the ambit of the English multiple monarchy (which already included the subordinate kingdom of Ireland), the vexed issue of locating authority in the British Isles was, if anything, intensified and rendered even more opaque and ambiguous. Moreover, the confessional divisions within British Protestantism acted

---

[17] Holinshed 1807–08, I, pp. 196–214.
[18] Craig 1695, esp. pp. 19–20, 418–24; Craig 1934.

as a further intensifier of the traditional jurisdictional divisions of the British world. Nor, following the failure of James VI and I's plans for a united British monarchy, did the Stuart rulers of England and Scotland manage to settle the question of where ultimate sovereignty — if any — resided within the British Isles. Indeed, the Stuart monarchy itself exhibited some uncertainty about the precise form of sovereignty within the Union of the Crowns. Did the Kingdoms of Scotland and England retain separate sovereignties or had they been merged into the dominions of a King of Great Britain? Although royal proclamations of 1604 changed the Stuarts' style to Kings of Great Britain, the English parliament continued to refer to the King of England, while the Scots parliament fluctuated between the British and the Scottish style. Official representations of sovereignty on Scottish seals and coinage were inconsistent in their renderings of seventeenth-century monarchs, who were sometimes described as Kings of Scotland and England, sometimes as Kings of Great Britain.[19]

Throughout the duration of the Union of the Crowns (1603–1707) the English claim over Scotland was not confined to a particular partisan or religious persuasion, but was espoused across the spectrum of English politics, Puritan as well as Cavalier, Whig as well as Tory. From the clericalist extreme, the Laudian geographer Peter Heylyn wove an English imperial superiority into his encyclopedic *Cosmography* (1652), incorporating numerous legal and historical examples in his account of Britain's political geography. Wallace, for example, had been executed by Edward I not because he was a prisoner of war, but because he was a traitor to the paramount crown of England. There was also a later body of pre-1603 case law which showed, Heylyn claimed, that Scots in England had been treated not as aliens, but as subjects of an English suzerain crown. Furthermore, Heylyn also explained the distinction between the English and Scottish crowns. Scottish kings, he noted, were merely styled *reges Scotorum*, thus 'intimating that though they are the kings of the nation, yet there is some superior lord (king paramount as we may call him) who hath the royalty of the land.'[20] On the other side of mid-century political and religious controversy, the Puritan antiquary William Prynne advanced a decidedly Erastian version of Anglo-British *imperium*.

---

[19] Anderson 1739, plates xciv–xcix and clxix–clxxiv; Burns 1887, II, pp. 414–525; Bindoff 1945, esp. pp. 196, 213–14, 216.
[20] Heylyn 1670, pp. 310, 324, 332, 339.

Prynne asserted 'the ancient right and sovereign dominion of our English kings over that realm and church [of Scotland], against all claims of usurping Popes or ingrate perfidious rebellious Kings of Scotland'. English sovereignty was first and foremost a matter of supremacy over the church, argued the anti-papalist Prynne. Indeed, he blamed the Papacy for having lent clandestine encouragement to the Scots in their rebellion against their paramount lord, Edward I. Moreover, Prynne was most insistent that the English crown — not the archbishop of York — held authority over the 'church' and 'clergy' of Scotland.[21]

By now, however, issues of ecclesiastical jurisdiction constituted only one component of the religious matter of Britain. From the Reformation onwards confessional differences overlaid older medieval debates about the location of ecclesiastical authority within the British Isles. British debates over ecclesiastical jurisdiction developed into disputes over church government, the relationship of church and state, and, by extension, over the location of sovereignty within the state. Questions of jurisdiction and autonomy retained their former importance, but were now rendered more urgent and immediate by the threat that a part of the British world might impose its own brand of religious conformity upon its neighbours. Scots Presbyterianism remained acutely vulnerable to the taunt of illegitimacy. Scots Presbyterians confronted the particular challenges posed by the Church of England, including an Anglican churchmanship which prided itself on the apostolic continuity of its episcopate, as well as the metropolitan claims of its archbishops to jurisdiction over the church in Scotland. In the face of these challenges, Scottish Kirkmen saw the need to establish an indigenous pedigree for their church polity as a means of reinforcing the legitimacy of presbyterian church government. Various indigenous myths proved useful in this regard.[22] These apparently provided material from the primitive era of the church which might substantiate the claim of Scots presbyterians to the crucial defining mark of antiquity, if not quite to perpetuity.

Acccording to the Presbyterian interpretation of Scottish history, the early church in Dalriada had been subordinate neither to the Pope nor to bishops, but had been governed by colleges of monks called Culdees. From the early seventeenth century Scottish ecclesiastical historians turned to the early history of Dalriada as a means of justifying the

---

[21] Prynne 1670, 'Epistle Dedicatory', pp. 487, 556.
[22] Russell 1990, ch. 2; Kidd 1995, pp. 163–5.

Scottish Reformation. Early seventeenth-century historians such as David
Buchanan (c. 1595–c. 1652) saw the potential to construct an illustrious
indigenous pedigree for Scottish Protestantism out of existing historical
materials. For example, in the writings of Tertullian (c. 160–c. 220) there
was an observation that a part of Britain which the Romans had failed
to conquer – presumed to be Scotland – had been won over to the
Christian gospel: *Britannorum inaccessa Romanis loca, Christo vero subdita.*
There was also an intriguing reference in Fordun to the effect that there
had been no bishop among the Scots until Palladius in the early fifth
century. The sixteenth-century historian Hector Boece had argued for the
conversion of the Scots around the year 200 in the reign of the fictitious
Donald I. In addition, Boece had transferred the Culdees, an eighth-
century Irish monastic reform movement, back into third-century
Dalriada. George Buchanan saw the potential in this to construct a
history of Scotland's early non-papal conversion by Johannine – rather
than Petrine – missionaries. However, it was only in the seventeenth
century that presbyterian historians concocted a full-blown history of an
ancient proto-presbyterian Kirk of Dalriada governed by Culdees –
rather than by Rome or by bishops. David Calderwood (1575–1651)
contended that a primitive Celtic Christianity without bishops had once
flourished in Scotland. David Buchanan set out the system of Culdaic
church government in more detail. The Culdees, who had been
established in the third century by King Cratilinth, had elected overseers
of the church from within their own ranks, but these superintendents had
not formed a distinct order within the church. According to Buchanan
full-blown diocesan episcopacy had only made its appearance in the
eleventh century.[23] This Presbyterian celebration of the ancient Celtic
church would continue into the eighteenth century, with the democratic
proto-presbyterian order of Culdees woven into the political myth of
Scotland's ancient elective constitution.[24]

   Scotland's supposed indigenous pedigree reinforced a more decisive
argument for presbytery by divine right. Scots Presbyterians did not

---

[23] Fordun 1871–1872, pp. 64, 93–4; Boece 1574, pp. 86, 99, 128; Buchanan 1715, *Rerum Scoticarum
historia*, lib. iv, R. 27 R. 35; lib. v, R. 42; lib. vi, R. 69; Calderwood 1842–1849, I, pp. 34–43;
Buchanan 1731, pp. lvii–lxxxiv.

[24] Dalrymple 1705; Wodrow 1842–1843a, 'Robert Wodrow to George Ridpath, Sept. 23, 1717', II,
p. 313; Wodrow 1842–1843b, II, p. 326; III, p. 383; Wodrow, 'Introduction, To our Scots
Biography . . .' (1727) (University Library, Glasgow, MS Gen 1213). For the continuation of this
tradition, see Brown 1845, pp. 17–18; Burrell 1964, pp. 1–24; Petrie 1662, pp. 55–6; Stevenson
1753–1757, I, pp. 3–26.

contend for presbytery as the peculiar church government of Scotland. While presbytery was celebrated as Scotland's historic form of church polity and the unfolding of Scottish history was attributed to the benign workings of providence, there was no suggestion that Scotland was unique, its presbyterianism an exception to the wider history of Christendom. In general, Scotland's earliest experiences of church government had conformed to the primitive norm, though perhaps such direct evidence was lacking for other places. Rather, it was understood that the history of the Scottish church provided a local example which crucially supplemented the lessons of scripture and the primitive fathers.[25]

Here Scotland's ancient ecclesiastical constitution and the religious matter of Britain intersected with wider European debates about church government. For Scottish history seemed to provide a compelling primitive example of non-episcopal governance. Such evidence was highly prized by Reformed defenders of the legitimacy of presbyterian government, not least for its scarcity value. Seventeenth-century Europe resounded to a major debate between Catholic antiquaries such as Denis Petau (1583–1652) who challenged the validity of presbyterian orders and Reformed scholars – such as Claude De Saumaise [Salmasius] (1588–1653) who argued that there had been no distinction between bishops and presbyters, or priests, in the early Christian church. However, decisive evidence was hard to come by. The polymathic English jurist, antiquary and orientalist John Selden (1584–1654), an opponent of prelatical episcopacy who was far from being an unqualified champion of divine right presbytery, identified a critical piece of evidence in the *Nazm al-Gawahir* [*Chaplet of Pearls*], a universal history of the world from Adam to 938 CE by Sa'id ibn Batriq (876–940), an Egyptian Arab better-known as Eutychius, the Melchite Patriarch of Alexandria. Eutychius argued in his history that at Alexandria there had originally been no distinction between bishops and priests. Selden's edition of a fragment from the *Chaplet of Pearls*, published as *Eutychii Aegyptii, patriarchae orthodoxorum Alexandrini, Ecclesiae suae Origines* (1642), provoked considerable controversy, attacked not only by Roman Catholic apologists but also in 1661 by the Maronite Christian Abraham Ecchellensis, who claimed that Selden had mistranslated the Arabic of the original. Interestingly, Selden also wrote elsewhere – in his *Judicium de decem historiae Anglicanae scriptoribus* (1653) – about the other

[25] See e.g. Jameson 1697; Jameson 1712.

remarkable example from the ancient world of presbyterian church goverment, the case of the Culdees, which he explicitly set in the international context of the controversy over Eutychius and the debate between Petau and Salmasius. The fact that the Scottish church had enjoyed a proper ecclesiastical polity without bishops for a full two centuries from the reign of King Donald around 200 CE through to the sending of Palladius to Scotland as — apparently — its first bishop around 430 was also seized on by the French Huguenot scholar David Blondel (1590–1655) in his *Apologia pro sententia Hieronymi de episcopis et presbyteris* (1646) as a telling piece of evidence. Similarly, the English Dissenter Richard Baxter (1615–1691) in his *Treatise of Episcopacy* (1681) cited the case of Scottish church government without bishops to bolster his argument for the legitimacy of presbyterian orders; indeed, Baxter argued, had not a succession of early English bishops received ordination at the hands of Scots presbyters from Iona?[26]

In the 1680s the issue of the Culdees provoked an intense round of debate over the matter of Britain, which embraced political as well as confessional and ecclesiastical differences. In his *Historical Account of Church-Government As it was in Great-Britain and Ireland when they first received the Christian Religion* (1684) William Lloyd, the English occupant of the Welsh bishopric of St. Asaph, identified the story of the Culdees as a dangerous lie. Of the various arguments deployed against the legitimacy of episcopacy, noted Lloyd, there was 'none that hath made more noise in the world, or that hath given more colour to the cause of our adversaries, than that which they have drawn from the example of the ancient Scottish church'. What was so disturbing about the way modern Scots Presbyterians used the legend of the Culdees was that it took the ground away from those critics who argued that presbyterianism was a dangerous radical novelty. Lloyd noted that when the Scots 'covenanted against episcopacy they had only used their own right; and thrown out that which was a confessed innovation, in order to the restoring of that which was their primitive government'. His assault on the Culdees was soon reinforced by Edward Stillingfleet in his *Origines Britannicae* (1685), and led to a wider attack on the credibility of the whole of Scotland's ancient history from 330 BCE through to the dark ages — not out of

[26] Selden 1726, *Eutychii Aegyptii, patriarchae orthodoxorum Alexandrini . . . Ecclesiae suae Origines,* II, tom. i; Selden 1726, *Judicium de decem historiae Anglicana scriptoribus,* II, tom. ii, esp. cols. 1130–1; Blondel 1646, p. 315; Baxter 1681, pp. 224–5. See also Hart 1952, p. 92; Champion 1992, p. 62.

English chauvinism *per se* but to further specifically Anglican ends through the subversion of the presbyterian interpretation of Scotland's past. Ironically, the works of Lloyd and Stillingfleet provoked fevered responses from Sir George Mackenzie of Rosehaugh, a Scottish episcopalian who shared the doubts of his English co-religionists about the Culdees, but who knew that to jettison Scotland's early history also challenged the proud boast of the Stuart kings to be descended from a monarchy established in Scotland 330 BCE.[27]

The Irish antiquary Roderic O'Flaherty did not accept the truth of the history either, and the mid-1680s witnessed an assault on the historicity of Scotland's ancient history from every other quarter of the British Isles.[28] Mackenzie, who was the King's Advocate in Scotland, declared it to be *lèse majesté* among the subjects of the Stuarts to question the antiquity of the Scottish royal lineage. After all, the antiquity of the Scottish royal line was implicated in the defence of Scottish independence from offensive English claims to a feudal superiority over Scotland. Mackenzie devoted a chapter of his *Observations on Precedency* to a demonstration 'That the Crown of Scotland was not subject to England'. Scotland, the royalist Mackenzie insisted, had always been a free monarchy. What evidence was there for the original constitution of the feu? Nor did history supply corroboration of the English boast that the Anglo-Scottish relationship was that of superior and vassal. The legal consequences of such an arrangement should be obvious: a vassal could not engage in diplomacy with a superior, nor could a vassal treat his own vassal as a foreigner. Yet British history gave the lie to such pretensions.[29]

The issue flared up again during the 1690s and haunted the negotiation of incorporating Union in 1706–1707. These intense historical controversies of the 1690s and 1700s on the subject of Scottish sovereignty have come to be known as 'the imperial crowns debate'.[30] In 1695, responding to the discovery and publication by Thomas Rymer, the King of England's historiographer, of archival evidence that Malcolm Canmore had performed homage to Edward the Confessor, George Ridpath published an edition of Thomas Craig's treatise on homage, *De hominio*, under the title *Scotland's Soverainty Asserted: Being a Dispute concerning*

---

[27] Lloyd 1684, 'Preface'; Stillingfleet 1685; Mackenzie 1716–1722, II.
[28] O'Flaherty 1793, I, pp. xix, lvii–lxvi, 225–92.
[29] Mackenzie 1716–1722, *Observations upon the Laws and Customs of Nations as to Precedency*, II, pp. 520–29.
[30] Ferguson 1974.

*Homage, against those who maintain that Scotland is a Feu, or Fee-liege of England, and that therefore the King of Scots owed Homage to the King of England.* Ridpath claimed that Rymer's Scottish sovereignty was presented in such a way that it answered the pretensions of those who questioned the existence of an independent Scottish sovereignty. Rymer had also questioned the historicity of the ancient alliance supposedly contracted between the Scottish king Achaius and Charlemagne, which functioned as compelling evidence of Scotland's historic sovereignty and independence.[31]

This phase of the debate was also fought over ecclesiastical terrain. Scots from both wings of their nation's Reformed tradition responded to slurs upon the historic autonomy of the church of Scotland, most notably James Dalrymple for the Presbyterians and Sir Robert Sibbald for an Episcopalian interpretation of Scottish church history which conceded nothing to his Anglican co-religionists.[32] The question of ecclesiastical jurisdiction was so closely intertwined with that of Scottish political autonomy that Episcopalians remained as staunch as Presbyterians on this issue. Just because there had been no Scottish archbishopric until 1472, it was argued, did not mean that the church in Scotland had been subject to an English metropolitan. The debate spilled over in another direction, being closely shadowed by an Anglo-Irish debate instigated by William Molyneux's *The Case of Ireland Stated* (1698), which insisted upon Ireland's full regnal status.[33]

The British succession crisis which ensued in 1700 at the death of Princess Anne's last child, and William's last direct heir within the Protestant family of James VII and II, further raised the stakes in Anglo-Scottish relations. In particular, Scottish sensibilities were appalled at the arguments of Molyneux's former opponent the English Whig polemicist William Atwood,[34] who, redirected his attention from the Anglo-Irish to the Anglo-Scottish relationship in his book *The Superiority and Direct Dominion of the Imperial Crown of England over the Crown and Kingdom of Scotland* (1704), which was followed by a sequel in 1705.[35] Atwood believed that as the crown of England held rights of superiority over Scotland, that the English Act of Settlement (1701) entailing the crown of England (and the subordinate crown of Ireland) on the Protestant Hanoverian line should thereby take effect in the vassal-kingdom of Scotland whether or not it gained the formal endorsement of a

---

[31] Craig 1695; Sibbald 1704b, p. 4.    [32] Dalrymple 1705; Sibbald 1704a.
[33] Molyneux 1698.    [34] Atwood 1698.    [35] Atwood 1704; Atwood 1705.

recalcitrant Scots parliament. Atwood claimed that the monarchs of England were heirs to an ancient pan-Britannic *imperium* and that the kingdom of Scotland was a feu held by the sub-kings of Scotland from an English feudal superior. The English Tory historian James Drake had also advanced a similar argument to Atwood's — though in a much less brazen manner — in his *Historia Anglo-Scotica* (1703), which recounted various examples of Scottish kings performing homage to their English suzerains. Drake began with Canmore's homage to William the Conqueror and also cited William the Lion's acknowledgement that he was the 'King of England's liege-man for the realm of Scotland, and his other lands, and for the same should do fealty to the said King of England, as to his sovereign lord.'[36]

The Scots parliament ordered Atwood's work to be burnt by the public hangman and encouraged the patriotic efforts of the lawyer and antiquary James Anderson,[37] who composed a direct riposte, *An Historical Essay shewing that the Crown and Kingdom of Scotland is Imperial and Independent* (1705) and went on to publish a collection of materials in vindication of this position, *Selectus Numismatum Diplomatum Scotiae* (1739). Anderson claimed that acts of homage to the kings of England had been performed only in respect of lands held by the Scottish kings in the northern counties of England, and did not involve any acknowledgement of the subjection of the kingdom of Scotland to an English imperial crown.[38]

It is worth paying some attention to the fascinating otherness of these late seventeenth- and early eighteenth-century debates about sovereignty. Heraldry, geography and literary criticism constituted crucial and understandably neglected adjuncts of the homage debate. Sir George Mackenzie's treatise, *The Science of Heraldry Treated as a Part of the Civil Law and the Law of Nations* had brought the ideological significance of heraldry into focus. In the tense years preceding 1707, the Scots parliament not only supported James Anderson's patriotic endeavours in the field of history, but also sponsored the heraldic researches of Alexander Nisbet.[39] For the matter of sovereignty had heraldic and armorial dimensions. Scotland's enclosed crown with four arches surmounted by a globe and cross, so the argument ran, provided crucial evidence of Scottish *imperium*. Alternatively, had the rulers of Scotland

[36] Drake 1703, pp. 4, 17.
[37] *Acts of the Parliaments of Scotland* 1814–1875, XI, p. 221. [38] Anderson 1705.
[39] *Acts of the Parliaments of Scotland* 1814–1875, XI, 85, 203; Nisbet, 1722–42.

been crowned with an unenclosed band, then this would have been evidence to confirm English claims to suzerainty over Scottish kings as a species of *sub-reguli* or viceroys.

The matter of Britain was also a matter of geography. Had the authority of the Romans over the province of Britannia devolved upon the kings of the ancient Britons, and then to the Saxon and Norman kings? If so, had Roman Britain been coterminous with the island of Britain? Did not Hadrian's Wall and Antonine's Wall suggest limits to the Roman province of Britannia?[40] There was also a huge and neglected debate over the interpretation of the geographical term Hibernia (or Ierne) in the *Panegyric on the Fourth Consulship of the Emperor Theodosius* by the Roman poet Claudian (*c.* 370–410). The upshot of this geographical vein of literary criticism was to discover whether the Scots had been in Scotland at the time of the Romans, as they should have been were the myth of a sovereign Scottish origin in 330 BCE reliable, or still across the sea in Ireland, and hence not in sovereign possession of Scottish territory. Scots argued that Ierne was the region north of the firths of Forth known as Strathearn. Ireland, Scots also contended, had never been ice-bound: therefore, *glacialis Ierne* must, they argued, be northern Scotland.[41] Nor should we forget about the debate over the location of Lodeney for which Scottish kings had performed homage to the English crown. Was Lodeney, as English historians argued, the Lothians, the very location of the Scottish capital? Or was Lodeney an area near Leeds in the north of England, and part of the English estates belonging to the Scottish crown, the performance of homage for which held no implications for Scottish independence?[42]

The debate overlapped with domestic English political controversies. Indeed, by this stage it is far from clear how representative Atwood's posturing was of English opinion. Queen Anne and her English ministry favoured a resolution of the crisis. Indeed, there was a danger that Atwood's inflammatory tomes might jeopardize the prospect of successful Anglo-Scottish negotiations. William Nicolson, bishop of the Border diocese of Carlisle, constituted a steadying influence, and deliberately distanced himself in his *Leges Marchiarum* (1705) from the feudalist

[40] Gordon 1726.
[41] Claudian 1981, pp. 30–33. For the patriotic Scottish rendering of Claudian, see Mackenzie 1716–22, *A Defence of the Antiquity of the Royal Line of Scotland*, II, pp. 370–78; Mackenzie 1716–1722, *The Antiquity of the Royal Line of Scotland, further cleared and defended*, II, pp. 404–10; Taitt 1741; Goodall 1773, pp. 2–16; Maitland 1757, pp. 99–105.
[42] Anderson 1705, pp. 214–22.

interpretation of Scotland's status. Indeed he insisted that commissioners for Union should 'treat as delegates on an equal foot' on behalf of two 'independent monarchies', not — as the feudalists would have it — 'as proctors and attorneys of a supreme lord of the fee and his vassals'.[43]

The defence of Scottish autonomy had devastating implications for the contemporary English Whig argument for an uninterrupted ancient constitution,[44] not least because the chronology of feudalism had come to assume considerable importance in Anglo-Scottish debate. If it could be shown, Scots antiquaries noticed, that the feudal law had only been imported into England in 1066, then this exploded Atwood's claims that Scottish kings had performed liege homage for Scotland since the folcmotes of King Arthur in the days of the ancient Britons. It also reinforced, from an unexpected quarter, the domestic royalist argument that England had been conquered by William I, and that its historic institutions existed not as integral components of a continuous ancient constitution, but rather by grace of the monarchy. English Whigs such as Atwood were keenly aware that Craig's arguments dovetailed with those of Robert Brady's Tory critique of England's ancient constitution, while Scots were equally aware that their chronology of feudalism challenged deeply-held English Whig shibboleths.[45] *Scotland's Soveraignty Asserted* rather pointedly observed that 'the kingdom of Scotland was always free, and did never acknowledge any superior lord (which is more than the English can say for themselves)'.[46]

The Articles of Union appeared to offer a partial resolution of the contested matter of Britain, in Scotland's favour it should be noted. But a Union negotiated on behalf of Queen Anne of Scotland with herself in her other regal capacity as Queen Anne of England was a cosily domestic sort of arrangement. Was Britain a new entity in international law created by a treaty between two equal sovereign powers, or merely the reincorporation of a feudatory kingdom within the original holding from which a British *dominus superior* had once granted the territory of Scotland as *dominium utile* to a vassal-king of Scots? The distinction between the Treaty of Union of 1707 and the Act of Union of 1707 is not mere pedantry on the part of the Scots. Terminological exactitude stands proxy for an informed understanding of the constitutional significance of 1707. Treaties belong to the law of nations; an Act is

---

[43] Nicolson 1705, p. vi.   [44] Pocock 1987a.   [45] Kidd 1993, pp. 44–8.
[46] Craig 1695, p. 260.

a piece of domestic law-making. Had Anglo-Scottish relations belonged
to the international sphere of the *ius gentium* or to a domestic realm
in which the *ius feudale* operated? Ironically, early eighteenth-century
Scots — the knowledge their juridical and academic leaders had of
Grotius and, sometimes, of Pufendorf notwithstanding[47] — did not
explicitly hitch the defence of Scottish independence to modern natural
jurisprudence: it was Scottish unionists who invoked Grotius, arguing
that incorporation involved not a loss of sovereignty but a mutual
communication of rights.[48] On the other hand, Scots of all stripes were
loudly insistent that the Anglo-Scottish relationship did not belong to the
feudal sphere.[49]

Other crucial ambiguities remained unresolved. Where did sovereignty
reside in the newly created united kingdom of Great Britain? Was this
new entity founded upon a fundamental law enshrined within the Treaty
of Union? Or did the authority embodied in crown-in-parliament trump
the Treaty guarantees given to Scotland in the Articles of Union? By what
mechanism, if any, might unhappy Scots seek redress from parliamentary
encroachments upon the Treaty of Union or the measures which
accompanied its passage, including the Act for the Security of the Church
of Scotland? Indeed, if the Kirk was secure in its unalterable privileges,
did this mean that an otherwise sovereign British parliament was
prevented from legislating within the sphere of the Kirk?

Henceforth, for Scots Presbyterians the matter of Britain was the
matter of the two kingdoms — not the relationship of Scotland and
England *per se*, but the uncertain relationship between the spiritual
kingdom and the temporal kingdom, as these were understood on either
side of a confessional border. For Scots Presbyterians held a more rigorous
conception of the separation of the spiritual and temporal kingdoms than
that practised within the Anglican polity. The Oxford Decrees of 1683 had
already borne witness to the intense differences in political theory which
separated Anglican and Presbyterian conceptions of governance and the
state. The Decrees singled out the canon of Scots Presbyterian political
thought for explicit condemnation: Knox, Buchanan, Calderwood,
Rutherford, the Solemn League and Covenant, *Naphtali*. The twentieth
Decree, in particular, which anathematized the doctrine that 'presbyterian
government [was] the sceptre of Christ's kingdom, to which kings as
well as others [were] bound to submit', was a harbinger of future

---

[47] Moore and Silverthorne 1983.   [48] Robertson 1995b, p. 221.   [49] Steel 1700; Belhaven 1705.

Anglo-Scottish disputation.[50] Although in 1710 the Whig prosecution of the offensively high Tory cleric, Henry Sacheverell, secured — at some cost — the burning of the Oxford Decrees,[51] there remained nevertheless an awkward gulf between Anglican and Scots Presbyterian conceptions of government. The issue of church-state relations came to function as a surrogate for the old causes of Scottish independence and English *imperium*. In particular, the parliamentary imposition of lay patronage on the Scots Kirk in 1712 provoked a long-running dispute on the nature and limits of sovereignty within the ecclesiastical realm, which would eventually culminate in the Disruption of 1843, when the Church of Scotland split asunder over its vexed relationship with an Erastian British state.[52]

This paper has focused upon the Anglo-Scottish aspect of the matter of Britain. But the matter of Britain is by no means reducible to the issues of Anglo-Scottish debate. An account of the Anglo-Irish matter of Britain would embrace some kindred issues, but would also engage more heavily with issues of ethnicity, civility and cultural difference.[53] There is also a fascinating story to be told about Scottish-Irish relationships. This involved not only themes of sovereignty and suzerainty — did the colonist Scots of Scotland pay tribute to the Scots of the Irish motherland? — but also cultural issues. The vexing Scottish appropriation of Irish Scots, most notably in the ecclesiastical and cultural realms, engendered a long-running dispute which eventually merged with the Ossian controversy.[54]

However, not only does the matter of Britain provide an alternative set of coordinates for plotting the contours of British political thought, it also challenges those historians of political thought who exhibit an unhealthy deference towards the norms and expectations of cognate disciplines. For deference of this sort can distort or obscure the history of political-arguments-as-they-were-once-deployed. Indeed, within the history of political thought concepts such as sovereignty sometimes seem overdetermined by their more settled definition in philosophy, jurisprudence and political science. This is, perhaps, unsurprising. After all, the history of political thought has a curious provenance, its origins

---

[50] Wootton 1986, pp. 120–26.
[51] Kenyon 1990, p. 141.
[52] Fry 1993.
[53] See e.g. Bradshaw, Hadfield and Maley 1993; Boyce, Eccleshall and Geoghegan 1993; Ohlmeyer 2000; Connolly 2000.
[54] Dempster 1829; Mackenzie 1708–1722; Leerssen 1986; Kidd 1999, pp. 156–7; O'Halloran 1989, pp. 69–95; O'Halloran 2004.

lying variously in history, philosophy, political science and law. In the
present case, however, their staple provisions are inadequate. The marrow
of the matter of Britain defies presentist analysis. Describing sovereignty
in early-modern British political thought is to participate in a messy
process of bricolage. At the very least, the matter of Britain summons the
historian of political thought down byways of ecclesiology, feudal
jurisprudence and heraldry unfrequented by political scientists or
philosophers. Indeed, while the history of political thought is certainly
capable of shedding light on current problems in political theory, is the
converse equally true? Is political theory a less useful aid to the historian
of political thought than ecclesiology or feudal jurisprudence, perhaps
even than heraldry or numismatics?

There is also an issue of congruence to confront. For example, do the
feudal concepts which so exercised late seventeenth- and early eighteenth-
century debates about sovereignty map directly onto the modern
discourse of sovereignty? Is *dominium directum* quite the same thing as
sovereignty, when, after all, the vassal holder of *dominium utile* — the
ruler of Scotland, say — is, arguably, presumed to control the fief in a
'sovereign' manner? The matter of Britain gave rise to distinctive and
peculiar idioms of political thought, which serve to illuminate not only
relationships among the four nations of the so-called British Isles, but also
the inadequacy of Procrustean approaches to the history of political
thought. Historians of political thought, it seems, need to construct their
own bespoke definitions from the materials of the past, eschewing
convenient off-the-peg formulations drawn from other disciplines.

# CHAPTER 4

# The Intersections between Irish and British Political Thought of the Early-Modern Centuries

*Nicholas Canny*

Irish political thought has scarcely had an independent history due to the thrust of academic history writing in Ireland. This discipline had dual origins: in an Irish Protestant liberal tradition dating back to W. E. H. Lecky, and in a conservative variety of English historiography cultivated in the 1930s at London, and in the 1950s at Cambridge.[1] Thus influenced, historians have had two principal concerns: to achieve a mean between denominational competition for the ownership of Ireland's past, and to understand the intersections between the histories of Ireland and Britain. In this light, the history of political thought has, until recently, focused on thinkers concerned with disputes over the constitutional relationship between Ireland and England, while Ireland's relationship with the European continent, and particularly with Catholic Europe, was left to Catholic (frequently clerical) historians writing to their own agendas.[2]

These distortions have been largely remedied by a new generation of historians who have delved into an ever-expanding range of sources concerning Ireland's multifarious links with Continental Europe. This work has also alerted scholars (including literary scholars) to the importance of printed and documentary sources in the Irish and Latin languages, while English language sources have shed fresh information following their re-interrogation by historians who have read more extensively on various historical experiences than their predecessors. Practitioners of both the new British history and Atlantic history have also been situating developments in Ireland (including the formation of political ideas) in ever widening contexts. The outcome has been a

[1] McCartney 1994; Brady 1994b, pp. 3–31; McIntire 2004, pp. 169–70, 306, 348.
[2] Clarke 1978; Clarke 2000; Simms 1983; Canny 2003b.

welter of publications on all aspects of Ireland's history including an appraisal of the political ideas fostered by the various elements of its population during the early-modern centuries.[3]

This chapter, drawing upon these fresh perspectives, has three objectives: (1) to examine how the steady increase in the power of the English state in Ireland impacted upon indigenous political culture there; (2) to assess how Crown involvement with Ireland, particularly between the 1580s and the 1650s, acted as a forcing ground for political thinking among English officials appointed there; and (3) to explain how Irish opponents to the designs of successive English governments drew more upon continental Catholic political ideas than upon English constitutional precedents.


### SIXTEENTH-CENTURY PROBLEMS

By indigenous political culture I mean those ideas that had prevailed in Ireland until the tenor of political life was disturbed, principally after 1579, by a determination of the English state to assert its authority over the political elites in all provinces. Previously, there had been two streams of political thinking in Ireland: one associated with those (the English Irish) who traced their origin to the Norman conquest of the twelfth century, and the other with Gaelic lords. Political discourse had a Hibernian piquancy only because contributors were divided over whether they accepted or rejected Gerald of Wales, who, in legitimizing the conquest of Ireland undertaken by King Henry II, had portrayed the Irish of the twelfth century as a barbaric people.[4] If we disregard this ideological cleavage, political culture on the island of Ireland at the mid-point of the sixteenth century was remarkably similar to that obtaining in Britain, even when Britain was not yet governed by a single monarch. The most articulate on both islands were those representing lowland interests. In Ireland these came from the English Irish population, and usually from within the English Pale close to Dublin. These, like lowlanders and townspeople in England and Scotland, were in favour of resolving disputes through reconciliation rather than by force, they were hopeful that a new educated generation of rulers would guide their

---

[3] Morgan 1999b; Ohlmeyer 2000; Connolly 2000; Boyce, Eccleshall and Geoghegan 1993; Ó Buachalla 1996; Palmer 2001; Rankin 2005.

[4] Cambrensis 1978; Cambrensis 1982; Gillingham 1993; Gillingham 1995; Morgan 1999b.

peoples to a more peaceful, prosperous life, and they derided lords who remained attached to lineage cultures, contending that their military exactions were destroying trade and manufacturing and compelling farmers to abandon their holdings.[5]

At the opposite pole was the political culture associated with the Gaelic polity of Ireland and of the highlands and islands of Scotland. Here, loyalty was focused on the lordship, with prime value attached to the prowess of the lord on the battlefield and to his entertaining his followers, especially after military victory. Each lordship was supposedly a self-contained political entity, but lords could purport to be promoting the security and enrichment of their followers when they led raids upon their neighbours which they could justify by citing the deeds of real or putative ancestors whose authority had been more extensive than theirs. Between these poles were the lineage cultures fostered by lords of Norman ancestry in the North of England, on Scotland's borders with England, and in the provinces of Munster and Leinster in Ireland where most noblemen were of Norman extraction. These lords cultivated loyalty to themselves but they differed from their Gaelic counterparts in recognizing a monarch (either of Scotland or England) as a superior authority.[6] The political culture on the two islands might be seen to have been even more similar if we recognize that the twelfth-century writings of Geoffrey of Monmouth, (as argued by Colin Kidd), fulfilled the same function for English people as did the writings of Gerald of Wales for the English Irish population in justifying the suppression of their Celtic neighbours.[7]

Political developments in Ireland over the sixteenth century took a different course from those of the other two kingdoms principally because the Protestant Reformation failed to establish significant native roots, whereas it did so in England and Scotland. Developing discrepancy in religious allegiances compelled the government to assert its authority over all elements of Ireland's population lest some become influenced by the continental enemies of Protestantism. This was achieved first by increasing the number of Crown troops in Ireland, and then by requiring that all potential officeholders take the oath of supremacy. This latter resulted in posts in the Dublin administration, customarily occupied by sons of English Irish families who had been to the London Inns of Court,

[5] Canny 1977; Canny 1979.
[6] Ellis 1995; Rae 1966; Maginn 2005, pp. 5–32; Edwards 2003, pp. 11–78.
[7] Kidd, in this volume, pp. 50–2.

falling to English-born Protestants. This meant that the character of government in Dublin became increasingly English, Protestant and military, and as the administration set about modelling Irish society to its wishes even Queen Elizabeth acknowledged it a 'thing impossible' to treat her loyal supporters in Ireland as 'any others of her Queen's Majesty's subjects'.[8]

Different elements of the Irish population reacted differently to the gulf that emerged between government and society, but three typical responses can be discerned. The most clear-cut English Irish response was that taken in 1569–1570 by James Fitzmaurice Fitzgerald (a cousin of the Earl of Desmond), and a decade later by Desmond and his adherents in Munster and by James Eustace, Viscount Baltinglass, and his followers within, and on the borders of, the Pale. These rejected the Crown's claim to wield authority in Ireland because, in 1570, Queen Elizabeth had been excommunicated by the Pope.[9] This justification for withdrawing allegiance proved unconvincing for most of the English Irish community, who wished to repair, rather than sever, connections with the English Crown, but Catholic clergy, especially those who had been educated in Catholic Europe, could hardly ignore a papal decree.

Hugh O'Neill, Earl of Tyrone, who emerged in 1594 as leader of a confederacy of Ulster lords intent on preventing the English from interfering in the internal affairs of this primarily Gaelic province, recognized that he could turn the excommunication of Queen Elizabeth to political advantage. Earlier Gaelic opposition to Crown encroachment, emanating from lords in Leinster, Connacht, the Gaelic midlands, and Ulster, had been piecemeal, inept and inchoate, and English officers in the provinces had held their ground with small complements of troops. The challenge presented by Tyrone was different because he, who had originally been a creature of the Crown in Ulster, had spent the greater part of his youth in English Irish and English company. These contacts provided him with experience with the Crown forces in Ireland, and he put this knowledge to good purpose when it became clear to him that his survival could be better achieved by opposing rather than assisting the Crown. Then he created a military alliance that included traditional enemies of the O'Neills as well as personal supporters.[10] As his challenge escalated, some Catholic bishops recognized him as the best

[8] Canny 1975, p. 24; Morgan 2004b.
[9] Coburn-Walshe 1990; Edwards 1992; Brady 1981; Brady 1994a, pp. 209–18.
[10] Canny 2003a.

potential champion of Catholicism in Ireland. This resulted in an alliance between the pragmatic, and possibly Protestant-leaning, Tyrone, and militant Catholic bishops, with Tyrone willing to represent his opposition to the crown as religiously inspired, and the bishops seeking to have Tyrone's struggle recognized by the Papacy as a Catholic crusade. They did succeed in persuading King Philip III of Spain to provide significant support to Tyrone, and they toyed with alternative modes of government, such as recognizing the Spanish king, or the ArchDuke Albert, as protectors of an Irish federation over which Tyrone might enjoy suzerainty.[11] However the English Irish community was not impressed by the call to arms, and the bishops also failed in their effort to persuade Pope Clement VIII (then suspicious of the increasing power of Spain) to compel Catholics in Ireland to support O'Neill's confederacy.

The more normal response of the English Irish community (with the exception of the few who became Protestant and intermarried with families of English-born officials) was, in Ciaran Brady's phrase, to become 'conservative subversives'. These individuals challenged officials whenever they breached customary practice or legal precedent, appealed over the government in Dublin to the Crown in England, or lobbied in London to have officials and even governors dismissed.[12] On the positive side they pointed to their, and their ancestors', records of loyalty, emphasizing their neutral stance during the insurrections of Desmond, Baltinglass and Tyrone. More particularly, they argued that religious and political allegiance were separable and to give substance to this rationalization they offered to take an oath of allegiance, pledging loyalty to the Crown, instead of the supremacy oath, hoping that this would qualify them for return to office. Therefore they seemed reconciled to Catholicism's being a clandestine faith, and appeared only to be seeking exemption from the legal consequences of not participating in Protestant services.[13]

Despite these stratagems of the English Irish population, the government persisted in requiring the supremacy oath of all nominees to office. The arguments launched by Protestant officials against any political rehabilitation of the English Irish (who they now dubbed as Old English) were more compelling. These contended that it was the Old English, rather than the Gaelic Irish, who were the primary

---

[11] Morgan 1993; Morgan 2004b.    [12] Brady 1985; Brady 1994b.
[13] Canny 1975; Lennon 1994, pp. 177–207.

opponents of Crown government, a charge they substantiated by reference to Old English associations with Catholic Europe, and to the endeavours of their priests to forestall Protestant missionary efforts in the Gaelic areas. To counter such trends, the New English (for so we shall call them) called for untrammelled state power to defeat the conspiracies that, they asserted, would persist so long as Irish people remained attached to Catholicism.

The common adherence of Old English and Gaelic Irish to Catholicism made it possible for New English commentators to conflate the two populations, but while Edmund Spenser (the most stentorian of the New English) was adroit at representing both populations as undifferentiated Papists, his primary purpose was to suggest that each was at the same cultural level as all twelfth-century Celtic peoples had been when their mores had been described by Gerald of Wales and Geoffrey of Monmouth. Reference to Geoffrey's text, which, as we know from Colin Kidd, was more usually invoked to assert English supremacy over Scotland, was pertinent to Spenser because it had alluded also to a British dominion over Ireland asserted by King Arthur.[14]

In *A View of the Present State of Ireland* (1596) Spenser followed two paths to his perverse conclusion that both populations of Ireland were a single barbaric race. First, he summarized the portrayal of the Gaelic Irish given by Gerald of Wales and concluded, from his own personal observations, that the Gaelic Irish remained as Gerald had described them, but that the Old English (the descendants of the Normans) had since degenerated to their level. Here he turned Old English rhetoric against themselves by referring to legislation that had been passed by the medieval Irish parliament to counter such degeneration, and claimed that the process had now culminated in the once civil Old English having become more depraved than their Gaelic opponents.

A state governed by a godly prince was, in the opinion of Spenser, necessary to counter this process of decay in Ireland. It was therefore consistent that he should dismiss the official position of the 1540s which held that the Gaelic population might be lured to civility by gradual means. Arguing the impossibility of this, Spenser became the prime advocate of increasing the military authority of the Crown to effect the destruction of all opposing elites in Ireland, and the redistribution of their property among committed Protestants from England who would

[14] Kidd, in this volume.

introduce further enterprising Protestants from England. These, in turn, would develop the economy and bring the indigenous population to civility and true religion. If the prince lacked the determination to see this programme to completion, Spenser predicted the instant destruction or degeneration of the New English, and the exposure of England to corruption from within and onslaught from without. What Spenser required was, therefore, a continuing cycle of military interventions both to advance civil conditions into previously barbaric regions, and to maintain the vigour and security of the civilizing parent body. The sequence of onslaughts on Irish lordships would end only when the more tractable elements of the population had been given the opportunity to engage with educational and evangelical endeavours. It was at this point, contended Spenser, that English common law would maintain this re-constituted Irish polity in a civil condition, and that England would become secure and prosperous, having fulfilled a providential demand.[15]

Therefore, by the end of the sixteenth century, a political culture had emerged in Ireland that was strikingly different from, and more variegated than, that flourishing in England. The extreme views being expressed by the New English had anticipated by half a century what Hobbes would have to say in England. The political arguments of the Old English community would have been equally foreign to an English audience who would have found them specious, unconvincing and untenable, especially since they were inconsistent with the more rigid political teachings of Catholics that were well known to, and reviled by, English political writers. In several respects Irish political discourse differed also from the political culture of Scotland, a kingdom that was destined, in 1603, to join England and Ireland in a common Union of Crowns. The Scots, more than the English, understood the aspirations for independence of Gaelic lords, but they would not have countenanced the virulent anti-English (and soon also anti-Scottish) sentiment that had entered into poetic discourse in Gaelic Ireland.[16] Scots would also have been shocked that many Gaelic lords had responded to calls from their priests and bishops to confront the English Crown, particularly when this meant countenancing over-lordship by a foreign Catholic prince. However, while such calls had been made, there is scant evidence that any

---

[15] Canny 2001, pp. 1–58; for companion texts see Beacon 1996; Herbert 1992.
[16] On this, see Maginn 2005, pp. 180–96; Bradshaw 1978; Brown 1992; Macinnes 1996.

Gaelic lords had any understanding of how such a foreign alliance would impact upon their existing claims to sovereignty. This conclusion indicates that the extreme, or implausible, political options that had been articulated in Ireland were the product of decades of uncertainty and that all who championed individual options were aware that their implementation awaited the outcome of the war that was in full flow in 1594–1603.

SEVENTEENTH-CENTURY SOLUTIONS

The new century brought victory for the crown over Tyrone and his Spanish allies but it also brought Queen Elizabeth's death in 1603 and the succession of King James VI of Scotland as King James I of England. The new monarch inherited a near-bankrupt state which explains why he immediately sought peace with Spain, effected by the Treaty of London in 1604. Taking account of these changes, the different political interests in Ireland put forward their preferred political options for royal consideration.

The Old English urban communities were first to put their preferences to the test. They welcomed the new king, but purported to believe that, as the son of Mary Queen of Scots, he would favour Catholicism. The mayors of the Munster towns, accompanied by priests in processional robes, made overtures to the victorious governor Lord Mountjoy, claiming an entitlement to hold Catholic worship within their towns, while professing loyalty to the new monarch.[17] By so doing the priests exposed the Old English homespun political philosophy as threadbare, and Mountjoy dissipated doubt by pronouncing King James to be a firm Protestant and that the Old English had to choose between conforming in religion or facing the rigour of the law.

This choice was stark in 1605 when the Dublin government, seeing its chance to enforce conformity, mandated named prominent people from the Pale to attend divine service on specified dates or face fines and imprisonment.[18] This action, which aroused public protests and created some martyrs, persisted until the king ordered a cessation lest it drive subjects into rebellion. However, it had a sobering effect on the Old English community who from 1605 to 1641 advanced no further demands for public Catholic worship, and ensured that all future

---

[17] Jones 1958, pp. 163–73.     [18] McCavitt 1990; McCavitt 1998, pp. 111–28.

negotiations over grievances were conducted by lay delegations chosen by Catholic landowners. With time, these Old English delegations began to speak for the entire Irish Catholic population, Gaelic as well as Old English, seeking only the right of private Catholic worship and tolerance for their priests to engage in pastoral work. Further ambitions that emerged at opportune moments were that an oath of allegiance should be substituted for the supremacy oath as proof of their loyalty, that, like subjects in England, they should enjoy secure title to estates which they had occupied for sixty years, and that the legal penalties to which Catholic landowners were exposed for not attending Protestant service should be disregarded. Later, the Old English sought, in return for their allegiance, to be appointed to government office and to plead before the bar.[19]

The willingness of the Old English to extend their protective umbrella to all Catholics provided but limited solace to Gaelic lords who were threatened by the government's intention to proceed with formal plantation schemes such as had been recommended in Spenser's *View*. The most intensive plantation was that in Ulster where the rebellious Ulster lords had once been dominant, but this was but a step towards proceeding with plantations aimed at the dispossession of Gaelic lords in all provinces. Faced with this challenge, individual lords had to choose between following into exile those Ulster lords who had already abandoned the country in 1607, or seeking an accommodation with the government.[20] Many, particularly from west Munster, fled to Galicia and Brittany,[21] while most who remained in the country took advice from their Old English co-religionists. On a secular level, the Old English provided legal advice and financial support (the latter backed by mortgages on property), while many Old English seminary priests accepted support from Gaelic landowners, and their wives, to further spread Tridentine Catholicism into these localities.

Thus, the political priorities previously associated with the Old English became common to all Catholics. The Catholic spokesmen were originally lawyers from the Pale but their efforts were later augmented by Galway lawyers (the most noteworthy, Patrick Darcy) whose education at the English Inns of Court was sponsored by the Catholic, but anglicized, Earl of Clanricard.[22] The ambitions of the Catholics, studied

[19] Clarke 1966.     [20] Canny 2001, pp. 187–242.
[21] O Scea 2004; Ó Cíosáin 1994; Ó Cíosáin 2001; Lyons 2003.
[22] Cregan 1970a; Cregan 1970b; Cregan 1995.

masterfully by Aidan Clarke, were couched in the language of English common law, and their pronouncements were constitutional when it came to defending the rights of the Irish parliament against incursions upon privileges by the Dublin executive, or challenging the pretensions of the Westminster parliament to legislate for Ireland. The texts of these authors, and especially those by Darcy, have been identified as precedents for the better-known political writings of Protestant authors of a future generation, especially William Molyneux and Jonathan Swift.[23] Ultimately, Catholics perceived that the principal challenge to them came from the Dublin executive, and their victories were in persuading successive monarchs, and especially Charles I, to hearken to their professions of loyalty and grant them concessions through his prerogative power, and against parliamentary wishes in England, Scotland and Ireland.

The Old English were concerned to maintain unity within the ranks of Catholics who remained in Ireland. They did this by both positive and negative means. On the positive side, the most potent text was *Foras Feasa ar Éirinn* [*A Compendium of Knowledge about Ireland*] composed in the Irish language in 1634–1635 by Geoffrey Keating, a continentally-trained priest of Old English lineage from County Tipperary. The text gained instant popularity in Catholic Ireland and circulated extensively in manuscript form, including in English translation. Here, Keating constructed an alternative antique past for Ireland to that depicted by Gerald of Wales and Geoffrey of Monmouth. His version of the past showed that social conditions in ancient Ireland were so humane that Christianity took root immediately following St Patrick's arrival. This interpretation enabled Keating to detail the exemplary Christian community that flourished until it was threatened by the onslaught of the Viking invaders who were eventually repulsed. Religion, in Keating's narrative, again prospered and, through a sequence of synods, the Irish church was brought into such conformity with Roman best practice that it merged successfully with the church of the Norman conquerors of Ireland. Thus, as Keating represented it, Irish society had always been in, or close to, a Christian condition until its tranquillity, as elsewhere in Europe, was disturbed by the Protestant Reformation. Thus he could argue that his own ancestors, 'the old foreign settlers in Ireland', and the Gaelic inhabitants were a single Christian people opposed by

---

[23] Clarke 1966; Clarke 2000; Simms 1983; Kelly 2000.

unprincipled foreign freebooters who lacked respect for the society and its traditions.[24]

Keating's text was, obviously, a refutation of 'the matter of Britain', that has been delineated by Colin Kidd, since Keating challenged all writers, including Stanihurst, Camden, Spenser, Fynes Moryson, and Sir John Davies, who wrote within that paradigm.[25] More particularly, Keating contended that his history was more authoritative that that of his opponents due to his superior citation of evidence, a point he sustained both by alluding to the inaccuracy of his rivals when they invoked authority, and their malevolent purpose when they vilified the Irish without evidence.[26]

With the appearance of Keating's *Foras Feasa*, history writing in Ireland became an equivalent of religious controversy with rivals from either camp claiming a monopoly on truth about Ireland's and Britain's pasts.[27] Historical writing, like theological disputation, was political, and Keating's purpose, besides discrediting the maligners of Ireland's populations was to argue (for reasons opposite to those of Spenser) that the two principal elements of stock — the Old English and the Gaelic Irish — were a single people. For these he coined the term *Éireannaigh* [Irish people], united by religion, consanguinity, and long sharing of the same space, against whom the New English (and the Scots) would always be foreign intruders. When exhorting his co-religionists to abandon their past differences he suggested that it was those of noble lineage from both the Old English and Gaelic Irish populations who were most likely to hearken to his call, thus implying his lack of confidence in social inferiors. Further such evidence emerged in another Irish language text, *Pairlement Chloinne Tomáis* [*The Parliament of Clann Thomas*], which, together with some Irish language poems expressing contempt for peasants who had risen above their station, suggests that wealthy Catholics feared their community would divide horizontally. It also establishes that those living in comfortable circumstances understood that English political ideas, practices, and vocabulary were being used by their social inferiors

---

[24] Keating 1902–1914, I, pp. 2–3; Cunningham, 2000.
[25] Kidd, in this volume; Keating, 1902–1914, I, pp. 12–13 where he specifically refutes the claim that Ireland paid tribute to King Arthur.
[26] Keating's references to Spenser's *View*, were specific, but it is unclear whether he was citing from a manuscript copy or the bowdlerized printed version of 1633, published in Dublin for the Protestant antiquarian Sir James Ware; Keating 1902–1914, I, pp. 24–31.
[27] On the parallel religious controversy of this time see Ford 1995, pp. 193–242.

to uplift themselves even as the peasants' imitation of English procedures provided the authors with material for ribald mockery.[28]

It is unsurprising that Old English lawyers and landowners feared that
their control over Catholic political discourse should be occasionally
challenged from below, especially since priests were essentially muzzled
after the debacle of 1605. Neither is it surprising, given the fluidity of Irish
society during decades of plantations, that some from the lower orders
should ride on the coat-tails of successful Protestants. However, the Old
English leaders proved themselves skilful at mobilizing delegations at
short notice either when danger threatened or opportunity beckoned.
Negotiations took place, sometimes, but not always, at fringe gatherings
to the Irish parliament in 1613–1615, 1634 and 1640. At these assemblies
they appraised policy and raised money to finance agents to lobby the
Privy Council, or individual Councillors, or the royal court. Moreover
they were also able, during the reign of King Charles I, to combine their
canvassing with that of Clanricard (or Viscount St Albans as he was in the
English peerage) who usually resided at Tonbridge in Kent, enjoyed
access to the Catholic Queen, Henrietta Maria, and who, as a Catholic
and the largest landowner in the province of Connacht, was a prime
target for government-planned plantation.

The pinnacle of Old English achievement was their negotiating from
King Charles I the package of concessions known at the Graces, conceded
in 1628 when war between England and Spain threatened. These
promised a tolerance, rather than a toleration, of Catholicism within
a Protestant state. This was an exceptional arrangement by European
standards, was considered implausible by some Catholics as well as by
Protestants and rested entirely on the promise of a monarch. The
shallowness of the Old English accomplishment was exposed when
Wentworth contemptuously dismissed the royal promises and when, in
the 1640s, the English parliament decided to legislate for Ireland without
reference to the Irish parliament. It was in response to these challenges
that Patrick Darcy put pen to paper, and formulated arguments on the
constitutional relationship between the two jurisdictions to which
reference would be made for generations to come.[29]

If the leaders of the Catholic community in Ireland refrained from
formulating fresh challenges, their exiled kin were attracted by every
political argument that might hasten their return to Ireland and their

---

[28] Williams 1981.     [29] Clarke 2000; Caldicott 1992; Ó Siochrú 2005.

recovery of the estates they had abandoned. Some who recorded their views were laymen such as Philip O'Sullivan Beare who, publishing from Portugal, rehearsed developments in sixteenth-century Ireland portraying the sequence of insurrections as a continuous war for the defence of Catholicism. For him, therefore, the issues that had been fought over would remain unresolved until Ireland had a Catholic ruler.[30]

This idea, consonant with Catholic political teaching, did not always enjoy support from Catholic clerics who offered political as well as spiritual advice to the exiled lords while acting as their agents to the Spanish court. These tailored their political doctrines to whatever strategy was favoured in Rome or Madrid for restoring Britain (as opposed to Ireland) to the Catholic fold. Consequently, the policies recommended by the clergy oscillated between advising people at home to take an Oath of Allegiance to the Stuart monarchy (hoping this would result in some tolerance of Catholicism both in Britain and Ireland), and rejecting the authority of the Stuarts because, logically, Catholics could not swear allegiance to monarchs who had previously taken an oath to uphold Protestantism. Historians frequently suggest that clerics from Gaelic background favoured the intransigent position, and that Old English priests were more conciliatory, but priests were usually guided by their superiors; thus, for example, the Old English Peter Lombard shifted from wishing to have Tyrone's rebellion declared a crusade, to expounding the merits of the Old English position of the mid-seventeenth century.[31] Moreover, all who were seminary-trained, whether they were in Ireland or on the Continent, knew that the conciliatory line went against Catholic norms.

If priests were inconsistent in their directives, Irish people also received mixed messages mediated through Gaelic literature. Some poets implicitly recommended loyalty to the Stuart monarchy (but not to the government in Dublin), and others rehearsed the wrongs that Irish Catholics had recently suffered, and they indicated that they hoped for redress. Thus while Breandán Ó Buachalla, in his monumental *Aisling Ghéar* (1996), identifies three Irish language poems congratulating King James on adding the crown of Ireland to those of Scotland and England, and can trace to 1788 a Gaelic literary tradition of loyalty to the Stuarts, all such professions (which after 1689 – and certainly after 1715 – were

---

[30] O'Sullivan Beare 1850; Carroll 2001.
[31] Silke 1955a; Silke 1955b; Lombard 1868.

statements of disloyalty to ruling monarchs) were counterbalanced by poems attributing Ireland's plight to particular rulers including James I and Charles I as well as Cromwell.[32] Also, Gaelic verse, like Catholic apologetics, was political in being laden with invective against Protestants who had come to Ireland with the plantations. Further political messages were transmitted in government proclamations (which were sometimes translated from English into Irish). Residents in Ireland would also have witnessed legal and parliamentary rituals evincing loyalty to the state, while those returning to Ireland from Catholic countries of Europe would have known alternate political pageants and symbols.

Protestant Ireland produced few who composed original political texts during the first half of the seventeenth century. One author who moved beyond regurgitation was Sir John Davies, a poet of distinction who held the posts of Solicitor and then Attorney General for Ireland during the reign of King James VI and I. Irish historians have long credited Davies with composing legal rationalizations for plantation in Ulster, and with designing the Irish circuits of assize. Also, in his best-known text *A Discovery of the True Causes...* (1612), Davies devised a new chronology for Ireland's history discarding the antique past and commencing with the Normans, who had brought the Irish into historical time that was about to end when, as Davies predicted, the Irish would 'in tongue & heart and every way else become English so there [would] be no difference or distinction but the Irish sea between us'.[33] Davies, as John Pocock has suggested, was, like Sir Edward Coke, an upholder of the authority of immemorial custom, but it has been made clear by Hans Pawlisch that not all custom was considered by Davies to be of equal merit.[34] Rather he, like Spenser before him, condemned Gaelic custom as corrupt and corrupting, and concluded that any claims legitimized by such custom should enjoy no standing in common law. Again, like Spenser, Davies invoked the right of conquest (which was anchored in Roman civil law) to justify his assertion, and he enforced it by judicial decree rather than by an act of the Irish parliament.

The authoritarian Davies is the more convincing figure because his views won acceptance from Protestants in Ireland, including his belief that decisions of Irish institutions, whether legal or parliamentary, might

[32] Ó Buachalla 1996; Ó Ciardha 2002; Canny 2001, p. 428.
[33] Davies 1612, p. 272.
[34] Pocock 1987a, esp. pp. 32–5; Pawlisch 1985.

be appealed for final resolution to their 'parent' institutions in England; a proposition that went undisputed until Thomas Wentworth, Earl of Strafford, began to use such appeals to challenge Protestant interests. Therefore, during the first half of the seventeenth century, Protestants no less than Catholics in Ireland, represented themselves as supporters of monarchical rule, and they association legal quibbling with Old English evasions. However the strident anti-Catholicism of Protestants, no less than the vehement anti-Protestantism of Catholics, indicated that, as with Catholics, their obedience to King Charles was conditional. The limit to Protestant deference to monarchical authority was exposed whenever the king (James VI and I as well as Charles I) sought, for political reasons, to concede religious tolerance to Catholicism. This raised a public outcry both within and without Protestant churches in Ireland with clergy sermonizing on such topics as the 'scandal of toleration' and religion being for sale.[35]

Protestant support for kingly rule became even more tentative when, as they perceived had happened during the government of Wentworth (a prominent supporter of King Charles), Protestants suffered persecution and Catholicism was tolerated. By this time also, the character and political outlook of Protestants had been transformed because many of the Scots planted in Ulster identified with the political and religious positions adopted by their Covenanter kinsfolk in Scotland, even to the point where the firebrands of militant Scottish Calvinism found refuge in Ulster. This led Wentworth to impose disciplinary measures upon Ulster Protestants and to raise an army in Ireland, which included Catholics, that he would convey into Scotland to suppress the Covenanters there. These events forced all Protestants to decide if they could continue to support the king's governor and his master; a choice that became more urgent when the rift between the king and his Scottish subjects became more acute, and when the king was at loggerheads with the English parliament. Ultimately, few Protestant leaders in Ireland gave unqualified support to monarchical rule, and those who did so experienced difficulty in controlling Protestant troops who, as well as being reluctant to fight against co-religionists, were frequently bound under oath by their clergy to withdraw from actions that were deemed to be in conflict with Protestant principles and interests.[36] Such obstruction points to the existence among Protestants in Ireland, including Protestants of modest

---

[35] Canny 2001, p. 267; Armstrong 2005.
[36] Forkan 2003; Armstrong 2005.

social position, of a keen awareness of political developments in England and Scotland as well as in Ireland. Moreover, in the increasingly uncertain circumstances of the 1640s, Irish Protestants began to commit their opinions to print at an unprecedented level in a deluge of political propaganda, much of it filed among the Thomason tracts.[37] Many pamphlets, addressed to English and Scottish readers, were sponsored by Protestants of high rank with an interest in Ireland. Most, however, was composed by clergy, merchants, officers, soldiers, and others who had been dispossessed by the insurrection of 1641, and who wanted their interpretation of what had occurred made available to the widest possible audience.

Most of this splenetic Protestant outpouring impresses by its quantity rather than its quality but it culminated in 1646 in Sir John Temple's *A History of the Irish Rebellion* which established itself as a fundamental pronouncement on the political preferences of many Irish Protestants. The 'execrable rebellion', was that of 1641 in Ireland which, according to Temple's interpretation, had been designed by the Papacy through its instruments the Catholic priests, and their pawns, the Catholic landowners of Ireland, to effect an extirpation of Irish Protestants analogous to the St Bartholomew's Day Massacre of 1572. The immediate occasion that provoked Temple to publish his *History* was the attempt in 1646 by the government of King Charles I to effect a cessation of hostilities between the royal army, commanded by the Marquis of Ormond, and the armies of the Catholic Confederates. These latter had been formed to maintain discipline within Catholic ranks in the aftermath of the insurrection of 1641, to uphold Catholic interests and to assist the king against his opponents in England and Scotland. Temple, opposed in principle to the political rehabilitation of those he held responsible for the deaths of Protestants in 1641, demonstrated the impropriety of any settlement with Catholics by citing selectively from Protestant eye witness accounts of the onslaught they had suffered in 1641.[38] Much of Temple's narrative fitted into previous Protestant presentations or presumptions: he shared Spenser's idea that Irish society had been corrupt from the outset; he endorsed Davies's argument that the English of the twelfth century had been the first to introduce civil conditions to the country; and he concurred with the presumption of both Spenser and Davies that evil would always prevail unless it was

[37] Lindley 1972; Armstrong 2005.     [38] On the composition, see Gillespie 2005b.

restrained by a superior force. But he differed from these in abandoning the notion that Irish Catholics could be transformed into useful subjects through a programme in social engineering such as had been detailed in Spenser's *View. The History of the Irish Rebellion* established that Irish Catholics were a perfidious, ungrateful and unregenerate people on whom Irish Protestants and the English Crown might rightfully wreak vengeance but must never admit into their society.

Some Protestants, English and Irish alike, of future generations, and including even some Cromwellians, aspired to contain Irish Catholics within their communities or even to reform them. However, most Irish Protestants had been convinced by Temple's argument that it was at their peril that Protestants would admit Catholics to positions of trust.[39] His opinions seem to have impacted also on English and Scottish Protestant thought if we are to judge from James Harrington's *Oceana* of 1656. Here Harrington displayed familiarity with Spenser's thinking on degeneracy, but instead of seeking in Spenserian fashion to improve the Irish through social manipulation, Harrington (in line with what Petty would recommend later) advised that the natives be removed to make way for Jews who might be invited from all parts of Europe to make Ireland their promised land.[40]

Such opinions were admissible into English, and indeed Scottish, political discourse because what happened in Ireland in 1641 and, more poignantly, what thousands of Protestant refugees from Ireland (who made their way to their home parishes in England and Scotland in the aftermath of the insurrection) alleged had happened to them during the course of the insurrection, made an impression upon the populations of those two kingdoms of a kind that no previous Irish episode had done. This explains why, from the outset, money had been made available by the Scottish Covenanters to recover Protestant authority in Ulster and why the military conquest of Ireland became the first priority of the parliamentary forces in England once victory over the king was assured. And what happened (or was believed by Protestants to have happened) in 1641, and the prolonged turmoil that stemmed from it, made it clear how closely bound were the destinies of the Three Kingdoms.

Perhaps most revelatory is the light that these actions and their legitimizations shed upon the political ideas, principles and expectations

[39] Temple 1646; Barnard 1993, pp. 173–86; Barber 2005; Barnard 2005; Gillespie 2005b.
[40] Harrington 1992, pp. 6–7.

of a broad cross-segment of the Catholic population of Ireland; glimpses that are as insightful as those offered by the Putney debates on the political priorities of common English soldiers. The first political idea universally shared by all Irish Catholics was that they had never been rewarded for their loyalty to the Crown, that they had been treated unfairly throughout the seventeenth century and that they had suffered the ultimate betrayal when Wentworth had denied landowners security in land which was the most tangible benefit promised by the Graces. Such factors added to their knowledge of how the Scots had taken their destiny into their own hands and their fear of what the English parliament was plotting against them indicates why such a large spread of Irish Catholics took up arms supposedly in support of the king. The shallow roots to such royalism were exposed by subsequent claims by the insurgents that they were the queen's soldiers (Queen Henrietta Maria being a Catholic) or that they wished to change their allegiance to a Catholic monarch, mentioning both the Kings of Spain and France as candidates, or that they would have one of the O'Neills as king, or that they would, 'have a free state of themselves as they had in Holland, and not to be tied to any king or prince whatsoever'.[41]

Any, or all, of such stated ambitions point to the widely shared desire among Catholics in Ireland for innovation, and particularly for a change that would restore power to Catholics and cancel that of the hated government in Dublin. Thus, unlike in England where leaders of the political nation showed a marked reluctance to take up arms either for or against their king, many discontented Catholic lords in Ireland took advantage of the first chink in the government's armour to seek after innovation and, by force of arms, to recover the property and positions that had come into the possession of English and Scottish newcomers either through plantation or commercial transactions. Moreover, as has been established by scholarly work of the past decades, those in England who did challenge the authority of the king in arms were responding to contingency and in the interest of upholding the *status quo*, and most did not acknowledge that they were seeking a new order until after the king's actions forced them to imprison him and ultimately to put him on trial and to death.[42] By way of contrast, those in Ireland who took up

---

[41] The course of events in 1641 and the explanations offered by Catholics for their actions are detailed in Canny 2001, pp. 461–550; deposition of William Fitton, Limerick, 1643 (Trinity College, Dublin, MS 829, ff 310–11).

[42] Russell 1991; Morrill 1980; Hughes 1987.

arms in 1641 (like those in Scotland who had done so some years previously) proceeded with alacrity and with ready-made explanations for their actions. Moreover it has been shown that in following the course they did, landowners were often driven by their social inferiors who seemed ready to overthrow their betters if they did not embrace revolution.

A reconstruction of events has indicated that the Catholic clergy, always depicted by Protestant propagandists as firebrands, were silent witnesses to the events of 1641. This is not surprising given that since 1605 the Catholic laity had insisted that they, rather than priests, should speak on matters political. However, once the insurrection was underway, priests became involved to discipline those they regarded as extremists and to direct the action towards godly purposes. They persisted in recognizing Charles I as their monarch, and the more his prerogative was challenged in Scotland and in England, the more they endorsed him as king of Ireland. But it soon became clear that their support for the king was conditional upon him accepting that Catholics were entitled to worship publicly, would recover property and churches confiscated at the time of the Reformation, and that Catholic clergy would be assigned official livings, presumably at the expense of existing Protestant ministers. What would be the position of Protestants within this Catholic Ireland was not clear.[43] However Catholic clergy were the prime movers throughout 1642 behind the creation of the Catholic Confederacy, which, with its armies, was to restore order, and secure a final agreement with King Charles after they had assisted him in overcoming his enemies.[44]

This package indicates the political gulf that separated the Irish Catholic clergy from the most accommodating politicians in England, Scotland and Protestant Ireland. It also highlights the differences that had always existed between clerical and lay interests within the Irish Catholic community that now came to the fore. Essentially, Old English leaders feared a Catholic church that would challenge them as natural leaders of their communities, and that would set demands that the king could not concede. This conflict of interest produced stalemate, with the Confederacy becoming divided, the king attempting to negotiate secretly with what he saw as the moderate faction, and the clergy using their powers of excommunication to enforce their political will.[45]

---

[43] Armstrong 2005.     [44] Ó Siochrú 2005.     [45] Ó Siochrú 1999.

Therefore the Confederacy episode is significant because it exposes the range of incompatible political ideas that had enjoyed currency in Ireland for a time before the mid-seventeenth century. Some potent Catholic ideas had been quiescent, at which times ideas anchored in English common law gained prominence. However the prospect of reversing the plantations, attaining a public status for Catholicism or achieving a Catholic jurisdiction for Ireland, had never been forgotten by those in exile, by seminary priests, or by the wider populace. Rather, it seems that the dream of a Catholic Ireland continued to hold appeal, and that the text best representing what Catholics might have wanted in 1641 (but not openly in the years of the Confederacy) is the *Disputatio Apologetica* (1645) by the Jesuit, Conor O'Mahony. This, like the pronouncements of those involved in the 'popular' insurrection, advocated the expulsion of all heretics from Ireland as the pre-requisite for making it a godly and Catholic society, and contemplated severing the connection with a Protestant monarchy.[46] The existence of such desires, however camouflaged, explains why the Catholic Confederacy could never arrive at a political consensus, and why the effort of Charles I to reach an accommodation for his three kingdoms was a forlorn hope.

## CONCLUSION

The study of political thought in Ireland has frequently been approached from a British perspective with attention given to authors who identified themselves with political discourse in England and even in Scotland. This chapter has remedied this bias by drawing upon the full range of historical writing on Ireland over time, and upon more recent writing that has been situated in wider contexts. The surprise has been that while political discourse in Ireland at mid-sixteenth century was but a provincial echo of political culture in Britain, that which flourished there a century later was radically different from British norms both in form and ambition. This conclusion has been enabled, first by a study of radical political arguments formulated by the servants of an expanding English/British state; arguments that had no equivalent in domestic English discourse previous to Hobbes. A second study, leading to the same conclusion, has been of the alternative political models inspired by writing in Catholic Europe and deployed by Catholics in Ireland to

---

[46] O'Mahony 1645.

counter the actions and ideas of British officials. In both investigations this chapter has demonstrated the relevance to the history of political thought of a wider range of sources than is customarily employed: histories, theological tracts, law tracts, oral legitimizations of political action and published and unpublished poetic compositions in several languages, in addition to political pamphlets (again in several languages) that conventionally fall within the purview of historians of political thought.

Despite the differences between the British and Irish experiences that have come to light, the chapter has a 'British' interest if for no other reason than because the actors accepted that Ireland's future would likely be linked to that of Britain. Obviously, to have such a relationship work satisfactorily would have necessitated either fundamental compromises, or the absolute dominance of one political culture within Britain and Ireland. Compromise solutions were usually favoured by Catholics (but not necessarily those in exile) and by the Crown during times of peace. However, compromise was never favoured by Protestants in Ireland or by more rigid Protestants in Scotland or England. Equally significant, all thought of compromise was forgotten when the exponents of any one position had the opportunity of establishing theirs as the dominant one. This impasse rendered the problem of governing a composite monarchy of three kingdoms more difficult than historians have appreciated.

The chapter is also 'British' because of the increasing Scottish presence in Ulster that was sympathetic towards the political priorities of the Scottish Covenanters. Their presence, living and interacting with sizeable Gaelic Irish, Old English, and English Protestant populations, meant that Ulster in the mid-seventeenth century was the world's quintessentially *British* space where a range of political voices clamoured, each seeking to become the loudest and, therefore, the dominant voice both on the island of Ireland and throughout the jurisdictions of the British monarchy. It is not surprising that this turmoil induced the people of Ulster to engage more readily than people elsewhere in bloody and prolonged conflict that resulted in a massive loss of life on all sides: initially in the 1640s but with a repeat performance in the 1690s. Since there were advocates in Ulster of almost every conceivable political option of the seventeenth century it is not surprising that the Ulster conflict spread rapidly to the other provinces of Ireland and to the other jurisdictions of the British monarchy. Thus it emerged that the issue of governance on the broader canvas of three kingdoms could be resolved only by further prolonged bloody conflict designed to effect the dominance of one set of political preferences over all competitors.

This chapter provides a practical demonstration of the variety of political opinions flourishing in Ireland and of the impact that political thought and experience there exerted on British politics. But it has also made the case that political thought within Britain and Ireland was but a dimension of European political thought, especially since the populations of Ireland and Scotland in the seventeenth, as in the twenty-first century were more outward-looking and continentally-linked than the population of England.

# CHAPTER 5

# In Search of a British History of Political Thought

## Tim Harris

Despite the Britannic turn that early-modern historiography has taken over the last couple of decades, what it means to write a British history of political thought remains an under-explored subject. Colin Kidd elsewhere in this volume shows how we might write a history of British political thought as a history of political thinking about the concept of Britain.[1] By a British history of political thought, however, I have in mind something different: how we integrate the study of political thought into the writing of the (so-called) new British history. We have been taught, of late, that many of the problems that afflicted the Stuarts in the seventeenth century, for example, stemmed from their problematic multiple-kingdom inheritance. Might not what contemporaries thought about 'the British problem' be characterized as British political thought, and is not the history of this thought that we proceed to write British history? If so, then what kind of a British history? John Morrill also observes that there are various broad types of British history currently being written — among them, the 'incorporative' (using the Britannic context to explain problems of English, or alternatively Scottish or Irish, history), the 'confederal' (parallel accounts of developments in all Three Kingdoms) and the 'perfect' (most notably, the study of important individuals, such as the Earl of Antrim, who saw their Irish, Scottish and English worlds as one) — and suggests that the incorporative approach is the one that has appealed most to historians of ideas.[2] Does this mean that a British history of political thought can at best only ever be an enriched type of English (or Scottish or Irish) history? Or might there be a history of political thought that is genuinely pan-archipelagic and which cannot be dismissed as Anglo-centric (or Scotto- or Hiberno-centric)?

This chapter will examine these questions with respect to the period from the Exclusion Crisis to the Glorious Revolution (covering the years

---

[1] Kidd, in this volume.    [2] Morrill, in this volume.

from the late 1670s to the early 1690s). Before proceeding, however, some general observations about my own position are in order. The first is that I have never been of the view that the Three-Kingdoms approach is *the* (in the sense of 'the only') way forward for seventeenth-century studies. The call for British history (or, more precisely, British and Irish history) has undoubtedly been of great value in forcing us to recognize the existence of a multiple-kingdoms dimension when such a dimension did exist but has been obscured by the blinkered approaches of traditional nationalist historiographies. Having said that, there is no point in trying to force a Three-Kingdoms approach where one does not make sense. Sometimes the appropriate unit of inquiry might be the nation or a locality. On occasion the trans-national perspective that beckons might be continental European or trans-Atlantic rather than British and Irish. Thus even though there might have been an important Three-Kingdoms dimension to the political history of the period 1678–1691, this does not mean that the Three-Kingdoms dimension provides *the* key to understanding the politics of this time: rather, it is just one of the contexts, and we need to keep our eye on the other contexts, whether they be provincial, metropolitan, or continental. Furthermore, the same range of sources might push in multiple directions; whether or not a Britannic centre makes sense will in part depend on the questions we intend to ask.

Historians of early-modern political thought – even when their work has focused exclusively on English-language texts – have long recognized the importance of the international dimension. For example, resistance theory as it developed in sixteenth- and seventeenth-century England, culminating with John Locke, had roots both Scottish (one thinks in particular of George Buchanan) and continental European (both Protestant and Catholic, pre- as well as post-Reformation).[3] Similarly, much English absolutist thought in the seventeenth century was actually European, in the sense of being derived from continental thinkers (such as Jean Bodin).[4] In some regards, it would not be accurate to style some (or perhaps much) of the political thought that was current in England in the seventeenth century as being English, in terms of its intellectual pedigree or ideological lineage – although historians have certainly acknowledged what were the recognizably distinctively English contributions to, say, the formulations of ideas about limited or unlimited

---

[3] Skinner 1978a; Burns 1993; J. Scott 2004, ch. 5.
[4] Sommerville 1986; Sommerville 1996; Goldie 1997.

government.[5] Yet in other regards political discourse in England, even when most explicitly derived from continental sources, must be labelled English political thought if it was (as much of it necessarily was) political thinking applied to specifically English problems and situations. If a Scotsman, writing from Holland, deploying ideas rooted in a continental European rather than a recognizably English intellectual tradition, nevertheless aimed to instruct the English how to react to an English crisis, surely his political thought is English in certain very central respects. One thinks here of Gilbert Burnet – although, as will become clear later in this essay, the case of Burnet is far from straightforward and illustrates the complexity of the issues involved.

This chapter will show that much of the political thought of the period 1678–1691 was indeed thought that addressed the British dimension to politics and worked at a pan-archipelagic level. Thinkers recognized that both the Exclusion Crisis and the Glorious Revolution held implications for all Three Kingdoms; they were aware that the later-Stuart monarchs pursued political strategies that were Britannic in conception rather than independent English, Scottish and Irish strategies; and the thought of this time period often reflected an assumption that the English, Scottish and Irish worlds were one. We do clearly encounter some form of British political thought here, and this is something which scholars have hitherto failed to appreciate. Yet it is not British political thought in any unproblematic sense: depending on the questions we choose to ask, we might style it British or alternatively not British. When writing British history – whether or not as historians of political thought – we need to be aware that there are going to be times when the British problematic takes centre stage and times when other perspectives displace the Three-Kingdoms one. This suggests the need for an alternative way of conceptualizing the subject of British history than those currently on offer: one that avoids compartmentalizations but rather recognizes and seeks to come to terms with the complex dynamic that shaped the interactions between the kingdoms of England, Scotland and Ireland in the early-modern era.

As I have demonstrated at length elsewhere, both the Exclusion Crisis and the Glorious Revolution were pan-archipelagic crises.[6] There were many reasons why this was the case, linked to the complex ways in which initiatives pursued by both Charles II and James II in any one of their

[5] Pocock 1987a.    [6] Harris 1998; Harris 2005; Harris 2006.

kingdoms had knock-on consequences for the other two. Yet there was
also a more fundamental reason: in a multiple monarchy, excluding the
heir to the throne or deposing the reigning sovereign in one kingdom
inevitably affected the other kingdoms that shared the same monarch.
Understandably, therefore, both crises generated a considerable amount
of political thinking that addressed the Three-Kingdoms dimension and
the problems of the Stuarts' British and Irish inheritances. For example,
concerns in England during the Exclusion Crisis were related not simply
to a fear of what might happen should Charles II's Catholic brother,
James, Duke of York, accede to the English throne; they were also set
against the backdrop of developments in Ireland (where the royal
administration appeared to be soft on popery) and Scotland (where the
government under the Duke of Lauderdale appeared to be acting in an
increasingly arbitrary manner, especially in its efforts to suppress radical
Presbyterian dissent). The Earl of Shaftesbury spelled out precisely these
concerns in a speech on the state of the nation delivered in the House of
Lords on 25 March 1679: 'Scotland and Ireland', he said, 'are two doors,
either to let in good or mischief upon us', but both had been 'much
weakened by the artifice of our cunning enemies'; in England 'popery was
to have brought in slavery', whereas 'in Scotland slavery went before, and
popery was to follow', while in Ireland the towns were so 'full of Papists'
that the kingdom would not 'long continue in English hands, if some
better care be not taken of it'.[7] Such concerns were to be reiterated by
various Whig spokesmen and pamphleteers as the Exclusion Crisis
unfolded.[8] Indeed, by failing to recognize that the Whigs were thinking
in Three-Kingdoms – and not just in English – terms, historians have
seriously misread Whig anxieties, seeing them as no more than imagined
fears, rooted in religious bigotry, of a possible threat in the future. In fact,
their fears related to what was going on in the present and the threat
was very real.

The Three-Kingdoms dimension is also vital to understanding the
Tory response to the Exclusionists' challenge. As we have now come
to understand, the Tories were highly successful in rallying public opinion
behind the crown and the hereditary succession in the face of the Whig
challenge. They did this, in large part, by portraying the Whigs as
nonconformist (especially Presbyterian) 'fanatics' who posed more of
a threat to the established Church of England and to English political

[7] Cobbett 1806–20, IV, cols. 1116–18.   [8] Harris 2005, pp. 168–74.

liberties than a Catholic successor would.[9] Within a purely English context, it is difficult to understand how this line of argumentation could have been persuasive. The English Presbyterians were not particularly radical or subversive, whereas York, when he became king, did (as the Whigs had predicted) use the royal prerogative to undermine the established Church and the rule of law. However, even the quickest perusal of Tory speeches, pamphlets, literature, and sermons from the Exclusion Crisis reveals that the Tories were not thinking within a purely English context. They were thinking of the threat posed by the Presbyterians north of the border: it was the Scottish Covenanter rebellion that had set in motion the train of events leading to the outbreak of civil war in 1642, and radical Covenanters in Scotland had launched two (albeit unsuccessful) uprisings since the Restoration (in 1666 and 1679). It was an easy step then for Tory journalists to allude to similarities between 'the Platform of the Scottish Presbytery' and that of the English Presbyterians, and to urge people 'to observe the Harmony betwixt Simeon and Levi'.[10] The claim that the Church of England would be safe under the Duke of York when he became king likewise seemed proven by York's record in Scotland, where he had effectively served as vice-roy during much of the Exclusion Crisis and shown himself a staunch ally of the episcopalian establishment against the threat of radical Protestant dissent. York should be judged by 'His Conduct', one pamphleteer insisted, pointing to his loving and wise rule in Scotland; another reported how York's 'noble Acts' north of the border had procured him 'a general respect' and tied the hearts of the Scottish people to him 'in Loyalty and Affection'.[11] Tories also argued that if the Whigs were not defeated, civil war was likely to break out again. Their logic here was in part related to their belief that, even if the English parliament succeeded in passing an Exclusion Bill, it would never be accepted by the Scots or the Irish (the former, indeed, had passed legislation in 1681 prohibiting tampering with the hereditary succession) and thus war between the Three Kingdoms would be bound to break out, as had happened in mid-century. One author even predicted that Scotland and Ireland would 'rejoice at another Civil War', in the hopes of freeing 'themselves from the Inconveniences of being Provinces'.[12]

---

[9] Harris 1987, ch. 5.     [10] L'Estrange 1678, p. 4.
[11] [J. S.] 1681, p. 1; *Plea for Succession* 1682, p. 2.
[12] *England's Concern* 1680, p. 10. For a general discussion of these issues, see Harris 2005, pp. 239–45, 251–2.

Pamphleteers, polemicists, political commentators and party spokesmen, in other words, thought about the crisis over the succession that
emerged in the late 1670s in Three-Kingdoms terms. (Why historians
should have been blind to this for so long remains puzzling, since the very
labels applied to the rival political interests, initially as terms of abuse by
their enemies, were Scottish and Irish: Whig referred initially to a
Scottish Presbyterian rebel, Tory to a Catholic-Irish cattle thief.)[13] Does
that mean we can categorize Whig and Tory political thought during the
Exclusion Crisis as British political thought? Yes and no. It was perfectly
possible for Whigs to make their case against popery and arbitrary
government, and hence for the need to exclude the Catholic heir, without
referring to either Ireland or Scotland. Indeed, many Whig writers and
spokesmen never once mentioned Ireland or Scotland. Frequently Whigs
looked at what was going on in France under Louis XIV – who had
consolidated the trend towards royal absolutism in France and also begun
to rescind the political and religious freedoms allowed to French
Huguenots under the terms of the Edict of Nantes (1598) – and warned
that a future Catholic ruler in England, especially one with the Duke of
York's temperament, would rule in exactly the same way. In much Whig
political thought, there is more of a continental European dimension
than a Britannic one. Moreover, Whig writers and polemicists were
able to point to political trends and developments in England under
Charles II and allege that popery and arbitrary government were already
on the increase at home, needing neither Ireland, Scotland, nor France to
make their points.[14] Of course, given that certain Whig spokesmen had
already done their best to bring the situations in Ireland, Scotland and
continental Europe to the public's awareness, others could choose not to,
confident in the knowledge that British and European developments
would still form part of the conceptual framework within which people
would interpret their arguments. It was not necessary for all Whigs always
to make the same points. Thus we might conclude that the terms of
discourse in which the debate over Exclusion was conducted might fairly
be characterized as British (and European), even if far from all of the
sources we examine in order to reconstruct this discourse make reference
to the British (or European) dimension. Yet, at most, what we are dealing
with here is surely an enriched English history. The perspective
presented enables us to understand how concerns, in England, about

[13] Willman 1974.    [14] Harris 2005, pp. 164–7, 174–83.

Irish, Scottish or continental European developments affected the way the English thought about the problems facing them — a still highly Anglo-centric British history at best.

Similar observations might be made about the Glorious Revolution. Critics of James II were all the more alarmed about what the Catholic king was doing in England because of what he was up to in Ireland and Scotland. In England, in fact, James was relatively cautious in his efforts to help his co-religionists and remained careful not to lay claim to an arbitrary or absolute power that the English monarchy could not be said to possess. In Ireland, by contrast, moves were rapidly made to Catholicize the military establishment and civil administration,[15] while in Scotland James unabashedly proclaimed his absolute prerogative to break or annul laws and his right to be obeyed 'without reserve', as he did in his Scottish Declaration of Indulgence of February 1687 (something he was able to do in part because the Scottish Parliament had itself acknowledged in an Act of 1685 that the Scottish monarch was absolute).[16] It was certainly possible for English people to regard James as a Catholic despot bent on overturning the rule of law and undermining the Protestant religion just by looking at what James was up to in England. The situation nevertheless looked much worse when set against what James was doing in the other two kingdoms over which he ruled. Here again, then, we have a British history of political thought that offers us a significantly enriched English history.[17]

Yet the situation is a little more complicated. This is in part related to the way that James II used Scotland as a laboratory for what he wanted to achieve in England: as his own daughter observed in June 1688, what 'has been done there [in Scotland], has been but a fore-runner of what in a short time has been done here [in England]'.[18] Because James knew he was theoretically absolute in Scotland, and because the crown in Scotland possessed greater control over the Scottish parliament than the crown in England did over the English parliament, he tried to force through his more controversial measures north of the border first, hoping that Scotland would provide a model that England would feel under pressure to follow. James was quite explicit about this. When he invited his Scottish Parliament in 1686 to grant liberty of conscience

[15] Miller 1977.
[16] *Acts of the Parliaments of Scotland* 1814–1875, VIII, p. 459.
[17] For a further exploration of these themes, see Harris 2006, chs. 3–5.
[18] Dalrymple 1790, II, 'Part I. Continued. Appendix to Book V', p. 176.

to Scottish Catholics, he told Scottish MPs that he expected them to 'cast England a good copie and example', as they had done, for example, back in 1681, when they had declared in favour of his 'right of succession'.[19] In fact, the Scottish parliament proved unexpectedly obstructive; hence James had no choice but to grant religious toleration to Scottish Catholics by dint of his prerogative. And with no 'good copie and example' for English MPs to follow, James had to abandon his English parliament and proceed by way of his prerogative also in England. Hence his Scottish Declaration of Indulgence of February 1687 and his English one of the following April. James's religious policies in Scotland and England were coordinated: James was pursuing a British strategy and the views expressed to criticize that strategy might thus justifiably be styled British political thought; certainly, our history of the political thinking about James's strategy has to be a British history. The situation is further complicated by the fact that the two most outspoken critics in print at this time were Gilbert Burnet and Robert Ferguson – both Scotsmen. In fact, both were writing from exile in the Low Countries, both were writing in the main for an English audience, and although they both addressed developments in Scotland it is difficult to see that there was anything distinctively Scottish about their arguments and there is no reason to suppose that the same arguments could not equally well have been made by Englishmen. Burnet condemned the Scottish Indulgence for its 'new designation' of the king's 'Absolute Power', implying, as it did, that there was 'an Inherent Power in the King, which can neither be restrained by Lawes, Promises, nor Oaths', and warned that 'we here in England' could now 'see what we must look for'.[20] Ferguson argued that the 'Absolute Power' asserted in the Scottish Indulgence amounted to 'an unpresidented exercise of Despoticalness, as hardly any of the Oriental Tyrants or even the French Leviathan would have ventured upon', and that it revealed James's true intentions for England, even though 'shame or fear' had prevented his ministers from putting the same claims to 'Absolute Power' into 'the Declaration for Liberty of Conscience in England'.[21]

Indeed, we might wonder how easily we can distinguish between English and Scottish (or indeed Irish) political thought when we are dealing with thought about a single monarch within a multiple-kingdom polity. The trickiness of the issue becomes readily apparent

[19] Fountainhall 1840, p. 234.   [20] [Burnet] 1687?, pp. 1, 5.   [21] [Ferguson] 1687, p. 28.

when we begin to explore the ways in which the legitimacy of the Restoration Stuart regime was defended by its champions and supporters. Let us start by asking where this defending was being done. The press in both Scotland and Ireland was far less developed than it was in England, but that did not prevent the emergence of vibrant Scottish and Irish public spheres, especially in the major urban centres.[22] People in Scotland and Ireland were reading what was coming out of London. We can reconstruct the contours of Tory political thinking about divine-right royal absolutism, indefeasible hereditary right, loyalty and allegiance, and the principles of non-resistance from an exhaustive examination of the outpourings of the London press, and we might well think of this as being English political thought; yet in fact this material was reaching people in Scotland and Ireland and was most certainly intended to influence opinion there as well.

To illustrate the point further, let us return to James II's effort to induce the Scottish parliament to grant Catholic toleration in 1686. The initiative was preceded by a government propaganda campaign: several pamphlets appeared in support of the policy, which were 'carefully spread ... about', we are told, in an attempt to sway Scottish MPs.[23] There was clearly a powerful Scottish dimension to the political thought advanced. Thus Thomas Burnet, professor of philosophy at the Marischal College of Aberdeen, produced a short Latin work, published in Aberdeen, arguing that the king of Scotland was absolute and could abrogate and annul laws, and that the three estates could not question his pleasure.[24] Such views accorded with the lengthy vindication of Scottish monarchical absolutism published in Edinburgh and London in 1684 by the Scottish lord advocate, Sir George Mackenzie of Rosehaugh,[25] and with the assertion in the preamble of the Scottish Excise Act of 1685 that the Scottish monarchy had historically always been absolute. Another pamphlet, this one in English and known to have circulated among Scottish members during the parliamentary session, sought to argue that since 'Kings in Scotland were before Parliaments ... all the legislative, as well as executive Power, did reside sovereignly in them' and thus that James could grant relief to his co-religionists without parliament's consent. It was an argument made in this context

---

[22] Pincus 1995; Mann 2000; Raymond 2003, ch. 5; Gillespie 2005a; Harris 2005.
[23] Wodrow 1721–1722, II, 594.
[24] Burnet 1686; Fountainhall 1759–1761, I, 415–16.
[25] Mackenzie 1684.

about Scottish history; but it was also one that could have been made — and indeed had been made — about the sovereign's power vis-à-vis English parliaments. Interestingly, the tract was said to have been written by Sir Roger L'Estrange (albeit with the aid of 'the Jesuits and Popish Priests, in and about Edinburgh'); L'Estrange, who hailed from Norfolk and was educated at Eton and Cambridge, was controller of the press in England and a key Tory ideologue in England during the Exclusion Crisis and the first couple of years of James II's reign.[26] Although this particular pamphlet did develop distinctively Scottish arguments for justifying the absolute power of the Scottish crown, appealing as it did to the specific nature of the royal supremacy over the Scottish church established under the Scottish Supremacy Act of 1669, the general principles articulated were similar to those which L'Estrange advanced in an English context, notably in his long-running London periodical *The Observator*.[27] Furthermore, as part of the same government propaganda campaign to promote Catholic toleration in Scotland, various pamphlets that had been published in England as part of the English debate over the dispensing power, and which set out to champion the royal prerogative and to show why Catholics deserved toleration, were circulated north of the border in order to influence Scottish public opinion.[28]

The question of subjects' allegiance and loyalty to the crown is especially useful for shedding light on the difficulties in trying to distinguish between English and Scottish or Irish political thought because of the ways in which allegiance and loyalty were rooted in a particular strand of Protestant episcopalian religious thinking that was common to all Three Kingdoms. We must caution against pushing comparisons between the Church of Scotland and the Church of England in the Restoration era too far: doctrinally and ceremonially the Scottish Church remained still quite Calvinist. Nevertheless, when it came to opposing Presbyterian resistance theory Anglicans and Scottish episcopalians thought along very similar lines. With respect to Ireland, the Church's teachings on allegiance and non-resistance were identical

<hr/>

[26] 'Reasons for Abrogating the Penal Statutes', in Wodrow 1721–1722, appendix no. 118, pp. 164, 166. For the attribution to L'Estrange, see ibid., II, p. 595. For similar arguments in the English context, see Weston and Greenberg 1981, ch. 8.

[27] L'Estrange 1684–1687.

[28] Fountainhall 1759–1761, I, 416. These tracts included: Cartwright 1686; *Popery Anatomis'd* 1686; C. 1686; [Gother] 1685; Sheridan, William (1686).

to those of the Anglican Church, for the simple reason that the Church of Ireland was indeed the Church of England in Ireland. Many of the clergy who staffed the Church of Ireland were Englishmen who had been ordained in England. And the oaths of allegiance that were required in Ireland by dint of Irish Acts of 1560 and 1666 were the same as those oaths enshrined in the English Acts of 1559 and 1662. Church of Ireland clerics made precisely the same arguments about non-resistance from the pulpit during the years of the Tory Reaction as did their counterparts in England. For example in July 1683 Anthony Dopping, Bishop of Meath, a Dubliner of English parentage who was educated at St. Patrick's Cathedral school and Trinity College Dublin, preached in Christ Church Dublin that the principles of passive obedience and non-resistance had been the 'constant opinion of the Church of England' and endorsed by the Irish Act of Uniformity of 1666, insisting that those who justified resistance to oppose the inundation of popery were not sons of the Church but borrowed their principles from Rome, Scotland, or Geneva.[29] At the time of James's accession Bishop Edward Wetenhall, an Englishman educated at Cambridge and Oxford who moved to Dublin in 1672 and became bishop of Cork and Ross in 1679, travelled through his diocese preaching sermons on the duties of obedience, offering the self-same conventional Anglican pieties heard so often from English pulpits at this time.[30] Loyal addresses that came out of Ireland during the latter years of Charles II's reign (signed almost exclusively by Church of Ireland Protestants) paralleled those of the loyal addresses drawn up in England at the same time (signed almost exclusively by Church of England Protestants).[31] In short, Protestant loyalist ideology in England and Ireland was largely the same. Irish Protestants were, of course, to rethink their positions on allegiance in the wake of the Glorious Revolution, an issue to which we shall return shortly. What is worth emphasizing here is that when Wetenhall, in 1691, discussed whether Irish Protestants were free from the oaths they had taken against resisting the king or anyone commissioned by him, the oath he specifically referred to was that embodied in the *English* Act of Uniformity of 1662 (not the Irish Act of Uniformity of 1666).[32] Wetenhall, it appears, was unaware of any need to distinguish between English and Irish political thought on this issue. Not that Wetenhall was being careless. While it is true that the

[29] Trinity College Dublin, MS 1688/1, pp. 61–77.    [30] [Wetenhall] 1686.
[31] Harris 2005, pp. 390–95, 403–5.    [32] [Wetenhall] 1691.

Irish Act simply adopted the oath enshrined in the English Act, the Irish
Act in fact required the oath only of clerics and teachers. However in the
absence of an Irish Corporation Act requiring such an oath of members
of corporations, many corporations in Ireland chose to adopt the non-
resistance oath themselves as a test for membership. Since the oath was
originally an English formulation and was adopted by some corporations
in Ireland before the passage of the Irish Act, Wetenhall was technically
correct in citing the English legislation.

To illustrate further the problems of how we might categorize loyalist
political thought in the 1680s, let us examine the Irish Act of Recognition
of 1689. This was passed by the parliament which James II summoned
to meet in Dublin in the spring of 1689 after he had already been
dethroned in England and Scotland. The parliament was an over-
whelmingly Catholic body: only six Protestants sat in the House of
Commons, and five Protestant lay peers and four Protestant bishops (one
of whom was Bishop Dopping of Meath) in the House of Lords.[33]
In recognizing James's 'Just and Most Undoubted Rights' to his 'Imperial
Crown', the act offered a forthright condemnation of the Glorious
Revolution in England — something which surely immediately qualifies it
as evincing British political thought. Thus it opened by complaining
about how James's treasonous subjects in England had 'forced [him] to
withdraw' from London and condemning the 'execrable' usurpation by
William of Orange as being 'against the Law of God, Nature and
Nations' (note the use of universalist language here, implying that the law
applied to all nations). Most of those who were guilty of helping to bring
it about, the act correctly alleged, had 'sworn that it was not lawful to take
up Arms against [James II] on any pretence whatsoever' (an English
particularist argument in this context; similar oaths renouncing resistance
had been taken by James's Protestant subjects in Scotland and Ireland,
though significantly not by Catholics). The act then proceeded to
rehearse the classic theories of indefeasible hereditary right and divinely-
ordained, irresistible monarchy: James had succeeded his brother,
Charles II, 'by Inherent Birth Right, and Lawful and Undoubted
Succession', and James's 'Right' to his 'Imperial Crown' was 'originally by
Nature, and descent of Blood, from God alone, by Whom Kings Raign,
and not from [his] People, nor by virtue or pretext of any Contract made
with them'. Neither the peers, the commons, parliament nor the people

[33] Harris 2006, pp. 437–8.

had 'any Coercive Power over the Persons of the Kings of this Realm' (an argument about Ireland now) and allegiance to the king was 'Indissoluble' and could not 'be renounced by us, or our Posterities'. In short, the act concluded, it was 'Utterly unlawful for your Majesties Subjects of this, or any of your Kingdoms' — now specifically a Three-Kingdoms argument — 'actually to resist your Majesty, or our Lawful, Hereditary King for the time being, by Violence, or Force of Arms; or to withdraw their Allegiance from your Majesty, your Heirs and Lawful Successors'. Instead, 'a misused Authority by our Lawful, Hereditary King (if any such should happen) must be left to the sole Judgment of God, the King of Kings, and only Ruler of Princes.' The ideology offered here was entirely conventional. It could well have been voiced by Tory-Anglicans in England during the final years of the reign of Charles II — only, of course, here it was being voiced by Irish Catholics in Ireland.[34]

How, then, should we categorize the ideology of loyalism we find articulated in tracts, pamphlets, sermons, and other writings during the 1680s? To style it simply English political thought is too restrictive. This political thought clearly applied, in crucial respects, across the whole of the Atlantic archipelago: at times it might be fashioned to fit distinctive Scottish or Irish contexts, but we are dealing with what was in essence the same ideology. One might make an argument about English intellectual and cultural hegemony, and maintain that this particular ideology of Stuart loyalism emanated from England and was imposed on the Irish and the Scots. (Certainly we should recognize the simultaneous co-existence of distinctive Irish and Scottish languages of Stuart loyalism.)[35] Yet this returns us to the thorny issue of the intellectual roots of divine-right theory: were they not, at least in part, continental rather than English? Do we label this ideology British? Perhaps, though it is not really thought about Britain — even if the ideology pervaded all Three Kingdoms and writers from one kingdom might on occasion relate their arguments to developments in the others. Pan-archipelagic might make more sense, apart from the ugliness of the word. One might call this ideology Tory-Anglican, except for the facts that Anglican cannot work for Scotland, Tory meant something very different in Ireland and Irish Catholics might on occasion embrace it. Yet perhaps we do not need to search for a label; we can recognize the processes at work

---

[34] *Anno V. Jacobi II. Regis.* 1689, pp. 1–5.     [35] Ó Buachalla 1993; Canny, in this volume.

and the variegated intellectual dimensions of the ideology and proceed
to write its history, without seeking to compartmentalize it.

So much for the ideology of loyalism. What about those who opted
not to stay loyal? When James II's regime in England collapsed in late
1688, it provoked a crisis that engulfed all three kingdoms. The vast
majority of Protestants in England, Scotland and Ireland had found
James's political and religious initiatives unwelcome, and they were faced
with the question of whether they could legitimately engage in acts of
resistance to their sovereign and/or renounce their allegiance to James II.
The crisis inevitably prompted considerable speculation on these issues in
print across the British Isles; whether in Scotland, Ireland or England,
writers confronted the same basic problem. Among the more prominent
protagonists in the debate were: Gilbert Burnet and Robert Ferguson
(Scotsmen writing mainly about England); James Canaries (a Scotsman
writing about Scotland who later retired to England and served in the
English Church); William King (an Ulsterman of Scottish descent
writing mainly about Ireland); Edward Wetenhall (an Anglo-Irishman
writing mainly about Ireland); and Charles Leslie (an Ulster Anglican
Jacobite writing in response to King who sought to explore the flaws
in his adversary's arguments by examining how they might apply to
Scotland). All of them recognized, in various ways, that the crisis they
were discussing was a Three-Kingdoms one. Yet although their thinking
was about a British problem, their thought was not always British. Each
tilted their particular arguments to address the concerns of the particular
national interest group they saw as their primary audience.

However, categorizing their political thought along national lines does
not make sense either. Let us take the three Scots on our list. Ferguson, an
Independent divine, embraced a brand of contractarian resistance that
fitted uncomfortably with Burnet's particular style of episcopalian
churchmanship. Burnet's views were closer to those of the Scottish
Williamite episcopalian Canaries, since both had to decide how their
support for the Williamite coup accorded with the Church's traditional
teachings on non-resistance. Canaries' arguments had more in common
with those of King and Wetenhall (for Ireland) than they did with those
of Ferguson — or of other Scottish writers who sought to apply contract
theory to the Scottish situation.[36] All of the above-named writers used
natural law arguments which they would have seen as being universalist,

---

[36] Examples of which being *Short Historical Account* 1689; *Salus Populi* 1689.

along with constitutionalist arguments that were particularist (though in fact the constitutionalist arguments could have applied equally well to England, Scotland and Ireland, since all the writers mentioned believed that the Stuart monarchy — whichever kingdom they were writing about — was limited by law). We have a discourse, in other words, about a crisis that had British and Irish origins and British and Irish implications, a discourse that recognized distinctive national particularities to the crisis but which nevertheless oftentimes sought to transcend national particularities. There were, to be sure, different types of argument advanced by different authors. When labelling this political thought, however, it perhaps makes most sense to use the categories developed by Mark Goldie in his analysis of the allegiance controversy in England in 1689 — contractual resistance; possession; abdication; conquest; providence; and resistance *in extremis* — and apply them across all Three Kingdoms.[37]

A brief examination of some of the more central tracts will help to illustrate what I mean. Let us start with Canaries, a Williamite epsicopalian who articulated his thoughts in a sermon preached in Edinburgh on 30 January 1689 (the anniversary of the regicide) which was subsequently printed in extended form. At the time of the accession of James II in 1685, Canaries had in fact preached a sermon against resistance,[38] and in 1689, like the good episcopalian he was, he began by affirming the Pauline doctrine of non-resistance. Yet subjects, he said, were 'upon their Conscience to yield their Soveraign all those Rights and Dues which by the peculiar Constitution in which they live, He can Legally exact of them'. The king could claim no more 'than what by the established Form of the Government he has a just Title to', and although the king was 'Superiour to the whole Body of the Subjects, when he Rules according to Law, when he deserts the Laws ... then the Subjects may look to themselves'. No 'private Subject' was allowed 'to resist' the government for any private act of injustice suffered; but 'when the Subject's Right in general is Invaded, and the Injustice reaches the Publick Interest of them all', then 'every particular Subject not only may', Canaries said, but 'ought to do whatever he can to contribute the relieving the whole Subjects Right in the Laws, from that Tyranny and Oppression it is falling, or fallen under'. The argument is made at the general level, a theoretical abstraction divorced from any

---

[37] Goldie 1980, p. 259; compare Jackson 2003, ch. 8.     [38] Canaries 1685.

specifically Scottish context; indeed, Canaries explicitly states that he has 'not presumed to condescend upon the particular Constitution of our own Nation', believing it inappropriate 'to mingle the Minister and the Lawyer together' — although he does add that 'it may be easie for every body concerned, to compare what has been said with our special Form; and so satisfie their Consciences'.[39] Interestingly, Canaries' main intellectual adversary — the author with whose ideas he engages most directly — is the English Anglican cleric William Sherlock, who had published a famous defence of non-resistance in 1684.[40] Sherlock's tract is normally (and correctly) seen as a classic articulation (by an Englishman) of the ideology of the Tory Reaction (in England). No one, to my knowledge, has ever styled it a text in British political thought. Yet, as Canaries makes apparent, it was undoubtedly a work that exercised considerable influence on Scottish episcopalian thinking. Canaries was confronting the English Sherlock in order to assure Scots that their scruples over resisting the king (of Scotland) could be overcome.

Canaries' views of 1689 are close to those articulated by Burnet as to why English Protestants might be free to resist James II. In his *Enquiries into the Measures of Submission* of the autumn of 1688, Burnet wrote that although 'Considerations of Religion' did 'indeed 'bring Subjects under stricter Obligations, to pay all due Allegiance and Submission to their Princes', they did 'not at all extend Allegiance further than the Law carries it'. Under the English system of government, the king's authority was limited: if the king acted 'beyond the limits of his Power', subjects lay under no obligation to obey; and if any one, acting illegally in the king's name, sought to 'Invade our Property' they were 'Violent aggressours' and the principle of self-preservation allowed for 'as Violent a resistance'. Burnet was also adamant that England was 'a free Nation' with 'its Liberties and Properties reserved to it by many positive and express Laws'; if 'we have a right to our Property, we must likewise be supposed to have a right to preserve it . . . against the Invasions of the Prerogative'.[41] Burnet might have been a Scot, but there was nothing particularly Scottish about his line of argument. A tract defending the northern resistance movement of November 1688 — attributed to the Yorkshireman and Tory-Anglican politician the Earl of Danby — argued in a similar vein to both Canaries and Burnet. In answer to the Pauline injunction that the powers that be were ordained of God and thus could not be resisted, the author

<hr>

[39] Canaries 1689, pp. 22, 28, 38, 39, 40.    [40] Sherlock 1684.    [41] [Burnet] 1688, pp. 2, 4.

maintained that governments had 'God's warrant to proceed according to the Frame of the Government, to the End of the Government, which is the publick Good', but 'if the Governor proceed neither according to the frame of the Government, nor to the End, but against it, such Process cannot be the Ordinance of God'. Just 'because I may not resist the Ordinance of God', it did not follow 'that I may not resist the powerless and inauthoritative, unjust, Attempts of Superiors upon me'. Understandably, our author seeks to apply his arguments directly to England, which he claimed was a limited monarchy, where the king was bound, by his coronation oath, 'to Govern by the Laws'. However, the argument would clearly apply to any limited monarchy – and thus by implication also in Scotland and Ireland, if the Stuart monarchy were deemed limited there.[42]

William King's *State of the Protestants of Ireland* of 1691 offers a detailed analysis of why Irish Protestants were justified in endeavouring to free themselves from James II's government and submitting themselves to William and Mary. Most of the tract is about the situation in Ireland. Nevertheless, before introducing the particularities of the Irish situation, King pitches his argument at the universal level. 'It is granted by some of the highest assertors of Passive Obedience', he states, 'that if a King design to root out a people, or destroy one main part of his Subjects in favour of another whom he loves better, that they may prevent it even by opposing him with force'. In such a case, the prince 'is to be judged ... to have Abdicated the Government of those whom he designs to destroy contrary to justice and the Laws', and his 'Subjects may desert their Prince, decline his Government and Service, and seek Protection where they find it'. Resistance was therefore justifiable 'in some cases of extremity': when the mischiefs of submitting to tyranny were more dangerous to the commonwealth than a war, then 'people may lawfully resist and defend themselves'. Irish Protestants were justified in renouncing their allegiance to James, King claimed, because 'James designed to destroy and utterly ruin the Protestant Religion, the Liberty and Property of the Subjects in general, the English Interest in Ireland in particular, and alter the very Frame and Constitution of the Government' – an argument which King chose to develop specifically in the Irish context but which is scarcely a specifically Irish argument. At one stage King asserts that 'It is a Maxim in our Law that the King can do no wrong, because he executeth nothing

---

[42] [Danby] 1689, pp. 4–5, 7–8.

in his own person, but has Officers appointed by Law to execute his Commands, who are obliged not to obey him if he command any thing that is illegal: If any Officer obey him in such unlawful Commands it is at his own peril, and he is accountable for it; the King's Command being no excuse or protection to any Man for his doing an illegal thing'.[43] This was an English maxim; indeed it is classic Sherlock. In 1688 Sherlock had written: 'It is a Maxime in our Law, That the King can do no wrong; and therefore if any wrong be done, the Crime and Guilt is the Minister's who does it; for the Laws are the King's publick Will, and therefore he is never supposed to command any thing contrary to Law'.[44] The British dimensions to King's political thought are revealed when he comments upon how James had issued a 'Declaration for Liberty of Conscience in Scotland', in which he had insisted he was to be obeyed 'without reserve', and how James in England had 'granted without any apparent Necessity ... several Dispensations', albeit (in contrast to Ireland) with 'some colour or form of Law'.[45] So is King's political thought Irish, English, or British? In some respects it is all three, yet by themselves none of these labels seems quite to fit.

The very fact that King's thinking, to be logically consistent, had to work equally well across England, Scotland and Ireland – given that the dynastic shift he was seeking to justify occurred not just in Ireland but also in England and Scotland – was picked up on by Charles Leslie. If King's fundamental premise – 'That if a King design to destroy one main Part of his People, in favour of another whom he loves better, he does abdicate the Government of those whom he designs to destroy' – were true, then it followed that 'the Episcopal Party in Scotland', who had lost out as a result of the Presbyterian settlement in the Church that accompanied the Glorious Revolution in Scotland, should be free 'from all Obligation to K. William's Government'. Moreover, Leslie points out, although King alleged that it had been James's intention in Ireland to overturn the established Church, in fact in Scotland William actually did overturn the Church 'by law established'. The Scottish Presbyterians might seek to justify their revolution settlement in the Church by saying that this was in accord with what the majority of the people had wanted, yet by this logic the Jacobites could argue 'That it was as just to set up Popery in Ireland, as Presbytery in Scotland'. Referring to King's doctrine of abdication, Leslie asserted that 'not only the Papists in

---

[43] [King] 1691, pp. 1–2, 3, 4–6, 20–21.   [44] [Sherlock] 1688, p. 2.   [45] [King] 1691, pp. 21, 70.

England, and Episcopal Party in Scotland, and the present Papists in Ireland, may justifie their taking Arms against the Present Government when they please', but 'the Irish Papists in 41 might have justified their Rebellion against King Charles I by this Author's Principles'.[46] In short, Leslie's tract demonstrates that one cannot justify the Glorious Revolution on King's grounds because King's reasoning does not fit all Three Kingdoms: implied is a recognition that a Three-Kingdoms problem needs to be discussed at the Three-Kingdoms level and the solution has to be found in British political thought (only, of course, Leslie's whole point was to insist that the Glorious Revolution could not be vindicated). In crucial respects Leslie was surely right. However, few contemporaries would have agreed with him. Supporters of the Revolution settlement across the Three Kingdoms found it quite easy to live with incompatible justifications of the Glorious Revolution.[47] There was, in fact, no text of British political thought (as opposed to English, Scottish or Irish political thought) that offered a coherent justification of the dynastic shift of 1688–1689.

This chapter has sought to raise questions and explore problems rather than offer definitive guidelines concerning how to proceed with writing a British history of political thought. However, a number of conclusions have emerged in the process. The central one is that scholars have often failed to recognize British political thought when they have encountered it for the simple reason that they have mistaken it for something else. Much of the English political thought of this period with which we are familiar, for example, on closer examination turns out to be British thought – either because, despite being articulated in English sources, it was intended to apply at the pan-archipelagic level (Tory-Anglican thought of the 1680s would be an important case in point here), or because the thought involved did indeed address the Three Kingdoms but this has been missed because the dictates of traditional historiography have forced us to focus on the national level (note both Whig and Tory thought during the Exclusion Crisis). The advantage of the recent Britannic turn in seventeenth-century historiography, therefore, has been to help us to see things we have missed and as a result to alter significantly our understanding of key historical developments and processes. The new British history, in short, has much to teach us. Yet this is different from saying that we should all become British historians or that there are

---

[46] [Leslie] 1692, sigs, d-d$^v$, p. 46.    [47] Harris 2002.

particular types of British history we should aspire to practise. Much of the political thought we have looked at in this chapter both is and is not British political thought. Depending on the questions we ask, sometimes the Three-Kingdoms perspective is going to come into sharp focus, at other times the national (or local or continental) will. This is why labels such as incorporative, confederal or perfect — even if accurately reflecting the various ways the new British history has tended to be written to date — are ultimately unhelpful. The time has surely come to move forward and get beyond such compartmentalizations. Those of us who want to write British history have to engage in many types of British history at the same time, while also being ready to recognize that in some (perhaps many) contexts the Three-Kingdoms dimension might not get us very far.

PART II

*British Political Thought and Literature*

CHAPTER 6

# Republicanism in Sixteenth- and Seventeenth-Century Britain

*Andrew Hadfield*

The study of political thought is too important to be left to political science and history alone. Of course, it would be odd if analysis did not start within these disciplines. However, the inability to establish more widespread, genuinely interdisciplinary modes of study has meant that ways of reading texts established by historians and social scientists have been accepted as the norm and then imported back into disciplines such as literary studies. Given that our understanding of the early-modern period has been transformed by the realization that people did not divide up the world and the books that represent it as we do, this is a seriously disabling problem for those concerned to reconstruct the past. If we are attempting to recover a world in which people read religious tracts, literary texts, scientific treatises, legal documents and other forms of writing alongside each other, we should recognize that our attempts to distinguish rigidly between subjects will not always yield fruitful results.

A case in point is the question of early-modern republicanism, a subject that has had little impact on the analysis of literature before the eighteenth century. This means that historical and theoretical debate about the existence and substance of republicanism has concentrated on the question of whether it was a language or a programme, a means of articulating an alternative to monarchical government, or a plan of action designed to replace hereditary monarchy.[1] The former definition has sometimes led to an over-inclusive understanding of republicanism that risks seeing any reference to 'virtue' as republicanism in miniature.[2]

---

[1] Pocock 1975b; Skinner 1978a.
[2] Peltonen 1995. For criticism, see Worden 2002, pp. 308–14.

The latter definition has led to a concomitant tendency for a rather straitened understanding of republicanism sprouting fully formed after 1642, with a clear programme that opposes Puritanism and royalism alike.[3]

Republicanism before the advent of the English republic is hard to define because it consisted of a number of inter-related themes, ideas and affiliations and there was no republican pressure group at or outside court that could easily be identified. Nevertheless, English republicanism might be described as a faith in the power of institutions to circumscribe the authority of the monarch, allied to a belief that such institutions — Parliament, the law courts, local and national government — had the means to make individuals more virtuous and so better able to govern.[4] Of course, it is often difficult to separate republicanism from a native 'commonwealth' tradition which had similar aims, but did not always place as much emphasis on the institutions as on the limiting of the monarch's prerogative.[5] Republicanism can be further distinguished in terms of the images, symbols and types of precedent that were cited to make a case.

We need to remember that republicanism was as much a literary as a political phenomenon, originating principally in the historical and poetic works surviving from the Roman Republic — Livy, Polybius, Ovid, Cicero, Lucan, and so on — studied by all boys at grammar school. It makes little sense to study the history of republicanism without examining the history of the representations of the rape of Lucrece, the banishment of the Tarquins and the protracted civil wars which ended the republic, and which included the deaths of Julius Caesar, Mark Antony and Cicero. Republicanism as a tradition was a fund of images, stories and motifs. The history of republicanism in England, I would suggest, makes little sense if we study it solely in terms of the definitions provided by historians and social scientists.

It would, therefore, be an eccentric reading of English or British political history and culture to see no republicanism before James Harrington outlined the property-owning oligarchy of Oceana in 1656, or Algernon Sidney was executed in 1683 in the wake of the Rye House Plot, leaving behind his voluminous manuscripts on the liberties afforded a people who accepted the principles of mixed government.[6]

---

[3] Worden 1981.     [4] Collinson 2003, chs. 1–2.     [5] Worden 2002.
[6] Harrington 1992; Pocock 1987a; Sidney 1996a; Sidney 1996b; Worden 1985; Scott 1988.

Harrington and Sidney made it clear that they looked back for inspiration to a corpus of monarchomach writers, principally George Buchanan; to well-known biblical writings on regicide (many of which were cited by writers such as Buchanan); the history of the Roman Republic; and the example of Venice, the key republican city-state that also formed the basis for the utopia of Oceana.[7] It would be reductive to claim that there was no political transformation between the late sixteenth century and the middle of the seventeenth, or that political thinkers did not read, reconsider, and often transform earlier texts. But there is a remarkable continuity in the points of reference that define a republican tradition, agreed on by its critics as well as its supporters.

Even the hostile to republicanism appear to have recognized its central role within the English political imagination. To take one example: Fulke Greville (1554–1628), the close friend of Sir Philip Sidney, Algernon's great-uncle, may have been a radical thinker in his youth, but he developed into a stern critic of republican thought.[8] Much of Greville's work remained in manuscript until after his death – the publication of *Mustapha* (1609) was without his consent – and he destroyed his play, *Antony and Cleopatra*, because it reflected rather too closely on the rebellion of the Earl of Essex, with whom Greville had been associated in the 1590s.[9] It is evident that his two surviving plays, *Mustapha* (c. 1594–1596) and *Alaham* (c. 1598–1600), neither of which were performed publicly, provide extensive discussions of resistance theory based on his reading of the monarchomach treatise, *Vindiciae Contra Tyrannos*, one of Sir Philip Sidney's favourite political works.[10] Greville, certainly when he revised his plays in the early 1600s, had little sympathy for armed rebellion.[11] He was, nevertheless, a keen student of Machiavelli, and had great faith in the value of parliaments.[12]

The plays are concerted attacks on the vices of overbearing rulers, but argue the case that anarchy is worse than tyranny. People need security and order, ideally under the law, and the worst ruler is a weak one, such as Alaham, who is more interested in his comforts and assisting his friends and allies than enforcing the law properly. Both plays stress the need for kings to heed wise counsel so that they realize when something untoward happens, an argument for the constitutional importance of parliament.

---

[7] Sidney 1996a, pp. 56, 112, 185, 187, and *passim*; Harrington 1992, pp. 8, 34, 218, and *passim*; compare Nelson 2004, ch. 3.
[8] Rees 1971, p. 42.    [9] Rebholz 1971, pp. 131–2.    [10] Greville 1939, vol. 2.
[11] Greville 1939, I, p. 4; Perry 1997, p. 106.    [12] Greville 1939, I, pp. 14, 17.

Greville also places emphasis on the need for true religion to play its part in good government, and favours the security of a hereditary rather than an elective kingship.[13]

There are many assumptions here in common with a number of political arguments made in the 1590s. In that decade there was a wide-spread fear that after the death of Elizabeth the process of hereditary monarchy, designed to preserve the nation's stability, might instead lead to the destruction of all that had been achieved under the Tudors, with the crown passing to an unsuitable candidate.[14] Greville values the need for counsel, for monarchs to obey the law, reason as the key principle of government, the fear that tyranny will erode the people's liberty and the concomitant fear of rebellion if a monarch treats subjects too harshly, the hope that religious differences can be either solved or placed to one side, and so on, all affirming a belief in the familiar principle of the 'mixed' constitution.[15] Nevertheless, the central political fear has changed from the need for subjects to force the hands of their rulers in order to ensure proper justice and liberty, to the need for rulers to behave well and be attentive to their kingdoms. As Greville's intellectual progress demonstrates, the concept of the 'mixed' constitution was inherently ambiguous. It could be used to argue that the people had the right to remind the monarch of his or her duties to them, as they shared power; or, more conservatively, that the monarch held power alone, but needed to listen to the advice of elected assemblies when he or she felt it was necessary.[16]

Greville's political opinions are meticulously laid out in his poetry, most obviously in 'A Treatise of Monarchy'. This long poem argues that hereditary monarchy is the best form of government.[17] It was prob-ably completed in the early 1600s, but was started in the 1590s.[18] Nevertheless, Greville's political anatomy and history is evidently touched by republican thought, as he uses the word 'republic' to describe states in stanzas 1, 14, 276, 325, and elsewhere. Greville charts the political progress of monarchy from its inception to its frequent degeneration into tyranny, warning his readers that 'thrones are not indefinite', that 'pow're bounded is with wrong and right' (40) and it is

[13] Perry 1997, pp. 106–11.    [14] Hadfield 2005, pt. 1.    [15] Sharpe 2000, chs. 1–2.
[16] Hadfield 2003, ch. 5.
[17] Greville 1965. Subsequent references to this edition in parentheses in the text.
[18] Rebholz 1971, pp. 146–7.

the duty of the good counsellor to 'lymitt the excesses of a Crowne' (45). The story of the end of the republic is told, yet again, with only a slight twist:

> *Caesar* was slaine by those that objects were
> Of grace, and engines of his tiranny.
> *Brutus* and *Cassius* worke shall wittnes beare,
> Even to the comfort of posterity,
> That prowd aspirers never had good end,
> Nor yet excess of might a constant frend (70).

Caesar is cast as a tyrant. But Brutus and Cassius are seen as equally ambitious and self-serving, tyrants who never got to rule, unlike Caligula and Nero (74). It is tempting to speculate how this verse read in the first version of the poem, assuming that Greville revised it. Whatever the genesis of the poem, it is clear that Greville felt the need to make use of the history of the Roman Republic as a central reference point for his readers. This would seem to indicate that it was difficult for any political writer from the 1590s onwards to ignore or summarily dismiss arguments for a republic. A contrary case could not be assumed but had to be argued. By a deft sleight of hand, in the verse cited above Greville transforms the story of the end of the republic into one of the end of constitutional monarchy, Caesar, Brutus and Cassius all being cast as enemies of the middle way. It is a neat manoeuvre, which testifies to the prominent role of the history of the republic in English political life.

Greville supported contemporary republics that opposed the might of Spain:

> The pride of such inferiors did constraine
> The *Swisse* against the *Austrians* cantonise;
> Soe were the *Belgians* likewise forc't againe
> A new *Republique* finely to devise;
> In which that Monarch [i.e., the King of Spain's representative,
> the Duke of Alva] was compeld to treat
> As with states equall free, not equall great (102).

The republics established here enable their citizens to stop tyrants whose desire is to 'Abridge our freedome, to lord over us' (100), and, in section 6 of the poem (192–238), Catholicism and tyranny are shown to have an identical agenda. The reference to Spain indicates that this verse was written in the 1590s when Spain's power was at its height and most Protestant European states devoted their foreign policy to halting Iberian imperial ambitions, and suggests that the poem may have been less obviously celebratory of monarchy in earlier forms.[19]

However, in the later stages of the poem, Greville weighs in against republicanism, as he compares monarchy favourably with alternative systems of government (aristocracy, in stanzas 580–609; democracy, in stanzas 610–640). The republic is seen as an unstable political form, veering from tyranny to popular rule, and the history of Athens is no less chaotic. Caesar was not without his faults, but 'he that brought back Monarchie / Err'd less, then he who sett the people free' (591). The banishment of the Tarquins was an unqualified good, but Rome soon degenerated from its unified state and 'fell shee into manie-headed powre', until the people eventually realized that they were better off with a 'brave Monarchall state' (592), a stable political form that could offset the dangerous swings that other states experienced. Greville's aim is to outplay the republicans at their own game and show that constitutional monarchy — which would in Greville's terms hardly limit the monarch's powers at all — is the best form of government that ensures stability and grants the people maximum liberty.

Greville's work would appear to suggest that a republican tradition in England could be assumed from the sixteenth century onwards, even if it became more developed and more clearly articulated as the prospect of a republic became a reality rather than a distant possibility considered in somewhat abstract terms by a few intellectuals and disaffected political commentators. Greville shows how important republicanism was within a literary tradition, hardly surprisingly given the role that literature played in political life.

Many educated people only had the chance to participate in public politics in any significant way by writing literary texts.[20] However, the implications of this relationship have not always been so carefully thought through. The question of republicanism has been controversial partly because the match between politics and literature has been imagined as one-way rather than two-way traffic. The result, I would suggest, is a distortion of early-modern intellectual culture which was far more able to countenance and so balance the complicated relationships between different fields of study.[21]

[19] Wernham 1984.        [20] Norbrook 1999; Bevington 1968.
[21] Woudhuysen 1996; Spiller 2004.

Republicanism has often been removed from the story of English political history because what has been observed does not match the retrospectively established definitions. The most sustained and cogent argument against the existence of republicanism before the English Civil War has been made by Blair Worden, who claims that, whether one defines republicanism as a language or a programme, its constituent elements are simply not present in Elizabethan England: 'In pre-civil-war England it was the abuse of monarchy, not the principle, that attracted complaint'.[22] Worden is convinced that classical republicanism was a clear and distinct strain in English political thought, and argues further that 'pre-war discontent ... was invariably directed towards the reform, and thus to the strengthening, of the monarchy'.[23] The inserted premise does not necessarily follow from the first. Reforming the monarchy did not always involve strengthening it, but, more often than not, limiting its powers in order to strengthen those of the people under the rule of law. As Markku Peltonen has reminded us, if English humanists took 'the princely context for granted, it did not prevent their adopting a number of "civic" and republican themes in their writings'.[24] If everyone did believe in the monarchy, there were clearly very different positions taken on its role and purpose, not just whether it was an institution worth preserving. Political debates in early-modern England cannot be reduced to this either/or formula. Worden rightly points out that major writers such as More, Sidney and Bacon did turn to 'non-monarchical models of government for guidance', and even if we can agree that 'constitutional collapse was the dread, not the hope, of the class of lay intellectuals to which these writers belonged', their exploration of alternative political institutions would appear to indicate that they did not necessarily believe that the monarchy had to remain static, and did not believe that a change of the constitution would make society better. There was a long tradition of commonwealth thought, placing emphasis on the needs of the people as well as the monarch, which could easily be mapped onto republican thought.[25]

We need to bear in mind how difficult it was for writers to say exactly what they meant in sixteenth- and early seventeenth-century England, as the case of the (eventually) cautious figure of Fulke Greville indicates: one reason why so many authors interested in political ideas, events and problems turned to literary forms to express their ideas in coded forms.[26]

[22] Worden 2002, p. 311.   [23] Worden 2002, p. 311; Worden 1981.
[24] Peltonen 1995, p. 9.   [25] Jones 2000.   [26] Clare 1999; Clegg 1997.

In adopting literary forms, narratives and modes of representation, writers did not simply disguise their political ideas, such as an interest in the ways in which a monarch ought to use the counsel of his advisers; the precise nature of the problematic formula of the king or queen possessing authority as a 'monarch in parliament'; the responsibility that a magistrate had towards those above and below him; the ways in which the succession should be managed; or, the exact form that the 'mixed constitution' should assume. They did, of course, comment on all these issues at appropriate times.[27] But it is important that we recognize that literature did not just exist as a disguised form of politics. Writers also made use of existing literary forms, styles and representations as political interventions in themselves. Nowhere was this more apparent than in the case of republicanism.

Republicanism was a literary phenomenon, as well as a matter of constitutional belief and doctrine, because it consisted of a series of stories. These were easy to narrate, repeat, retell and refigure, signalling a republican subject matter, style or area, without *necessarily* entailing a commitment to any programme. This particular aspect of republicanism is another reason why it is hard to define and isolate, and why some historians have been sceptical that the scraps and fragments of republican culture that undoubtedly exist in pre-Civil War England can be accorded any substance. Nevertheless it is a mistake to argue that historical documents and evidence precede literary evidence, as if the latter were simply derived from the former as a supplementary discourse.

The basic stories of republicanism were well known, and were often repeated. The two fundamental stories dovetail neatly, representing the birth of the republic, and its prolonged death, linked through the name that has perhaps become the most republican of all names, Brutus. The first story is that of the rape of Lucrece, whose abuse at the hands of Tarquinus Sextus, son of the tyrannical king of Rome, Tarquinus Superbus, results in the end of the dynasty of the first kings of Rome, and the founding of the republic when Lucius Junius Brutus leads the revolt that has them banished. The most familiar source for readers in the English Renaissance was Livy's *The History of Rome from its Foundation*.[28] Of course, the story could be inflected in a variety of ways, often being used as a paradigmatic example of female virtue and chastity, as in Chaucer's *The Legend of Good Women* (reprinted in the complete edition

---

[27] Axton 1977.     [28] Livy 1960, pp. 80–85; Donaldson 1982; Shakespeare 2002.

of Chaucer in 1561). More often, however, it possessed a clear political charge, as it did when alluded to in the most widely cited Huguenot treatise advocating the assassination of tyrants who opposed the will of God and the people, *Vindiciae Contra Tyrannos, or, concerning the legitimate power of a prince over the people, and of the people over a prince* (1579). The author of *Vindiciae Contra Tyrannos* went out of his way to advertise the link between republicanism and Protestant resistance theory. The text was supposedly written by 'Stephanus Junius Brutus, the Celt', translating the name of the founder of the republic, Lucius Junius Brutus, to Scotland and so signalling support for those radical Protestants, such as John Knox, who opposed the imposition of Catholic rule by Mary Stuart.[29] The text ends with a plea for the tyranny of Iberian Catholicism to be overthrown and the author stating in block capitals: 'O BRUTUS, YOU WERE MY TEACHER'.[30]

The fact that the text could refer to the story of the foundation of the Roman Republic in such a fleeting manner indicates its status as a key element of what a 'culturally literate' reader might be expected to recognize, as well as its significance within early-modern political culture (evidence that might be read alongside attacks on republicanism as signs of its existence and importance). Exactly the same political connotations are provided, albeit more cautiously, in William Painter's *The Palace of Pleasure*, one of the most popular works of fiction in the second half of the sixteenth century, which, like the even more successful *A Mirror for Magistrates*, went through a variety of editions and ever expanding versions after its initial publication in 1566. Painter's sub-title, 'with pleasaunt histories and excellent novelles, selected out of divers good and commendable authors', makes the work sound innocent enough, but this influential compendium of prose tales started life when it was entered in the Stationers' Register in 1562 as what must have been a more politically oriented work entitled *The Cytie of Civilitie*.[31] Painter derives a number of tales from Livy, as well as contemporary Italian and French collections. The second novel in the collection is 'The Rape of Lucrece', a narrative that may have influenced Shakespeare's poem, especially given the use of Painter's work by other dramatists to provide source material for their plays (most famously, John Webster's *The Duchess of Malfi*).[32]

[29] *Vindiciae Contra Tyrannos* 1994, p. 3; Knox, 1994.
[30] *Vindiciae Contra Tyrannos* 1994, p. 187.
[31] Painter 1890, I, p. xxxix; Hadfield 1998, pp. 147–62.
[32] Shakespeare 1960, pp. 193–6; Webster 1995–, I, pp. 675–705.

Shakespeare's decision to publish a version of the legend in 1594 was certainly a bold move and would have marked him out as a writer keen to explore political ideas and themes, however he chose to tell the story.

Shakespeare's *Lucrece* stands as part of the well-established English tradition of complaint poetry, where a female voice eloquently laments her fate.[33] Lucrece's journey from servile subject of the king to an outspoken critic of the excesses of monarchy, prepared to use violence, absorbs the political transformation which she had traditionally been seen to cause. There is little need for Brutus in Shakespeare's version, not because the poem has no interest in the republican significance of the story, but because Lucrece has already done all the work for the reader. Hence it is a sign of the poem's sophisticated political character, rather than the interference of a heavy-handed editor, that it has a prose description of the establishment of the republic as a preface to the poem as 'The Argument'.[34] Shakespeare, making use of the accounts in Ovid's *Fasti*, as well as Livy's *History of Rome*, ends with the standard political moral as read by earlier writers such Buchanan, Painter and William Fulbecke. Brutus, speaking next to Lucrece's body, makes 'a bitter invective against the tyranny of the King. Wherewith the people were so moved, that with one consent and a general acclamation the Tarquins were all exiled, and the state government changed from kings to consuls'.[35] However, the poem itself simply ends with the memorable, but potentially bathetic, two feminine couplets:

> And so to publish Tarquin's foul offence;
> Which being done with speedy diligence,
> The Romans plausibly did give consent
> To Tarquin's everlasting banishment. (ll. 1852–5).

The use of these feminine rhymes is perhaps a means of reminding us that the republican case is based on the actions of a woman. Shakespeare's representation of Brutus's speech (ll. 1818–41) does not have the dramatic character that it does in Ovid's *Fasti*, Livy or Painter because Lucrece has already reached the conclusion that Rome needs to re-establish its 'country rights' (l. 1838).[36] In transferring the political significance of her violation to the victim herself, Shakespeare refashions and combines two distinct poetic traditions, establishing the virtuous, beautiful, politically agile and literate Lucrece as a republican heroine.

---

[33] Kerrigan 1991.     [34] Shakespeare 2002, p. 48.     [35] Shakespeare 2002, p. 66.
[36] Ovid 2000, *Fasti* 2, lines 841–4.

In terms of this reading of the poem, Tarquin's attempt to persuade Lucrece to yield to his desires is probably its most significant section. We do not witness the conflict of two mutually exclusive political languages, that of absolutism and that of contractual theory, as we might expect if republicanism is considered as a language or a programme.[37] Rather, both protagonists accept that a constitutionally limited monarchy is a desirable political form. The problem is that Tarquin cannot confine his appetites within the boundaries established, and Lucrece is consequently forced to consider more revolutionary action. Tarquin is represented as a tyrant, admitting to himself that his 'will is strong past reason's weak removing' (I. 244). The narrator elaborates on this clash between reason and appetite, referring to Tarquin as a traitor, whose 'greedy eyeballs' commit 'high treason' in misleading his heart (II. 369–70). Given that the expanded treason statutes that were passed by the Tudors all sought to strengthen the power of the monarchy and define more forms of verbal opposition to the regime as treachery than had been prohibited in the late middle ages, the extent of Tarquin's arrogant abrogation of constitutional powers is clear enough.[38] While still attempting to persuade Lucrece to commit adultery he proposes a means of circumventing the law that will satisfy his desires, confirm his real power and leave the constitution intact:

> 'But if thou yield, I rest thy secret friend;
> The fault unknown is as a thought unacted.
> A little harm done to a great good end
> For lawful policy remains enacted'. (II. 526–9)

Tarquin's argument is that Lucrece should submit to him as a means of preserving Roman liberty; the barely suppressed threat is that if she does not yield to him he will undermine the state when he becomes king.[39] Tarquin's reason informs him that he is acting in a manner ill befitting the heir to the throne; his will is too strong for him to control. Any monarch who cannot limit his appetites is a tyrant and leaves himself vulnerable to being overthrown in the interests of the people, as monarchomach and republican theories often claimed. In a discussion about kings who seize kingdoms 'by violence and without the consent of the people', Buchanan argues that tyrants often disguise their true natures because they are aware of the consequences of their actions,

[37] Sommerville 1986, 'Introduction'.    [38] Bellamy 1979, p. 15.
[39] On the political implications of disguise in the poem, see Dzelzainis 1999, pp. 111–13.

'For the hatred aroused by a single misdeed loses them all gratitude for their ostentatious generosity'. Their aim is to act 'for the sake of their own absolute power rather than the advantage of the people' and to 'enjoy their own pleasures' instead of governing in the interests of the people they are supposed to serve.[40] This dishonest and closed form of government encourages the further vice of bad rule, flattery, the 'nurse of tyranny and the most grievous plague of lawful kingship'.[41]

Lucrece refuses to remain silent and dares to challenge Tarquin. His desire to separate his private act from his public person produces a corresponding division in Lucrece's understanding of him: 'In Tarquin's likeness I did entertain thee:/Hast thou put on his shape to do him shame?' (ll. 596–7). Lucrece tries to separate the private from the public body of the future king. Lucrece then explores the consequences of Tarquin's as yet uncommitted crime in lines that show her political ideas changing as we read:

> 'Thou seem'st not what thou art, a god, a king:
> For kings like gods should govern everything.

> 'How will thy shame be seeded in thine age,
> When thus thy vices bud before thy spring?
> If in thy hope thou dar'st do such outrage,
> What dar'st thou not when once thou art a king?
> O be remember'd, no outrageous thing
> From vassal actors can be wip'd away:
> Then kings' misdeeds cannot be hid in clay.

> 'This deed will make thee only lov'd for fear;
> But happy monarchs still are fear'd for love.' (ll. 601–11)

Lucrece stands as the ideal subject in these lines, perhaps we might even argue that she transforms herself into a citizen when threatened by the illegal actions of the monarch, a role that prefigures her representation as the body politic itself when Tarquin rapes her. In the first lines cited here she sees kings as God's representatives on earth, able to govern everything, the familiar statement of absolutist theory in Europe, and an interpretation of the role of the monarch within the English constitution which the Tudors intermittently asserted as theirs.[42] In the second stanza she develops her ideas, speculating on what Tarquin might do when he has become king if he is prepared to act so badly before he has assumed

[40] Buchanan 2003, pp. 85–7.    [41] Buchanan 2003, p. 3.    [42] Sommerville 1991.

power. The implications of this train of thought undermine the premise with which she started. If kings need to be suitable for their office, then they have no absolute right to rule. If they rule to serve the people then the people have a right to expect proper regal behaviour. The last line of this stanza might have been written with Buchanan's recently published *History of Scotland* in mind.[43] Buchanan's long work was designed in part to show that history exists to record the misdeeds of kings so that their subjects can learn how to choose their monarchs wisely and to depose those who show signs of being unsuitable to rule.[44] Lucrece's actions lead to the deposition of the Tarquins before Sextus Tarquinius has a chance to rule, the implication being that prevention may be better than cure.

Lucrece travels a vast journey in her debate with Tarquin. She starts off accepting that the king is like a god, and ends one step away from articulating the monarchomach position, that the monarch who fails to rule justly in the interests of his subjects can be legitimately overthrown. This political awakening is then applied — by implication — to the poem itself: 'For princes are the glass, the school, the book, / Where subjects' eyes do learn, do read, do look' (ll. 615–16). Anyone who learns from the behaviour of Tarquin, as Lucrece suggests, will almost certainly come to the conclusion that the Romans came to, that they would be better off without kings ever again.

Lucrece's rhetoric, as Colin Burrow points out, 'is a textbook example of political oratory in this [i.e., Elizabethan] period', designed to counsel the monarch against a destructive course of action.[45] Lucrece explains that she sues for 'exil'd majesty's repeal' (l. 640), and her pleas are unsuccessful. Nevertheless, the lines point to a very different future. Lucrece means here that Tarquin is exiled from himself in his duty as king. But we all know that Tarquin and his line really are banished from Rome at the end of the poem, and that even a protracted war with the newly established republican armies fails to restore the dynasty.[46] The eventual effect of Tarquin's base desires is to make Romans value their freedom even more: 'The hard-won liberty of Rome was rendered the more welcome, and the more fruitful'.[47] Lucrece's failure at this stage does not imply that resistance to tyranny is futile; rather, it suggests that the rhetoric of counsel may have to be abandoned in favour of more drastic — that is, republican — measures.

---

[43] On Shakespeare and Buchanan, see Norbrook 1987.   [44] Buchanan 1690.
[45] Shakespeare 2002, p. 52.   [46] Livy 1960, pp. 84–5.   [47] Livy 1960, p. 89.

*The Rape of Lucrece* contains a series of ironies, or displacements, that require us to read its status as myth and history with due care and attention. Lucrece speaks for more than half of the poem and develops a sophisticated understanding of political issues in the course of her argument with Tarquin and subsequent meditations on her unhappy fate, yet she concludes that argument is futile and that she is too polluted to carry on living (ll. 1021–2, 1700–22). Her death, not that of the king, paves the way for the establishment of the republic, with men acting to expunge the faults of men over the dead body of a woman.[48] Yet the real establishment of the republic occurs through the words of Lucrece and the intellectual journey she undertakes.

The second story is a little more complex and involved, but is easy enough to recognize. The republic ended and imperial Rome began when Octavius Caesar assumed control after defeating the republican forces led by Brutus and Cassius. Just as the republicans had to fight a series of wars with the forces of the Tarquins to retain control of the body politic they wished to control, Octavius had to defeat his former ally, Antony, now in league with the Egyptian queen, Cleopatra. When he managed this feat, he was left in sole command and assumed the title of Augustus. The Roman Empire was born. Augustus's triumphant moment, as all readers of Tacitus, Suetonius and Plutarch would have known, was all too brief, and he was succeeded by a series of horrible tyrants whose names were a byword for cruelty and excess – Tiberius, Caligula, Claudius and Nero – eventually killed off by a popular coup, leading to the rule of the Flavian dynasty. The cyclical nature of Roman history was, as always, apparent.[49]

The events leading up to this political transformation were just as important as elements of the story in the Renaissance imagination. The decay of the values and morals of the republic led to a bloody civil war between the former allies, Pompey and Julius Caesar, which Caesar won. The story of this struggle was told in Lucan's epic/anti-epic poem, *Pharsalia*, their author becoming a republican martyr when he participated in a plot against Nero, and was forced to commit suicide.[50] Caesar then seized control of Rome, and, although he was not actually crowned, he became its sole ruler, following in the footsteps of the dictator, Sulla. Caesar was then assassinated in a republican coup

---

[48] Kahn 2003, p. 271.     [49] Holland, 2003.
[50] Lucan 1992; compare Norbrook 1999, pp. 23–62, 83–92.

by Brutus and Cassius, who hoped to restore the values of the Roman Republic, but only succeeded in unleashing a further wave of destructive violence.[51]

A large number of the most significant writings that told the history of Rome narrated these events and their consequences. They encapsulate the common perception that its history was a cycle of diametrically opposed forms of government. There were other significant narratives, moments and images too, and a list might include the attempted coup of Sejanus against the emperor Tiberius, narrated in a variety of Roman histories, including Tacitus and Dio Cassius's *Roman History*, and represented in Ben Jonson's *Sejanus His Fall* (1603);[52] the conspiracy of Catiline, governor of Africa, narrated in Sallust's well-known work, and represented in Jonson's *Catiline His Conspiracy* (1611);[53] the suicides of Lucan and Seneca during the reign of Nero, the first narrated in Tacitus, Cassius Dio, and Suetonius's *Twelve Caesars*, the latter also in Suetonius, but more importantly in his letters, and through the profound influence of his tragedies on early-modern drama;[54] the murder of Cicero at the hands of Mark Antony's agents in 43 BCE, as his work was ubiquitous and impossible to avoid in Elizabethan England, the biography being most readily available in Plutarch's *Lives*.[55] Taken together these stories and events represent a general historical picture.[56] The historical lesson given declares that the republic is a far more desirable form of government than the empire, although the latter may be preferable in times of decay and corruption, taking its political cue from Aristotle's belief that tyranny could be a plausible form of government if the world had become bad enough.[57] The republic is thought to be not always strong enough to incline men to virtue and so sometimes be vulnerable to the attack of the wicked, desperate and corrupt, such as Catiline, whose attempt to seize power was thwarted by the republican hero, Cicero. Eventually, if the guardians of the republic are not vigilant enough, an oligarchy will seize power and end the republic, promoting their own interests at the expense of the general citizens. Of course, the danger of imperial government is tyranny, as Rome soon discovered, when the reign of the problematic but essentially

---

[51] Crook, Lintott and Rawson 1994.
[52] Tacitus 1956, pp. 153–221; Jonson 1990; Worden 1994.
[53] Sallust 1963, pp. 151–233; Jonson 1972.
[54] Suetonius 1957, pp. 209–42; Barbour 1998.
[55] Jones 1981.    [56] Miola 1983.    [57] Aristotle 1946, pp. 243–50.

public-spirited Augustus was followed by those of Tiberius, Caligula and
Nero. And, as the works of Tacitus so frequently demonstrate, secrecy,
plotting and conspiracy become the way of life under the rule of a tyrant.
Roman history shows that it is better to try and make the republic
function properly, and then to defend it against its enemies, than to throw
one's lot in with the imperialists. Everybody knows where the assassination of Julius Caesar leads, but it is not clear who is really to blame: the
assassins who despatch the putative tyrant, or Caesar and his followers,
who have already killed off the republic by promoting their champion at
the expense of everything else, including the republic?

Shakespeare narrates more of the republican story than any other
dramatist working in Elizabethan and Jacobean England, as well as
applying the lessons of a history of the republic to the English crown.
Having told the story of the birth of the republic in *The Rape of Lucrece*,
he then narrated the story of the death of the republic in *Julius Caesar*
and *Antony and Cleopatra*, which show the rise of Julius Caesar leading
eventually to the assumption of power by the colourless Octavius Caesar,
the future Augustus. The play concludes with Octavius arriving in
Egypt to find the dead Cleopatra and Antony, announcing that 'Our
army shall / In solemn show attend this funeral, / And then to Rome'
(5.2.362–4).[58] Octavius's bland lines depend on the audience knowing
exactly what has passed and what the future holds in store for Rome.
And, perhaps, there is a pointed contrast to the concluding lines of
*Hamlet*, a play that contains a king with the name of one of Augustus's
successors, Claudius, whose underhand behaviour leads to the end of
his family's rule in Denmark. There, Fortinbras, another foreign martial
king who arrives on the scene to find a mass of dead bodies, arranges
the funeral of Hamlet before assuming power himself in an equally
deadpan manner:

> Take up the bodies. Such a sight as this
> Becomes the field, but here shows much amiss.
> Go, bid the soldiers shoot. (5.2.406–8)

In *Hamlet*, the audience cannot possibly have any idea of what the future
will hold for Denmark, and whether the burial of the dead will bring
peace and political stability or a renewed cycle of violence.

The comparison between the plays should also alert us to the fact that
the influence of Roman history on Shakespeare's imagination was not

---

[58] All references are to Shakespeare 1997.

simply confined to the works he wrote using the relevant source materials. Early in his career Shakespeare was confident enough a dramatist to produce a play, *Titus Andronicus*, written sometime before 1594, possibly much earlier, that invented a Roman history.[59] *Titus* would appear to be set in very late Rome, as the empire was being overrun by the barbarian Goths and shows either the last chance of the empire to revitalize itself through the establishment of its republican government, or that it has decayed too much to be saved.[60] Later on, he meticulously analyses the electoral process in Rome in *Coriolanus*, relating the Roman constitution to electoral practices he may well have observed in London.[61]

But if Shakespeare seems to have exhibited a particular interest in the history and meaning of republican Rome, he was by no stretch of the imagination alone. Many of his contemporary writers, including Christopher Marlowe, Ben Jonson, Edmund Spenser, Sir Philip Sidney, Samuel Daniel, Michael Drayton, George Chapman and Fulke Greville were also extremely aware of the importance of republican politics and history, even if some were less than enthusiastic about its viability as a political form. However, it would be a mistake to imagine that only argument and belief are what matters in early-modern political debates.

Republicanism and early-modern literature are interlinked in two fundamental, interrelated ways. Literary texts adopt and adapt stories from republican history and literature. They also contain republican ideas with which they engage. Not only were there a great number of literary texts inspired by republican ideas and history, but there were also works, such as Shakespeare's *Lucrece*, which represented key republican moments, alerting readers to the need for close and careful reading of the text in order to determine its political significance. Such literature is perhaps best read as one of the arts of persuasion, like the speeches of Cicero, not as an autonomous, free-standing artefact.

We are back to some familiar issues of definition. If we define republicanism in terms of a political or historical culture that insists on a clear sense of its existence as a programme, or as an articulated political language, then we risk a historical narrative that sees it emerge almost *ex nihilo* (like Sin from Satan's head in *Paradise Lost*) unless we speak in terms of a proto-republicanism, which perhaps risks confusing and blurring the issues and forcing us to distinguish between two things

---

[59] Shakespeare 2000, pp. 69–79.  [60] Rhodes 2003.
[61] Kishlansky 1986, ch. 1; Barton 1994, ch. 1.

which may well be virtually the same (like the of idea of a sort of 'pre-sin' in the Garden of Eden in the same poem). If we define republicanism in terms of a literary culture of poetry and translation we risk an all-inclusive definition that fails to distinguish between the allusive and the substantial, the real and the imagined. However we try to sort out this problem it is clear that we are not going to get much further unless we debate these issues from the perspectives of different disciplines. Scholars of early-modern literature need to try and see their work as part of a larger intellectual culture if they wish to continue using words such as 'political'; historians and political theorists need to consider more literary texts as evidence in their work. And we all need to stretch our definition of 'politics'.

CHAPTER 7

# Dramatic Traditions and Shakespeare's Political Thought

## Jean E. Howard

Like a prism, Shakespeare's plays are shot through with the political thought of his time; but like a prism, they omit no single ray, but refract a multitude of colours. In the much-cited 1993 volume, *The Varieties of British Political Thought, 1500–1800*, John Guy, Donald Kelley and Linda Peck delineate many of the recurring topics that informed political thinking before the Civil War of the mid-seventeenth century.[1] The role of counsel in good governance, the proper education of a prince, the body politic as concept and informing metaphor, Tacitus, Ovid, and republicanism, resistance theory, Machiavelli and the new statescraft: these are but a few of the topics discussed throughout the sixteenth and early seventeenth centuries, and hardly one fails to make an appearance in Shakespeare's works.

Of course, Shakespeare might not to everyone seem the most obvious source of political reflection on the Elizabethan stage. After all, it is Marlowe in *The Jew of Malta* who brings Machiavelli on stage, vaunting his free-thinking ways:

> To some perhaps my name is odious,
> But such as love me, guard me from their tongues,
> And let them know that I am Machevill,
> And weigh not men, and therefore not men's words
> (Prologue, ll. 5–8).[2]

But it is Shakespeare, in *Richard III*, who creates a villain hero who, 'set[ting] the murderous Machiavel to school',[3] embodies the new philosophy as a means to power and a principle of rule and not just as the signature of an exotic Italian villainy. Similarly, in play after play

[1] Guy 1993, pp. 13–46; Kelley 1993, pp. 47–79; Peck 1993, pp. 80–115.
[2] Marlowe 1966, p. 9.
[3] Shakespeare 1997, p. 336 (3.2.193). All further quotations from Shakespeare's plays will be taken from this edition.

Shakespeare explores what I would call the problems of political rule. In *Macbeth* and *Winter's Tale* he anatomizes the tyrant;[4] in *Richard II* he considers the difficult issue of resistance to a sitting king;[5] in *Henry IV, Parts* 1 *and* 2 and *Henry V* he traces the education of a prince; in *King Lear* he examines the dangers of dividing a kingdom, of the king's separation from good counsel, and of the evil of flatterers; in the Roman plays he explores the possibilities of republicanism, in a number of plays (*Julius Caesar, Coriolanus, Henry IV, Part 2, Henry V*) he meditates on the role of 'the people' in the body politic.

These are all themes and topics that appear in the non-dramatic political writing of the period, and they form the bedrock of Shakespeare's political imagination. Almost from the first moments of his career, he seems not to be able to avoid thinking politically, if by that one means thinking in terms of how power is exercised within the complex social structures of the household and the kingdom. And yet, as many have noted, it is hard to pin down anything that we might call 'Shakespeare's own politics' though he has been labelled a 'traditionalist', 'a monarchist', *and* a sympathizer with republican thought.[6] In truth, one does not quite know where to have him. That is fundamentally, I think, because even more than most dramatists Shakespeare does not use his plays to elaborate a consistent political position. He never wrote an overtly polemical play like John Bale's *King Johan*, for example.[7] Nor did he write a prose treatise in which he offered advice to a monarch or a great man on affairs of state.

The popular stage, however, was important to the elaboration of political thought because it provided resources for juxtaposing one strand of political thinking with another and for subjecting each to critical examination, partly by the creation of contrapuntal and multi-vocal dramatic effects that simulated the structures both of debate and of cultural struggle and negotiation. The stage gave political ideas embodiment and put them in motion and in conversation.

---

[4] Bushnell 1990.

[5] Kantorowicz 1957 famously analysed this play in terms of a split between the mystical and natural bodies of the king, the one which never dies, the other which is both mortal and fallible. For a critique of this reading of the play see Norbrook 1996.

[6] Dzelzainis 1999, pp. 100–16, explores some of the reasons why critics have taken a sceptical view of Shakespeare's political originality and consistency before going on himself to place Shakespeare within the new humanism of the second half of the sixteenth century.

[7] For an excellent discussion of the profound animus to Catholicism that informs Bale's representation of John's reign, see *King Johan* 1969, introduction.

The first book of criticism I wrote, *Shakespeare's Art of Orchestration* (1984), explored how Shakespeare built plays, how he made them, so that they would have effects on audiences.[8] I would not write the same book today, but it still represents my deep commitment to understanding the link between the many things a play might 'mean' and how it is made: the way it draws on what, for example, Rosalie Colie called 'resources of kind',[9] generic templates that pre-exist the author's employment of them; on resources of language, such as the rhetorical tradition of the Elizabethan grammar schools; and, perhaps more than any other, on resources of the stage, on prior traditions of structuring embodied action and voicing thought in relationship to other voicings. Whatever strands of political thought entered Shakespeare's imagination from his culture, they were both expressed through the transforming medium of the stage and partly derived from it. Shakespeare did not invent drama concerned with political matters. *Fulgens and Lucrece, Respublica, Gentleness and Nobility, Health and Wealth, Gorboduc* and *Jack Straw* – these are but a handful of the many plays on the sixteenth-century stage that dealt with right rule, the role of counsel and the possibility of popular rebellion.[10] Shakespeare certainly knew *some* of this drama first-hand; and he certainly knew, in general, the possibilities for making plays on the Elizabethan public stage – what I like to think of as the toolkit of resources he had been bequeathed and to which he added much in the course of his long and fruitful career.

When, in fact, Shakespeare started out to be a stage writer, his very earliest works included a number of his English histories and political tragedies like *Titus Andronicus*. In short, he was drawn both to comedy – the genre in which he worked his whole career in one form or another – but also, immediately, to history and tragedy and thus to the dramatic representation of kingship, of struggles within the body politic, of counsel, consent and rebellion. While the formal elegance, the sustained lyricism and the formal shapeliness of *Richard II*'s examination of the fall of one king and the rise of another has long been considered to mark the moment when Shakespeare reached a certain stage of maturity as a dramatist of the political world, I want to go back to the beginnings, to look at earlier plays, especially *The First Part of the Contention of the Two Famous Houses of York and Lancaster* (also known as *The Second Part*

---

[8] Howard 1984.    [9] Colie 1973.
[10] There are many books dealing with this material, but perhaps none so influential as Bevington 1962.

*of Henry VI*), to talk, not about Shakespeare's political thought as if it were separable from particular traditions and conventions of theatrical representation, but precisely about the dramaturgy within which anything we can call his political thought was embodied. If Shakespeare was not a programmatic political thinker, he was, nonetheless, gifted at what I would call the dramaturgy of politics in action.

It is often said that his early history plays are baggy monsters, desperate attempts to carve from sprawling chronicle sources something resembling a coherent two-hour traffic for the stage.[11] I do not wish to defend the formal comeliness of these early plays as much as to suggest that they are built on discernible dramaturgical principles of considerable effectiveness, many of which persisted in more elegant form in Shakespeare's later histories, and which are the means by which he was able to put political ideas in motion and in conversation. Take *The First Part of the Contention*. It is in many ways an anatomy of the sources of social disorder in a kingdom. Its general themes are to some extent dictated by Shakespeare's sources which were unanimous in depicting Henry VI as a weak king and his reign as a disaster for England's control of its French domains. But *The First Part of the Contention* focuses not on losses abroad, but on social disruption at home. And from the beginning, Shakespeare had at his disposal a device from the morality play of flanking a protagonist with good and bad counsellors to give a basic structure to his material. In *The Contention*, Henry is a young king, and he rules surrounded by a bevy of advisors and courtiers. But from the first scene — involving the announcement of the terms of Henry's disastrous marriage to Margaret of Anjou — those counsellors divide into two camps. Some, like Warwick and Salisbury, support the Good Duke Humphrey in his attempts to keep the king from folly, including the folly of this marriage. Others, led by Cardinal Beaufort and the Duke of Suffolk, plot to bring down Gloucester and control the King. Until the middle of the play, when Gloucester is murdered in his bed, one overarching tension is thus provided by the dialectic between good counsel and bad, and the triumph of the latter in Act III leads directly to the decisive plunge into a disastrous civil war.

In the 1475 morality play, *Mankind*, the protagonist is flanked by Mercy on one side, and by Mischief, New Guise, Nought and Now-A-Days

---

[11] Among those critics who see the complexity of these early plays, in terms both of dramaturgy and political content, see Rackin 1990; Riggs 1971; Manheim 1973.

on the other.[12] As David Bevington has pointed out, gradually these allegorical figures give way in the course of the sixteenth century, in plays such as *King Johan*, to historical figures.[13] Sedition, Mischief, and Insolence become Pandulphus or, in Shakespeare's case, Beaufort and Suffolk. But what persists is a structure of juxtaposition by which one can see the struggle for the good of the commonweal determined by the rhetorical skill of the counsellors and the ethical judgement of the king. And, of course, when Henry decides at a climactic moment to require from Gloucester his staff of office as Lord Protector, the young king's essentially tragic fate is sealed. The play thus has a before and after structure, before and after the fall of Gloucester, before and after Good Counsel holds sway.

This pattern, of structuring action around the choice between those on the one hand and those on the other, deeply informs much of Shakespeare's political drama. It is as true for *King Lear*, poised between good daughter and bad, Kent and Oswald, as for the young Prince Hal.[14] It is a structure derived from the dramaturgy of the moralities but secularized to put considerable emphasis, as in humanist discourse, on the monarch's capacity for virtue, for wise choice, and for a receptive response to critical counsel. That Shakespeare's kings so often fail to rise to the implicit standard encoded in the structure both makes for good drama and also contributes to the sense, emphasized by some critics, of his drama's frequent, implicit scepticism about the operations of monarchical power and his experiments with representing other models of kingship, those based, for example, on more Machiavellian principles which subordinate ethics to successful manipulation of power and appearances as seen in the play in question by the rise of the Duke of York: instigator of Cade's rebellion, author of the fiction of Cade's royal birth, and devious manipulator of those around him.

But Shakespeare's political dramaturgy in *The Contention* is more complex than I have so far indicated. Competing dramatic structures supplement the before and after template that pivots around Gloucester's fall. Throughout *The Contention*, Shakespeare alternates low scenes with high, scenes involving the common people, often but not uniformly presented in a comic vein, with scenes devoted to affairs of state understood as the prerogative of the nobility, of the king and his counsellors.

---

[12] *Mankind* 1907, p. 2.     [13] Bevington 1962, p. 132.
[14] For discussion of the morality underpinnings of *King Lear* see Mack 1965.

This, too, is a technique adopted from the morality drama, and is found in plays such as *Lusty Juventus* with its alternations of vice and counsel scenes. It is a technique that in the secular historical drama becomes, in Dermot Cavanagh's fine phrase, a way of staging 'an argument with history' or, put differently, a way of using dramatic form to embody political debate outside a debate form.[15] Consider briefly, for example, three of the incidents involving commoners in the first half of the play, the dark comedy in 2.1 of the false 'miracle' of Simpcox, the man who claims to have been cured of his blindness at St. Alban's shrine; the incident in 1.3 in which several commoners misdeliver petitions to Suffolk instead of Gloucester; and the subsequent moment in 2.3 when one of those petitioners, Peter Thump, engages in combat with his master, Horner, over Peter's accusation that Horner had said the Duke of York was heir to the throne.

Much could be said about each of these episodes, but I want to say two things about them collectively. First, they expand the implicit conception of the political nation on the stage to include figures such as apprentices and commoners like Simpcox and to put their actions in a complicated relation to those of surrounding actors. In regard to the first of these scenes, for example, the petitioners who believe they are addressing their grievances to the Good Duke Humphrey are taking part, as much as Cardinal Beaufort or Warwick, in affairs of state, though from a different position. They make complaint against Suffolk for unlawful enclosures and against those who treasonously espouse the legitimacy of York over that of the sitting King. They come as suppliants, certainly, expecting redress, and not as governors, but their actions happen within a predictable structure of mutual obligation by which their loyalty is to be matched by a corresponding care for their grievances. Inattention to their ancient rights of petition, such as that expressed by Suffolk, who tears up one of their documents, rends the fabric of the body politic as it is established in the play. When this same Duke later masterminds the death of Gloucester, it is members of the commons who burst into the court under the aegis of Salisbury to demand his banishment (3.2.243–71). What the 'low scenes' do first, then, is to force consideration of the commons as political actors in the sense of those who have a role in the operations of the commonweal, who must sometimes be sternly governed, as when Simpcox attempts to blear the eye of justice with

---

[15]  Cavanagh 2003, p. 12.

a false miracle, but whose ancient rights must also be defended. This technique, of examining the actions of the great in view of the lives, the rights and the actions of the common people, is one Shakespeare continued to pursue in his later histories, though perhaps in no other play does he explore with such imaginative force the consequences of a breakdown of the bond uniting people, counsellor and king with the eruption of Jack Cade's rebellion.

The second consequence of this alternation of high and low scenes is to produce certain critical or ironic effects, enabled by the arguments they set in motion and the questions they elicit. In 1.3, for example, the actions of the commoners, bringing their petitions in orderly fashion before the man they assume to be the Lord Protector, contrast sharply with the subsequent disorderly behaviour of members of the court. The commoners' part in the scene is immediately followed by a conversation between the adulterous Margaret and her lover, Suffolk, and that, in turn, is followed by a fierce dispute among the court faction over whether York or Somerset will be sent as regent to Ireland. Irony emerges from the juxtaposition of orderly behaviour among the low and the chaos, disorder and competition among the high. More complex still is the actual combat later carried out between Peter and Horner. It is an event wedged in between the moment when King Henry strips Gloucester of his staff of office (2.3.23) and the scene (2.4) when Gloucester's wife passes in shame through the streets of London for her part in unlawful conjuration. The frame events stage the fall of the house of Gloucester, a fall masterminded by York and Suffolk, the Queen and Beaufort. The comic battle between master and man, by contrast, reveals the truth of the apprentice's accusations in that they fight a single combat, and the master loses. In this case, treason has been revealed and defeated among the lowly while it continues to flourish at court.

The continuing irony to which the actions of the 'high' are submitted by these juxtapositions corrodes the latter's authority and privilege as does the very *form* that the fight between Horner and Peter assumes. They fight, not with swords, but with sandbags fastened to staffs, and Horner is horribly drunk. Master and man perform a travesty of a courtly ritual – trial by single combat – that simultaneously seems to mock the rituals of the privileged and to move the locus of honourable action considerably downward on the social scale. Collectively, the juxtaposition of high and low in its many iterations implicitly submits pieties to critical examination, including pieties about the coincidence of virtue and high birth, and puts in motion a debate about the nature of right rule and the role of the commons in the commonweal. Does such an ironizing dramaturgy make Shakespeare an anti-monarchical writer? No; its effects are much subtler than that. The resources of the dramaturgical and rhetorical tradition Shakespeare inherited allowed him to use the stage to create dialectical structures in which political positions and assumptions were implicitly allowed to critique or comment on one another, where the actions of one set of political actors had to be judged in their relationship to and effects upon another set of actors.[16] That this was done on a commercial stage in front of an audience mixed in its social composition, is not a fact that can be too often recalled, since the scene of representation made more likely the appreciative uptake of the play's ironic juxtapositions. Such a stage, in Shakespeare's hands, was less a space to espouse certain political ideas than to test them, to make them the subjects of an implicit public debate which the stage was uniquely situated to promote.[17] It was a stage that in its openendedness could lead to various appropriations of the ideas it put in motion.

This is certainly true of what is probably the play's most memorable part, the eruption of the popular rebellion led by Jack Cade in Act IV. The Cade episodes, so often debated as to their political import,[18] again owe much to the dramatic traditions upon which Shakespeare was drawing, particularly his use of Vice and clown as stage types through which to give shape to the character of Cade. To the extent that he is a Vice, Cade both articulates disorder and simultaneously establishes affinities with the audience through laughter and through the intimacy of speech acts situated in the liminal space of the plateau where clowning, direct address to the audience and the irreverent travesty of high behaviour regularly occurred.[19] Though Cade does to some extent represent the allegorical concept of Disorder writ large, he has also been transformed and humanized into a foul-talking, funny and violent

---

[16] Altman 1978 skillfully explores the effect on sixteenth-century drama of the rhetorical tradition of arguing *in utramque partem*, that is, on each side of a question. Influenced by this tradition, Shakespeare frequently allows dramatic structure to set up an implicit debate among different points of view rather than having two characters engage in face-to-face disputation.

[17] For my fuller discussion of the social role of the public stage in Elizabethan and Jacobean England, see Howard 1994.

[18] Good discussions of the Cade rebellion and Shakespeare's representation of it include Greenblatt 1983, pp. 1–29; Patterson 1989, pp. 32–51; Helgerson 1992, pp. 195–245; and Cartelli 1994, pp. 48–67.

[19] For the *locus classicus* of the by now familiar distinction between plateau and locus as symbolically and sometimes physically distinct playing areas on the Elizabethan stage, see Weimann 1978, pp. 73–85.

clothier who aspires to be a king. By modelling the rebel on the pattern of a comic Vice, Shakespeare *places* him, morally speaking; Cade is bad, someone who sacks London, is the tool of the Duke of York and would dethrone a king. Yet by drawing on this prototype, Shakespeare also draws on the performative power of the role to produce effects quite in excess of any homiletic function.

For example, Cade engages in a running imitation of kingly behaviour at once funny, horrifying, and deeply demystifying of what it evokes. In 4.2, comically assuming the powers of a king, Cade knights himself (l. 106), proclaims his Plantagenet lineage while his followers, in asides, speak of his actual descent from a bricklayer and a midwife (ll. 33–43), and condemns a man to death because he can write his name instead of making a mark 'like an honest plain-dealing man' (4.2.90–91).[20] Cade continues to send to their deaths those who show signs of privilege and proclaims 'My mouth shall be the Parliament of England' (4.7.12–13). When he dubs himself a knight, Cade is ridiculous but also appealing in his wild energy. By submitting the prerogatives of kingship to rough and energetic appropriation, Cade desacralizes those actions, makes them imitable in the low theatre of his public acts and invites critical reflection both on the role of king and on kingly prerogatives.[21] Who should have the right to condemn men to death and to elevate others to privilege on the field of battle? In this play the man who is supposed to play the king, Henry VI, though less brutal, is no less an imperfect actor of the role than Cade. The disproportion between ideal and embodiment is forced into view by Cade's burlesque as is the reality of the awesome power over life and death that is part of the daily operation of high office.

Cade's devastating performance of kingship is, moreover, not without its own informing ideology. Even while wishing to be king, Cade articulates the watchwords of a popular radicalism with roots in the late medieval period.[22] He praises the inherent nobility of working men, stressing that those who labour in their vocations should be magistrates; and he orders that when he is king, 'all things shall be in common' (4.7.16). His position is incoherent, and the violence he spawns reprehensible, but he speaks throughout to the material needs — for bread and

[20] All quotations are from *The First Part of the Contention* in Shakespeare 1997.

[21] This is David Scott Kastan's central observation about how the stage removes the sacred aura of kingship by making it an act a man might play. See Kastan 1986, pp. 459–75.

[22] See, in particular, Hobday 1979, pp. 63–78; Manning 1988, pp. 187–219; and Patterson 1989, pp. 32–51.

beer — of those whom the nobility in this play have been all too frequently ready to ignore or to scorn. The insolence of Suffolk in ripping
up a commoner's petition and his class-based contempt for the seamen
who eventually capture and behead him suggest just how far short of
Gloucester's benevolent paternalism members of the ruling class have
fallen.

In fact, the placement of Cade's rebellion in the fourth act of the play
after the murder of Gloucester casts it in a very different light than if it
had erupted earlier. In the dramatic logic of the play, the rebellion seems
to follow on from that death and from the corruption of the particular set
of commitments and political beliefs that adhere to the Lord Protector in
the play. Without Gloucester to hold together a popular-aristocratic axis
in support of the traditional hierarchical conception of the commonweal,
something much more radical is spawned in Cade's wholesale attack on
privilege: the privilege of those who can read, wear silks and write on
parchment.[23] It is the wrong question to ask if Shakespeare 'believed' in
or advocated for or against this strain of egalitarian political thought.
That is ultimately unknowable, though unlikely. However, through the
figure of Cade, the Vice-like clown, he can conjure this body of thought
in order to set it, critically, in view of the positions marked by
the paternalistic Gloucester and the Machiavellian Duke of York. The
before and after two-part structure of the play, stemming from Henry's
failure to heed good counsel, produces a dramatic logic in which popular
rule seems to emanate from an abrogation of the responsibilities of
the monarch and his peers and to bear a direct relationship to the
machinations of York, Cade's sponsor. At the same time, the events
in which Cade is involved mirror features of the dominant order, but
in such a way as to subject them to parodic imitation that empties them
of their aura. These features include, for example, aristocratic investment
in lineage and ritual to legitimate privilege, their use of 'parchment'
to control resources and their use of force to effect their wills.
The presence of low scenes throughout the play forces the question of
the role of the commons in the political nation; the Cade scenes intimate
both the power of the commons to challenge the traditional order when
their privileges within it are ignored and also the power of common men
to submit the privileged to their withering critique.

---

[23] For an acute discussion of the strategic intelligence informing peasant attacks on documentary
records, see Justice 1994, esp. pp. 13–66.

The effect is very different from a play such as the anonymous *Jack Straw*, printed in 1594 and thus nearly contemporaneous with *The Contention* and dealing with some of the same matter. While historically Jack Cade's rebellion occurred in 1450, in staging it Shakespeare drew on popular accounts of other peasant rebellions including that of 1381 when Wat Tyler invaded London, burned London Bridge and sacked the Savoy, John of Gaunt's palace. *Jack Straw* stages this rebellion directly, but uses quite differently the resources of the popular dramatic tradition of which it is also a part. The anonymous play begins when a group of commoners, upset by the rude treatment of the King's tax collector, kill him; then, urged on by the preaching of Parson Ball, who argues against 'this difference in degrees' and laments that 'The Rich have all, the poore live in miserie' (1.1.85, 103),[24] they gather 20,000 men and march on London. The play pivots around a simple opposition between King and rebels. Many of the rebels are comically portrayed and speak with great colloquial vigour about the economic grievances that spur them to take up arms, but the King is never anything but solicitous of their complaints. When he hears their demands for 'Wealth and libertie' (3.1.707), he promises to grant them all they ask and pardons to boot. When Cade and a few followers persist in their desire for 'spoile' (3.1.757), Cade is killed by the loyal Mayor of London, and the rest are condemned to death. While sympathetic to the humanity of the rebels, the play starkly separates the incorrigible rebels from those who respond to the attentions of the king and moves swiftly to depict the restoration of order.

The play is not only different in length and complexity from *The Contention*, but also different in the degree of dialectical pressure its dramatic structure exerts on the opposing terms of the political debate it implicitly stages. Jack Straw's rebellion tests the mercy and goodness of the King, but it does not critically refract the principles upon which kingship rests. It draws on the energies of clowning to make rebellion funny and to make it theatrically exciting, but not to make it subversively mirror what it opposes. Nor does it use the overarching structure of the play to relate rebellion to the abrogation of an implicit social agreement in which all parties had a stake, an abrogation coincident with the King's separation from Good Counsel. In *Jack Straw*, there is little to contradict the Bishop's initial assertion that 'The Multitude [is] a Beast of many

---

[24] *The Life and Death of Jack Straw* 1957.

heads' (I.2.188), a grotesque and unnatural anomaly, at least insofar as the chief rebels are concerned.

In closing, I want to explore one final way Shakespeare uses the performative resources of the stage to embody political thought in compelling and disturbing ways. Unlike the anonymous author of *Jack Straw*, Shakespeare eschews the overt use of metaphors that define the rebels as a many-headed beast or that even present the commonweal as a body composed of many interconnected but hierarchically organized parts. Instead, he foregrounds actual bodies in ways that use performance indirectly to evoke and to pressure the meanings traditionally encoded in such overworn political metaphors. Heads and hands are of particular importance in the Cade scenes. In Act I, commoners had come to Suffolk with petitions in their hands, deferentially asking for redress. In Act IV, the commoners who surround Cade have weapons in their hands, and they are no longer deferential. As artisans, these men have time out of mind used their hands to make what the kingdom needs: cloth, shoes, food. But in an uncanny transformation, these artisans now turn the tools of their trade to the tasks of murder and mayhem.[25] The axe with which a butcher slaughtered a calf now beheads a nobleman or cuts out his tongue. Jesting among themselves, the rebels talk about the nobles' scorn for honest labour and about how as workmen they can turn the skills of their trades from production to violence.

SECOND REBEL: The nobility think scorn to go in leather aprons.
FIRST REBEL: Nay more, the King's Council are no good workmen.
SECOND: True; and yet it is said 'Labour in thy vocation'; which is as much as to say as 'Let the magistrates be labouring men'; and therefore should we be magistrates.
FIRST: Thou hast hit it; for there's no better sign of a brave mind than a hard hand.
SECOND: I see them! I see them! There's Best's son, the tanner of Wingham —
FIRST: He shall have the skins of our enemies to make dog's leather of.
SECOND: And Dick the butcher —
FIRST: Then is sin struck down like an ox, and iniquity's throat cut like a calf.

[25] I owe this insight to my former student, Ronda Arab, whose dissertation on the bodies of working men dealt not only with Jack Cade but with Bottom and other dramatic characters whose physical strength and artisanal skills define a masculinity in competition with aristocratic bodies: see Arab 2002. The next several pages of this chapter draw on ideas I develop in Howard 2006.

| SECOND: | And Smith the weaver — |
| FIRST: | Argo, their thread of life is spun. (4.2.10–26) |

Just as Cade knights himself, usurping the King's prerogative, so his followers imagine themselves in the roles of magistrates and executioners, tanning noble hides and slitting noble throats, rather than labouring to produce the food and the clothing that will feed and adorn noble bodies. The hands of labourers have suddenly become frightening and the heads of the nobility vulnerable. In one of the most memorable moments in Act IV, Cade orders Lord Saye beheaded because of his dedication to grammar schools, printing presses and papermills, and then orders his son-in-law, James Cromer, killed as well. The heads of Saye and Cromer are put on poles, and Cade orders these heads be borne through the streets, kissing one another as they go.

In a disorienting reversal of traditional status hierarchies and political assumptions, the 'hands' of the Commonwealth have become the 'head', forcing their way to rule; and the mighty have been subordinated, the 'headwork' associated with the printing press and the grammar school devalued, their bodies desecrated and torn apart, echoing a prior scene in which the seamen who capture Suffolk cut off his head and send it back to Henry's adulterous Queen. Something other than a simple reversal, or world-upside-down, is occurring here, however. This is not just about the mighty being brought low and the lowly exalted; rather, the insistent theatrical focus on body parts invites a critical rethinking of the terms of authority and privilege encoded in metaphors of the body politic and in hierarchical social structures in which hand is subordinated to head, clouted shoon to silken coat, handwork to headwork.

The performance traditions of popular theatre would have reinforced the political handy-dandy enacted in the represented action in yet a further way. Popular acting troupes depended, especially in the 1580s and 1590s, on the particular skills of their clowns. Cade's part, for example, would have been performed by such a company clown, and his physical skills would have been one of the chief sources of theatrical pleasure offered to spectators. We are not sure which company first performed *The Contention*, but the play was probably in the possession of Pembroke's Men before 1594, after which it passed into the hands of the Chamberlain's Men.[26] After 1594, the part of Cade might have

---

[26] For a discussion of the theatrical provenance of the plays before 1594 see Shakespeare 1990, pp. 36–8 and Gurr 1996, pp. 261–2.

been assumed by Will Kemp, the famous acrobat, dancer, and actor who was a member of the Chamberlain's Men between 1594 and 1599 and played such roles as Peter in *Romeo and Juliet*, Dogberry in *Much Ado About Nothing*, and probably others such as Bottom, Costard and Falstaff. As one of the most famous clowns of the 1590s, Kemp had an independent reputation as an improvisational entertainer who could play instruments, perform jigs, as well as act, often in parts requiring an emphasis on physicality and the assumption of a rustic or lower-class persona.[27] In 1599, when he left the Chamberlain's Men, Kemp did a celebrated morris dance from London to Norwich which was commemorated in an illustrated pamphlet entitled *Kemp's Nine Daies Wonder*.

Even though Shakespeare probably did not create the part 'for' Kemp, he would certainly have been familiar with the talents of Kemp and of the other stage clowns from the 1580s and early 1590s and would have written the part of Cade with their clowning skills in mind. These skills, developed through decades of theatrical performance, were themselves part of the particular resources of the stage upon which Shakespeare could draw, and they were not innocent of political implication. Because actors were drawn from the artisan class from which Cade derives, in the fused stage body of Cade/clown, the theatre would have been showcasing the bodily skills of its own artisan performers. And if Kemp at some point *did* perform the part of Cade, he would have infused the part with a particularly celebrated athleticism and comic skill. Many scholars have argued that in the 1590s, in particular, the clown often returned to the stage to dance a jig when the formal play had ended.[28] It is enticing to think of the implications of such a jig at the end of *The Contention*, perhaps especially if performed by Kemp. Within the fiction of the play, Cade is himself beheaded in Act V. But if, in the person of the clown, he returned to dance a jig, then Cade/clown would be the only decapitated character, of the many in *The Contention*, to undergo a kind of onstage resurrection (an anticipation, perhaps, of Falstaff's 'resurrection' at the end of 1 *Henry IV*). As so often in the Elizabethan theatre, the

---

[27] For the fullest account of Kemp's life and theatrical parts, see Wiles 1987; and also Grote 2002, pp. 31, 231, who argues that Kemp definitely played Cade during the Chamberlain's revival of Part II.

[28] Wiles 1987, pp. 43–60.

presentational elements of performance carried within them the capacity to disrupt and complicate the ideological thrust of representation.[29] The character Cade may have died a traitor, seemingly ending his political career in disgrace, but in the artisanal energies of the jigging clown he lived on, a powerful exemplar of the skills and the persistent presence of hard-handed men within the commonweal and within the theatre. If the history plays are most centrally about kings, they are enacted by commoners and assign commoners important roles within their multi-vocal political explorations. In this and other ways, drawing on the resources of the stage traditions he inherited, Shakespeare submitted the political thought of his time to the test of embodied representation.

It is important, then, when thinking of Shakespeare's contribution to political thought, to consider not only the ideas debated in his plays, but also the particular vividness with which the stage brought them home to the ordinary people who frequented the theatre and the degree to which the political thinking they embodied was inseparable from the dramatic forms and conventions through which they were expressed. The commercial theatre was a public and popular London venue, and in the 1590s, the English history play, which Shakespeare helped to establish as a recognizable stage genre, became an important part of this theatre's repertory. It not only gave playgoers a sense of their national past, but also let them experience a uniquely dialogic and complex exploration of political ideas that circulated in different forms in other quarters of the national culture. Written somewhat later than his English histories, both Shakespeare's Roman plays and tragedies exhibit a similarly complex capacity to investigate ideas of tyranny, right rule, and popular participation in the commonwealth. What is unique about the history plays, I would argue, is not only how early Shakespeare penned the first of them, but also how directly they insert political debate into an explicitly English context. As theatregoers confronted their national past in dramatized form, they were invited to understand it in the context of implicit debates about the limits and powers of the sovereign or the proper relationship of the people to their rulers. I would submit,

---

[29] For a discussion of the gap between representational and presentational levels of performance, see Howard 1994. For sophisticated discussion of how the actor's body, his stage position and performative skills affected early-modern theatrical meaning, see also Weimann 1978.

therefore, that without attention to such venues as the public theatre, we will never fully understand the way in which political ideas percolated through Elizabethan and Jacobean culture and the perhaps unexpected forms of their expression.

# CHAPTER 8

# Irony, Disguise and Deceit: What Literature Teaches us About Politics

## Steven N. Zwicker

Here is the problem: the texts studied by historians of political thought are almost invariably systematic and discursive; they are rarely poems or plays or novels, and who could blame historians for such a choice. The careful unfolding of political thought is rarely the business of playwrights, poets or novelists, and who could blame them for failures of analytic rigour or argumentative transparency as they make their specialized, interested, often polemical, at times uncertain, ironic, and rarely even-handed interventions into political systems – that is of course not their job. There seems then a gap difficult to bridge between interests and texts – on the one side, historians who are anxious to get on with their business and go to places where they can work efficiently and without the distractions of figuration, uncertainty or irony; and on the other, students of literature who feel an obligation to explicate the political ideas that so often erupt in their texts with a sense of their genealogy, force and currency, their status and character in the master-pieces of political thought, but for whom those masterpieces are rarely objects of devotion. The recognition of this gap is no great insight into disciplinary divides, but our own moment of heightened inter-disciplinarity and an awareness of the early-modern implication of politics in aesthetics suggest the importance of probing such divides and of considering the ways in which reading literature enhances our understanding of politics.

My aim in this chapter is, then, to think about literary language and literary strategy, and especially about irony, and to ask what irony and figuration enable language to do, and why such doing might interest students of political thought. This effort will take the form of a series of panels or expositions that runs from Tacitus through Dryden, Donne, Marvell and Congreve, texts that I have arranged neither as a strict chronology nor teleology, but as a display that unfolds irony's full armoury of complication and compromise. I begin with a scene from Tacitus because of its brilliance and its deep ironies but also for the ways in which it raises questions about the function of irony in the exposition of political themes, and for the display it makes of the body politic – a trope that preoccupies early-modern writers at the centre of this study. I also choose Tacitus for a beginning because he raises the problem of genre and allows us to ask whether irony may have a greater affinity with some genres than others, and whether we might be able to contemplate irony's performance more fully in literary texts than in those of political theory or political philosophy.

Of course the equivocal generic status of the *Annals* – the way it seems to hover between literature and history – and the extraordinary subtlety of Tacitus' prose may well suggest that irony and figuration, indeed subtlety of mind and inwardness of expression, are not the exclusive property of those genres we identify as literature, and that fully to understand relations between irony and politics we might want to explore, and with an equal attentiveness to irony and figuration, the discursive prose of political history and political philosophy. But for the moment I want to affiliate irony and figuration with what we conventionally think of as literature even while allowing that such affiliation is made for experimental or argumentative purposes. The generic uncertainty of the *Annals* suggests too how difficult it is to make a hard and fast distinction between literature and the discursive modes that we associate with political history, political philosophy and political theory. In another setting and for different purposes we might situate poems, plays, novels, histories and philosophical prose along a continuum that allows both proximities and gradations of difference. Here I want to stress distinctions and to argue that the freedom and indeterminacy and the pleasures of the literary text, the pleasures, that is, of fiction – of repetition, variation and the unsettling of anticipated returns – allow a different quality of life for language than that warranted and organized by tract and treatise.[1]

### 'MORE OF OSTENTATION, THAN OF UPRIGHT MEANING'

Early in book I of the *Annals* Tacitus records, or should we say imagines or invents, the language, ceremonies and circumstance of Tiberius's accession to power, and the psychological currents released by the event.[2]

[1] On literature and pleasure see Barthes 1975.
[2] The episode, *Annals*, I, II–12, can be most easily consulted in the Loeb Library edition: Tacitus 1931, pp. 265–9.

We are still uncertain whether 'records' or 'invents' is the right word since the status of this text as history is in doubt, though its literary quality is not. As Tacitus's most recent editor remarks of the scene: 'a literary masterpiece ... but at the same time very imperfect history'.[3] Elsewhere Tacitus had described Tiberius as a master of dissembling who 'studied nothing save anger, hypocrisy, and secret lasciviousness'; here he depicts political change with an acute sense of its dangers. But Tacitus also heightens the ambiguities that surround the shift in power, the temptations of ambition and compliance, and the desire and fear that bound Tiberius to those who would suffer or profit from the new regime.[4] When Augustus's funeral rites had run their course,

... earnest Supplications were address'd to Tiberius; who, on his side, spoke ambiguously concerning the Greatness of Empire, and the Diffidence he had of his own Abilities; Saying, 'That nothing but the Soul and Genius of Augustus could support so great a Burden of Affairs; and that having sustain'd some part of them during the Life of the Emperour, he was sensible by his own Experience, how difficult and dangerous it was to charge his Shoulders with the Weight of Government. That in a City, which abounded with the Choice of great and able Persons, all Things ought not to be intrusted to the Management of one; since Publick Functions were better exercis'd, when many join'd their Cares and Labours.' But there was more of Ostentation, than of upright Meaning in these Discourses. And besides, if Tiberius, whether by Nature or by Custom, spoke obscurely even on those Subjects, where he had no occasion to dissemble, his Words at this time became more intricate and doubtful, when he studied altogether to disguise his Thoughts. Then the Senators, who were all equally afraid of seeming to divine his Meaning, broke out into Tears, Complaints and Vows; holding out their Hands to the Gods, and to the Image of Augustus, and embracing the Knees of Tiberius.... In the mean time, the Senate still descending to the most abject Supplications, it happen'd that Tiberius said unwarily, He found himself uncapable of Governing the whole Empire, but if it pleas'd them to commit some part of it to his Administration, whatsoever it were, he would accept it. Then Asinius Gallus laying holding of the Word, 'And what part of it, O Tiberius', said he, 'wouldst thou undertake?' He not expecting such a Question, and not having his Answer in a readiness, for a while stood silent: But having recover'd the use of his Reason, answer'd 'That it was unbecoming of his Modesty to choose a Share of it, when he had rather discharge himself altogether of the Burden'. Asinius, who discover'd in his Countenance, that he had stung him, replied, 'That the Demand which he had made, tended not to the sharing of that Power,

[3] Goodyear 1972–1981, I, p. 176.
[4] The classic study of Tacitus's presentation of Tiberius is Syme 1958, I, pp. 410–11.

which could not be divided, but to draw the Acknowledgment from his own Mouth, that the Commonwealth, being but one Body, could only be governed by one Soul'.[5]

Sharply observant of tactics and obscurity in others, Tacitus himself proved a master of the difficult style, a brilliant tactician of dark sentences and equivocations. Perhaps the cultivation of ambiguity had made him more alert to the ways in which utterance could shade and conceal as well as reveal intentions and to the multivalence of language itself, its unsteadiness and uncertain character; or perhaps Tacitus' extraordinary sensitivity to the performance of irony in others shaped his own style. In either case, this passage is a superb analysis of the devices of rhetoric, of the mixed messages of power, and of the intricate play between the nature of rule and the linguistic conditions in which, at this moment of change, its fundamentals are acted out. The unitary, even organic nature of political authority was a concept already sustained by a substantial body of commentary.[6] What Tacitus adds to our understanding is an awareness of the subtlety and force with which the language of the organic and indivisible body of the state might be deployed in a scene of risk and danger, and on all sides. To Tiberius's assertion that he aims but at one place within the whole, Gallus responds with a question that takes at face value the argument of modesty and incapacity, not, seemingly, to catch Tiberius out and curb his power but merely to draw from Tiberius – so Gallus claims and Tacitus reveals exactly how tactical is this claim – an acknowledgement of the properly unitary nature of authority in the state. Here is a scene of multiple deceptions in which false modesty, a not very well hidden craving for acclaim, and the manipulation of political and moral commonplaces are answered by an equally false naïveté that takes words at face value and substitutes the pretense of one kind of incomprehension for another.[7] 'And what part of it, O Tiberius, wouldst thou undertake?' Gallus asks, and by asking exposes Tiberius's intricate fabric of dissembling – or perhaps self-delusion or real self-doubt. In the end Gallus would resolve the whole through the comforting escape of a commonplace that neutralizes the

[5]  Tacitus 1698, 1, p. 35–38. The translator of Book 1 of *Annals* was John Dryden; on the character and politics of the many-handed translation of the three volumes and on Dryden's translation in particular, see Zwicker and Bywaters 1989.

[6]  On this theme, see Goodyear 1972–1981, 1, p. 180, n. to I.12.3.

[7]  For Syme, the entire scene was 'a solemn comedy'; Syme 1958, 1, p. 411. A dissenting view of Tacitus on Tiberius's 'sincerity' is presented by Woodman 1998, pp. 43–53, and, as well, Woodman's translation and annotations: Tacitus 1998, pp. 9–10.

dangerous thrust of his seeming innocent query and naturalizes Tiberius's ambitions for rule.

What Tacitus allows us to hear, and it is quite audible, perhaps in fact heightened, in the turns and counterturns of Dryden's late seventeenth-century translation, is the unsteadiness of language, the difficulty of controlling meaning, the leakage of implication between intended argument and unintended effect, and the subtlety and flexibility with which maxims or commonplaces, political idioms and languages, form the means of negotiating status and power. It is not that these idioms and languages have no overt or stable set of meanings, but rather that such meanings are complicated and compromised, their valences altered by the stream of duplicity, fear and desire in which they are immersed. The themes of Roman political thought can of course be grasped without reading such inimitable scenes, but here and elsewhere in the *Annals* Tacitus aims to convey something to which treatise and tract do not aspire, and that is the way in which irony, disguise and deceit at once inflect political speech, contribute to its strategic life and alter its formal or structural stability by allowing the simultaneous play of meanings that are if not wholly contradictory not perfectly aligned. Knowledge of political systems and ideals and of their languages is of course crucial to an understanding of the life of politics in the Roman or early-modern or indeed modern commonweal, but such knowledge is incomplete without an understanding of the life of politics in the street, in whispered exchange, in the privacy and indeterminacy of meditation, as well as in scenes of publicity and public affairs – knowledge, that is, of the life of politics endowed with all the subtle inflections of the voice and con-tradictions of the psyche. It shall be my argument that such a life can best be caught from within literature, not of course the only site of irony, disguise and deceit but surely a domain that both privileges their display and makes them available, indeed fixes them in place, for our study and reflection, and for our pleasure. Nor should we underestimate the signi-ficance of pleasure in this scheme for it signals exactly the imaginative freedom and poise, the reflective leisure, and the opportunity for surprise and play that allows irony a space for its unsettling, compromising, work.

## 'IF THE BODY POLITIQUE HAVE ANY ANALOGY TO THE NATURAL'

Tacitus alludes to the indivisibility of political authority in a Roman context; that theme and its transformation into the metaphor of the body

politic has a very long life, and I should like to pause over another display
of its idioms and implications for rule, now in an early-modern and
English context. In this instance Dryden unfolds the commonplace and
provides us with a further understanding of the interplay of literature
and political languages and beliefs.

> The true end of Satyre is the amendment of Vices by correction. And he who
> writes Honestly, is no more an Enemy to the Offendour, than the Physician to
> the Patient, when he prescribes harsh Remedies to an inveterate Disease;
> for those, are only in order to prevent the Chyrurgeon's work of an
> *Ense rescindendum*, which I wish not to my very Enemies. To conclude all; if
> the Body Politique have any Analogy to the Natural, in my weak judgment, an
> Act of Oblivion were as necessary in a Hot, Distemper'd State, as an Opiate
> would be in a Raging Fever.[8]

The 'all' getting here concluded is the superb little preface to *Absalom
and Achitophel*, Dryden's complex meditation on the bounty and safety of
'patriarchalism', a meditation made in the uncomfortable shadow of the
publication of Sir Robert Filmer's *Patriarcha* (1680) – that arch defence
of divine right rule and anatomy of relations between the family and
the state which invested the originary force of paternity in the political
authority of the king. Not only was *Absalom and Achitophel* composed
in the shadow of *Patriarcha*, it was made in the even more discomfort-
ing circumstances of a political crisis brought on by a king who had
managed to act out his paternal energies in any number of unsanctioned
circumstances but who had not, by 1681, succeeded in producing a legitimate heir.[9] Why Dryden was willing to conjure with patriarchalism in
defence of one of its less promising exemplars is an obvious puzzle, and I
want to return to this question. But for the moment what we might note
in the concluding sentence above is the tentative nature of its assertion,
the studied and, I shall argue, dissembled caution with which Dryden
proposes and tests the implications of the metaphor of the body politic.
The poised diffidence is not I suspect a real uncertainty as to whether
the metaphor still holds; whether it continues to name a system of
political beliefs that can sustain and naturalize political authority.
The caution is rather a way of seeming to soften the remedy folded into
the metaphor. Once we accept the unobjectionable, indeed unimpeach-
able, metaphor, a rather different and more dangerous implication
follows: 'an Act of Oblivion were as necessary in a Hot, Distemper'd State

---

[8] Dryden 1958, I, p. 216.
[9] On the Exclusion Crisis, see Kenyon 1972; Scott 1991; Knights 1994.

as an Opiate. . . in a Raging Fever'. The body under siege of a distemper is in need first of 'harsh remedies', and, failing those, of the 'Chyrurgeon's work of an *Ense rescindendum*' [an amputation]; it is only the narrator's diffidence that prevents him from naming exactly which limb the surgeon might excise to cure the inveterate disease of rebellion.

Dryden's cultivation of the conditional with its attractive restraint and uncertainty allows the emergence of the powerful and unpleasant consequences of a metaphor whose multivalence covers one kind of argument with another. Within the folds of a traditional and tempered and unitary metaphor is concealed a course of action neither tempered nor unitary, for amputation or dismemberment surely undermines the argument of an indivisible state. The brief passage manages to invoke the soothing familiarity of the political commonplace with its assurances of wholeness, harmony and hierarchy while at the same time, and with a seeming straight face, sharply to qualify its argument. The passage seems in fact the very model of irony which works by allowing the yes and no of assertion, by balancing idealized content against compromises and distortions that alter but do not wholly deny or render unrecognizable the innocent or ideal form of an argument. Irony, properly constituted, works by preserving some semblance of innocence in the linguistic transaction; if the ideal is wholly denied, then irony has nothing to resist, nothing of value to weigh in the balance, and we have descended into the simpler arguments and emotions of derision, debasement and mockery.

Perhaps Dryden's performance in the preface to *Absalom and Achitophel* asks if we are at a juncture in the history of a political language that exposes a faultline in its authority, a weakening of the capacity of the metaphor to sustain political argument and contain the disintegrative forces of different and challenging metaphors and myths – fictions that urge contractual or voluntaristic imaginings of the relations of parts and whole. But perhaps the sleight of hand within this sentence is less an indicator of tectonic shifts or even a piece of nostalgia than a momentary and strategic regrouping, a pause, a dissimulation of uncertainty, an act of politesse that invites reflection, perhaps even acknowledges the possibility of dissent, all the while aiming to foreclose that possibility and narrow the remedies for a state recoiling from the very act of reimagining the foundations that the conditional 'if' seems to invite and imply. The dissimulative arts of this sentence, and more largely of the preface, and more amply of the poem as a whole, allow us to hear linguistic play and political manoeuvering as they take place in real time – as, in this instance, a series of events unfolded into a political crisis which turned out to have revolutionary implications.

The literary text may enhance our understanding of the life of political languages in time imagined as a horizontal dimension, but the horizontal dimension is not its main argument and literary texts do not form the most efficient or effective archive for mapping the changes of political language over time. Within the freedom and with the linguistic resources of literature, what we discover is an opening onto the vertical dimension of political languages, their performance at specific moments and under particular strain, their subtlety and operative power, their ability to sustain and simultaneously undermine argument, to provoke both scandal and assent. The capacity of literature to allow this contradictory spectacle adds significantly to our understanding of the performativity of political language, and in a way not easily available outside the freedom and authority of the literary. Irony and contradiction, dissimulation and outright deceit may not be the exclusive domain of literature – and surely a number of examples of the ironic and dissimulative capacities of language in other forms come quickly to mind – but there is something about the gifts of the literary, its concentration and artful and studied character, its capacity to sustain both play and polemic, both irony and sublimity, and perhaps too its indeterminacy and its access to pleasure, that make literature the most economical and rewarding domain within which to explore the vertical dimension, that is the life and reach, of political languages.

We have touched on the meanings of the body politic in the closing sentences of Dryden's preface to *Absalom and Achitophel* and on the extension of that metaphor into a patriarchal subtext. But patriarchy turns out to be less a subtext of the poem prefaced by those sentences than one of its crucial exhibits. With fatherhood the poem begins and concludes, and fatherhood in its psychic and sexual and in its domestic and civic dimensions forms the poem's central theme. But what might be the rewards for invoking patriarchy in defence of a political regime whose responsibilities towards patriarchy might seem to have been so negligently squandered? In answering this question we must of course acknowledge *Patriarcha*, the book whose print publication in 1680 inserted the fixtures and fundamentals of patriarchalism into the crisis looming over the succession once Charles II had been gathered into the arms of his lord.[10] That publication made it difficult wholly to avoid

---

[10] On the dating and original context of *Patriarcha*, see Filmer 1991, pp. x–xxi.

the arguments of Filmer's systematic defence of the sanctity and authority of patriarchal rule, but *Patriarcha* seems a text nearly devoid of irony and *Absalom and Achitophel* is bathed in irony from beginning to end, from its initial punning and joking to the slightly hollow and irreverent prophecy at its close. Filmer's work had put the cards of patriarchy on the table, but *Patriarcha* is not a report on their status during the Exclusion Crisis. The most subtle and responsive report is in fact Dryden's poem which tells us something about the political landscape in which patriarchalism had come into play but more importantly reveals the nature and capacity of this language to absorb and refashion, to manage and deflect political crisis. And that is because Dryden deploys the resources of political language so deftly and with such a full measure of irony. His poem works as a serious-minded argument about the social cohesion and psychological comforts of a political arrangement that imagines kingship as patriarchy in an organic commonweal. Simultaneously *Absalom and Achitophel* is a daring, witty and resourceful defence of a particular instance of patriarchy in the person of a king for whom very little by way of sanctity, solemnity, indeed even sexual fecundity could at this point in his rule straightforwardly be invoked.

That this poem with its system of veils, innuendos and puzzles was designed as an entertainment – and an entertainment that might appeal both to the esoteric and exoteric communities of its readers – is certainly true. But puzzles and allegories, veiling and innuendo in no way diminish, indeed, they rather enhance, its value as a report on the condition and capacities of political language. The poem is a register of the state of play among political languages and models of governance in the midst of the Exclusion Crisis. It is also a demonstration of irony's nimble if unsteady truths. *Absalom and Achitophel* carefully diminishes, even at points dismantles and certainly ironizes, what is hegemonic or overbearing and wearisome, and of course dangerous, about the argument of the divine donation of royal authority to Adam and its undiminished lustre as it passed from generation to generation of fathers and kings finally to devolve onto the person and office of Charles II and, by a not so shadowy extension, onto the Roman Catholic person and patriarchal capacities of the Duke of York. It allows us to ask – and allowed contemporary readers to contemplate – whether or not, two decades after the Restoration and some thirty years after the beheading of Charles I, and in the wake of a flamboyant series of sexual scandals and political crises – whether or not the crown could be sustained by the systematic if late born defence of its authority articulated in *Patriarcha*.

Locke's *Two Treatises of Government* is certainly evidence – and it was not alone – that this was a question worth asking, but the answer was neither simple nor obvious.

Or rather *Absalom and Achitophel* allows us to say that the answer was both yes and no, and simultaneously yes and no. The shimmering uncertainty of the opening lines of this poem has been often and beautifully parsed, and in ways that show us how divine sanctity and authority, creative energy and sexual abundance, paternal indulgence and political generosity might provoke both laughter and more serious kinds of assent, and the poem as a whole seems a meditation on both these possibilities. What the much studied sequence of images and ironies establishes is the possibility that a serious political claim and one with a sharp polemical edge might be made in a way that spends some of the ideological capital of its assertion: that the sanctity of lineal descent, the divinity of kingship or the abundance and social generosity of a particular system of governance might be proffered, and simultaneously, as a serious argument and as a joke. The joke does not disallow the patriarchal argument but rather converts it into legal tender, into a fungible proposition; yes, devaluation takes place but not the utter evacuation of value; yes, a reduction of some of the high-toned authority of the argument but a reduction that means it might be traded on the open market of ideas rather than put aside or lofted on high as a burdensome treasure or as a target of refutation or demolition. That is what irony is doing not only at the opening of this poem but throughout all of its brilliant parts.

### 'ALL PARTS FULFILLED OF SUBJECT AND OF SON'

Listen for a moment, and on this very subject, to Absalom's discourse of paternal authority and kingly rights, as Dryden, the master's hand hidden partly behind a veil, acknowledges some delicate and embarrassing, perhaps dangerous, themes: an indulgence grown into negligence; a feminization of authority through sensual play; debility; political dependence on France; and the distinction between kingship and paternity in the matter of authority and obedience:

> 'My Father, whom with reverence yet I name—
> Charmed into Ease, is careless of his fame:
> And, brib'd with petty sums of Forreign Gold,
> Is grown in Bathsheba's Embraces old:
> Exalts his Enemies, his Friends destroys:
> And all his pow'r against himself employs.

He gives, and let him give my right away,
But why should he his own, and yours betray?
He only, he can make the Nation bleed,
And he alone from my revenge is freed.
Take then my tears, (with that he wip'd his eyes)
'Tis all the Aid my present power supplies:
No Court Informer can these Arms accuse;
These Arms may Sons against their Father use,
And, tis my wish, the next Successors Reign
May make no other Israelite complain. (ll. 707–22)

We should note, though it is perhaps the least interesting aspect of this passage, that this speech emerges from the mouth of a character weak, indulged, and ambitious beyond his station. The truth claims of Absalom's charges are, in consequence, partly denied or delimited – but only in part. But such damage control cannot wholly deny the cogency of these charges, their truth value in a world where they were rumoured and acknowledged and not simply as a way for the emergent opposition to discredit Stuart political authority. And now the proximity of this scene to the opening manoeuvres of the poem comes into view. The passage mingles truths and lies and exaggerations, and blurs them in such a way that they are difficult wholly to disentangle. They are mixed purposefully, and not simply to apply a bit of camouflage, but rather to suggest that truth and deceit, integrity and bad faith, assertion and irony are more intimate with one another than we might allow. More important than their distinction and disaggregation is an obedience to the overriding sentiments of the domestic and civic system, to the power of affect, to the authority of a love and loyalty that even the compromised character and impure psychology of an ungrateful son might acknowledge, 'my Father, whom with reverence yet I name' (l. 707). And that sentiment hovers over the whole, masks the impurities and foibles and follies even of this father and his son. This is not an invocation of the patriarchalism of Sir Robert Filmer, but the conjuring of fatherhood as political authority mingled with domestic sentiment. Even the suggestions of sexual weariness and spent energies contribute to the conversion of the high rhetoric of patriarchalism into an idiom of restraint and flexibility, of diminished expectations but heightened rhetorical efficacy.

The closest that the poem comes to the unembarrassed spectacle of fatherhood as sustaining political and cultural institution is the elegy for Ossory that Dryden folds into the portrait of the Duke of

Ormond: 'Barzillai crown'd with Honour and with Years'.[11] So begins the argument of fatherhood, properly constituted, and the word 'honour' recurs as a leitmotiv in the elegy for the son. The assertion of honour and reputation was of course one of the central concerns of early-modern aristocracy, hence Dryden's emphasis on Ossory's achievements and fame as warrior – Ossory's contribution to the aristocratic ethos of his class and to the reputation of his family. And these terms are doubled when Dryden crowns Ossory's achievements as the very embodiment of civic duty and domestic affection and affiliation: 'All parts fulfill'd of Subject and of Son' (1. 836). In a poem which designs Exclusion as a primal assault on patriarchy and portrays Absalom's ambitions for the crown as filial ingratitude, Dryden's braiding together of these roles is strongly purposive and resonant.

And yet something of irony's contradictory logic is to be found even in this deeply un-ironic scene, for the argument of binding political loyalty and filial affection is endangered or rendered vulnerable by this scene, and not only by its recording of the death of Ormond's son, but by its complex web of associations and alignments that link Ossory with the heroic dignity and civic promise but as well with the early death of Marcellus, and the Duke of Ormond with Augustus and with Charles II. The problem of succession and the fragility of the male line tie the Duke of Ormond to both 'Caesars', hence to the crisis of succession then unfolding in the Exclusion controversy, and to the political culture put at risk by the betrayal of the natural ties of paternal affiliation and affection. Of course it is also true that Dryden uses this scene to associate himself with Virgil who had read *Aeneid VI* to Augustus and Livia after the death of Marcellus and to link the affective power of his poem with Virgil's elegiac verse. He would use exactly this beautiful Virgilian moment in the elegy for John Oldham – 'Once more, hail and farewel; farewel, thou young / But ah too short, Marcellus of our Tongue'.[12] And all of these arguments and associations work together, culminating as an acknowledgement of the uncertain prospect of succession through the male line – exactly the shadow that falls across Virgil's evocation of Marcellus's death, the fate of the Ormond line, the question of literary lineage, and, of course, the not altogether certain prospects of Stuart succession. Hovering over the elegy is a powerful affectivity linking civics and domesticity, but the whole is shadowed by vulnerability and loss.

[11] On Dryden's relations with the Ormonds, see Ohlmeyer and Zwicker 2006.
[12] Dryden 1958, I, p. 389, II. 22–23.

Ossory's death was the culmination of a series of losses; the Duke of Ormond had fathered eight male children; in 1681 only one son remained, and the poignancy of fatherhood is beautifully caught by Dryden's lament, 'His bed could once a fruitful issue boast: / Now more than half a father's name is lost' (ll. 829–30). The passage on Ormond and Ossory balances lineage against loss and vulnerability.

This set of motifs informs the argument of patriarchy throughout the poem and works not as a simple piece of Tory triumphalism but as the subtle assembling of a case for patriarchalism that conjoins natural and civic affections, domestic affinity and political loyalty, and the cultural properties of Latin poetry and modern epic and elegy. The case is counter-pointed against the corruption of patriarchy put on display at various points in the poem and vividly so in Dryden's brief slur on the generative and political capacities of the Earl of Shaftesbury:

> Else, why should he, with Wealth and Honour blest,
> Refuse his Age the needful hours of Rest?
> Punish a Body which he could not please;
> Bankrupt of Life, yet Prodigal of Ease?
> And all to leave, what with his toyl he won,
> To that unfeather'd, two leg'd thing, a Son:
> Got, while his Soul did hudled Notions try;
> And born a shapeless Lump, like Anarchy. (ll. 165–72)

The slur folds physical deformity into political rebellion, intellectual aridity and sexual incapacity, but oddly slur and sentiment depend on one another. The poem layers together wit, scepticism and satire, and as sharp a capacity for cartoon and cleverness as Dryden was ever to display. But these instruments of attack depend on the poem's unguarded moments of sentiment and celebration. In fact one element cannot properly work without the other, they exist simultaneously, and they are surprisingly interdependent. It is of course the very model of irony that I hope has been emerging in these remarks, a model whose argument is always simultaneity, association and similarity but as well paradox, difference and distance. Irony allows a diverse and paradoxical or contradictory aggregation of feelings to haunt arguments and ideals. Its effect is not wholly to discredit those arguments and ideals but to render them less hegemonic. The application of irony's skeptical intelligence to narratives and arguments allows parallel though divergent stories to emerge from a single narrative or argumentative point. Irony changes their tone and tenor; it makes them less certain, less self-satisfied, more negotiable in the marketplace of stories and explanations, of arguments, ideas and ideals.

'MAKE YOUR RETURNE HOME GRACIOUS'

Indeed the texts of systematic political philosophy – Hobbes's *Leviathan* or Locke's *Two Treatises of Government,* for example – seem at a disadvantage for the display of such acts and arts of linguistic play, for the spinning of an abstract system of argument into a mobile and refined instrument of meditation and persuasion. This is in part because compromise and negotiation are at odds with systematic discourse, but it is also true because suggestion, innuendo and irony are not the familiar tools of discursive and philosophical prose, though Hobbes certainly understood the uses of derision and even Locke can indulge occasional mockery at Filmer's expense. But in early modernity irony and innuendo are more regularly the domain of those genres that we identify as literature. To paraphrase Sir Philip Sidney, because literature is limited neither by the narrowness of historical events nor by the barren abstractions of philosophy it can afford different kinds of truths – the inimitable truths of irony that tell us the yes and no of things, that report on the status of ideas in all the uncertainty and flux of the moment, of ideals in tainted and prejudiced circumstances, of the always only partial truths that emerge from particular needs and urgencies and desires. Listen for a moment to the exploration and exploitation of a theological truth in the midst and on behalf of what we might think of as a fairly crass act of clientage. Here John Donne is fishing for the favour of that quite glamorous, elevated and busy aristocrat and courtier, Lucy, Countess of Bedford:[13]

> Reason is our Soules left hand, Faith her right,
> By these wee reach divinity, that's you.[14]

The woman whom Donne later in this poem calls 'The first good Angel, since the world's frame stood' is the object of such relentless and embarrassing exaggeration that it scarcely occurs to us that clientage and patronage could be conducted within this linguistic system. What Donne's verse epistle to the Countess of Bedford also explores with a kind of overbearing, almost intolerable wit is the altogether serious proposition that the human form bears the stamp of the divine, that love and desire, need and admiration, generosity and condescension are

---

[13] On the relationship between Donne and Lucy Harrington, Countess of Bedford, see Donne 1967, p. 253.
[14] Donne 1967, p. 90, ll. 1–2.

instruments with which we can approximate knowledge of God's goodness and grace, and indeed in this fallen world are the best, perhaps our only, hope for experience of the divine.[15]

These serious propositions are gathered into the embrace of the most familiar, indeed trite, kind of courtly compliment in order to refashion and to force a serious consideration both of fundamental theological truths and of all too human needs for privilege and favour. Not that the Countess of Bedford, for all her wealth and authority, her position and favour among the 'elect', is herself the divinity (though Donne seems to come dangerously close to that blasphemous proposition), but rather that what we can know of the divine with our fallen capacities of apprehension and understanding can only be through the limited instruments of reason and faith, that the 'human' for all its imperfections – and God recognized this through his descent into the metaphor of flesh – is the only condition for our knowledge of the divine. So all the brilliant strategies of this poem – its wit and fantastic exaggerations, its brash kidnapping of the language of divinity on behalf of interest and need – that is, the text's bold literariness – act as a form of negotiation between the language and ideals of a system of thought and momentary historical needs and circumstances. It is not the case that need and circumstance and the compromises that they force must cut against theological ideals or reduce or deform their truths. But there is a transaction between need or desire and idealization that we can hear in the subtle and bold inflections of Donne's appeal that bears a family resemblance to the exchange that irony proffers between realities and ideals, and that family resemblance colours the exchange and reduces the embarrassments of need in a manner that has a formal, though not a tonal, kinship to irony:

> Make your returne home gracious; and bestow
> This life on that; so make one life of two.
> For so God helpe mee, I would not misse you there
> For all the good which you can do me here. (II. 35–38)

For all the pressure that Donne puts on last things and eternal truths, on sin and grace and salvation, the poem ends not in heaven but in the present tense, not in the contemplation of eternities but with that lovely remembrance and reminder of '... all the good which you can

---

[15] On Donne's exploration and exploitation of theological symbolism in the verse letters see Lewalski 1973.

do me here'. And 'here' is the last word of this poem. Like the pun on
'gracious', the last line opens simultaneously onto material and spiritual
beneficence, and our knowledge of the poet's physical, and domestic,
and economic circumstances *c.* 1608 makes 'all the good which you can
do me here' ring with some poignancy.[16]

In the freedom of its favoured devices, its figures and metaphors,
its partialities, its acts of concealment, compromise and disguise – and
with all of its ironies – literature proffers a report on the condition of
systems of thought – politics, civics, the nature of rule of course, but
as well theology, morals, ethics, the law – as they are experienced in the
particularity and sensuality and partiality of the here and now, of, let's
say, 17 September 14 CE in the instance of Tacitus's report on Tiberius's
accession, or December of 1608 in the case of Donne's appeal to the
countess of Bedford, or the early days of November 1681 for Dryden's
Exclusion Crisis masterpiece. We cannot of course live in the past, but
literature enables us to listen to its varied inflections and uncertainties,
its boldest affirmations as well as its most nuanced compromises.

The immensely learned and comprehensive system of study that has
constituted John Pocock's work makes clear that we can learn a good deal
about the civic languages which people spoke in the past, their singularity
and forcefulness as well as their complexity, their hybridity, the ways
in which they might be purposefully layered over and joined to one
another. No less important, the study of political languages as argumentative paradigms allows us to grasp their horizontal dimension, their
evolution over time, their genealogies, their inheritances and legacies,
the ways, for example, in which civic humanism is embedded in the rich
linguistic resources of the Florentine republic and then transformed by
its migrations between and among peoples, places and times.[17] For this
work, the kind of text that we have so far examined may seem if not
inconsequential then certainly of a secondary order of interest, indeed,
perhaps even contra-indicated because of the ambiguous or contradictory,
even indecipherable, qualities that render literature a suitable archive for
a different order of knowledge.

And if we would ask after that different order of knowledge, if we
would ask what these languages sounded like when they were being
handled not in the form of systematic or philosophical exposition, not
in transit between Medician Florence and Jeffersonian America, but on

---

[16] On the dating of this poem see Donne 1967, p. 253; also Bald 1970, pp. 172–5.
[17] Pocock 1975b.

behalf of business – and in human affairs that business is often the grasping acquisition and violent redistribution of goods and authority – in answer to that question, the texts of systematic or philosophical discourse may not be our best guide. We cannot want the knowledge that discursive exposition supplies, but just as surely that knowledge, for all of its order and authority, is partial, abstract, removed from the sordid particularities of need and desire in the midst of which domestic and civic negotiation so often take place. Literature might then be considered as a report on a different but no less fundamental kind of knowledge, on what I have earlier suggested as the vertical rather than horizontal dimension of language, its complex behaviour at particular moments rather than its articulation across time, a report on the capacity of words to occupy puzzling or paradoxical or contradictory positions within the same linguistic space and on the capacity of language simultaneously to embrace and deny the logic of particular systems of thought, to say both yes and no, and to imagine the stasis achieved by compromise and complicity.

### 'O HORRID PROVISOS'

Compromise and complicity lie at the heart of William Congreve's *The Way of the World*, and more especially of the wonderful little treatise on provisos that forms the centre of the play's fourth act. We can read the scene as a report on changing social and gender relations, on the rewriting, towards the end of the seventeenth century, of female authority and autonomy, including the autonomy of female pleasure. There is of course a history of such scenes and so we ought not to overstate the boldness or originality of Congreve's orchestration of this dance of prenuptial arrangements, though it can hardly be bettered for wit. But what we might notice is that Congreve re-imagines domestic negotiation in the shadows of a quite powerful challenge to the status of covenants and contracts, of oaths and obedience, and of patriarchal authority. The year of the first performance and of the publication of Congreve's play is 1700 and so the proviso scene was first acted out not in the deepest shadows cast by the debates over those arrangements known as the Glorious Revolution, but more on their margins.[18] Yet the scene is resonant with the implications of those debates. While it is clear that

---

[18] See Congreve 1967, p. 387.

Act 4 of *The Way of the World* is not political allegory, the scene does gather force from its proximity to ideas propounded and interrogated by sermons and broadsides, and by tracts and treatises that addressed the nature of covenant and contract in the wake of the Revolution. But the traffic moves in more than one direction. If the events of 1688–1689 and the debates and philosophical writings that reflected on and interpreted these events add a kind of ballast to Congreve's scene, just as surely the scene itself acts as commentary on the languages of the Revolution. We might think of this commentary not as ridicule, not as a send-up of the idioms of the Glorious Revolution, but as a witty and ironic examination and application of some of its central terms, a display of what 'liberty' and 'property', 'contract' and 'covenant' sound like when they are shorn of some of their ponderous weight and when the site of their application has shifted from the public sphere to the private domain, from affairs of state to those of the heart, though we understand at once that the private and the public cannot be wholly disentangled in this scene:

MILLIMANT:  Ah! I'll never marry, unless I am first made Sure of my will and pleasure.
MIRABELL:  Wou'd you have 'em both before Marriage? Or will you be contented with the first now, and stay for the other till after grace?
MILLIMANT:  Ah don't be Impertinent – My dear Liberty, shall I leave thee? My faithful Solitude, my darling Contemplation, must I bid you then Adieu? ... my morning thoughts, agreeable wakings, indolent Slumbers, all ye *douceurs*, ye *Someils du Matin*, adieu I can't do't, 'tis more than Impossible – positively *Mirabell*, I'll lie a Bed in a morning as long as I please.  (4.1.1.80–91).

Millimant adds other conditions as well: a liberty to pay and receive visits at will, to correspond without interrogation, to 'wear what I please; and choose Conversation with regard only to my own taste ... Come to dinner when I please ... have my Closet Inviolate; [and] be sole Empress of my Tea table'. As Congreve heightens the negotiation, the scene progresses towards sexual union and reproduction, the centre of the civic and sacred meanings of marriage. And here the debate makes a daring inroad on the logic of patriarchy:

MIRABELL:  *Item*, I shut my doors against all Bauds with Baskets, and pennyworths of Muslin, China, Fans, Atlases, &c. – *Item*, when you shall be Breeding –

MILLIMANT:  Ah! Name it not.
MIRABELL:  Which may be presum'd, with a blessing on our endeavours –
MILLIMANT:  Odious endeavours! (4.1.252–59)

Perhaps sensing that he had moved to dangerous or subversive territory, Congreve allows the scene to turn from the reproductive to the less fraught matter of taste and the tea-table, but sexual autonomy, indeed reproductive rights, however guarded or baffled by wit, by the rhythm and rapidity of exchange, has been deposited at the centre of the scene, and it cannot be wholly effaced by what follows. We ourselves hardly need any tutoring on the political volatility of such a subject, on the centrality of the reproductive to the civic and sacred meanings of matrimony – how much more central then were these issues to a society in which the sanctity of lineal descent, of crowns as well as of lesser properties, turned on purity of the bloodline, an inviolability secured by marital union whose most sacred duty was the reproductive.

The resonance of this moment in the play was surely heightened by that series of late seventeenth-century political crises which turned – one after the other – on the reproductive failures, scandals and sensations of royal union. If the comedy defuses or diminishes the dangerous subversion of that sanctity, it also holds out the possibility of refashioning or hearing anew the whole vocabulary of patriarchal authority in all of its idioms and arguments. While Congreve seems willing to go a certain distance in that direction, such irony, such subversion, is also here delimited by the structure of the comedy, indeed by the rhythm of this very scene which Congreve carefully breaks just before the contract is sealed. Millimant cries out – with a bit of her tongue in her cheek – 'O horrid provisos! Odious Men! I hate your Odious proviso's' and Mirabell counters, understanding that perhaps Millimant doth protest too much, 'Then we're agreed. Shall I kiss your hand upon the Contract? And here comes one to be a witness to the Sealing of the Deed'. The scene is broken at this point, the plot rejoined, and the comedy of manners re-emerges, but not without Congreve's having allowed a daring glance – and in the space of a mere hundred lines or so – at contract and consent and the matter of patriarchy. The languages of provision and proviso and the sanctity of patriarchy have not just been smiled on but ironized in a way that changes and challenges their political valence.

We might expect the diminution of patriarchy from the Whiggish and compliant William Congreve, but the Revolution settlement had hardly aimed at the debunking of patriarchal authority. Indeed, some might have thought that Charles II had done a good enough job of that, and the sharpest attacks on William III aimed not to raise constitutional issues but to question in a quite vulgar manner the king's generative capacities and sexual tastes.[19]

Of course the fact that attacks on William III were couched in the language of deviance and incapacity is its own testimony to the continued importance of patriarchalism to political mythologies. But both Dryden as Tory apologist and Congreve as celebrant of the new regime suggest that patriarchalism – and the system of analogies between the body and the state – might be seen in a subtly recalibrated light, seen that is in ways that acknowledge both the continuing presence and the limitations of patriarchalism as a system of politics. For Dryden and for Congreve irony forms the principal instrument of recalibration, and we might think of irony's nuances, contradictions and alternatives as the principal mechanism for complicating and refining, for more perfectly tuning, the idioms, styles and languages of political argument.

'WHAT FIELD OF ALL THE CIVIL WARS / WHERE HIS WERE NOT THE DEEPEST SCARS?'

It may seem odd to have written of politics and irony in the early-modern period without mentioning what is surely irony's political masterpiece: Andrew Marvell's *Horatian Ode upon Cromwell's Return from Ireland* (1650). The productivity of this poem's ironic modes to our understanding of mid seventeenth-century English politics is so well appreciated that our reading of the poem hardly needs more help. But I want to invoke this text in order to raise the subject of puns which seem to function as a perfect – if not very exalted – miniature of irony, an emblem of the ways in which irony and ambiguity work to deepen the vertical or contrapuntal dimensions of language, allowing contradictory or equivocal or imperfectly aligned meanings to surround, in the case of puns, a single phoneme, or in the case of irony larger narrative units. Puns replicate the structure of irony by making possible in one linguistic site the counterpoint of contrary meanings. What happens in the brief, explosive simultaneity of puns or in the larger

[19] See, for example, the satires on William III which depict him as catamite or gelding in Lord et al. 1963–1975, vols. V, VI.

narratives of irony is something like a flood of equivocation that touches the life of all the terms and meanings in play. One meaning may remain dominant, but no meanings are untouched by these transactions. 'What field of all the Civil Wars, / Where his were not the deepest Scars?'[20] This example – an interrogative in which the meanings of 'his' unfold to indicate the scars that Cromwell suffered as well as those he inflicted – may be imperfect since the phoneme does not double in the classic homonymic manner of the pun, but it is a perfect example of the ambiguities and equivocations that arise from puns and ironies and that allow so many different understandings of the figure of Cromwell to play across the surface and within the deep structure of this poem. The pun is I believe a strong exemplification of irony, but I raise this subject not to extend that exposition but to address a final argumentative point, one that emerges from Quentin Skinner's work on the relevance of language philosophy and in particular the concept of illocutionary force to the study of politics and political languages.[21]

At the centre of Skinner's argument lies the notion that the performative implications of language need not coincide with language's more overt meanings; to understand the political work that particular languages perform we must not only grasp their denotative schemes but as well their 'take-up' implications, their illocutionary force. Of course irony may come to play a part in the illocutionary act, it may be one of the agents of disjunction or distance between the denotative and performative values of language, but the concept of illocutionary force – which always implies agency and intention – does not exhaust irony's range of work which can of course include the intentional but does not rely on agency and intention since irony can emerge from the equivocal nature of language itself. Perhaps this comes clearest in the instance of the pun which may be deployed, and quite self-consciously, on behalf of argument, but whose nature does not depend on agency and intention, as is surely the case above: whether or not Marvell intended ambiguity, ambiguity is irreducibly located within syntax and semantics. With or without Marvell's intentions, the couplet's disruption of meaning and disturbance of certainty come into play. And now of course we have come close to Derrida's work on language.[22] We need not embrace deconstruction's wholesale erasure of agency and intention in order

[20] Marvell 1971, I, p. 92, ll. 45–46.   [21] Skinner 1969, pp. 3–53.
[22] Derrida 1974, pp. 44–53; or, more explicitly, Derrida 1991, pp. 64–6.

to acknowledge a linguistic essentialism that points to irony's 'timeless' structure, not merely its dependence on agency or intention. This seems particularly important to an appreciation of the ways in which irony always operates along the vertical axis of language, disturbing certainties and redistributing settled meanings, and this is as true of irony in Horace or Martial as in irony's masterful embodiments in the literature of early-modernity and well beyond.

## 'THE HISTORIOGRAPHY OF THE HUMAN HEART'

I have stressed in these remarks the role of literature in exposing the vertical dimension of language, but I do not want to deny literature's function as a marker of change over time. It is certainly possible to make an argument that in *Absalom and Achitophel*, for example, Dryden is observing and recording and with unusual perspicacity a particular moment in the long history of patriarchalism, perhaps a turning point in its evolution from the central language of masculine civic authority to a mere idiom of domestic sentiment, and the poem's ironies might be seen as playing a role in that softening or subversion of meanings. There are however other ways of doing such work, of archiving the horizontal dimension of political languages, and John Pocock's theorizing of the archive and fashioning of a model of political history educate us in how we might properly perform such work.[23] But writing the history of the horizontal dimension of political languages need not exclude the vertical dimension of those languages, and most especially the dimension of irony, though in the practice there seems to have been a disciplinary, perhaps a temperamental, divide between those who have looked after one dimension or the other. Pocock's histories seem to fall to one side of that divide; yet in his most recent work Pocock suggests a way of binding together these different dimensions of language and history. Urging the Tacitean inheritance of Gibbon's *Decline and Fall*, Pocock describes Tacitus's rendering of Roman politics as a study of the 'deviousness, perversity, brutality, and recurrently suicidal folly, which have made [Tacitus] renowned in the historiography of the human heart as we wish it were not but know that it is'.[24] In that wonderful

---

[23] The theoretical work is most easily consulted in Pocock 1971; both Pocock 1975b and the case studies in Pocock 1985b provide extraordinary models for tracing the history of change in political languages over time.

[24] Pocock 1999-, II, p. 20.

phrase the intersection between the vertical and horizontal dimensions of political language is perfectly caught. Here is a historiography constituted of different kinds of records, one set that chronicles events and the languages in which they were performed, and a second that may refer, incidentally, to events but whose primary business is with the affects in their complexity and contradiction and in their simultaneity and indeterminacy, a set of records that opens, through the offices of irony and deceit and disguise, both the comedy of sudden juxtapositions and the poignancy of contingency and simultaneity. Poems and plays, romances and novels are not the primary archive for political history as we know it, but if we would write 'the historiography of the human heart' they are indispensable, and this is a historiography – and a history of politics – that we should not willingly do without.

CHAPTER 9

# Poetry and Political Thought: Liberty and Benevolence in the Case of the British Empire c. 1680–1800

*Karen O'Brien*

If the history of political thought is, as John Pocock argues, a 'history of the terms of discourse in which debate about politics has been carried on', Restoration and eighteenth-century poetry has a very good claim to be read as a part of that history.[1] This is not simply to state the obvious point that the poetry of this period was intensely engaged with politics, nor even to settle for the claim that political ideas were given complex imaginative embodiment in the medium of poetry. It is, rather, to assign a role to poetry in the generation and elaboration of political concepts as part of a sustained conversation with political thought conducted in other forms of writing, such as treatises, dialogues, parliamentary speeches and pamphlets. I would like to argue that this inter-generic conversation constitutes the broader frame of discourse within which eighteenth-century political thought developed, and that it becomes more fully intelligible if one attends to the contribution of poetry. Historians of political thought are fully accustomed to approaching Milton in this way, but subsequent (and often earlier) poets are more usually analysed in terms of political allusion — a second-order kind of political thought — or of their instigation or unconscious reflection of dominant ideologies. The argument here is that early-modern literature was one domain within which political ideas — as they related to party politics, but still more to abstract, overarching questions — were meaningfully contested and transformed; and that poetry, in particular, provides something more than an enlargement of the evidence for the historical 'terms of the discourse' of political thought, and yet, also, something more decisive in its impact than a dramatization of politics. This, as I hope to show, had much to do with the vocabularies, positions of address and acute sense

[1] Pocock 1985a, p. 284.

168

of ethical responsibility habitually assumed by those attempting to write poetry. The case for this kind of approach could be made very generally, but is particularly compelling in relation to the political thought of the first and early second British Empires. Here, I will argue, poetry had a significant bearing, in the metropolitan context, on the political theorization of imperial trade and colonization. It not only provided a sort of echo chamber in which the key concepts of empire could resonate and settle upon the public ear, but also advanced new, humanitarian theories of empire which would find favour in decades to come.

Some of what I have to say about late seventeenth- and eighteenth-century poetry in relation to political thought does apply to early-modern literature in general. Not until the nineteenth century did literature conceive of itself as normatively belles-lettristic, essentially different in kind and concern from other modes of public writing. Seventeenth- and eighteenth-century poetry was part of an earlier, less specialized and more inter-communicative republic of letters. It was nevertheless distinctive in the kinds of public voice it adopted, and in the ways in which it thematized its own search (within the constraints of patronage or commercially sponsored publishing) for an independent position of address from which to speak to the realm of politics. More than any other species of literary writing, poetry promulgated itself as an agent, not only of party politics, but of political ideas. Horace, Juvenal, Pindar and Lucan were models, respectively, for stances of detached evaluation, righteous anger and (in the last two cases) enthusiastic encouragement towards a public culture of liberty. In a world of party politics, pamphleteering and political corruption, poets promoted their work as a medium in which the underlying principles and concepts of politics — freedom, the common good, justice, legitimate sovereignty — retained a degree of pristine abstraction. Alexander Pope ended his 'Epilogue to the Satires' (1738) with the defiant lines, 'Yes, the last Pen for Freedom, let me draw, / When Truth stands trembling on the edge of Law'.[2] Political concepts gained further clarity from the poets' intense imaginative engagement with the historical contexts in which they had emerged (Ancient Greece, the Roman Republic, Anglo-Saxon England and so on), and the ways in which the generic resources of mock-epic, Juvenalian satire and Horatian epistolary verse permitted stark juxtapositions of past and present epochs. Whatever we think of their claims, many poets

---

[2] Dialogue II of the 'Epilogue to the Satires', Pope 1938–1968, IV, II. 248–9.

of this period did consider themselves to be the unacknowledged
legislators, if not of mankind, then certainly of Great Britain. They
asserted and enjoyed a special relationship to the idea of liberty, nurtured
and refined by the poetic pen, and some of the period's most extensive
discussions of the social dimensions of liberty are to be found in the
works of poets such as Dryden, Pope and James Thomson.[3] A major
theme of eighteenth-century poetry is how liberty — as a stimulus and
agent, rather than as an end in itself — is related to artistic achievement,
social cohesion and commerce. Another is the need for liberty to
be tempered by a proper regard for social harmony in both the domestic
and colonial political contexts. It was in relation to questions of liberty
and social harmony that poets aspired to the rank of philosophers, and
explored the foundations of the social order in man's inner impulses
to selfishness, sympathy and altruism.

In relation to empire, poetry played an important role in bringing
together a nexus of concepts, including commerce, liberty and
international community, as part of a coherent national idiom, and in
helping the British metropolis to imagine itself as an imperial polity.
This was a poetry orientated and addressed to a home audience. Poets
did frequently incorporate the disruptive voices of indigenous peoples
and enslaved Africans; but, to the extent that they were based on an
uninformed ventriloquizing of an external point of view, they never
enabled genuine non-European participation in the debate about empire.
I have written elsewhere of the involvement of poets in the creation of
an elastic, morally accommodating idea — one might even call it a
'White Legend' — of peaceful empire.[4] From the poet-diplomat Matthew
Prior, in the late seventeenth century, to Robert Southey at the end of
this period, poets collaborated in the formulation of what David
Armitage has characterized as the 'classic' conception of the British
Empire as Protestant, commercial, maritime and free. Armitage, Richard
Koebner and other historians of seventeenth- and eighteenth-century
imperial ideology have rightly made extensive use of literary source
material, and have recognized the role of imaginative writing in
conceiving of disparate geographical locations and peoples as part of
a single entity.[5] Georgic poetry, in particular, supplied many of the
metaphors of organic community used to embellish this theoretical

[3] See Mehan 1986 and Griffin 2002.    [4] O'Brien 1997.
[5] Armitage 2000; Koebner 1961.

enterprise, along with an idea of cultivation as the basis of national virtue and imperial entitlement. It was a classical reflex for poets to measure instances of territorial expansion against the Virgilian ideal of peaceful, universal *imperium*. Where many political theorists saw only an assortment of trading posts, planted provinces and fortresses, poets presaged, very early in its history, the coming of a new global empire to rival or surpass that of Rome. Where many saw profitable networks of staple production, manufacture and re-export, poets sought to characterize the economic interdependence of the empire in terms of mutual ethical obligations. The fact that poetry was seen and practised in this period as a self-reflexively ethical activity also led many to publicize the fact that these obligations had been breached by the practice of slavery, illegal territorial seizure and other derogations from the baroque ideal of an empire for liberty.

In general, poets adopted a rhetorical stance of humane Horatian civility, rarely endorsing either slavery or the forced displacement of native peoples. They were often at the forefront of what one might call 'anti-conquest' thinking in the late seventeenth and eighteenth centuries, that is a principled opposition to all forms of military vainglory and violence. It was in origin, a form of Jacobite or Tory opposition to the campaigns of William III, and a product of Tory unease at the extent of Marlborough's campaigns, but was given enduring embodiment in Johnson's *Vanity of Human Wishes* (1749), after which opposition to aggressive warfare was often worn as a badge of poetic professional ethics. In many cases (though not that of Johnson), a principled anti-conquest poetic stance went hand-in-hand with an alternative ideal of peaceful, maritime empire. Poets revived and modernized the Ciceronian idea of empire as a protectorate maintained through acts of kind service, and were often harshly critical of the imperial activities of Caesar, Trajan and other Roman generals and emperors.[6] Others, notably Oliver Goldsmith and Charles Churchill, were more fundamentally opposed to the very idea of territorial empire, and its diminution of the human to the economic. Milton's anti-imperial vision in *Paradise Lost* and, especially, in *Paradise Regained* was at the fountainhead of a poetic tradition, submerged at first but surfacing in the works of poets from Blake to Shelley, which sought to imagine a world liberated from all forms of imperial power.[7]

---

[6] Quint 1993; also Weinbrot 1993, esp. part 2, ch. 7.     [7] O'Brien 2002.

Poets entered the national conversation about the nature and meaning of empire at many points during its long history, and were from the outset deeply exercised by the idea of the colony, in the sense of a discrete community, set up at a location already populated by native peoples, and retaining legal and other ties to the mother country. From *The Tempest* onwards, the colony, especially of the island variety, occupied a special place in literature, providing an experimental space for the imaginative unsettling of social, gender and racial hierarchies. Colonization was very much to the fore, both as a literary *topos* and a pressing political question, in the late seventeenth to early eighteenth centuries, a period during which royal charters were granted for American plantations in Pennsylvania, New York, the Carolinas and Georgia. The questions raised by the advent of these new proprietary colonies were not new, but they were reformulated by political theorists, particularly in the light of William Penn's efforts to set a new standard for the treatment of native peoples, and then throughout the eighteenth century as the American crisis slowly came to its head. By what right, it was frequently asked (conquest, occupation, cession) does a country gain colonies? What were colonies for (strategic reasons, economic)? There was some debate about the relationship of the plantations to the state. Most characterized them as possessions, rather than as territorial extensions of Britain, but this left the status of the colonists somewhat uncertain. They were subjects of the Crown, certainly, yet not fully a part of a British community since few thought that their interests were anything other than subordinate to those of the British at home. Many were anxious about colonies depopulating and depleting their mother country, though others, notably Charles Davenant, argued that, within bounds, colonial emigration and the colonial trade would add significantly to the national wealth.[8]

A new element entered the colonial debate with the chartering of Pennsylvania, and later, Georgia, as specifically philanthropic provinces, set up to provide a refuge for the persecuted and indigent. The possession, by English proprietors, of philanthropic colonies also raised wider questions about both private and state involvement in matters of welfare. In this part of the debate poets played a particularly important role, seizing upon the notion of the welfare colony as an expression of a national aspiration for a more just society. As often as they engaged imaginatively with the plight of displaced or conquered indigenous peoples, they looked back to home, considering the colony as a rehearsal

---

[8] See Multamaki 1999; Knorr 1968.

for a more benevolent or paternal domestic state – one which might provide a broader outlet for the self-realization of elites and artists through the practice of public virtue. The imaginative space of the colony in this period was, then, not so much a remote *locus amoenus*, or a Renaissance-style lubber-land teeming with sensory indulgences, but an outlet for poetic fantasies of a fair or redeemed social order. To the perennial questions as to whether territorial expansion is detrimental to liberty at home, and whether this erodes the very public virtue which gave rise to it in the first place, most answered no: colonization ought to and could be, instead, an opportunity to consolidate national virtue. The virtue promoted by poets from Pope and Thomson to William Cowper was on the classical model of selfless devotion to the public weal (Pope insisting all the while that 'Self-love and social are the same'), but with a Christian and sentimental emphasis upon care for the needy as its highest manifestation. They dwelt upon the socially integrative potential of the exercise of this virtue by all, and its role in the preservation of the form of liberty secured by a mixed constitution. Moreover, in an era when little could be expected of the state in the welfare arena, the idea of colonization provided an imaginative outlet for a new vision of politics. It was in this context that virtue metamorphosed most readily into benevolence, and in which benevolent government was most easily imagined.

## THE COLONIZATION OF ANCIENT BRITAIN

Through a series of examples, I am going to try to give substance to my contention that poets were instrumental in the fashioning of ideas of imperial trusteeship far in advance of their flowering in the nineteenth century, and that this was achieved by inserting the notion of benevolence into the language of political theory and by characterizing benevolence as an outgrowth of liberty. The first is the attempt to imagine colonization from the point of view, not of indigenous peoples, but of the pioneering colonizers trying to establish a new and fair political order in unfamiliar lands. This often proceeded through an act of inversion whereby it was Britain that was imagined as a province colonized by Normans, Saxons, Romans, and, before that, in the mists of time, by the grandson of Aeneas and his Trojan followers. Central to this literary enlargement of the ethical debate about colonialism was Dryden's translation of the *Aeneid* (1697), a work permeated with the translator's ambivalent attitudes to conquest, empire and the potential complicity of art with both of these.

Steven Zwicker has revealed the extent to which Dryden's *Aeneid* dramatizes Aeneas' conquest of Latium in terms that invite comparison with William III's usurpation of James II's crown.[9] Dryden's troubled exploration of the issue of illegal seizure resonated not only with contemporary British domestic politics, but also in the context of the colonization ventures undertaken in the recent past by James and his clients.[10] Dryden had long taken a sceptical interest in such questions. In his version of Shakespeare's *Tempest* (adapted with some input from William Davenant, the father of Charles), the drunken sailors Stephano, Mustacho and Ventoso appoint themselves 'Vice-Roys' over the island, establishing fundamental laws, boasting about their prerogatives and staggering around in search of native subjects.[11] In his translation of the *Aeneid*, Dryden describes Aeneas and his comrades as comprising a 'navy' of imperial adventurers and would-be colonizers.[12] Dryden converts Virgil's Mediterranean scenery of cultivated landscapes and sophisticated peoples into a harsh geography of frontier settlements, desolate seas and hostile, uncivilized natives. Aeneas visits Dido's rival 'Tyrian colony' on the 'wild uncultivated shoar' of Carthage, before proceeding to the 'inhospitable coast' of Latium where Palinurus the helmsman is butchered by a 'cruel Nation' of savages.[13] In the end when Jupiter decrees:

> The Natives shall command, the Foreigners subside.
> All shall be *Latium*; *Troy* without a Name:
> And her lost Sons forget from whence they came.[14]

Aeneas will ultimately be obliged to adopt a strategy of peaceful settlement and ethnic coexistence, and will become more of a William Penn than a William of Orange.

Aeneas and the Trojans' eventual settlement in Latium is at once a conquest, an exile, a homecoming, and a restoration of lost empire on terms of peace and co-operation.[15] Just as Dryden finds contemporary

[9] Zwicker 1984, ch. 6. Also see Thomas 2001, ch. 2.
[10] See O'Brien 1999, pp. 164–5.
[11] Dryden with William Davenant, *The Tempest, or the Enchanted Island. A Comedy* (1670, first performed 1667) in Dryden 1956–2002, x, pp. 32–4.
[12] The *Aeneid* is in Dryden 1956–2002, v–vi. The translation will be cited by book and line number.
[13] *Aeneid*, I, I. 425; VI, II. 490–92.
[14] *Aeneid*, XII, II. 1213–15. Virgil, XII, I. 836 has 'subsident Teucri' but nothing to support Dryden's phrase 'The Natives shall command'.
[15] On this idea of restoration and homecoming in Dryden's translation of Virgil, see Hammond 1999, pp. 233–40.

British echoes in the tension between illegal seizure and legitimate settlement, he also hints at parallels between the *Aeneid* and legends of the founding of Britain, including the myth of the Arthurian re-conquest of ancient Britain. Dryden had made plans for Arthurian epic in which Arthur has to beat back the Saxons.[16] One of his younger contemporaries, Richard Blackmore delivered just such an *Arthuriad*, depicting in *Prince Arthur* (1695) the young Arthur's re-appropriation of Britain from the Saxons in overtly Whig, bellicose terms that found little favour with contemporary readers.[17] Blackmore may have put the next generation of poets off the Arthurian idea. Instead, they seem to have found a more propitious legend of national founding in Geoffrey of Monmouth's account of the colonization of pre-historic Britain by Aeneas' grandson Brutus. This had been considered as possible epic material by Milton, and in turn, would provide poets with a potent analogue for colonial activities in their own time.[18] In the Galfridian source, Albion (as it was before Brutus renamed it) is uninhabited except by a few wicked giants, destroyed by the Trojan invaders who then partition and settle the country. This is the version of events adopted by Spenser, and (with reservations) by Milton in his *History of Britain* (1670—1671).[19] Pope had long been interested in this story, having supplied the English version of Brutus's prayer to Diana for Aaron Thompson's 1718 translation of Geoffrey of Monmouth.[20] He planned his own epic version of the Brutus legend, significantly adding a new dimension to the story in the form of native inhabitants needing protection from the marauding giants. The poem was never written, of course, but eighteenth-century readers could have learned about it in some detail from the account given in Owen Ruffhead's biography of 1769.[21] Pope's Brutus is not so much an exile as a colonial adventurer, though strictly of the disinterested, benign variety. His defining virtue and motivation is 'benevolence', and he travels

---

[16] Dryden, 'Discourse concerning the Original and Progress of Satire' (1692) in Dryden 1956—2002, IV, p. 22. Milton also made similar plans. See 'Mansus', II. 80—84 in Milton 1997. Spenser's *Faerie Queene* (1590—1596) set out to promote the Elizabethan restoration of Arthurian empire in Ireland.

[17] Blackmore (1695). On the Whig martial idiom of this time, see Womersley 1997 and Williams 2005.

[18] 'Epitaphium Damonis', II. 163—5 in Milton 1997. On Geoffrey of Monmouth and the 'matter of Britain', see Kidd, in this volume.

[19] *Faerie Queene*, II, canto X, II. 5—9; *The History of Britain* (1670—1671) in Milton 1953—1982, V, p. 16.

[20] Monmouth 1718. The prayer was supposedly by Gildas, an ancient British poet.

[21] Ruffhead 1769, pp. 410—20. A manuscript draft by Pope is in the British Library: MS Eg. 1950 ff. 4—6.

the world in search of an outlet for his philanthropic impulses in order to introduce good government 'among a people uncorrupt in their manners, worthy to be made happy; and wanting only arts and laws to that purpose'.[22] To this end, he lands at Torbay and helps the native Celts expel the giants. Geoffrey had implied that the Trojans' *imperium* in Britain was by right of cultivation, but for Pope their occupation is justified by their moral motivation and generous conduct. After Brutus establishes his military authority in Britain, one of his young kinsmen argues in favour of 'treating the people who submitted to him as slaves'.

But Brutus gives it as his opinion, not to conquer and destroy the natives of the new-discovered land, but to polish and refine them, by introducing true religion, void of superstition and all false notions of the Deity.[23]

The planned epic promised nothing less than a rewriting of the *Aeneid* as a parable of Enlightened colonization, one which would have made the benevolence of the colonizing power the main criterion of its political legitimacy. It would thus have extended into the imperial arena Pope's idea of the 'close system of Benevolence', elaborated in *An Essay on Man* (1733–1734) and central to his theodicy.[24] At the very least, Pope would have written the poem in such as way as to encourage readers to draw parallels between the founding of Britain and the present-day conduct of empire, a subject which exercised Pope throughout his career.[25] There were a number of other poets in this period who thought the legend worth attempting, all of whom made the connection between the Brutus story and Britain's contemporary pursuit of empire. Among these was Hildebrand Jacob who published the first part of the epic *Brutus, the Trojan* (1735) in which Diana predicts the coming of a British empire of liberty: 'a *Dardan* Line, / *Riches*, reviving *Liberty*, and *Arts*, / The *Muses* Seats, and new discover'd *Worlds*'.[26] At the very end of the century, the so-called 'milkmaid poet' Anne Yearsley published her 'Brutus: A Fragment' in direct imitation of Pope. Her Brutus is a benevolent colonizer and legislator, bringing liberty and the prospect of maritime empire to a benighted land.[27] And there was John Ogilvie's

---

[22] Ruffhead 1769, p. 410.   [23] Ruffhead 1769, p. 420.
[24] *An Essay on Man*, IV, l. 58 in Pope 1939–1969, III-i.
[25] See Erskine-Hill 1998.
[26] Jacob 1735, p. 77. Only the first five books were ever published, and the poem breaks off before Brutus reaches Albion.
[27] Yearsley 1796 discussed in Griffin 2002, pp. 280–85.

*Britannia* (1801), which linked Britain's original settlement by Brutus to its eventual destiny as a global empire of liberty.[28]

## GEORGIA ON THEIR MINDS

Pope drafted the Brutus fragment around 1740, at a time when he was also writing the fourth book of *The Dunciad*, a work which imagines an altogether more sinister imperial take-over of Britain, this time by the oppressive, mind-contracting and malevolent forces of Dullness.[29] The contrast between benevolent and malevolent empire had been on Pope's mind throughout the previous decade. He took a keen interest in James Oglethorpe's Georgia venture, and characterized Oglethorpe as the very type of benevolence, famously alluding to him in these lines in his *Imitations of Horace*: 'One, driv'n by strong Benevolence of Soul, / Shall fly, like *Oglethorp*, from Pole to Pole'.[30] Oglethorpe undoubtedly provided Pope with the model for Brutus, and for responsible colonial stewardship more generally. Pope's close associate Bolingbroke exhorted his ideal patriot king to 'to improve and keep in heart the national colonies, like so many farms of the mother country', something both of them felt Walpole had failed to do, especially when, in 1738, Oglethorpe had to brow-beat the Prime Minister into giving him the resources to defend the province against the Spaniards.[31] As a public figure Oglethorpe enjoyed a special relationship to poetry, and the Georgia venture was, from the outset, celebrated in verse. One example will suffice: an anonymous poem 'To James Oglethorpe' (1736), which mentions Pope's endorsement, and the pacific intent behind the creation of the colony:

> Let Twickenham's bard, in his immortal lays,
> Give thee the humble tribute of our praise.
>
> [. . .]
>
> No verdant plains of Georgia we view
> With blood discolour'd, or a purple hue;
> But cities founded, and new conquests made
> Without the slain that Marlbro's triumphs shade.
>
> [. . .]

---

[28] Zwierlein 2002, pp. 200–3.    [29] See O'Brien 2002, pp. 285–7.

[30] 'The Second Epistle of the Second Book of Horace Imitated' (1737), ll. 277–8 in Pope 1939–1969, VI. Pope also knew Benjamin Martyn the secretary to the Georgia trustees and playwright (see Mack 1985, p. 925 n.).

[31] Bolingbroke 1997, p. 278. See Thomas 1996, p. 9 and Ettinger 1936.

> The wand'ring emigrant may now descry
> A land that sacred is to liberty.[32]

The Georgia colony secured a royal charter in 1732 as the result of the
fundraising efforts of Oglethorpe and a group of trustees, and quickly
became just such a beacon of benevolent empire. The charter entitled the
trustees to administer for twenty-one years a non-profit-making colony
for the poor and persecuted, after which it was to revert to the Crown.
The charter emphasized the colony's philanthropic and Christian
missionary purpose, referring warmly to the precedent of Pennsylvania,
although the Crown clearly stood to benefit from Georgia's strategic
position as a bulwark against Spanish expansion from the south.[33] It was
Oglethorpe who fashioned its political mission by taking personal
charge of the colony on the ground. He prohibited slavery, insisted
upon religious toleration and just dealings with the native peoples,
and instituted agrarian laws restricting the size of land holdings and
inheritances. All was done on an expressly Roman model (with perhaps
a nod to James Harrington), in an attempt to revive the ancient virtues,
though without any of the ancient representative institutions.[34]

Oglethorpe may have started out with a Ciceronian idea of imperial
protectorate in mind, but the project for a philanthropic colony took
his thinking in new and surprising directions. Addressing the House of
Commons in 1732, he articulated a vision of the people of the British
metropolis and colonies as members of one community, equally entitled
to be governed in their own interest:

in all cases that come before this House, where there seems to be a clashing of
interests between one set of people and another, we ought to have no regard to
the particular interest of any country or any set of people; the good of the whole
is what we ought only to have under our consideration: our colonies are all a part
of our own dominions; the people in every one of them are our own people, and
we ought to shew an equal respect to all.[35]

To MPs accustomed to thinking of the colonies as possessions and of
colonists as inferior, mainly Scotch Irish, wastrels, this must have seemed

---

[32] 'To James Oglethorpe, Esq; on his late Arrival from Georgia', appended to *A New Voyage to Georgia by a Young Gentleman* 1737. This is not mentioned in the otherwise comprehensive Boys 1947.
[33] Force 1836–46, I, no. 2, pp. 4–7. Also Reese 1963.
[34] For instance, his observations on the 'wisdom of the Roman State', in Oglethorpe 1732, p. 52. On Oglethorpe's authorship of this, see Baine 1988.
[35] Quoted in Ettinger 1936, p. 101.

revolutionary. Oglethorpe's views certainly had an impact upon Edmund Burke, who knew him well in his later years, and whose speeches on the American crisis articulated similar, if less thorough-going, ideas of imperial community and colonial privilege.

In his administration of Georgia, Oglethorpe was a paternalistic, somewhat authoritarian figure, little preoccupied, as Burke would later be, with the transposition of liberty from mother country to colony. It fell to Whig poets to take on the problem of reconciling liberty and benevolence in the colonial context, and none more prominently than the Scottish poet and author of 'Rule, Britannia' James Thomson. Thomson gave extensive treatment to the question of morally sanctioned empire in works such as *The Seasons* (final authorial edition 1746) and *The Castle of Indolence* (1748), often as part of an implicit narrative of the development of liberty over time. His fullest statement on the Georgia project occurs in the context of *Liberty, A Poem* (1735–1736), a long, five-part overview of the progress of liberty from ancient Greece to modern Britain. The poem treats liberty as a supra-historical abstraction that finds embodiment in various historical guises, but only fully realizes its true form in Britain's mixed constitution. For most of the poem, it is she who does the talking, and her status as a goddess reinforces the notion that political liberty links the state to the metaphysical order of things. Liberty is shown to be the object of enthusiastic Shaftesburian adoration by free peoples everywhere; by worshipping her they acquire the ability to burst 'the Bounds of Self' and meld the public weal out of 'the mix'd Ardor of unnumber'd Selves'.[36] Such an inspired capacity for self-transcendence is the essence of public virtue, the 'social Cement of Mankind'.[37] It is by analogy with this self-transcendence that Thomson imagines the reaching out of the British people into philanthropic colonies. Oglethorpe's Georgia provides the operative example:

> 'Lo! Swarming southward on rejoicing Suns,
> Gay COLONIES extend; the calm Retreat
> Of undeserv'd Distress, the better Home
> Of Those whom *Bigots* chase from foreign Lands.
> Not built on *Rapine*, *Servitude* and *Woe*,
> But, bound by *social Freedom*, firm they rise;
> Such as, of late, an OGLETHORPE has form'd,
> And, crouding round, the charm'd *Savannah* sees.'
> [Liberty is speaking here.][38]

[36] *Liberty, A Poem*, III, ll. 107–110, in Thomson 1986; see also Mehan 1986, p. 10.
[37] *Liberty*, v, l. 95.    [38] *Liberty*, v, ll. 638–46.

The passage appears straight-forward until one starts to wonder what 'social freedom' might mean here. Thomson goes on to discuss other philanthropic schemes at home to relieve orphans, the unemployed and the destitute ('No starving Wretch the Land of *Freedom* stains').[39] It seems clear that Thomson has broadened the terms of liberty to include freedom from the dependence of poverty and lack of opportunity, and that 'social freedom' means, at least in part, the enabling of individuals within the social sphere. Liberty may create the conditions for philanthropy at home and welfare colonies abroad, without necessarily entailing the extension of formal liberty to its beneficiaries.

## COOK, LIBERTY AND BENEVOLENCE

Thomson was one — and by far the most widely read — of many poets who attempted to fashion a poetic language of liberty equal to their aspirations for a kinder domestic social order, for an expanding empire and for the progress of the arts. Poets assumed a special role in the philosophical consideration of the social dimensions and operations of liberty. William Collins, for instance, in his 'Ode to Liberty' (1746) a decade or so later, urged the 'Laureate Band' of poets to 'sooth' Liberty in order for her 'to gain' 'Blithe Concord's social Form'.[40] In a similarly Pindaric vein, the popular mid-century Whig poet Mark Akenside made lofty claims for the bard as the preserver and reformer of a social order built upon foundations of liberty.[41] The empire features in such works as a by-product of British liberty and its struggle with French absolutism. The expansion of Britain corresponds metaphorically with the imaginative expansiveness of the poet, since both are stimulated by liberty, and both give liberty expressive form. It was thus possible to imagine the empire as an outgrowth of British liberty, without ever implying that it was a community of shared liberty in which colonists and native peoples enjoyed the same freedoms as those at home. There were many poems, especially georgics such as John Dyer's *The Fleece* (1757) or James Grainger's *The Sugar-Cane* (1764), that celebrated the American and West Indian colonies as part of a community of production and consumption, but here too what they offered to overseas imperial subjects was economic rather than political participation.[42]

[39] *Liberty*, v, l. 656.
[40] Collins 1979, ll. 129–32. See also Rowe 1739, 'An Ode to Liberty'.
[41] See the excellent discussion of Akenside in Griffin 2002, ch. 4.
[42] See, for example, Dyer 1757, IV, ll. 525–41.

During the American Revolutionary War, the idea of the colonies as part of a community of liberty — in Richard Price's words, 'a multitude of free states branched forth from ourselves' — featured prominently in the dissenting campaign for conciliation.[43] Schemes, such as that of the 'Country Association' (a coalition of radical friends of America) for a new kind of imperial federation held out the possibility of an entirely new vision of empire.[44] Yet these were no more successful in the short term than Burke's idea that the American colonists, for too long infants under the protection of the modern country, should be allowed some of the privileges of adulthood. 'Never again', Eliga Gould has argued 'would the British think of any part of their empire as an extension of their own nation'.[45] Yet, at the point where the loss of America seemed inevitable, writers were fashioning a regenerated language of empire in the wake of the three Cook voyages of 1768—1780, the published accounts of the discoveries, and the melodrama of Cook's murder, in Hawaii, in 1779.[46] The literary attempt to make moral and political sense of Cook's achievements came at a moment of particular imperial pressure. In addition to the American crisis and war, it coincided with the beginning of the anti-slavery campaigns, and followed a period of parliamentary and public concern about the activities of the East India Company in the wake of the devastating Bengal famine of 1770. Much has been written about the decisive roles played by poets in the campaign for abolition, and something has been said about poets' mythologizing of the South Seas discoveries, and a little about the overlap between these roles.[47] Poets mythologized the voyages as examples of the workings of an imperial benevolence hitherto absent in the nation's dealings with its African subjects, often in terms which divulged an incipient evangelical language of moralized global capitalism. It was Cook himself who bore the symbolic brunt of this artistic search for imperial regeneration, as a figure embodying both disinterested scientific rationality and humane Christian values.

The most widely read poem in this vein was the *Elegy on Captain Cook* (1780) written by the radical Whig poet Anna Seward, possibly with some input from her friend Erasmus Darwin. In the elegy she celebrates Cook's disinterested pursuit of discovery and science, rather than

---

[43] Price 1776, p. 27.
[44] Gould 2000; Miller 1994.     [45] Gould 2000, p. 214.
[46] The voyages took place in 1768—1771, 1772—1775 and 1776—1780.
[47] See Veit 1972; Smith 1992; Wilson 2003; Russell 2004; and Fulford, Lee and Kitson 2004.

empire and gain, a pursuit motivated (as Seward states repeatedly) by 'Benevolence' (or, in the earliest versions, 'Humanity'):

> Say first, what Power inspir'd his dauntless breast
> With scorn of danger and inglorious rest,
> To quit imperial London's gorgeous domes
>
> [. . .]
>
> It was BENEVOLENCE! — on coasts unknown,
> The shriv'ring natives of the frozen zone,
> And the swart Indian, as he faintly strays
> 'Where Cancer reddens in the solar blaze',
> She bade him seek; on each inclement shore
> Plant the rich seeds of her exhaustless store;
> Unite the savage hearts, and hostile hands,
> In the firm compact of her gentle bands.[48]

Seward ends the poem by addressing Cook's widow, the private embodiment of the nation's public grief. The poem's domestication of Cook very effectively enhances his status as an imperial hero, and it enables Seward to take shrewd advantage of her femininity. It is indicative, more generally, of the late eighteenth-century feminization of patriotism, and the process by which women laid claim to moral authority and proximate political influence in the shaping of the nation.[49] Emboldened to speak on national matters from a domestic position of address, women poets, including Seward, Yearsley, Hannah More (discussed below), play an increasingly prominent role in the articulation of Britain's imperial duties and destiny. Seward's focus upon the domestic pathos of Cook's death here detracts from the official aspects of the voyages as pre-emptive assertions of the right of discovery against future territorial claims by rival European powers. The President of the Royal Society, Lord Morton, had reminded both Cook and Joseph Banks before they set out that the native inhabitants were 'the natural, and in the strictest sense of the word, the legal possessors of the several Regions they inhabit' and had insisted that 'no European Nation has a right to occupy any part of their country, or settle among them without their voluntary consent'.[50] Yet Cook took possession

---

[48] Anna Seward, 'Elegy on Captain Cook' (1780), 1810 version, in Kelly 1999, IV, p. 36; the quotation is from Thomson's *The Seasons*. See also Fitzgerald 1780; *Ode to the Memory of Captain James Cook . . . By a Sea Officer* 1780.
[49] Guest 2000.    [50] Quoted by Williams 1998, pp. 560–61.

of Queen Charlotte Sound in New Zealand after the most cursory explanation to the local Maori, and claimed the east coast of Australia on the grounds that it was *terra nullius* (no man's land). The dimensions of illegal territorial acquisition and European rivalry were usually missing from poetical accounts, even the more critical ones, which like Seward's emphasized entitlement by benevolent intent or focused instead on the experience of the encounter between Europeans and indigenous peoples.[51]

In the years leading up to the creation of the first penal colony at Botany Bay, the posthumous Cook grew in stature into 'a figure capable of reconstituting British imperial authority'.[52] His respect for indigenous culture continued to be held up for poetic praise, in contrast to the practice of slavery and abuse elsewhere in the empire. The difference was not so much between the freedom and rights accorded to the South Sea islanders and those withheld from black slaves, as one between exploitation and collective social responsibility. Filtered through the language of Evangelicalism, this idea of responsibility became one of brotherhood and sisterhood, and the brothers and sisters of the empire were imagined as members of a virtual global congregation. The influential Evangelical writer Hannah More, in her *Slavery, A Poem* (1788), distinguished Cook from earlier explorers whose discoveries had lead only to destruction and slavery:

> Whether of wealth insatiate, or of pow'r,
> Conquerors who waste, or ruffians who devour:
> Had these possess'd, O COOK! thy gentle mind,
> Thy love of arts, thy love of humankind;
> Had these pursued thy mild and liberal plan,
> DISCOVERERS had not been a curse to man!
> The, bless'd Philanthropy! thy social hands
> Had link'd dissever'd worlds in brothers bands;
> Careless, if colour, or if clime divide;
> Then, lov'd, and loving, man had liv'd, and died.[53]

Both Cook and William Penn find a place in More's pantheon of imperial philanthropists, although Oglethorpe and his benevolent colony, long since given over to slave-owners and large plantations, appear forgotten. The 'Conquerors who waste, or ruffians who devour' include slave traders and Spanish conquistadors, notably Cortez.[54]

[51] See, most famously, Cowper, *The Task* (1785), I, ll. 620–77 in Cowper 1980–1985, II.
[52] Wilson 2003, p. 62.    [53] More 1788, ll. 233–42.    [54] More 1788, l. 220.

More's negative and positive typologies of greedy conquerors and philanthropic colonizers were utterly standard by this time, and often formed part of much fuller accounts of the benefits of voluntary economic exchange as against the disadvantages of forced labour and indiscriminate plunder. For instance, William Cowper in his poem 'Charity' (1782) observed: 'While Cook is loved for savage lives he saved, / See Cortez odious for a world enslaved!'[55] These lines follow Cowper's consideration of Cook's fair dealings with the native peoples of the South Seas:

> Wherever he found man, to nature true,
> The rights of man were sacred in his view:
> He sooth'd with gifts and greeted with a smile
> The simple native of the new-found isle ...[56]

The soothing gifts are not merely gifts; they initiate the 'simple natives' into a system of property and commerce which in turn gives them a point of access to the global operations of charity through international exchange:

> The band of commerce was design'd
> T'associate all the branches of mankind,
> And if a boundless plenty be the robe,
> Trade is the golden girdle of the globe.[57]

Cowper sees commerce as a redemptive activity, potentially capable of engendering fraternal interdependence between peoples where before there was isolation or exploitation. Cowper, a strident and influential critic of both the slave trade and the East India Company, was far from optimistic that he would ever live to see a regenerated empire, but he never doubted that imperial commerce and colonization were potentially compatible with benevolence.[58] Others who, like Cowper, advanced the idea of commerce as form of global sociability, were more confident that empire could be salvaged for the cause of humanity. The former slave, Olaudah Equiano concluded his popular autobiography with the argument that the abolition of slavery would open up a 'commercial Intercourse with Africa' which would bring both financial and moral benefits to all concerned.[59] Equiano was a government commissary

---

[55] 'Charity', in Cowper 1782, p. 182.    [56] Cowper 1782, pp. 181–2.
[57] Cowper 1782, pp. 184, 186.
[58] On Cowper as an 'imperialist', see Faulkner 1991 and more sceptically, O'Brien 1998.
[59] Equiano 1995, p. 333.

and enthusiastic supporter of the period's most experimental benevolent colony, the 'Province of Freedom', established in 1787 in the Sierra Leone estuary, as a home for settlers and ex-slaves of African descent. Its founder, Granville Sharp, received active encouragement from the elderly James Oglethorpe, as well as from Hannah More, for his aim of creating a self-governing colony and beacon of British humanitarianism.[60] Naturally, there were poetic outpourings of support, including a poem, published in the *Morning Post*, by the future poet laureate Robert Southey celebrating the colonial settlers and authorities: 'Their minds enlarged, their hearts humane, / They come to break the oppressive chain ...'.[61] Southey's belief that Sierra Leone offered an enlightened model of colonization and an alternative way for Britain to deal with Africa was widely shared, but, in this case, at least, there is substantial evidence about the quite different feelings and views of the intended recipients of colonial paternalism. The settlement (which became a shareholding company in 1791) recruited a group of escaped American slaves ('Nova Scotians') who, throughout the 1790s, consistently petitioned the government and the company authorities for their full civil rights: as they wrote to governor John Clarkson, 'we are willing to be govern by the laws of England in full but we do not Consent to gave it in to your honer hands without haven aney of our own Culler in it'.[62] Far from submitting cheerfully to the yoke of benevolence, these imperial subjects demanded, and continued to demand, the right to representation implicit in their original consent to the governing authority.

### CONCLUSION

In the decades that followed, the idea of benevolence as both the moving spirit of British imperial egress and the outcome of British trade went through more Dissenting, Evangelical and Anglican permutations, and gained its familiar hold. Literary writers were engaged very early on in an attempt to integrate the ideal of benevolence into the language of political thought, and they identified the colonies as a promising sphere in which both private and state benevolence could be exercised and tested for its viability at home. To a degree, benevolent colonization represented

---

[60] Sharp 1820, pp. 157–8.
[61] 'On the Settlement of Sierra Leona' (1798), in Southey 1994, I, p. 169.
[62] Fyfe 1991, p. 25. In general, see Coleman 2005, chs. 1–3.

a trial-run for a new idea of the paternal state, one that might charter, underwrite, finance or supervise the voluntary efforts of high-minded individuals. In both the domestic and imperial contexts, liberty (in the sense of protection from arbitrary government by the constitution) was essential to the benefactor, much less so to the beneficiary. The first generation of Romantic poets bolstered the moral case for empire, partly by characterizing white colonial emigration as a remedy for the Malthusian perils of over-population, and partly by depicting colonizers, not as the standard-bearers, but as the casualties of the British imperial state. Wordsworth's vagrants and displaced poor are Britain's internal and external migrants, deserving of sympathy and state support. They have been deprived of a productive relationship to the land, and are different therefore, in quality and in kind, from the property-less, pre-social native Americans who figure so frequently in his poems. Southey, too, depicted colonial migration sympathetically as an activity issuing from Britain's Celtic, economic or political margins. In his *Madoc* (1805), the eponymous hero, a medieval Welshman, is pushed out of his native home by the forces of corruption and Anglicization. Madoc turns into a Brutus figure when he migrates to Florida, takes benevolent control of the local native population and cultivates the land. In later life, Southey argued vigorously for government-assisted colonization of the 'unculti-vated parts of the earth', and he has a good claim to be considered as a precursor to the colonial reform movement of the 1830s.[63] The Romantic emphasis upon man's natural property in the land he cultivates — which coincided, not by chance, with the first settlements in New South Wales and the acquisition of the Cape Colony — added a Lockean element to a moral case for empire built upon notions of responsible metropolitan trusteeship. Duncan Ivison has explored, in his chapter, the exclusionary implications, for indigenous subjects of the empire, of Locke's agriculturalist notion of property rights, and the ways in which the lack of such forms of property disqualifies native peoples from collective political agency.[64] His argument allows us to see, at the moment of the formation of the second British Empire, the implication of the Romantic figure of the free, noble, nomadic native in imperialist conceptions of human political competence. Lockean ideas of property entitlement by cultivation, as well as by first occupancy, played an enduring role in the eighteenth- and nineteenth-century debate

---

[63] Southey 1832, I, p. 154.    [64] Ivison, in this volume.

about empire, both to justify dispossession and to challenge it.[65] Despite their potential complicity with native dispossession, Locke's ideas of natural rights, consent and self-determination, as Ivison suggests, retained their potential as the basis of a thorough-going critique of empire. The language of benevolence — central to the campaigns against slavery and the slave trade — was highly effective when geared to the amelioration and regeneration of empire; but it was not created to offer a similarly fundamental critique of empire, and ultimately informed a nineteenth-century idea of imperial trusteeship. David Armitage has written of how the mid-eighteenth-century notion of the empire as Protestant, commercial, maritime and free, when recast as liberalism, lingered into the nineteenth century, less as an ideology by which policy was governed and measured than as a corner stone of British national identity.[66] It might also be said that the nineteenth-century idea of the empire as morally purposeful, benevolent and humanitarian had deep roots reaching back to the late seventeenth century — roots which found an early and fertile soil in the writings of poets. It is certainly essential that we recognize their contribution to this area of political thought if we are to understand the entanglements of ideas of empire, liberty and benevolence.

[65] Armitage 2000, pp. 96—8.    [66] Armitage 2000, pp. 195—8.

# PART III

# British Political Thought and Political Theory

# CHAPTER 10

# The Nature of Rights and the History of Empire

## Duncan Ivison

I

This chapter is a study in the globalization of the history of British political thought. What do I mean by 'globalization' in this context? If the history of British political thought has been deconstructed into something more than the history of English political thought — and the idea of 'political thought' itself into more than just explicitly political treatises, speeches or pamphlets[1] — then what happens when we extend this multi-centred approach beyond the edges of the British Isles to the settler-colonial contexts of North America and Australasia, for example? British political discourse, now a complex of discourses as opposed to one, engages with and becomes part of a new bundle of discourses that includes but is not reducible to either English or British political thought.

To illustrate this approach, I shall consider the genesis and afterlife of one strand of the discourse of rights. The language of rights — especially that of 'subjective rights' or, as we call them today, individual rights — was one of the most powerful and influential modes of political discourse to emerge in the early-modern period. Historians of rights have pointed out that although the emergence of subjective rights in the seventeenth century is closely associated with attempts at limiting the authority of states, this legacy is somewhat ambiguous.[2] First of all, rights discourse was used to justify *submission* to authority as much as limits against it, insofar as it entailed the discretion of individuals to submit absolutely. Secondly, there are deep connections between the language of rights and processes of state-formation,[3] and especially the link between the

---

[1] See O'Brien, in this volume.
[2] Tuck 1979; 1993; 1999; Haakonssen 1996; Haakonssen 2001; Foucault 2003.
[3] Tuck 1999; Armitage 2000; Braddick 2000.

emergence of the 'modern' idea of natural rights and European expansionism.[4] For Richard Tuck, the autonomous rights-bearing agent at the heart of liberal individualism is a product of seventeenth-century theorizing about the nature of the autonomous state acting in the international sphere. The sovereign individual is the 'traditional cousin of the sovereign state', argues Tuck, and especially the aggressive, violent, and minimally constrained relative described by Hugo Grotius, Thomas Hobbes, John Locke and Emer de Vattel.[5] Thus the connection between liberalism and imperialism, on this reading, is not merely chronological or historical but metaphysical. The analogy between the sovereign state and the sovereign individual acting on the basis of their natural rights, constrained by the recognition of the basic rights of others (but not much more than that) represents an influential vision of liberal freedom. This minimalist account of freedom represents only one vision, however, and Tuck's account of the pre-history of liberal rights has to be balanced against other conceptions, including more emancipatory ones.[6]

My aim in this chapter is thus to take the complexity of our histories of rights as seriously as the nature of rights themselves. Let me say immediately that the point is not to satisfy our sense of moral superiority by smugly pointing out the prejudices found in arguments made over three hundred years ago. We have more than our own share of problems and prejudices to deal with. Rather, in coming to grips with this history, and especially how early-modern political theorists struggled with the extension and application of natural rights to the 'New World', we may learn something about our own struggles to extend human rights beyond the boundaries of the state system of which Grotius, Hobbes, Locke and Vattel were among the key intellectual architects.

II

But first, let me summarize some of the key claims involved in the repositioning of the history of the emergence of the language of subjective rights in seventeenth-century British political thought from the mainly domestic and intra-European stage to the global stage.

---

[4] Tuck 1987, pp. 99–122; Tuck 1994, pp. 159–70; Mills 1997.
[5] Tuck 1999, pp. 14–15, 84, 195–6, 226, 233–4; Schneewind 1998, pp. 3, 483.
[6] Compare Ivison 1997; Muthu 2003; Pitts 2005.

Amongst the cluster of philosophical and political problems which the great sixteenth- and seventeenth-century rights theorists struggled with, one of the most important was dealing with social and cultural difference, both within their own communities (after the Wars of Religion) and beyond (between competing European powers and between them and the indigenous peoples they encountered in these lands). One influential strategy that emerged, pioneered by Hugo Grotius, was to try and identify a minimal set of propositions that, whatever else one believed, one must accept if any kind of human society was to be possible.[7] The belief in the right to self-preservation (and correlative to that, the right to defend oneself), the cornerstone of 'modern' natural law theory, was a universal claim in just this sense. The aim was to minimize the objective content of both natural morality as well as religion, in order to minimize the scope for contestation and thus civil and international conflict. The natural ethics of Grotius then, on this interpretation, was not intended to be a comprehensive account of man's moral life, but rather — especially in the international context — to be the basis for 'inter-national or inter-cultural negotiation, by providing the common ground upon which the rival and conflicting cultures could meet'.[8] The thought was that the law of nature and the law of nations could be bridged on the basis of a minimalist core of morality observable by all rational creatures, whatever their cultural or religious beliefs. But this in itself said little about the conduct or quality of such negotiations and interactions, or who exactly would be accorded the appropriate standing such that they could be said to possess these fundamental rights in the first place. The famous Spanish debates in the sixteenth century over the status of Aboriginal peoples made that very clear.[9] Francisco de Vitoria, for example, was able to ascribe natural rights to the American Indians in virtue of their shared humanity and evidence of their civic life but, at the same time, justify declaring war on them if they barred his fellow Spaniards from travelling and trading on their lands, as a violation of the natural right of 'commerce'.[10] Even Las Casas, who defended the Amerindians against various brutalizing aspects of Spanish imperialism, still thought the overall project was justified, given the cultural inferiority of the Amerindians and their need for Christianity.

---

[7] Tuck 1994; 1999; for critical discussions of Tuck's argument and alternative readings of Grotius, see Tierney 1997; Haakonssen 1996; Haakonssen 2001.
[8] Tuck 1994, p. 167.     [9] See Pagden 1986.     [10] Vitoria 1991, pp. 278–84.

Thus we arrive at a paradox about the nature of rights and empire. Natural rights did not merely coexist with imperialism, as if the latter was an unfortunate departure in practice from a basic acceptance of the moral equality of all human beings. Instead, they were actually used to justify imperialism. How could this be?

John Locke's place in this debate is instructive precisely because he works within a natural law framework that contains, at its heart, a strong presumption of equality.[11] It is true that his anti-essentialism about species in the *Essay* makes it seem as if who counts as a 'man', and thus eligible for the attribution of equality, will be mainly conventional, which means the boundaries of humanity could be drawn very narrowly indeed.[12] But Locke also makes it clear that, for moral purposes at least, all we need is the complex idea of a 'corporeal rational Creature; What the real Essence or other Qualities of that Creature are in this Case, is no way considered'.[13] It constitutes an 'immovable and unchangeable Idea'. So equality is associated with the real resemblance of corporeal rationality between beings; those beings who exhibit corporeal rationality are entitled to be seen and treated as equals, which for Locke means basically not being subject to the non-consensual control of others. But this raises another question; what is the threshold associated with these capacities? Lunatics and 'idiots' fall beneath the line,[14] but what about any others? There is considerable debate in the literature here, but the basic idea seems to be that men are equal in the sense that each has reason 'enough to lead them to the Knowledge of their Maker, and the sight of their own Duties'.[15] It does not follow, therefore, that not actually knowing God's law is grounds for falling below the line, since many of us do not and we will get there via different paths. The capacity for abstract thought is what is crucial, at least for moral purposes.[16] We are capable of relating to God's existence and thus to a law that is to govern us, and from that to a set of duties and rights that apply to our conduct, however difficult it might be to actually grasp it.

---

[11] Locke 1988, II.4, 6, 54.
[12] Locke 1979, III.6.26; IV.7.16; see Ayers 1993, II, pp. 65–90; Waldron 2002, pp. 62–82; Grant 1987; Bracken 1984, pp. 54–6.
[13] Locke 1979, III.II.16.
[14] Locke 1988, II.60.
[15] Locke 1979, p. 45. That it is 'men' who are equal should also be taken literally, since although Locke thinks the natural rights of men and women block absolutism in the political sphere, there is a 'Foundation in nature' for the legal subjection of women to their husbands (cf. Locke 1988, II.65 with I.47).
[16] Locke 1979, III.II.16.

Do indigenous peoples fall below the threshold for corporeal moral agency, according to Locke? Is the appropriation of their lands, or the subjugation of their forms of government possible because they are not owed basic equal respect in the first place? Much depends on what one thinks follows from the notion of 'equal respect'. Today we often associate equal respect with respect not only for individuals, but sometimes the cultures and ways of life they construct and value, either as a product of their freedom or as a necessary condition for its realization.[17] Does Locke offer any intimations of such an argument in the *Two Treatises* (or elsewhere)? Hardly. But is his argument for possession based on denying the indigenous inhabitants of the Americas *any* attribution of equality? He does refer to indigenous peoples in the *First Treatise* at one point as 'irrational and untaught'[18] (a passage I shall return to in a moment), but does this entail that they are incapable of possessing natural rights?

We now have a sophisticated account of both the domestic and international context in which Locke made his arguments concerning property and civil society in the *Two Treatises*.[19] The basic structure of these Lockean arguments goes something like this. First, Locke ties ownership of property very closely to labour and to use. And labour is linked in relation to land and to cultivation: 'As much Land as a man Tills, Plants, Improves, Cultivates, and can use the Product of, so much is his Property'.[20] Thus if someone simply roams over unimproved land, or grazes his flock over it, he secures no property in the land he uses. This clearly entailed that, beyond the animals they catch, or the crops they sow, the indigenous peoples of America had no genuine property in their territories, and thus could not exclude Europeans from them, or demand negotiations over land use. It is no coincidence that Locke's point of comparison in discussing the difference between productive and unproductive practices to do with land is with Amerindian societies — wherein a 'King of a large and fruitful Territory there feeds, lodges, and is clad worse than a day Labourer in England'.[21] The argument

---

[17] See for example Kymlicka 1995.
[18] Locke 1988, 1.58.
[19] Armitage 2004b; Keene 2002; Tuck 1999; Tully 1993a; Tully 1979; Wootton 1993.
[20] Locke 1988, 11.32.
[21] Locke 1988, 11.41. On the background to Chapter v, see Tully 1993a; Tully 1993b; Arneil 1996; Armitage 2004b.

is a general one about increased productivity through the efficient use of land (reflecting his reading and translation of Pierre Nicole,[22] among other things), but its specific application to America has striking consequences.

The second crucial argument Locke makes is that the Indian 'Nations', as he refers to them, 'exercise very little Dominion, and have but a very modest Sovereignty'.[23] What societies they do have are not *civil* societies, and they remain, for all intents and purposes, in a state of nature (especially with regard to other European nations). Locke's argument here is sometimes assimilated with the 'four-stages' stadial theory of human history — linked especially with Adam Smith — whereby humanity progresses from wandering tribes or families to settled, commercial societies. I think this assimilation is somewhat premature, however crucial the stadial theory is to understanding European/ indigenous relations.[24] But Locke certainly does associate the 'Indian nations' with a pre-agricultural, nomadic existence, which entailed a limited set of desires and modes of interaction (and conflict) characteristic of more settled, agriculturally developed societies, and thus without the complex social and political institutions he assumed grew up around agriculture and monetarized exchange. For Locke, sovereignty is derived from the consent of members of civil society to incorporate themselves into a collective body — a people — and then be bound by majority will, exercised through a government justified on the grounds of protecting their natural rights.[25] To be sovereign, in other words, a collection of individuals, families or tribes — what Hobbes would call a 'multitude' — has to be converted into a people. Sovereigns can recognize and make treaties with each other and declare war, but the Indian nations, at least on their own, cannot. They can be acted on but lack the moral and political agency to be counted as genuine political actors themselves. (It is important to note, however, that the British Crown did, in fact, engage in treaty-making with various indigenous nations throughout the seventeenth and eighteenth centuries.)[26]

---

[22] See Locke 1993, p. 107; Ivison 1997, p. 120.

[23] Locke 1988, II.108; see also II.36. As Laslett points out, the discussion here mixes quasi-anthropological and biblical history freely, as Locke draws analogies between the 'Kings of the Indians in America' and the early kings of Israel.

[24] See Meek 1976; Haakonssen 1981, ch. 7; Pocock 1999; Pitts 2005, pp. 25–58; cf. Hont 1987.

[25] Locke 1988, II.95–8.

[26] Williams 1997; Slattery 1991.

Although the history of European-indigenous relations in the early-modern period is a complex and multi-faceted matter, this 'agriculturalist' justification of property rights was absolutely central to international and domestic law in colonial contexts well into the nineteenth century.[27] Even in Australia, for example, where only a tiny fraction of the country was under cultivation — or ever could be — the Sydney *Herald* declared (in 1838) that for the Aborigines, '[t]his vast country was to them a common — they bestowed no labour upon the land — their ownership, their right, was nothing more than that of the Emu or the Kangaroo'. The settlers had a 'perfect right', the *Herald* continued, to take possession of the land, 'under the Divine Authority, by which man was commanded to go forth and people, till the land'.[28] The language and culture of 'improvement', among other things, was what was supposed to distinguish British imperialism from others (especially the Spanish). Productivity was valued over religious conversion and cultural assimilation. And the flexibility of the common law, in theory at least, was supposed to help coordinate the customs and norms of Aboriginal peoples with the newly introduced European law.

It is important to see the moral argument Locke was appealing to. The emphasis on labour follows from Locke's understanding of human beings as rational creatures and yet dependent upon God. God commands us to labour, not just for the sake of it, but because it is the most appropriate mode of our supporting and sustaining his creation: 'God commanded, and [man's] Wants forced him to labour'.[29] We need to appropriate to fulfil our duties to God, and labour is the natural mode of appropriation.[30] Moreover, God gave the Earth to mankind to produce 'the greatest conveniences of life'.[31] It turns out that, with the introduction of money and the division of labour that occurs, 'improvement' helps produce more conveniences than in any other system, especially one in which land is left vacant. Cultivation and industry does not merely produce more stuff, but more opportunities for people to labour, and thus greater opportunities for more people to preserve themselves and serve God.

---

[27] See especially Vattel 1916, I.vii, pp. 76–8; II.vii, pp. 326–7; for more background see Weaver 2003; Keal 2003; Armitage 2000; Pagden, 1995.

[28] Cited in Karsten 2002, p. 257; see also Reynolds 1992, pp. 74–6.

[29] Locke 1988, II.35, II.42.

[30] Locke 1988, II.26; see also I.86.

[31] Locke 1988, II.34.

Now it is true, as Jeremy Waldron has emphasized, that these are *arguments* and not merely assertions, and that someone who seeks to justify their claims to someone else at least thinks they are entitled to a justification. Locke has at least produced an argument that *purports* to respect equality and to treat the Native Americans as persons.[32] But here I think a powerful set of intuitions associated in contemporary moral and political philosophy with the link between egalitarianism and the demand for mutual justification are in danger of being read back into Locke.[33] For although it is true that Locke's arguments were indeed intended to compel the agreement of Amerindians, in fact, their validity did not depend on their actual (or even counterfactual) consent. Failure to recognize the natural duties that flowed from the right of self-preservation – namely, refusal to cede their lands, allow settlement or use them more productively – legitimated the use of coercive force against them.[34] The centrality of the language of war with regard to relations between settlers and indigenous peoples in North America (and elsewhere), is a striking feature of this literature in the seventeenth century.[35] Nor, *pace* Waldron, was there any genuine option to 'co-exist side-by-side with European agriculture',[36] since, as we have seen, any recognition of the mutual capacity of both indigenous peoples and European settlers to determine coordinate rights of jurisdiction was explicitly denied by Locke (although he had once been attracted to a more explicitly contractual account of the nature of property).[37]

It might seem at this stage that any attribution of basic equality to indigenous people is barely self-evident in this discussion in the *Two Treatises*. Certainly the attribution of any form of collective right – either natural or positive – to indigenous *peoples* is absent. But what about his writings on toleration? Locke is very clear in the *Letter Concerning Toleration* (as well as in the *Fundamental Constitutions of Carolina*) that 'Not even Americans are to be punished either in body or in goods, for not embracing our faith and worship. If they are persuaded that they please God in observing the rites of their own country ... they are to be

---

[32] Waldron 2002, pp. 168–9.
[33] On the connection between equality and mutual justification see Rawls 1971; Rawls 1993; Scanlon 1998.
[34] Locke 1988, II.8, 9, 16; also I.130.
[35] See especially Tuck 1999.
[36] Waldron 2002, p. 169.
[37] See Locke 1997, pp. 268, 180; for more detail on how Lockean arguments were deployed against treaty-based relations in colonial America, see Tully 1993a, pp. 267–78; Armitage 2004b.

left unto God and themselves'.[38] He then goes on to provide a startling genealogy of the consequences of settlement, in which after a point when the settlers and inhabitants 'all joyn together and grow up into one Body of People', a magistrate 'becomes a Christian, and by that means their Party becomes the most powerful. Then immediately all Compacts are to be broken, all Civil Rights to be violated, that Idolatry may be extirpated ... And unless these innocent Pagans, strict Observers of the Rules of Equity and the Law of Nature ... forsake their ancient Religion, and embrace a new and strange one, they are to be turned out of the Lands and Possessions of their Forefathers, and perhaps deprived of Life'.[39] The dangers of using civil power to promote religious orthodoxy are the same 'both in America and Europe': how 'easily the pretence of Religion, and of the care of Souls, serves for a Cloak to Covetousness, Rapine and Ambition'.[40] There is a similar almost Rousseauian moment in the First *Treatise*. Following a sensationalist account of indigenous cannibalism taken from the *Commentarios Reales* of Garcilaso de la Vega, intended as part of a rebuttal of Filmer's assertions concerning natural paternal authority, he suggests that the 'Woods and Forests, where the irrational untaught Inhabitants keep right by following Nature, are fitter to give us Rules, than Cities and Palaces, where those that call themselves Civil and Rational, go out of their way, by the authority of Example'.[41] Locke is obviously concerned about the alliance between religious enthusiasm and temporal power, not only because magistrates are often incompetent when it comes to promoting true belief, but also tend to corruption.

Locke's argument for toleration is often said to rest mainly on his distinction between public and private, or at least between the domain of the magistrate and that of the church. But this distinction, central as it is to modern liberalism, is perhaps too blunt for making sense of Locke's own arguments. For one thing, Locke calls for the pursuit of religious freedom with 'charitable care'; 'every man has commission to admonish, exhort, convince another of error, and *by reasoning* draw him into truth' (my emphasis). He also insists that toleration entails a change in the behaviour of citizens and churches, as much as it does constraints on the magistrate. Thus it is not enough that 'Ecclesiastical men abstain from Violence and Rapine', but also 'admonish [their] Hearers of the Duties of Peace, and Good-will towards all men ... [they] ought industriously to exhort all men, whether private Persons or Magistrates to Charity, Meekness and Toleration . . . and diligently endeavour to allay and temper all that Heat, and unreasonable averseness of the mind, which either any mans fiery Zeal for his own Sect . . . has kindled against Dissenters'.[42] Locke is not merely drawing a distinction between public and private here, but also offering a possible mode of inter-action between different religious groups, one based on a form of public reasoning rather than force. In this sense his account of toleration is more 'political' than it is often given credit for, in the sense that Locke is here looking for a way of shaping disagreement rather than simply privatizing it.

But only just. For the main purpose of the *Letter* was to provide Locke's thoughts on the 'mutual Toleration of *Christians* in their different Professions of Religion'.[43] Atheists were clearly beyond the pale, since they could not be trusted to uphold the basic 'Bonds of Humane Society', given the crucial roles that contract and promise play in Locke's argument, and the deep theological structure underpinning it. The argument concerning toleration also clearly presupposes that the boundaries concerning the nature of *civil* interests are relatively fixed, and about which there is little scope for reasonable disagreement, although Locke's theory of resistance does mean the magistrate is subject to the countervailing threat of resistance if he is judged to have violated them (i.e. the 'life, liberty, health' and property of his subjects)[44] – the justification of which is ultimately up to the people to decide. So it goes without saying that *Locke's* argument for toleration is not addressed to the kind of pluralism we find in multicultural societies today – of life-styles, cultural and ethnic groups, religious sects, linguistic groups, migrants – however much a *Lockean* argument could be made that radically expanded freedom of conscience from religious matters to matters of public morality more generally.[45] And so although the basic premise of equality implicit in Locke's theory of religious toleration is indeed extended to indigenous peoples, it has limited political consequences. Their faith, or perhaps even the lack thereof, cannot be grounds for denying them their liberty. But their failure to put their lands under cultivation, and their lack of proper political institutions, mean that they lack both *imperium* and *dominium* over their traditional territories.

[42] Locke 1983, p. 34.    [43] Locke 1983, p. 23 (my emphasis).
[44] Locke 1983, p. 26.    [45] See for example Rawls 1993.

It is sometimes suggested that Locke's natural rights argument offers a powerful resource for indigenous peoples today, once we remove his prejudice against their land-holding practices and forms of civil government.[46] And so a rejection of Lockean arguments for denying indigenous peoples' land claims seems to yield a Lockean premise for recognizing them — namely, first occupancy. The indigeneity of first peoples — that they are 'tangata whenua', in the Maori phrase, 'people of the land' — is coupled with a principle of first occupancy that yields a claim for the restoration of their traditional lands, or significant compensation in lieu. Although Locke is talking about individual rights to property, presumably legitimate forms of collective property could be accounted for in the same fashion.

The problems with this approach, however, are considerable.[47] First of all, there are problems with the principle of first occupancy itself. Many of those who might support indigenous peoples' claims for land would probably not be happy with adopting an historical entitlement approach to property rights more generally, since it severely constrains the scope of distributive justice. Second, and more importantly, it is not clear the principle of first occupancy as it is elaborated by Locke — and by his latter-day followers[48] — sits easily with the political theories of indigenous peoples themselves, at least as I understand them. Although they have sought to use the common law to protect their property interests, it is not clear the dominant modes of occupancy and use therein best explain or help justify indigenous peoples' conceptions of property.[49] The natural rights approach essentially extends the conception of agency articulated by Grotius, Hobbes and Locke — one linked to the notion of sovereignty and a spatial metaphor of an inviolable sphere or boundary of non-interference — to the rights of indigenous peoples. It is not that indigenous peoples and their supporters do not often refer to the importance of prior occupancy for consideration of their claims; they do, and some version of it plays an important role in the contemporary jurisprudence of native title.[50] But it does not follow that Locke's account best captures the interests at stake. Also, it is one thing to explain ownership, but another to explain jurisdiction. Locke's argument struggles to explain the latter. And yet the wider and more important claim indigenous peoples are making refers to

---

[46] See Simmons 1995.     [47] Waldron 2003.     [48] Nozick 1974; Simmons 1992.
[49] But cf. Pocock 1992.     [50] See especially McNeil 1989.

self-government, and flowing from this to their standing in international custom and law. We need a more complex, multi-centred account of not only the history of international and constitutional law in these contexts, but of our regulative conceptions of political legitimacy too.

IV

What lessons then can be drawn from the connections between this Lockean language of rights, toleration and empire? What does this history of rights teach us about our theories of rights?

One of the most intriguing and potentially controversial claims made by proponents of the 'new history' of political thought emerging from the path-breaking studies of Quentin Skinner and others, was that a specific way of doing the history of political thought could contribute to addressing the paradoxes and antinomies thrown up in contemporary debates over the nature of rights and freedom.[51] For example, James Tully, in a review of Richard Tuck's *Natural Rights Theories* (1979), wrote that Tuck's history of natural rights offered a potential solution to a problem bedevilling contemporary debates about the nature of rights. The conclusion of Tuck's survey, Tully argued, was that the concept of a right is fundamentally ambiguous between different modes, and thus that various combinations thereof are possible in ways that many contemporary philosophers tend to rule out by conceptual fiat. Even more, Tully argued, 'once we know that a right can be used in such and such a way, the way out is to ask "*why* it is being used in such and such a way"' (quoting Tuck).[52] The answer will involve excavating a complex combination of the existing linguistic and normative resources available to the theorist, as well as the practical and political circumstances they find themselves in and responding to. The point is not that we should substitute history for theory, but that history provides a critical resource for surveying the uses of various concepts and theories over time, and especially the conflicts and choices that were made around the concepts and values we now take for granted.

One paradox subject to sustained scrutiny in recent years has been the idea of 'citizen's rights'. Some argue that the very idea is paradoxical, since the language of rights was articulated precisely in order to defend the moral claims of individuals *against* the positive order of the *civitas*. As Annabel Brett has summarized it, a 'negative locution' (rights) is used

---

[51] See Skinner 2002a.     [52] Tully 1981.

to fill out a 'positive concept of belonging' (citizenship), and the application of the former threatens to hollow out the latter.[53] Thus Brett interprets Locke as offering an 'essentialist notion of extra-civic humanity' with rights founded on the possession of reason, which put a 'natural limit on what kinds of political arrangements were legitimate'. Rights, according to this view, are mainly defensive and 'purely negative', dictating when a wrong is done but not any prescription for a 'moral life together with others in a society, nor any prescription concerning religion' except some kind of belief in God. Even his use of the republican language of liberty against arbitrary government or tyranny, Brett argues, 'amounts to little more than a common protection of individual private rights'.[54]

On the other hand, others have argued that Locke does, in fact, offer a potent combination of natural law and republican arguments – a ' "constitution-enforcing" conception of rights' – in which the people subject their rulers to the rule of law through the threat and practice of resistance.[55] According to this reading, rights can promote republican forms of civic liberty, however much they may be compatible with non-republican forms of government.[56] Liberty as non-interference may indeed remain the primary moral good of such a society, but the range of what counts as a constraint on a citizen's liberty is expanded to include living in a state of dependence upon others. And thus various forms of non-arbitrary 'interferences' – for example, to do with enforcing the rule of law, or ensuring people have the capacities to make effective choices and decisions about their ends – may be required, either from the state or other social and political actors.[57]

We have been examining yet another possible paradox in relation to Lockean rights, this time not only as a means of criticizing *imperium*, but also justifying it. Thus, Locke's influence on Thomas Jefferson's drafting of the *Declaration of Independence* extends not only to the language of natural rights, but also to the fact that the American indigenous peoples were denied 'the separate and equal station to which the Laws of Nature and of Nature's God entitle[d] them' claimed by the American 'people' against the *imperium* of the British Crown.[58]

---

[53] Brett 2003, p. 100.
[54] Brett 2003, pp. 110–11.
[55] Tully 1993a pp. 259–61; Skinner 1998, pp. 18–21, 55.
[56] Skinner 1998, p. 55, n. 177.
[57] Skinner 1998, pp. 84–5; Pettit 1997.
[58] From the first paragraph of the *Declaration*.

It seems clear then that in order to define the nature and scope of rights, claims have to be made about the nature of persons, and particularly about those qualities or powers to which the rights refer, or are intended to protect. This means drawing a distinction between those who are eligible for rights and those who are not, and between those who display and are capable of exercising the relevant powers and capacities and those who are not. Second, all theories about rights ultimately depend on claims about the wider purpose of rights and how they fit into more general conceptions of moral and political order and human sociability. In both instances, the filling out of claims about the subjective rights of persons against arbitrary treatment by the state (and their fellow citizens) provides ample room for the introduction of thicker constraints on who is eligible to claim certain rights, and ultimately, what kind of society the language and practice of rights is meant to promote and protect. As Sankar Muthu has put it (echoing Hannah Arendt), no sooner had the Inca or Iroquois been granted a minimal humanity, as against being classified as an Aristotelian natural slave, 'than the privileges and protections of such a classification were abrogated'.[59] The more natural and less cultured the account of human agency, the easier it was to depict their societies and *mores* as radically different and then as either uncivilized and requiring improvement, or debased and subject to punishment or control according to natural law.

Hence the apparent paradox of moral universalism: that is, how universalistic premises applied to politics (for example, that 'all Men by Nature are equal'),[60] can end up justifying particularistic and exclusive practices and institutions.[61] Thus, as Uday Mehta has put it, 'what is concealed behind the endorsement of these universal capacities are the specific cultural and psychological conditions woven in as preconditions for the actualization of these capacities', and that these can often be discriminatory against racial and cultural minorities, amongst others.[62] As we saw above, it was a basic tenet of early-modern natural jurisprudence that although the individual played a crucial role in the foundation of civil society, 'he' (again, usually always meant literally) was also under-developed outside of it. Humanization comes with appropriation, social interaction, norms and culture; the state of nature denotes precisely the absence of these conditions. The problem lies in what is

---

[59] Muthu 2003, p. 273.     [60] Locke 1988, II.4, II.116–19.     [61] Mehta 1997, p. 60.
[62] Mehta 1997, pp, 61–2; Arneil 1996, pp. 210–11.

said to count (or not) as an appropriate set of institutions and norms for a properly human life. Locke naturalized the relation between labour and property in such a way that it excluded other forms of use and occupation, and by implication, a more historicized approach to human culture. This converted cultural and societal differences into hierarchical differences, and opened up a gap between 'egalitarian interpersonal morality and inegalitarian political and international morality'.[63] A theory of human development over time need not include claims about the moral or cognitive superiority of the societies occupying one stage compared to another, as arguably Adam Smith's did not.[64] But by the end of the eighteenth century, and certainly by the nineteenth, it almost always did.

One thing that was occurring was the complicated unravelling of the law of nature from the law of nations, which is increasingly conceptualized as obligatory between *Christian* nations, and as the product of interaction between *states* (especially after the Treaties of Westphalia and the various responses to the French Revolution). This intermingling of the civilizational standard and positivism in international law arguably continues to shape our understanding of the universalizability of rights today.[65] First of all, once international law begins to be associated mainly with the reason of states, then non-state actors, such as indigenous peoples, have even less standing in the system than what little they had before. For example, between 1600–1800, literally hundreds of treaties were signed between various Aboriginal nations and British and French authorities. How these treaties are understood will depend importantly on the political and legal authorities considered relevant. Are they international treaties between equal sovereign entities? Or are they a species of domestic contract or statute imposed by a legitimate political authority on its citizens?[66] However much middle ground may have been carved out between indigenous nations and European powers on the ground in various parts of North America between 1600 and 1800, it was clear that by the nineteenth century it was rapidly disappearing, and the residual sovereignty of Aboriginal peoples was either flatly denied, ignored, or subsumed under 'domestic dependent' status. This meant that it was hard to see (public) international law as anything but the

---

[63] Parekh 1995, p. 92.
[64] See the excellent discussion in Pitts 2005, ch. 2; and Haakonssen 1981, ch. 7.
[65] Gong 1984; Keene 2002; Anghie 2004.
[66] Slattery 1991, p. 684; Williams 1997.

law of a broad but still culturally specific civilization, as opposed to an emergent set of genuinely global — or at least cross-cultural — public norms.

This blurring between nature and culture in rights discourse is perhaps best exemplified by the *Déclaration des droits de l'homme*, which also returns us to the paradox of 'citizen's rights'; that is, the welding together of a negative locution with a positive conception of belonging.[67] The 'rights of man' still *sound* like natural rights — 'natural inalienable and sacred to man' — and yet they are declared in the name of a sovereign people, 'constituted in a national assembly'. Moreover the most basic rights are civil and political rights and, as Anthony Pagden points out, seem to 'derive from the status of their holders as citizens ... and can only have any meaning, within the context not merely of civil society but of a society constituted as a nation'.[68] They could only be made intelligible in the terms of a specific political order, and thus were 'increasingly useless as a notion in international or intercultural relations'.[69] The conclusion to be drawn from this, argues Pagden (echoing many others) is clear: what we think of today as the international law of human rights, are 'cultural artefacts masquerading as universal, immutable values'. It follows that if 'we wish to assert any belief in the universal we have to begin by declaring our willingness to assume, and to defend, at least some of the values of a highly specific way of life' — basically, those found in a liberal democratic state.[70] Thus, for example, Pagden argues, 'a liberal democratic Islamic state is an oxymoron', and the changes required to enable the kinds of freedoms associated with the international law of human rights 'can only come about from outside Islam'.[71]

I hope (and think) Pagden is wrong about this *particular* case, but he is raising an important point. Our modern conception of human rights, embodied in documents such as the *Universal Declaration of Human Rights* that emerged in the aftermath of the Second World War, are often said to be the modern analogue of early-modern natural rights. But the analogy is imprecise at best, deeply misleading at worst. For one thing, modern human rights presuppose a whole range of modern social and political institutions, and have been shaped by an emerging set of global political structures and dangers since 1945. Taken as a

---

[67] Scott 1996; Pagden 2003.      [68] Pagden 2003, p. 189.
[69] Pagden 2003, p. 190.      [70] Pagden 2003, pp. 172–3.
[71] Pagden 2003, p. 199.

whole, they also aspire to do much more than secure the bare liberty and security of the person, and look much broader and richer than the Grotian framework we examined above.

For some, the mere fact that our conception of the international law of human rights originated in a distinctive cultural context and ethical tradition is enough to suggest that its accessibility and acceptability to those embracing other comprehensive ethical traditions will be severely limited. And it is a familiar charge today that the discourse of human rights, when conjoined to a justification of armed intervention or pre emptive war — a prominent feature of early-modern natural law dis-course that is once again prominent in an age of the 'war on terror' — is simply an extension of the imperial 'standard of civilization' in a new guise. An even sharper version of this critique is a variation on Marx's argument against liberal rights in 'On the Jewish Question': human rights were born not only in the aftermath of World War II, but also in light of the globalization of neo-liberal economic institutions. This explains, so this argument goes, the emphasis in extant international law and practice on political and civil rights over social and economic equality. The broader point is that human rights are entwined with the very relations of power against which they are supposed to provide critical leverage.

These are powerful criticisms. But they are ultimately too reductive and posit, I think, a far too simplistic picture of the relation between the practice of human rights as it is developing amid social and cultural pluralism, as well as in relation to concerns about global poverty and economic inequality. The criticisms lead in two broad directions. First, they might entail simply rejecting human rights in general as a vacuous form of moral theorizing, and limit appeals to rights to those which are embedded in a legally enforceable framework.[72] But this under-estimates the aspirational and imaginative appeal of human rights claims. Rights are valuable sometimes just because they are unenforceable by ordinary legal and political means, as a way of drawing attention to the purported unacceptability of those circumstances. Moreover, although plagued by the self-important rhetoric of human rights lawyers and activists who assume international law exists just because they say so, the demand for human rights has emerged in part because of the kinds of social, political and economic challenges people actually face in the world today — whether in the north, south, east or west. So another

---

[72] See Geuss 2001, pp. 138–52; James 2003b.

direction this critical approach might lead us is to try and craft a practice
of human rights that takes cultural and ethical differences seriously, and
that is sensitive to the history of imperial expansion and intervention
(both in the distant and more recent past) that shapes the beliefs and
attitudes of so many people in the world today. One way to do so is to
take the value of toleration seriously as a principle of international law
and governance. But this only serves to dramatize what is a fundamental
tension when thinking about the foundations of international law
today; between a principled respect for, and recognition of, the collective
agency or self-determination of peoples and states and individual human
rights. This is partly because this tension is written into the various
international Treaties, Declarations and norms that make up the complex
of modern human rights instruments today (e.g. Article 1 of the *UN
Charter*; and Article 27 of the *Optional Protocol of the Convention on
International Civil and Political Rights*). These treaties and norms emerged
out of inter-*state* negotiations, after all. But the issues at stake are
fundamentally normative as well. How can a principle of toleration be
reconciled with a commitment to human rights? How can we both accept
the idea of the existence of a global basic structure that suggests the need
for some form of transnational distributive justice, and yet recognize
the equality and value of the collective agency of states and peoples?

An influential strand of recent work on global justice denies that
there is any such tension, since the moral significance of states or peoples
is entirely derivative from their contribution to achieving justice.[73]
Although the details of the theory of justice to which these arguments
appeal vary, they all place a significant emphasis on individual autonomy.
Thus self-determination and the right to non-intervention are owed
to states or peoples only on the grounds that observing them contributes
to the realization of individual autonomy. It might be that there are
pragmatic or prudential reasons to adhere loosely to principles of non-
intervention and self-determination, but not any principled ones. The
best understanding of our commitment to human rights dissolves any
principled tension between toleration and human rights. When states
violate justice, toleration must yield to remediation and rectification.

The danger of this approach — admittedly, for some, its primary
virtue — is that it insists there is basically no difference between
the standards of transnational justice and a liberal theory of justice.

---

[73] See Beitz 1979; Caney 2005. Cf. Buchanan 2004.

It presupposes that such an account can be given that is sufficiently determinate for international society, and that the best conception of human rights will feature as an important component of such a theory. However, a theory of rights cannot just ignore social and cultural difference, as if it were a regrettable feature of the world, but has to try and make sense of it and tell us something about how we should relate to each other given this diversity.[74] The point is not then that toleration itself is a foundational value for the justification of human rights, but that it is an appropriate response to the diversity of views about the good and the right that characterize both domestic and international political life. The basic thought is this: as the scope of our moral principles grows, so should our sense of the boundaries of reasonable disagreement, and the need to create institutions and practices within which it can be played out peacefully and without false expectations or impositions of consensus.

It is for something like these reasons, I think, that John Rawls and others have argued recently for a very different approach to justifying human rights as a way of thinking about the moral foundations of international law. And it has a Grotian ring to it. This approach involves appealing to a form of *moral* or *justificatory* minimalism; that human rights be justified in such a way that they can be acceptable to those within very different ethical traditions, including societies which have suffered domination in the past by those states most vocal in promoting human rights today. It is important to distinguish *justificatory* minimalism from what we might call *empirical* minimalism. The latter entails that human rights be grounded at the intersection between various actual religious and ethical traditions, as a kind of lowest common moral denominator between them. Although this might yield important constraints to do with prohibitions on torture or genocide, for example, it generates a far smaller set of basic rights than is assumed in current international practice. Actual agreement is far too strong a condition to impose on the justification of critical standards; it ties them too closely to those existing moralities, whatever their particular content, and presupposes they remain relatively static and immune to internal and external challenge and disruption.[75]

So justificatory minimalism need not imply minimalism about the *content* of human rights. It entails, roughly speaking, that the grounds

---

[74] Rawls 1993; Jones 2001.
[75] Beitz 2001, pp. 273–4; Cohen 2004, p. 200.

for human rights can be found not in a particular doctrine of individual autonomy or Lockean natural law, but in terms that are accessible from within the vantage points of various different moral and religious traditions. But at the same time, that the language of human rights discourse can help shape these local traditions and practices too, faced as they are with the challenges of the global political structure. To justify human rights in this sense is to accept that it is a *constructive* task; of constructing, in Joshua Cohen's helpful phrase, a 'shared terrain of argument' (and obligation) between different moral traditions and societies about the kind of standards suitable for holding political societies to account for their treatment of individuals and groups.[76] In fact, for these reasons talk of minimalism is misleading. We should aim for a common standard, not a minimal one.

What does this mean? 'Common' falls somewhere between comprehensive and minimalist and implies the ongoing activity of constructing a common point of view, not simply positing one. All rights regimes are culturally mediated in various ways. They rest on a structure of moral beliefs about the urgency or appropriateness of the interest in question to receive the institutional and political attention sought by identifying it as a 'right' in the first place. And so we need to explore much more carefully the dynamic relation between rights and social and cultural norms; the way rights not only reshape local norms and practices, but also how these in turn (for better or worse) shape the language of rights. Why is this important? If we want rights to be effectively enforceable claims — 'real freedoms', in other words — then we require effective institutions that can allocate and enforce the rights we care about. And we need people with the appropriate dispositions, attitudes, knowledge and resources to be able to make claims in the first place, and respond appropriately to those made by others.[77] We tend to associate these conditions above all with the well-defined authority and political and legal order of a state. And this is one reason why the state is far from dead, despite the claims of globalization enthusiasts. But it is also the case that the conditions required for realizing the effective enforceability of the most urgent interests of many people in the world today — including those basic civil, political and economic interests often associated with citizen's rights — will require collective action and institution-building across borders as much as within them.

[76] Cohen 2004, p. 195.      [77] James 2003b.

And the struggle to articulate the moral grounds of modern human rights, as well as to question the adequacy of existing human rights instruments and institutions is part of the process of trying to realize these conditions.

Michael Ignatieff has referred to arguments over human rights in these contexts as involving the construction of a kind of 'hybridized moral vernacular', not necessarily cut loose from liberalism, but not as dependent on it in the way critics suppose. He seems to mean this is a descriptive claim, which may well be overly optimistic. But I think it offers a potential normative vision too, and one that is well worth trying to spell out in greater detail.[78] Studying the development of the language of subjective rights in tandem with changing conceptions of the justification of empire between 1600 and 1800 helps us see the cluster of assumptions that surround rights claims; theories of rights always exist within broader discourses of state-formation, citizenship and international order. Taking the history of rights seriously helps us see both the possibilities — and crucially the constraints — this language offers us today, as we try to make sense of and respond to new conjunctions between rights and *imperium*.[79]

---

[78] Ignatieff 1999; Ivison 2006.

[79] I am grateful for the comments and advice I received from the participants in the Folger conference, and especially to David Armitage, Nicholas Canny, Kirstie McClure, Karen O'Brien, John Pocock and Quentin Skinner.

# CHAPTER 11

# Reading the Private in Margaret Cavendish: Conversations in Political Thought

## Joanne H. Wright

In a recent essay on women writers and the early-modern British political tradition, Hilda Smith identifies the 'perpetual state of schizophrenia' that arises from working at the intersection of women's intellectual history and British political thought in the early-modern era.[1] There is little agreement between these fields of inquiry on approaches, significant texts or accepted interpretations. Emblematic of this scholarly schizophrenia is the literature surrounding the dichotomy of public and private and its proper use and interpretation. If we are to achieve some synthesis of this disparate literature toward a more nuanced understanding of public and private, we need to generate further conversation among feminist political theorists, historians of political thought and gender historians.

The meanings of public and private — including their gendered character — are contested in at least three scholarly conversations about early-modern Britain. First, beginning in the 1970s, feminist political theorists drew attention to the gendered power relations inscribed on the traditional division between the two spheres. Second, historians of social and political thought have examined male early-modern theorists and their ideas of the private in context and primarily in connection to politics, religion and economic relations. And third, early-modern gender historians have enhanced and refined our perspectives on the fluidity of public and private life for women and men in this period. Within these three literatures, there has not been, however, sustained investigation of how the private might look different, and be experienced differently, from the perspective of women thinkers. This chapter will illustrate how such an investigation might be more broadly conducted by examining the reflections on the private offered by Margaret Cavendish, Duchess of Newcastle.

---

[1] Smith 1998b, p. 1.

In several of her works, Margaret Cavendish reveals her perception of the potentially dichotomous nature of the private realm for seventeenth-century women. Perhaps most striking are her reflections in the drama, *The Convent of Pleasure* (1668). For the female protagonists of the play who have chosen to establish a life of communal retirement in the company of women only, the retreat into the private affords them the pleasure of freely cultivating their minds in the absence of marital and societal pressures. This choice is framed by the entirely negative experiences of marriage and male companionship, which, for these particular women, are associated with violence, infidelity and relentless breeding. While *The Convent of Pleasure* invites many readings, and goes some measure to re-establish the validity of heterosexual marriage at its conclusion, the premise of the play rests on the contention that domesticity brings such misery to women that they must construct an alternative to free themselves from its most pernicious aspects.[2]

Although Margaret Cavendish did not publish a systematic analysis of politics — the political treatise being a genre that she considered inappropriate for women writers — she was nonetheless a political thinker and an acute observer of social and political life. Evidence of her critical eye for power relations in early-modern society is woven throughout her literary and dramatic works as well as her orations and letters. Taken together, these diverse published works are no less apt an arena for investigation of political ideas as they formed part of a broader public discourse — an 'inter-generic conversation', as Karen O'Brien describes it — in which political questions were 'meaningfully contested'.[3] In particular, Cavendish's writings offer us a view of the private that is distinct from that of male political theorists as well as that of the domestic advice manuals of the seventeenth century. Indeed, in Cavendish's many published writings we see a persistent and incisive critique of oppressive private relations and their effects upon women. Yet Cavendish's powerful analysis of the darker side of the private is counter-balanced by her frequent assertions of the virtue of a carefully constructed, closeted, intellectual life for women. Through her defence of a retired life, Cavendish actively and publicly constructs an alternative meaning of the

---

[2] What Cavendish intended in the conclusion of the play has been thrown into question by the discovery of an inserted note by her in some of the existing versions informing readers that the play's final two scenes were 'Written by my Lord Duke'. For a synopsis of interpretation, see Wood 2004, pp. 435–7.

[3] O'Brien, in this volume, p. 168.

private and its potential benefits for women. In this reading of Cavendish, I suggest that it is her understanding of the dichotomous character of the private realm — its dangers and its possibilities — that is politically (and epistemologically) significant.

The origins and popularity of the feminist analysis of public and private relations in Western public discourse are inseparable from the politics of the Second Wave feminist movement itself. In its earliest writings in the 1960s and '70s, the Women's Liberation Movement in North America declared that 'the personal is political', thus politiciz-ing formerly private relations and exposing their injustices to public scrutiny. The development of the analysis of public and private was connected to the radical feminist practice of consciousness-raising, wherein women began to connect their own private experiences of subordination with those of other women. As Redstocking Carol Hanisch argued, consciousness-raising was not a form of group therapy meant to make women feel better about their circumstances: 'One of the first things we discover in these groups is that personal problems are political problems. There are no personal solutions at this time. There are only collective solutions'.[4] Indeed, consciousness-raising politicized women into feminists, causing them both to interrogate private relations and to organize to disrupt long-standing and unjustified male privilege in the intimate sphere.

Influenced by the attention to public and private within the Second Wave Women's Liberation Movement, early feminist political theorists made the gendered division between the two realms the subject of academic study. For example, in her influential *Public Man/Private Woman* (1981), Jean Bethke Elshtain sought to enhance the debate, to elevate its theoretical and historical sophistication by using the dis-course of public and private 'as a conceptual prism through which to see the story of women and politics from Plato to the present'.[5] Elshtain understood public and private as conceptual categories that have been deployed 'in some form' by most thinkers; as deeply-felt imperatives, 'public and private ordered and structured diverse activities, purposes, and dimensions of human social life and thinking about that life'.[6]

---

[4] Hanisch 2000, p. 85.      [5] Elshtain 1993, p. xv.

[6] Elshtain 1993, p. 9. Elshtain explains that she tried to think '"really honestly" from the vantage point of a political theorist who has been influenced, for over fifteen years, by her involve-ment with the feminist movement'. The result, she warned, is that *'Public Man/Private Woman* is a nasty book' (p. xi).

Public and private were, in fact, so deeply rooted, and so fundamental to Western societal organization, in Elshtain's view, the point was not to eradicate the distinction but to address its gendered dimensions.

Also seizing upon the political moment of the Second Wave, Carole Pateman's *The Sexual Contract* (1988) took aim at the ideological association of women with the private realm of naturalized subordination. For Pateman, men in liberal societies had been able to construct themselves as individuals and citizens to the extent that they could shed their association with private, familial work and obligations, a fact that creates serious problems, in her view, for admitting women into full liberal citizenship in any straightforward way.[7] Pateman drew attention for the first time to the fact that, in accounting for the birth of the public realm, the early-modern social contract had missed half the story. The social contract had nothing whatsoever to say about the origins of the private realm or how the relationships within it came into being. And for their part, contemporary political theorists had done little to shed light on this question. Rather they continued to treat public and private as divisions '*within* civil society itself, within the world of men'. The debate about public and private in political theory, she argues, had often been wrongly cast in terms of a bifurcation of ' "society" and "state", or "economy" and "politics", or "freedom" and "coercion" or "social" and "political" ', thereby completely eliding the other, shadowy private sphere on which the public sphere rests.[8]

Spawned by the politics of the Second Wave, then, feminist political theory developed critical insight into the gendered discourse(s) of public and private. Of course, as Elshtain and Pateman, among others, make clear, the relationship between public and private has a long history in Western culture, dating as far back as ancient Greece and the writings of Plato and Aristotle. However, what is distinctive about the feminist approach is that it exposed the power relations *within* the private realm, treated them as politically significant, and integrated them into the larger story about the public. Moreover, feminist theorists argued that an analysis of the division between public and private was necessary because the process of articulating the line between the two was essential to a thinker's conception of what was properly considered political. No picture of women's (or men's) relationship to the state — or to citizenship — could be complete without it.

---

[7] Pateman 1988. See also Brennan and Pateman 1979.
[8] Pateman 1989, p. 122.

While the early analyses developed in Second Wave feminist political
thought are still recognized as groundbreaking, Joan Landes points out
that 'feminists are no longer united in their evaluation of the public/
private split, or in their approach to its study'.[9] While the critiques of
public/private analysis are multifarious, my concerns with its efficacy as
a conceptual tool are historical. In my own analysis of Hobbes, for
example, I have identified the problems that arise in Pateman's straightforward imposition of the idea of a masculine public sphere and
a feminine private one onto early-modern England.[10] Although Hobbes
(along with his contemporaries) certainly used gender to think about
politics, at this point the private realm was not womanly in the way that
it came to be for later social contract thinkers such as Rousseau. While
rightly focused on the *politics* of public and private, early feminist analysis
may not have been as attentive to differences in historical contexts as it
could have been.

A departure from the early analysis of public and private is particularly
evident within the field of women's or gender history. In that field,
attempts to understand public and private as divisions between the worlds
of men and women — the 'separate spheres' analysis — has given way to
a general dismissal of the utility of the terms altogether. For women's
historians, looking at women's experiences through the lens of public
and private imperatives — in the way that Elshtain suggests — has the
effect of keeping our inquiry purely at the level of ideology, accepting
a view of the past that is constructed, for example, through the works
of political thinkers and the domestic advice literature. As Laura Gowing
points out, '[t]he gulf between prescriptions for the ideal household
and everyday life for men, women, children, and servants was manifestly
wide'. Moreover, she states,

Despite the precepts of advice literature, in the early-modern world masculinity
and femininity were not equatable with publicity and privacy; nor was the
household a private sphere. The domestic world had a well-established correla-
tion with the public and the political; disordered households had implications
for the moral order of society.[11]

In short, the social history of early-modern England consistently undermines the descriptive veracity of separate spheres for men and women,
and reveals the family as 'a structure deeply implicated within the social
order'.[12]

[9] Landes 1998, p. 16.    [10] See Wright 2004.
[11] Gowing 1998, p. 269.    [12] Hinds 1996, p. 105.

Women's historians caution as well that we need to be mindful of how to interpret strong gender imperatives in prescriptive literature. A public focus on proper roles for women in the private realm may indicate women's *expanding* roles outside the domestic sphere and men's desire to limit them.[13] For Amanda Vickery, rejection of separate spheres analysis is connected to the need to avoid pervasive generalizations about women's diminished public status in the nineteenth century. A separate spheres analysis falls short, in her view, in its ability to represent the complexity of gender relations; even within the context of the private, it 'fails to capture the texture of female subordination and the complex interplay of emotion and power in family life'.[14] Gowing and Vickery, among many others, highlight the conceptual and theoretical difficulties with a straightforward mapping of public and private onto separate spheres, and the historical problems that arise from assuming *a priori* the power of public and private discourse to determine the fate of women's lives within a given historical context. Since thinking in terms of separate spheres has little descriptive value, it seems futile to continue to allow this approach to govern our thinking about women's past.

The rejoinder to be appropriately historically sensitive in our analyses of public and private in the early-modern era might also be extrapolated from conversations in the history of political thought. Unlike women's historians, historians of political thought have not engaged in an explicit critique of the public/private analysis developed in feminist political theory. Nevertheless, the imperative within historical readings of political thought to avoid imposing contemporary concerns onto the past could be instructive in this conversation. Historians of political thought guide their inquiry with vigilance to prevent the reading of history backward. For example, in his study of the Medieval roots of the concepts of consent and coercion, Arthur Monahan urges caution 'against reading material through modern lenses.' The concepts into which he is inquiring, he explains, 'usually have a different, less specific, meaning for thinkers in the Middle Ages than in contemporary thought'.[15] In other words, past and present terms might look the same, but their present meanings cannot simply be grafted onto the past. Gender historians and historians of political thought agree that we should recognize differences in the historical contexts in which terms such as public and private are employed.

---

[13] Vickery 1993, p. 400.    [14] Vickery 1993, p. 401.    [15] Monahan 1987, pp. xvii–xviii.

The question at this point becomes, can we continue to talk in terms of public and private at all? Does the use of this terminology necessarily indicate that we are in fact reading history backward? Although feminists no longer agree in principle on how or if public and private should be used, Landes argues that there is little use in exaggerating the differences between feminist positions, for that would 'risk freezing, or perhaps "essentializing" the positions within feminist theory that have generated an ongoing conversation about the contours of public and private life'.[16] Nevertheless, since my purpose is to stimulate further conversation among these fields of inquiry, it is necessary to point to areas where women's historians, feminist political theorists and indeed historians of political thought could mutually benefit from more cross-pollination. Recognizing the problems associated with public and private thinking, and building upon the insights gleaned so far, might it yet be possible to bring these 'evanescent notions ... down to earth', to anchor them 'in the particularities of history and the specificities of theory'?[17]

I suggest that, as important as the historical corrective is, something vital is lost to our analysis of the political when we move away from the terms public and private altogether. Recognizing that the construction of public and private is complex and interwoven with other discourses, that their meanings are essentially contested, and that the lines between the two are blurry and often permeable, we need further inquiry into these terms, more nuanced and historically-sensitive inquiry, not less of it. Political theorists cannot simply abstain from the use of these terms, however unsatisfactory they might be, precisely because they are part of our inherited discourse; the negotiation of the boundary between the two has involved 'profoundly political struggles'.[18] Within feminist political theory, public and private were not used merely to describe men's and women's locations in a given historical context. Far more than simple descriptors, public and private are understood to be important ideological constructs in the early-modern period, which have a powerful influence on historical actors above and beyond what the advice literature dictates. There is no denying that the analysis of public and private developed within feminist political theory emerged from the specific historical circumstances of the Second Wave. Still, these questions are not brand new: they have been asked in other ways and in other contexts. The benefit of the Second Wave analysis is that it has the effect of opening our

[16] Landes 1998, p. 16.    [17] Elshtain 1993, p. 4.
[18] Ackelsberg and Shanley 1996, p. 217.

eyes to the politics of public and private that may have been identified by historical women – and more importantly in this context, women thinkers – but to which we have been inattentive.[19] Reading history forward means making no assumptions; rather, it requires that we investigate *whether* these terms were meaningful to seventeenth-century women such as Margaret Cavendish, and if so, pursuing further inquiry as to *what* the terms meant to them.

## CAVENDISH'S 'GRAVE OF LOVE'

Perhaps the most compelling reason to retain the language of public and private in our analyses of early-modern England is that the terms were used frequently by, and had meaning for, Cavendish and her contemporaries.[20] A brief look at Cavendish's *The Life of the Thrice Noble ... William Cavendishe* illustrates the regularity with which she uses the discourse of public and private to describe the nature of their affairs. For example, she frequently refers to the Duke's personal, economic matters (the 'prudent mannage of his private and domestick affairs'; and 'his private affairs [which] he orders without any noise or trouble') in contrast to his public service to the commonwealth (he 'never ventures upon either publick or private business, beyond his strength'). And, in keeping with another common usage of private, to denote something secret, something that ought not to be revealed, Cavendish 'cannot forbear to mention' the advice book written by Newcastle to King Charles II, but explains that, 'it being a private offer to his sacred Majesty, I dare not presume to publish it'.[21] In *Orations of Divers Sorts*, she uses public and private to demarcate acceptable religious practice; debating the issue of conscience and the religious sects, she queries, if they 'disturb not the public weal, why should you disturb their private devotions?'[22] For Cavendish, the discourse of public and private was both a meaningful and useful one, accounting for differences in the sorts of business being attended to.

Cavendish also uses the terms to refer to spatial locations, which are implicitly gendered. She deplores those who, in the future, will attempt

---

[19] I am thankful to Gordon Schochet for sharing his thoughts on method in the history of political thought, especially as found in Schochet 1999.
[20] The range of meanings of private and privacy in early-modern England is discussed in Huebert 1997.
[21] Cavendish 1916a, pp. 128–9.    [22] Cavendish 2003, p. 168.

to tarnish the Duke's 'heroick actions, as well as they do mine, though yours have been of war and fighting, mine of contemplating and writing: yours were performed publickly in the field, mine privately in my closet: yours had many thousand eye-witnesses, mine none but my waiting-maids'.[23] Cavendish's apparently benign distinction here between the Duke's public contributions as against her private ones belies her darker view of the private for women. Ronald Huebert argues that women and men experienced the private differently:

... private life in the early-modern period, however companionate, was at all times inflected by the semiology of male privilege. In a world where one gender was expected to govern and the other expected to obey, it could not have been otherwise.[24]

Patriarchal authority in the family and within the private context of the domestic realm was a widely-recognized social fact in seventeenth-century England. There was virtually no thought that marriage might function democratically, as all relationships were assumed to require a hierarchy of power to work properly.[25] Cavendish determines that, as far as the judiciary was concerned, relations between husbands and wives were indeed private, and the 'prerogative of a husband' to rule the wife — being analogous to that of master over servant and parent over child — was grounded in 'Nature, God, and morality'.[26] Of course, in practical terms, marriages varied tremendously, then as now. Sara Mendelson and Patricia Crawford identify 'an affectionate but hierarchical relationship' as 'the dominant ideal',[27] and indeed, this may have even been the norm. However, Cavendish's writings bring the power relations of the private realm into sharper focus, revealing that women's experiences of subjection had the potential to be much harsher.

In contrast to the advice literature, which encouraged women's acceptance of their place in the marital hierarchy, and to the justifications for masculine authority found among early-modern political theorists, Cavendish's depiction of marriage is stark and unsentimental. In *The Convent of Pleasure*, a series of vignettes that form a play-within-a-play

---

[23] Cavendish 1916a, pp. 7–8.    [24] Huebert 2001, p. 63.
[25] Sommerville 1995, pp. 84–7.    [26] Cavendish 2003, 'Oration 49', pp. 178–80.
[27] Of course, the data for what plebeian wives expected and derived from marriage is much scarcer than for women of Cavendish's social class. See Mendelson and Crawford 1998, p. 132.

reveals a group of 'gossiping women' whose conversations detail a litany of abuses experienced by women in marriage: physical violence, husbands who gamble all their money away, the taking of whores and mistresses, the expectation of relentless breeding, the threat of infant and maternal mortality, to name a few. Upon being told that a neighbour's husband has run off with another woman, one woman responds,

> I would to Heaven my Husband would run away with Goody *Shred* the Botcher's Wife, for he lies all day drinking in an Alehouse, like a drunken Rogue as he is, and when he comes home, he beats me all black and blew, when I and my Children are almost starved for want.[28]

Through their shared stories about marriage and childbirth, the female characters undermine the dominant narrative of their natural subjection within marriage, and lay the foundation for choosing a communal life of retired contemplation.

In *The Convent of Pleasure*, Cavendish gathers and synthesizes the common knowledge, or folk wisdom, about women's marital experiences and develops it into an incisive analysis of power relations within the private realm. Although Cavendish is critical of women's gossip else-where, especially in her *Sociable Letters*,[29] she casts these vignettes, not as trivial or malicious, but as an important – yet insufficiently recognized – site of knowledge production. This is not the university or the Royal Society, but the knowledge acquired here is not available anywhere else; moreover, it makes sense of women's experiences, both public and private, in a way that other, more publicly-validated institutional knowl-edge cannot.[30] That Cavendish explores the theme of women's oppres-sion within marriage in a dramatic medium allows her to give these ideas, in Jean Howard's terms, an 'embodied representation':[31] rather than having their stories described, the characters within the vignettes

---

[28] Cavendish 2000, p. 112. The vignettes are found in Act II, Scenes II–IX, with Scene X being a declaration of the curse of marriage and the decision to enter a life of retirement.

[29] Cavendish 2004, 'Letters 91, 103', pp. 143–4, 157–8.

[30] My discussion of the epistemological significance of gossip and women's talk is informed by Code 1995; and Dalmiya and Alcoff 1993.

[31] Howard, in this volume, p. 143. Cavendish's dramas were never performed publicly, yet Straznicky 2004 problematizes the traditional categorization of plays according to audience, with some plays intended for commercial performance and others written as closet dramas. The division between the two does not take account of household performances of plays, which, although not fully public, were also not completely private either. She argues that the closure of theatres to public performance during Cavendish's writing career blurred the distinction between commercial and closet drama and had the effect of politically charging private readings of plays.

give voice to their own experiences. In viewing this series of female conversations, the audience-within-the-play is led to a truth about the oppressive aspects of marriage and motherhood for women that confirms their commitment to remain 'incloystered'. The one opinion in exception to this, and the only defence of marriage found in *The Convent of Pleasure*, is offered immediately after the vignettes by the Princess, a character whom we discover at the end of the play is actually a man. While Cavendish rarely places herself 'among the women' — most often she seems anxious to distance herself from them, especially those of her own class and status — in *The Convent of Pleasure* she makes it clear that it is from women's talk and from women's experiences that her knowledge of the perils of the private is derived. And this is indeed why the private looks different from Cavendish's purview.

Even as an economically and socially privileged woman, Cavendish was not herself immune to the potential hazards of a disastrous marriage.[32] In a patriarchal society before the advent of divorce, marriage was essentially all-determining for women: one might be 'lucky' or not. Indeed, women understood that marriage would be life-altering for them, 'a violent discontinuity' from their former, single state.[33] As Sara Mendelson and Patricia Crawford note, 'marriage was experienced in bodily as well as social terms', since men expected sexual access to their wives and could subject them to physical 'correction' if they saw fit.[34] Physical violence by men against their wives was socially acceptable as long as it was within moderation, and in fact such violence was thought necessary to the proper maintenance of order in early-modern households.[35] It was generally assumed that 'a man could do what he liked inside his own home, that his wife was his sexual and physical property'.[36] Except in extreme cases, death was the only end to a marriage: 'there can be no Honourable Divorce but by Death, for all other Divorces are Marked with some Disgrace'.[37] In her judicial oration on domestic violence,

---

[32] Disrupting the dominant romantic view of intellectual harmony in the Cavendish marriage, Smith 1997a draws attention to several divisive issues, including William's infidelities and financial difficulties, the tensions between his children and their stepmother, and perhaps most importantly, her inability to produce further heirs. On the latter point, see Cavendish 1916a, p. 63; Turberville 1938.

[33] Mendelson and Crawford 1998, p. 129.      [34] Mendelson and Crawford 1998, p. 126.

[35] See Fletcher 1995, pp. 192–7; and Sommerville 1995, p. 93.

[36] Fletcher 1995, p. 196.      [37] Cavendish 2004, 'Letter 201', p. 273.

Cavendish describes the plight of a wife who makes a case for divorce on the grounds that her husband 'not only beat her often, but so grievously and sorely as she is weary of her life'. The defendant justifies his actions accordingly:

a wife is bound to leave her parents, country, and what else soever, to go with her husband wheresoever he goes and will have her go with him, were it on the dangerous seas, or into barren deserts, or perpetual banishments, or bloody wars, besides child-birth; all which is more dangerous and painful than blows . . .[38]

As the head of the household, his authority over his wife, servants and children is, for all intents and purposes, beyond question.

Against the backdrop of the social acceptability, normality, and effective legal sanction of physical coercion of wives within marriage, William Cavendish's promise to Margaret that, as a husband thirty years her senior, he would not have the same inclination to dominate her that a younger spouse might, takes on heightened meaning. In fact, as much as Cavendish portrays her own marriage as nothing short of idyllic, in regards her impending union with William Cavendish she states, 'I did dread marriage'.[39] It was not that Cavendish thought all husbands necessarily bad and violent,[40] but that one never knew which way it might go. Her critique of the potentially tyrannical power of husbands comprises a persistent theme throughout Cavendish's works, but it is nowhere more evident than in her funeral orations: 'death is the far happier condition than marriage; and although marriage at first is pleasing, yet after a time it is displeasing, like meat which is sweet in the mouth but proves bitter in the stomach'.[41] Similarly, about a recently deceased virgin, Cavendish remarks,

'tis true, her husband, Death, is a cold bedfellow, but yet he makes a good husband, for he will never cross, oppose, nor anger her, nor give her cause of grief or sorrow, neither in his rude behaviour, inconstant appetite, nor lewd life . . . for there is no whoring, gaming, drinking, quarrelling, nor prodigal spending in the grave.[42]

---

[38] Cavendish 2003, 'Oration 49', p. 179. For similar historical accounts, see Crawford and Gowing 2000, ch. 6.
[39] Cavendish 1916b, p. 195.
[40] Although her statement that 'where One Husband proves Good, as Loving and Prudent, a Thousand prove Bad . . . ' does beg the question. See Cavendish 2004, 'Letter 93', p. 146.
[41] Cavendish 2003, 'Oration 100', p. 219.     [42] Cavendish 2003, 'Oration 99', p. 218.

In her own distinctive language and tone, and in a manner unparalleled in seventeenth-century discourse, Cavendish exposes and lays bare the power relations within marriage.

Her scrutiny of traditional female roles is not limited to marriage, however; it extends to pregnancy, childbirth and childrearing. Disliking the whole culture of breeding, Cavendish chastises pregnant women for their pride and self-indulgence, for revelling in, and exaggerating the effects of, their condition.[43] In *The Convent of Pleasure*, bearing children causes women nothing but pain and sorrow, for even if both mother and child survive, children grow up to be ungrateful. Connecting the experience of childbirth to the larger injustices against women, 'A Child-bed Womans Funeral Oration' celebrates the deceased's happiness 'in that she lives not to endure more pain or slavery', for women 'endure more than men', and they 'increase life when men for the most part destroy life'.[44] Perhaps owing to her own experience, Cavendish reserves particular ire for the societal expectation that second wives produce more heirs for husbands who already have sons. While their widower-husbands are motivated by the desire to perpetuate their family name, 'a Woman hath no such Reason to desire Children for her Own Sake'.[45] Although she suffers the pain of childbirth, and has the greatest share in raising them, the mother loses proprietary interest over her progeny when the child receives its father's last name.

Aside from Cavendish, the only mid-seventeenth-century theorist who questions the natural basis of these traditional roles for women is Thomas Hobbes, but he does so for different reasons. For Hobbes, every human relationship, even that between mother and child, involves a rational calculation and some measure of consent. Hypothetically, at least, he entertains the notion that women may decide to walk away from a newborn: 'she may either nourish, or expose it'.[46] But this is purely hypothetical for Hobbes; having reduced all relationships down to their basic contractual parts, his unstated assumption is that women will still agree to the terms of the conjugal contract. Cavendish does not. In fact, Cavendish's language about the feminine roles of wife

---

[43] Cavendish 2004, 'Letter 47', p. 97−9.
[44] Cavendish 2003, 'Oration 108', p. 226.
[45] Cavendish 2004, 'Letter 93', pp. 145−6. Cavendish is frank about Newcastle's desire for more children, blaming herself for failing to produce further heirs despite the fact that Newcastle was being treated for impotency at the time.
[46] Hobbes 1991, p. 140.

and mother — roles which seventeenth-century women were expected to assume without a great deal of deliberation (beyond consent to the marriage contract) — implies that these are things that women might legitimately choose not to do. Hobbes, provocative as he is on this subject, is engaged in a political exercise to undermine opposing constitutional theories.[47] In contrast, Cavendish's interest in the subject is anything but abstract; hers is an interested inquiry into a matter that affected the well-being of other women and her own as well. After seriously weighing the advantages and disadvantages, she finds marriage and motherhood to be so potentially dangerous for women that they are not worth the risk. In light of this calculation, she advises her sister against marriage altogether.[48]

Although Cavendish's modern interpreters cannot but take notice of her provocative language about marriage and motherhood, systematic attempts to make sense of her darker view of the private, or to treat it as a matter of political import, have been harder to come by.[49] The difficulty in this regard may legitimately arise from Cavendish's own apparent inconsistencies on the subject of gender relations as a whole. On the one hand are her evocative statements to the effect that men 'would fain Bury us in their Houses or Beds, as in a Grave; the truth is, we Live like Bats or Owls, Labour like Beasts, and Dye like Worms'.[50] On the other hand, she presents a convincing case that she believes women to be indulged, weak, lacking in intelligence, and that, where marriage is concerned, there is 'no Life I Approve so well of'.[51] Of course, we must understand some of her commentary about women's appropriate deference in the ironic spirit in which it is offered. Moreover, on the issue of gender relations, part of Cavendish's gift, Susan James observes, is 'a truly rhetorical ability to see the issue from many points of view'.[52] As a royalist who believed it 'an Honour to Obey the Meritorious',[53] Cavendish is as able to provide a convincing defence of societal hierarchies as she is to critique them. That she was steeped in a culture that perceived women to be intellectually inferior must also

---

[47] On Hobbes's instrumental use of gender, see Wright 2004, chs. 4, 5.
[48] Cavendish 2004, 'Letter 201', p. 272.
[49] Although see Smith 1997a and 1997b.
[50] Cavendish 2003, 'Oration 129', p. 248.
[51] Cavendish 2004, 'Letter 201', p. 273; 'Female Orations' debates woman's virtue, see Cavendish 2003.
[52] James 2003a, p. xxix.
[53] Cavendish 2004, 'Letter 201', p. 273.

be considered in the assessment of her many rationalizations for her own inferiority and her other disempowering language.[54]

Still, if her critique of power relations in the private realm is not entirely *consistent*, it is nonetheless *persistent*. Her critique emerges as an important theme in several of her works and spans her relatively compressed writing life, from *A True Relation* (1656) to *Divers Orations* (1662) and *Sociable Letters* (1664), culminating in *Plays, Never Before Printed* (1668), of which *The Convent of Pleasure* is one. She is determined to show that, even in the most initially blissful of unions, marriage can prove to be the 'Grave of Love'.[55] I suggest that a consideration of the epistemological challenges facing Cavendish as a woman thinker may help us account for some of her inconsistencies on the issues involving women's traditional roles. Cavendish had developed an embryonic political understanding of the oppressive aspects of private life for women but the rhetorical space available for such a perspective in seventeeth-century England was very limited. As Lorraine Code has argued, the context in which truth statements are made impacts their perceived veracity. Rhetorical spaces 'structure and limit the kinds of utterances that can be voiced within them with a reasonable expectation of uptake and "choral support"'.[56] Knowledge, in this view, is not produced in abstract circumstances by 'no one in particular', but is instead generated within 'textured locations where it matters who is speaking and where and why'.[57] In speaking against, but nevertheless within the context of, early-modern patriarchal culture, Cavendish cannot be assumed to have had the receptive audience that would be required to refine and develop a systematic argument about marriage and motherhood. Moreover, with no precedent for her views, Cavendish also had no discourse to tap into, no extant critique of gendered power relations to draw upon which might have forced her to take sides, to consider her views further, and thus encouraged her consistency. Cavendish was, on this front especially, an unaffirmed intellectual whose critique of private relations stood so far outside acceptable discourse that there was simply no possibility of 'choral support'. Therefore, what she offers are persistent references,

---

[54] Among the most pronounced examples of disempowering language about women's abilities is found in Cavendish, 'The Preface to the Reader', in Cavendish 1655. She was not alone in her use of such language, as the female religious activists of the Civil War period often tempered their demands to be heard by professions of their own inadequacy and inferiority vis-à-vis men. See Mack 1992.

[55] Cavendish 2004, 'Letter 89', p. 141.

[56] Code 1995, p. ix.      [57] Code 1995, p. x.

hints of a critique which do not, in fact, get taken up until much later and are not perhaps fully developed until the Second Wave Women's Liberation Movement.[58] We need not draw any simplistic historical lines between Cavendish and the feminists of the 1960s and 1970s to identify and foreground what is, in my view, a distinctively political view of the private realm in Cavendish's writing.

### A RETIRED LIFE: THE OTHER SIDE OF THE PRIVATE

Among the many things that separate Cavendish's use and understanding of the private from, for instance, that of the Second Wave feminists, is her disinclination to seek social change to remedy its evils. Here again, there is no existing discourse for Cavendish to fall back upon; restructuring private relations was simply a non-issue. And the only women who are making any sort of plea for greater public roles in the mid-seventeenth century, the many and diverse religious activists, are doing so to legitimate either the authority of their public biblical interpretation or their attempts to plead for their husbands' release from captivity.[59] Cavendish makes it clear that she neither shares their interests nor sanctions their methods. Her reflections on her trip to London to petition for some monies from her husband's estate – as only wives and family members were allowed to – illustrate Cavendish's inability to accommodate herself to the image of a Parliamentary petitioner. Thus she asked her brother to petition on her behalf, reporting unequivocally: 'I did not stand as a beggar at the Parliament doore'. When refused by the committee, Cavendish recalls, 'I whisperingly spoke to my brother to conduct me out of that ungentlemanly place'.[60] Cavendish is anxious to distinguish her public advocacy, done discreetly and for legitimate economic reasons for her noble husband, from the activities of other women who 'become pleaders, attorneys, petitioners and the like, running about with their several causes, complaining of their severall grievances, exclaiming against their severall enemies, bragging of their severall favours they receive from the powerfull'.[61]

Unwilling to position herself in any official public political role, however minor or justified, but clearly rejecting traditional female roles and activities as well, Cavendish chooses a different path. For herself

---

[58] For discussion of Cavendish's inconsistencies and how to place her in the history of feminist thought, see Smith 1997b, pp. 122–5.

[59] See Mack 1992; Crawford 1992; Crawford 1993.

[60] Cavendish 1916b, pp. 200–1.    [61] Cavendish 1916b, p. 201.

and for other women, she advocates instead a retired existence, divorced from the noise and chaos of the public realm and from the demands of aristocratic social life, and yet separate from the tedium of the domestic. 'She shut herself up at Welbeck alone', in Virginia Woolf's famous description.[62] Perhaps due in part to Woolf's characterization, Cavendish's choice in this regard is typically seen as the act of an eccentric who was in the end more ridiculous than serious. However, when interpreted in light of her dismissal of aristocratic female culture, her views about the Civil War, and her reflections on human mortality, her defence of a private life for women takes on greater political and metaphysical gravity.

For Cavendish, the private is not just a space or a location, but a choice as to how to live one's life. It is a choice grounded in the history of her family life; as a child she favoured contemplation over other activities, if anything 'inclining to be melancholy'.[63] Cavendish's mother, too, 'made her house her cloyster, inclosing herself as it were therein', after her husband's death.[64] In her adult life, Cavendish feels herself completely free to do anything and go anywhere, yet '[t]his course of Life [retirement] is by my own voluntary Choice'.[65] Offering an account to her friends of 'how I spend the idle Time of my life, and how I busie my Thoughts, when I thinke upon the Objects of the World', Cavendish writes:

For the truth is, our Sex has so much waste Time, having but little imployments, which makes our Thoughts run wildly about, having nothing to fix them upon, which wilde thoughts do not onely produce unprofitable, but indiscreet Actions; winding up the Thread of our lives in snarles on unsound bottoms.[66]

The contrast between Cavendish's chosen employments and those of other aristocratic women is elaborated by Richard Flecknoe, a frequent guest at Welbeck who flatters Cavendish as being a woman elevated high above other members of her sex:

> Is this a Ladies Closset? 't cannot be,
> For nothing here of vanity we see,
> Nothing of curiousity, nor pride,
> As most of Ladies Clossets have beside . . .

---

[62] Woolf 2001, p. 74.    [63] Cavendish 1916b, p. 208–9.    [64] Cavendish 1916b, 196.
[65] Cavendish 2004, 'Letter 29', p. 76.    [66] Cavendish 1653, p. [A5].

> ... Here she's in rapture, herein extasie,
> With studying high, and deep Philosophy.[67]

From Flecknoe's epigrams, Cavendish's self-descriptions, as well as from portraits of Cavendish at her desk, we derive an image of the philosophical, writerly woman revelling in her private closet.

Cavendish articulates her vision of the contemplative life by pitting the vanities and excesses of aristocratic women against a romanticized depiction of working women. Whereas she finds 'Idle Time is Tedious' and 'Luxury is Unwholesom', by contrast,

Labour is Healthful and Recreative, and surely Country Huswives take more Pleasure in Milking their Cows, making their Butter and Cheese, and feeding their Poultry, than great Ladies do in Painting, Curling, and Adorning themselves.[68]

As much as Cavendish had rejected traditional female roles and the labour accompanying them, in the household labour of women, she finds something enviable: it is removed from the social world of the upper classes; it is domestic and private; and it is active.[69] Taking great pains to distance herself from other sociable women, especially the kind with whom she served at court,[70] Cavendish valorizes the intellectual life as itself active and meaningful, as an appropriate diversion from the frivolities and excesses of social life. Although the women whom Cavendish romanticizes are the least able to take her suggestion to actively employ their minds, in her rendering, they need it the least *because* they actively labour. Aristocratic women are most in need of some active employment; they have no legitimate excuse *not* to think, 'for Thoughts are free', therefore we 'may as well read in our Closets, as Men in their Colleges'.[71]

Cavendish's retreat, however, does not take the form of a quiet escape into her closet. Cavendish wishes to convey publicly, in fact through her many publications, her 'Retirement from the publick Concourse and Army of the World'.[72] Indeed, the private is given meaning in and through her rejection of the public, her 'public gesture of withdrawal'

---

[67] Flecknoe 1670, p. 26.    [68] Cavendish 2004, 'Letter 55', p. 107.

[69] Cavendish 2004, 'Letter 34', p. 85 describes wives' maids who make more pleasant company 'as they do not have time to think of their Splenes, besides, they are forced to Labour and Work for their Living, which keeps them from such Obstructions or Disease, and the Splene is a Disease which is onely amongst the Noble and Rich, whose Wealth makes them Idle ...'

[70] See Turberville 1938, p. 122.    [71] Cavendish 1655, p. [A5].

[72] Cavendish 2004, 'Letter 29', p. 79.

signifying her critique of what she wishes to leave behind.[73] The quasi-public social world of women, with its incipient gossip, vanity and superficiality; the noise and disruption associated with too much company; and the disorder and turbulence of the public, political world: these are the things from which Cavendish wishes to abstain. Whereas the private formerly connoted a lack, a deficiency and something potentially destructive to public order, Cavendish is active in reshaping the meaning of the private, positing it as a virtuous, even superior, choice of how and where to spend one's time. In *The Convent of Pleasure*, Lady Happy asks, 'what is there in the publick World that should invite me to live in it?'[74] Why choose the public when the private offers a more authentic life that is not necessarily deprived? The virtuous women who choose this convent will *only* lack the company of men; in no other way shall it be an ascetic life, or a 'Cloister of restraint'. With beds of velvet, floors strewn with flowers, and the décor changed according to the season, Cavendish describes a 'place for freedom, not to vex the Senses but to please them'.[75] Indeed, in much of Cavendish's writing, from the autobiographical to the fictional and dramatic, her portrayal of private retirement has a celebratory tone.[76]

Still, her retreat is not just a social and intellectual choice, but a political and philosophical one as well. At the conclusion of *A True Relation*, after stating that she could 'most willingly exclude myself, so as to never see the face of any creature but My Lord, as long as I live . . .',[77] she addresses the question of why she chose to write her memoirs at all since, in all likelihood, nobody would care 'whose daughter she was, or whose wife she is . . . or how she lived.' Her reply is revealing:

to tell the truth, lest after-ages should mistake, in not knowing I was daughter to one Master Lucas of St. Johns, near Colchester, in Essex, second wife to the Lord Marquis of Newcastle; for my Lord having had two wives, I might easily have been mistaken, especially if I should dye and My Lord marry again.[78]

---

[73] On the public and private as defined in and through each other, see Brewer 1995. Stewart 1995, pp. 80–81 discusses the construction of the closet as, at one and the same time, a 'place of utter privacy' and a 'very public sign of privacy' — its privacy was made public by the fact that early-modern retreats to its recesses were often enacted in full public view.

[74] Cavendish 2000, p. 98.      [75] Cavendish 2000, p. 101.

[76] Straznicky 2004 elaborates the relationship between Renaissance women's closet drama and constructions of the private.

[77] Cavendish 1916b, p. 213.      [78] Cavendish 1916b.

Her memoirs, and indeed all of her publications taken together, are a kind of insurance against the oblivion of mortality. Deeply distraught by the events of the English Civil War, having personally experienced some of its worst abuses, Cavendish is all too aware of the temporality of human existence. Yet, never having produced the heirs that the Duke so desperately wanted, she has no progeny by which she can be remembered. Should the Duke remarry after her death and have more children, she well understood how easily her memory would be eclipsed – 'mistaken' – between two reproductively successful wives.

Current interpreters emphasize the devastating impact of the Civil War on Cavendish and her tendency to personalize its events in relation to her own family.[79] Her mother, although having chosen to live privately, was forced out of her home 'by reason she and her children were loyall to the king'. Barbarous to the extent that they 'would have pulled God out of Heaven, had they had power, as they did royaltie out of his throne',[80] Parliamentary soldiers ravaged the Lucas home, forcing members of her family out, defacing the house and gardens, killing the livestock, and plundering the Lucas family vault: 'the Urns of the Dead were Digged up, their Dust Dispersed, and their Bones Thrown about'.[81] Listing her several family losses, including her mother, who 'lived to see the ruin of her children, in which was her ruin', and the execution of her brother, Charles Lucas, Cavendish writes, 'I shall lament the loss so long as I live'.[82] Having lost most of her family members while in exile, Cavendish reflects abstractly on the nature of civil war:

If the Change of Government had been likely to Alter their Religion, to Destroy their Natives, to Torture their Friends, to Disperse the Ashes of their Dead Ancestors, and to Pull down their Monuments, and his Country to be Enjoyed, Possess'd, Ruled, and Governed by Strangers, he had Chosen Well, to have Voluntarily Died, rather than to Live to see those Miseries, Calamaties and Destructions . . .[83]

Cavendish's experiences of the wars in England shaped her personal, philosophical and political perspective. On the political front, she staked out a position that was fundamentally opposed to war, variously blaming men who 'for the most part destroy life' and, in a strikingly Hobbesian tone, those whose vanity, pride and envy drove them to create factions

---

[79] See Williams 2002; and Battigelli 1998.   [80] Cavendish 1916b, p. 196.
[81] Cavendish 2004, 'Letter 119', p. 174.   [82] Cavendish 1916b, p. 198.
[83] Cavendish 2004, 'Letter 187', p. 253.

in the first place.[84] Preferring to live a life of peaceful exile than confront the despair of war again, Cavendish points out that 'those that
never had the Sweetness of Peace, or have not known the Misery of
War, cannot be truly and rightly Sensible of either'.[85] Although she
never wavered in her commitment to the royalist side in the Civil War,
and indeed she devoted much effort to defending it and, particularly,
to restoring her husband's reputation following his exile,[86] she also
distances herself emphatically from civil affairs when she questions
why women should be 'Subjects of the Commonwealth' at all when
they are not considered citizens. Cavendish's political claim here is less
for women's rightful inclusion in the public realm, and more for their
outsider status, since they are 'neither Useful in Peace, nor Serviceable
in War'.[87]

The wars also forced Cavendish to confront the inevitability of death
in an immediate way. Indeed, the theme of death is a powerful one
throughout her works, well beyond her funeral orations: 'there is nothing
I Dread more than Death', she writes in *Sociable Letters*. Yet she makes
clear that it is not the pain of death that she dreads 'but the Oblivion in
Death, I fear not Death's Dart so much as Death's Dungeon'. In another
passage she explains that there is no terror in death, nor pain; rather
'it is Life that is Painful both to the Body and Mind ... for the Mind
in Life is Fearful, and the Body is seldom at Ease'.[88] Moreover, since
the life of the body is 'like a Flash of Lightening, that Continues not,
and for the most part leaves black Oblivion behind it',[89] one must
contemplate whether it is better to live a long and idle life or a short
and productive one.

---

[84] Cavendish 2003, 'Oration 28', p. 156.
[85] Cavendish 2004, 'Letter 185', p. 251.
[86] Turberville 1938, p. 145 notes the 'monstrous sin of ingratitude' toward her husband by the
restoured monarch as a recurring theme in Cavendish's work, emerging most clearly in her
biography of him. Chalmers 1997, pp. 217–24 argues that to 'act as a dutiful mouthpiece for
grievances which her husband himself cannot voice' was Cavendish's primary political purpose.
Her many publications, then, were a kind of 'wifely self-display' which served to affirm the
couple's 'aristocratic status in the aftermath of the Civil War'. Yet the content of her work
indicates that she had political and social concerns well beyond those of her husband's
reputation; moreover, it seems problematic to assign to Cavendish no self-driven motives for
her writing and publishing career.
[87] Cavendish 2004, 'Letter 16', p. 61.
[88] Cavendish 2004, 'Letter 119', p. 173.
[89] Cavendish 2004, 'Letter 90', p. 142.

Cavendish's preference to 'Leave a Little to After Age', in effect to employ her short time profitably rather than 'Wast a Great Deal of Time to no Purpose', is vitally connected both to her desire for fame and her choice to live her life in private contemplation. If the physical body must die, and worse, if its remains can be desecrated at will, better that she leave an idea behind — her 'paper bodies', her 'castles in the air' — something that will continue to live in the memory of others.[90] The private is the space uniquely suited to thought, and 'those my Mind likes best, it sends them forth to the Senses to write them down', and subsequently 'out to the Publick view of the World'.[91] Her desire for fame is not necessarily in conflict with her professed desire for privacy, since the kind of fame she seeks is not that associated with 'Rich Coaches, Lackies, and what State and Ceremony could produce'. These things are connected to the temporal world, but her 'Ambition flies higher, as to Worth and Merit, not State and Vanity'.[92] The public sphere is noisy and oriented to things superficial, but the private life is serene, a place where her 'Mind lives in Peace', and 'calm Silence' prevails.[93] Cavendish wants to actively and publicly defend the private as a legitimate choice as to *where* and *how* to live one's life, connecting it to tranquility, creativity[94] and ultimately, immortality.

While we have reason to be cautious about the language of public and private — an insight that is engendered by debates within women's history and, implicitly, the history of political thought — an understanding of Cavendish's political import is incomplete without it. It is evident in reading Cavendish that the discourse of public and private was one that resonated deeply for her. This is not to say that the terms *circumscribed* or even *described* her own experience; as the most published English female author of her time, she clearly did not reside exclusively in the private realm. Nevertheless, the terms had significance for her as

---

[90] Cavendish 2004, 'Letters 143, 113', pp. 203, 167.

[91] Cavendish 2004, 'Letter 29', p. 77.

[92] Cavendish 2004, 'Letter 82', p. 136. Cavendish interpreters tend to agree that there is some tension between her desire for privacy and her desire for fame. Jagodzinski 1999, p. 130 argues that Cavendish resolves the anxiety that surrounded her quest for privacy by publishing, that for Cavendish, 'publication is the only true sign of virtue'. Conversely, I suggest that Cavendish exhibits more anxiety about publishing her works than she does about writing them in private; publication is indeed a virtuous outlet for one's ideas, but Cavendish's many defences of private life suggest that virtue can also be found within it.

[93] Cavendish 2004, 'Letter 29', p. 77.

[94] See further Huebert 1997, p. 26.

means of making sense of social and political life. She was acutely aware of the power relations within the private — she saw their gendered dimensions — even if she had no immediate solution to them. At the same time, she was anxious to affirm a distinction between public and private, to emphasize the private itself as a site for intellectual auton-omy and a more authentic life. Defined in relation to the public — and often in opposition to it — the private could be a woman's ruin or her salvation. For Cavendish personally, it was likely a bit of both. As modern interpreters we neither share her precise concerns, nor see public and private from her perspective, but her language is not so different from our own that we cannot gain some insight from her analysis. In continuing to ask questions about public and private, feminist political theory will come closer to an understanding of *how* the discourse(s) have changed over time, and refine our sense of *why* it looked different from the perspective of thinkers like Margaret Cavendish.[95]

[95] I wish to express my thanks to Gordon Schochet, Lorraine Code, Leah Bradshaw, David Bedford and Kate Bezanson for their helpful feedback on various parts of this chapter; to the participants in the Folger Institute conference on British Political Thought in History, Literature and Theory for which this chapter was written; and especially to David Armitage for his valuable editorial suggestions.

CHAPTER 12

# Reflections on Political Literature: History, Theory and the Printed Book

*Kirstie M. McClure*

Over the last four decades, historians, political theorists and literary scholars have substantially, if gradually, shifted attention away from histories of ideas understood as a sequence of great texts by great men and literary histories concerned principally with the life and works of noted authors of drama, poetry and fiction. Scholars of political thought today — historians and theorists alike — are more likely to speak of political languages or ideologies, discourses or traditions, contingently situated in time and place. The energies of literary studies, too, have been similarly extended to the political or ideological dimensions of literary works, often informed by one or another variant of 'new historicism', inflected by various forms of critical theory, or indebted to sundry perspectives in the philosophy of language.

In this chapter I want to raise the question of the relation between these various developments and recent perspectives on the history and historiography of the printed book. If, as many now argue, the history of 'political thought' is a matter of distinctive languages or discourses, the material vehicles of such thought remain the various forms and genres of print culture. To note this is to suggest that, despite the often exemplary work that has been done in shifting the object of histo-riographical inquiry away from 'unit-ideas' or 'the work itself' as a self-sufficient whole, this focus on the emergence and persistence of such languages tends to a level of ideological generality removed from the welter of polemical struggles at the 'ground level', so to speak, between writers and readers at particular moments of intense political engage-ment. The political languages at issue, however, are neither self-enclosed nor self-limiting. As Anthony Pagden has noted, writers might 'employ the idiom or vocabularies of one language while speaking predominantly in another', as well as 'combine different languages in the same text'.[1]

---

[1] Pagden 1987b, p. 2.

And this, in turn, may spark the transformation of such languages, 'almost to the extent of constituting new languages by their exposure to other discursive practices and changes in the external circumstances they seek to describe'.[2]

To acknowledge both the hybridity of particular texts and their capacities to change or inflect a 'political language' — even to the point of 'almost' generating 'new languages' — is to suggest the potential fecundity not only of the broad terrain at the intersection of *langue* and the instances of *parole* through which a political 'language' is worked out over time, but also of repeated acts of *parole* — that is, of the inventive pressures upon political languages exacted by the *reiteration* of particularized textual performances.[3] Attention to such particularities reintroduces neither 'the work' or 'the author' as a principal focus of inquiry, but rather opens the field of investigation to the sometimes strange dynamics of polemical reception — not, perhaps, as they inflect or modify a larger *langue*, but instead as they incite specific orientations to action in the successive presents of particular times and places. In this context, the phenomena of multiple editions of particular works and their associated paratexts (introductions, prefaces, critical apparatuses and the like), in some cases over broad temporal and geographic expanses, might offer a productive site for considering these dynamic aspects of 'political thought' as it finds new readers, new venues of critical reception and new contexts of political controversy. Translations, too — both from classical languages and between European vernaculars — are part of this dynamism, and raise similar issues of reception, appropriation and critical deployment over time, as do the many instances of plagiarism, epitomizing and emendation (scholarly or otherwise) that characterize the culture of print to this day.

In raising this issue, I mean to follow up on a number of J. G. A. Pocock's observations regarding 'texts as events'. We cannot, he observes, 'write history in terms of the great texts', but there is nonetheless 'a sense in which the great texts are difficult to reduce to history'.[4] In part, this is because 'they continue to be read and used by people who are not historians' — and hence by readers unconstrained by professional canons of interpretation. But further, texts are historical events because

---

[2] Pagden 1987b, p. 2. See also Tuck 1987, pp. 99–119.
[3] The point is made at length by Pocock 1985b, pp. 12–28 and Pocock 1987b, pp. 29–31.
[4] Pocock 1987b, p. 29.

'they outlive their authors'. Here, Pocock raises the issue of reception in time as one that necessarily exceeds the question of authorial intentions, even in the revised form characteristic of the Cambridge adaptation of speech-act theory. The reader, too, is an 'actor ... in a historical process', an actor that 'reenacts the text' often in ways quite removed from whatever its author may have intended. Analogizing readers to performers of a dramatic work, Pocock argues that, in this respect, 'readers' consciousness is no less active than the authors'; they 'respond' to the author of a text and thus 'preserve the independent activity of their consciousness' by reading 'as they intend, which may or may not be how the author intended to be read'. Finally, and emphasizing the value of interdisciplinary *exempla*, he notes that while 'students of literature know that text-reader relationships are complex and unpredictable affairs', those who study the ' "history of ideas" may need to be reminded that they are a very large part of what they are studying'.[5]

In what follows I shall offer select examples that I take as supple instances of this phenomenon. My purpose is not to propose alternative methods for historians, but rather to suggest that there are political and theoretical stakes involved in attending more closely to the nexus of 'history, theory and the printed book' suggested in my subtitle. Because, however, each of these examples replicates elements of ostensibly 'classic' texts, I will draw on a view of texts as 'utterances' different from the notions of language-games and speech acts that inform Cambridge contextualism, that of Mikhail Bakhtin. My reasons for this choice will be briefly elaborated in the first section of the chapter, while subsequent sections will focus on significant moments in the print history of three originally pseudonymous or anonymous books: the *Vindiciae Contra Tyrannos,* the *Two Treatises of Government,* and the *Vindication of Natural Society.* The strange history of the *Vindiciae,* I shall argue, is one example of the dynamism of *parole* in the sphere of print culture, and the creative anachronism of twentieth-century constructions of what we now know to be Locke's *Second Treatise* as a paragon of liberalism is another. So too, I will suggest, is the stranger-still publishing history of Edmand Burke's originally anonymous satire in the *Vindication.* By considering such things not only in terms of Bakhtinian 'utterances'

---

[5] Pocock 1987b, pp. 29–30. That this dynamic of 'responsiveness', in narrative texts in particular, is a matter of orientation to action is a central concern of Ricoeur 1984–1986, I, ch. 3; and Ricoeur 1981, pp. 145–64.

but also in light of an older notion of 'literature' as 'letters' and printed works, I want in the phrase 'political literature' to pursue what might be called the life of political languages or, alternatively, the political life of books. In this I hope to blend the tasks of history and theory into a broader perspective on print culture as both site and symptom of the vicissitudes of political community in time.


## I.   OF BOOKS AND 'UTTERANCES'

Books can be understood as material vehicles of the political languages, discourses, traditions and ideologies of interest to historians, critics and theorists of all sorts. Recent work in bibliographical and textual studies, however, has called attention as well to the signifying dimensions of books that are little noticed in the history of political thought – among them, size, typography and paratexts of various sorts, both in the original and across multiple editions.[6] Readers, too, have now taken shape as agents in the production of meanings that may or may not accord with the intentions of a book's original author.[7] In light of such insights into the production, circulation, and uses of books, the question of the relation of the book to the notion of a political 'utterance' might be considered in terms other than those of the words, phrases, sentences and vocabularies that come to comprise a discernible 'language' of political thought. This is not to deny the significance or appropriateness of such constructions of political languages as historiographical objects. Rather, in order to glimpse something of readers at work across time and place, it is to suggest the potential usefulness of Bakhtin's dialogic notion of the 'utterance' as unit of speech communication that entails both an 'actively responsive understanding' and, importantly, *'a change of speaking subjects'*.[8] By thus conceiving a text as a completed 'utterance' and including attention to the activities of its respondents, Bakhtin opens the question of addressees as links 'in the chain of speech communion in a particular sphere of human activity or everyday life'.[9]

---

[6] See McGann 1983; McKenzie 1986; and Genette 1997.
[7] Most generally, see the reader–response criticism of Iser 1974; Iser 1978; Jauss 1982; Fish 1980. Significant, too, are numerous works that emphasize less the authority of interpretive communities than the peculiarities of acts of reading, and I have profited especially from Chartier 1988; Darnton 1985; de Certeau 1984; Ginzburg 1992; Jardine and Grafton 1990; Sherman 1997; Zwicker 1998.
[8] See Bakhtin 1986, esp. pp. 67–100.
[9] Bakhtin 1986, p. 83.

For my purposes, the virtue of this approach is twofold. First, it opens a field of historical attention to idiosyncracies and conflicts in the reading and appropriation of books over time. Whether in writings of later authors or, alternatively, in later editions sporting paratexts absent from the original, repeated appearances of whole or partial texts offer sites where that 'change of speaking subjects' is itself inked on the printed page. Further, however, Bakhtin's formulation also offers an opportunity for reflection on the ways in which our own contemporary attentions to historical texts participate in the history of active responsiveness to particular works, for the chain of speech communication in time necessarily includes such scholarly practices as quotation, citation and paraphrase under the rubric of 'a change of speaking subjects'. So, too, might it extend to internet postings of historical texts, as these suggest a kind of active, even vital, contemporaneity despite the passage of time. In recasting such aspects of usage as 'political literature', perhaps we can not only discern things as yet unrecognized in our textual inheritance, but also consider what we are doing in writing of them as a further dimension of their historical persistence.

## II. TRANSLATION AND NATURALIZATION: THE STRANGE ADVENTURES OF THE 'VINDICIAE CONTRA TYRANNOS'

The place of the pseudonymous Junius Brutus' *Vindiciae Contra Tyrannos* of 1579 in the history of Huguenot resistance right is by now well-known to theorists and historians of political thought alike.[10] As Quentin Skinner pungently notes, however, in the broad development of erstwhile 'Calvinist' theories of resistance, 'there are virtually no elements in the theory which are specifically Calvinist at all'. With the resources of scholasticism, Roman law and Lutheranism (itself drawing on canon and civil law) drawn together by the pressures of political contingencies, the 'main foundations of the Calvinist theory of revolution were constructed entirely by their Catholic adversaries'.[11] In this paradoxical history, one might say, the *Vindiciae* was but one player among many as its arguments migrated from its original Gallic context

---

[10] Most notably, through Franklin 1969, and the expansive discussion of 'Calvinism and the Theory of Revolution', in Skinner 1978b, part 3.

[11] Skinner 1978b, p. 321.

into a more expansive, more radical and eventually more secular language of resistance across the European Republic of Letters.

The print history of the *Vindiciae*'s Englishing adds a new dimension to this story, for it discloses a series of early-modern readers at work amidst the vicissitudes of political time in the place now called Great Britain. It was these readers who, as writers, pitched the *Vindiciae* itself into that larger history. And their diverse translations and appropriations naturalized significant parts of the original text into commonplaces of British polemics that percolated across the eighteenth and beyond the cusp of the nineteenth century.

To start near the beginning: it is not only the case that the 1579 *Vindiciae* as originally published contributed to the development of modern theories of resistance right. The scholastic and Catholic foundations of that developing language made the use of the *Vindiciae* a risky business in the context of English political and religious controversies, and the process of its partial secularization extended well into the last years of the seventeenth century.[12] A portion of the text, however – specifically its fourth question, 'whether neighbor Princes may, or are bound by law to aide the Subjects of other Princes, persecuted for true Religion, or oppressed by manifest tyranny' – was first Englished in 1588, with a title that made its translator's intentions clear. In full, that title was *A short apologie for Christian souldiours: wherein is conteined, how that we ought both to propagate, and also if neede require, to defende by force of armes, the Catholike Church of Christ, against the tyrannie of Antichrist and his adherentes: penned by Stephanus Iunius Brutus, and translated into English by H. P. for the benefite of the resolution of the Church of England, in the defence of the gospel.*[13] The translator's purpose, of course, was to urge English intervention in favour of The Netherlands' struggle against Spanish rule, and for this the *Vindiciae*'s justification of resistance against the Antichrist was eminently useful. This, however, was but the beginning of the book's adventures in print culture. Roughly half a century later, in 1643, William Prynne made the next energetic Englishing by including in the appendix to *The Soveraigne Powers of Parliaments and Kingdoms*[14] a swatch of the third question of the *Vindiciae*, that asked 'whether it be lawful to resist a Prince which doth

---

[12] This discussion is much indebted to Tutino 2005. I am grateful to Prof. Tutino for her generosity in sharing this manuscript.
[13] H. P. 1588.
[14] Prynne 1643.

oppress or ruine a publike State, and how far such resistance my be extended, by whom, how, and by what right or law it is permitted'.[15] Here, Prynne translates that portion of the original that emphasizes the covenant between King and people and royal subordination to the laws, but is notably silent on the *Vindiciae*'s first covenant, the covenant between God and the people. This, as Stefania Tutino argues, 'constitutes the embryo of the English *Vindiciae* and will "set the tone" for the future reading and understanding of the text'. Although Prynne himself was no republican, and though his *Vindiciae* was hardly pitched as a 'republican' text, it nonetheless paved the way for the production and reception of the first full translation of the book, in the late heat of civil war radicalisms, in 1648.[16]

But even this is not the end of the story. While another edition of the *Vindiciae* appeared in 1689 – seemingly the same text as that of 1648 with a new title page – a more interesting, and finally more long-lived appropriation of the text arrived, initially under the title *Political Aphorisms: or, The True Maxims of Government Displayed*, in 1690.[17] The author of the *Aphorisms* remains unknown, but the text is remarkable for its pastiche of snatches, sometimes extending to whole passages, of the *Vindiciae*, the then-anonymous *Two Treatises of Government* and various other pamphlets of the allegiance controversy.[18] More remarkable still is not only that it reappeared in two more editions by 1691, but that it was repeatedly reprinted – with occasional augmentations – under two successively new titles in no less than twelve editions between 1709 and 1810. In this process of reprinting and partial redaction, *Political Aphorisms* first reappeared as the *Vox Populi, Vox Dei* of 1709,[19] itself the target of numerous polemical replies. But it found renewed life as

[15] The materials from the *Vindiciae* appeared in July, 1643, appended to *The fourth part of The soveraigne power of parliaments and kingdoms*. In August the full four-part text appeared, again with the appendix demonstrating the superiority of parliaments and other collective bodies over and above individual rulers.

[16] Tutino 2005, pp. 15–16.

[17] A gesture in the subtitle of the first edition specifies its target and addresses by describing it as '*a challenge to Dr. William Sherlock, and Ten other New Dissenters, and Recommended as proper to be Read by all Protestant Jacobites*'. The editions of 1691 excised the 'challenge' to Sherlock *et al.* from the title.

[18] The latter are Burnet 1688; Ferguson 1689; and the anonymous pamphlets *The Doctrine of Passive Obedience and Jure Divino Disproved* 1689 and *The Letter which was sent to the Author of the The Doctrine of Passive Obedience and Jure Divino Disproved, Answered* 1689. For discussions see Goldie 1999, I, pp. xxxiii, 2; Ashcraft and Goldsmith 1983.

[19] *Vox Populi, Vox Dei* 1709.

*The Judgment of Whole Kingdoms and Nations*, a book issued in various formats in 1710,[20] 1713, 1714, 1716, 1747, 1771, 1773, 1774, 1781, 1795, and 1810. These, as some have noted, doubtless contributed to the dissemination of 'Lockean' ideas and to the association of the *Treatises* with the radical or populist wing of Whig politics. But so, too, did they extend the critical edge of the *Vindiciae* long beyond its last early-modern Englishing of 1689.

Here we have the curious phenomenon of an ostensibly ephemeral text, a stitched-together mélange of assorted fragments on resistance and the limits of obedience, that retained political currency for more than a century. Unlike earlier appropriations of the *Vindiciae*, these editions soon took on a relatively stable discursive form. Their temporal and geographical spread, however, as well as their varied material forms, spun their orientation to political action into increasingly diverse venues of political controversy. Whoever may have been their original compiler, a succession of subscribers and printers in England, Ireland and three American colonies continued to find the work either politically attractive, commercially vendible or, perhaps more likely, both. Thus despite, or rather because of the stability of its contents, this too becomes a matter of interest, for the vernacular Englishing of the book made it resonate both within and against the politics of the metropolitan core of a growing empire.

The original editions of *Political Aphorisms*, as well as the 1709 editions of *Vox Populi* and the initial issue of *The Judgment of Whole Kingdoms and Nations*, were nasty little pamphlets. Printed on poor paper, their text was crowded, sometimes over-inked and compressed into cheap tracts of between thirty-one and seventy-one pages.[21] In 1710, however, the publisher announced the upscaling of the book in the preface to the fourth edition: 'Many gentlemen having desired to have this book in a large print, this is to give notice that it is now printed on nine sheets and a quarter, of very fine paper at 1s. per book'.[22] Soon after, a fifth edition appeared, a full 131 pages in octavo with fourteen pages of

---

[20] *The Judgment of Whole Kingdoms and Nations* 1710.

[21] *Political Aphorisms* 1690 and 1691 runs thirty-one pages in quarto, not including the title page and advertisement; the 1709 *Vox Populi* ran forty-one pages in octavo. Containing minor emendations and additions, the smaller formats remained cheap tracts, crowded with print. For details see Ashcraft and Goldsmith 1983.

[22] Quoted by Ashcraft and Goldsmith 1983, p. 794. As they observe, the notice 'also declared that any person may buy this book of most booksellers in London and Westminster and read it for two days for nothing, provided they do not damage it'.

prefatory materials and another advertisement – a performance that was repeated in one printing of 1713. Numerous other 'editions' of 1710, 1713, 1714, and 1747 retained the smaller and less expensive material form with little if any alteration of content. While doubtless the better-off could purchase the cheap tracts, the finer and more expensive variants were unlikely to find their way into the hands of the poorer sort; thus these differences speak in part to the book's circulation at different levels of the social hierarchy. But with each sale a bit of the *Vindiciae* lived on, sharing a spine with the bits of other works to which it had been bound.

As *The Judgment of Whole Kingdoms and Nations* found diverse readers in England, it also migrated outward, first to Ireland, then to various American colonies. Another large octavo saw print in Dublin in 1716, while a flurry of further substantial octavos – on good paper with large print and wide margins – appeared in the 1770s not only in London (1771), but in Boston (1773?), Philadelphia (1773), and Newport, Rhode Island (1774). This format marked a Dublin edition of 1781 as well, and the run of these better printings suggests that the book was finding an audience in all these places among those with the wherewithal to buy it. Finally, amidst the Irish echoes of the French Revolution, another cheap print edition was issued in Dublin in 1795. Again titled *The Judgment of Whole Kingdoms and Magistrates*, this variant cited the London original of 1710 and noted that it was being 're-printed by an enemy of despotic power, for the information of the swinish multitude'. Neither the addressees nor the intentions of the anonymous printer are easy to mistake, for this was one of a number of pamphlets that took direct aim at Burke's recent reference to 'the swinish multitude' in his *Reflections on the Revolution in France* (1790).[23] By the late eighteenth century, in short, the pamphlet had ridden the centrifugal and centripetal eddies of English, British and colonial politics alike, and its justifications of resistance were promiscuously open to all suitors with an interest in such possibilities.

III.  GLOSSING, EDITING, AND UPDATING: A SLICE OF THE
LIFE OF 'THE SECOND TREATISE OF GOVERNMENT'

If, in the print history of the *Vindiciae*, the change of speaking subjects that marked its rearticulation as a political 'utterance' was largely

---

[23] For a sparkling discussion of these polemics see Herzog 1998, esp. ch. 12.

populated by translators, compilers, subscribers and printers, that of the *Two Treatises of Government* both included and extended beyond these to other sorts of appropriations. Let me take my starting point, though, from that odd centaur of a creature, half-man, half-beast, generally known today as 'Lockean liberalism'. The term itself should be irritating to the historically minded. From the time of the text's composition through the first century of its history it was simply not possible to *be* a 'liberal'. There were, of course, the liberal arts and sciences. And it was indeed possible to possess the virtue of liberality, just as it was possible to offer liberal interpretations of Scripture. 'Liberal', however, was not a term of political art as a marker of partisan identity or political positioning. It became one, to be sure, in the nineteenth century, as Locke's writings on toleration and education figured prominently in what was then being built as a liberal tradition. Even at the turn of the twentieth century, however, Sir Frederick Pollock could voice his regrets that Locke's *Treatises* were neglected by scholars and confidently characterize them as part of the heritage of 'ancient constitutionalism'.[24] It was in short, rather later and quite posthumously that the author of the *Treatises* became a 'Lockean liberal' – in the United States, as best as I can tell, in the decade following the Second World War.[25]

It is nonetheless the case that Locke's *Two Treatises*, and more particularly the *Second Treatise*, had long served many as a thorny critique of arbitrary power and privilege.[26] This, as we saw with its pairing alongside the *Vindiciae* and other resistance tracts in *Political Aphorisms*, was clearly an important part of its eighteenth-century dissemination and reception. It was, of course, also printed in a number of eighteenth-century editions, most of them either octavos including a portrait of the by then famous Locke, or expensive folios of his *Works*. But while the

---

[24] See Pollock 1903–1904, pp. 237–49. In recent scholarship Locke appears as a 'modern constitutionalist', equally curious given the print history of the *Treatises*: see McClure 2003.

[25] The phrasing is characteristic of F. S. C. Northrop: see Northrop 1946 and Northrop 1947. The term, of course, may have circulated outside the academy, but going back to the late nineteenth century the J-STOR journal archives have no record of it. Though Laski 1936, and others had associated Locke with various ideological currents within liberalism, the precise terminology of a 'Lockean liberalism' achieves solid scholarly currency in the USA by the mid-1950s through the challenge of, and responses to, Hartz 1955. But see also Hartz 1948, which explores 'The Myth of Laissez-faire' economics as a deeply rooted American phenomenon and ties the ideology of economic individualism to Locke through a case study of Pennsylvania.

[26] Strangely, there seems to have been no American edition of the work between 1773 and the 1880s, a period roughly corresponding to that which Hartz identifies with the rise of laissez-faire economics and corporate power.

*Treatises* were both generally known and widely read, their publishing history independent of periodic editions of the *Works* tends to follow the vicissitudes of British politics, and this on both sides of the Atlantic. Here, then, I shall focus on three publications that suggest some of the ways in which the 'utterance' of the *Treatises* could be transformed by later readers.

The first, and one that runs sharply against the grain of the radical positions woven into *Political Aphorisms,* was an anonymous pamphlet of 1753 that advertised itself as a 'Theory' that had been 'extracted from Mr. Locke's *Essay* on Civil Government'. Titled *Of Civil Polity,* it offers what might best be called a flat but creative gloss on the *Second Treatise.*[27] Like *Political Aphorisms* and its successors, the tract is richly larded with other sources, now including an array of works by latitudinarian and Whig churchmen. The 'theory' here 'extracted' substantially reorganizes the *Treatise*'s order of presentation into ten short topical sections and, as Goldie aptly notes, it significantly domesticates the earlier book 'into a series of Hanoverian commonplaces'. Its discussion of divorce, for instance, makes Locke 'more ethically respectable', while its section on '*the Establishment* of RELIGION' turns him 'into a pillar of the Established Church'.[28] Of note here, too, is a distinctly eighteenth-century emphasis in an opening section on 'the Social Nature of Man', drawn verbatim from William Parker's 1752 sermon on *The Grounds of Submission to Government.* A good part of the publication, to be sure, takes its language and often whole sentences from the *Second Treatise*; but there is little said, and that with little emphasis, on any of the *Treatise*'s discussions of resistance right save for the tract's brief treatment of conquest. There we find that the vanquished might 'find it prudent' to consent to the protection of their conqueror. The conqueror too might follow prudence by 'quieting the minds' of the 'conquered Vassals from the Fears of Oppression', even to the point of 'consenting to some Limitation in the Exercise' of power. But should these recommendations of prudence fall on deaf ears, 'Insolence and Oppression on the Part of the Governors would naturally occasion Remonstrance and Resistance on the Part of Subjects'. This discussion, however, ascribes to such 'remonstrance and resistance' the origin of 'those several *Forms* of Civil Government which are established in different Parts of the World',

---

[27] A slightly abbreviated version is printed in Goldie 1999, II, pp. 359–77.
[28] Goldie 1999, I, p. 358.

as well as the 'Distinction of Authority into its *several Branches*' –
arguments notably absent in its ostensible source.[29]

Subsequent years saw various sorts of engagement with the *Treatises*,
but let me focus on two examples of the kinds of 'responsive understanding' to which the latter work opened itself in the last decade of the
eighteenth century. The first of these, published in 1794, is *The Spirit
of John Locke on Civil Government, revived by the Constitutional Society
of Sheffield*. This, too, is a creative appropriation, albeit one that runs
in a political direction quite contrary to that of *Civil Polity*. And yet,
at the same time, it remains in a sense more faithful to the text of the
*Second Treatise* – at least, to those parts of the text that it reproduces.
But of that more in a moment, for there are a few initial aspects of this
text that merit attention.

*The Spirit* is a short pamphlet of forty-two pages, introduced by
a preface addressed 'TO THE PEOPLE'. Noting that the publication
was promised at a public meeting, that preface observes that, given the
times, 'no apology should be made to the Public for reducing, into as
small a compass as possible, every popular writing which has a tendency
to improve or confirm the reasoning and morals of our Countrymen'.[30]
On the whole, the preface is a paean both to Locke and to late
eighteenth-century radicals' interpretations of the Revolution of 1688.
The 'immortal' Paine comes off well; Filmer, '*Dagger* Burke', and the
clergy come off badly, principally for their support of passive obedience.
The first of Locke's *Treatises* is dismissed as essentially obsolete, while
the second, called *The Discourse on Civil Government*, is touted as
'applicable to the present times' for its capacity 'to open the eyes of our
deluded Countrymen, who are persecuting and hating us because we are
vindicating the ancient liberties of our Country'. Indeed, it will 'expose
the fallacious reasoning of those who would persuade the People that
they have no other rights but what their rulers choose to give them', and
will 'prove passive obedience to be folly, and RESISTANCE AGAINST
OPPRESSION to be the duty of the people'.[31] Mentioned, too, are the
examples of Nero, Caligula and Claudius, as well as 'the tyranny of
Tarquin' – and the argument is that God approves of resistance to such
abusive rulers. The preface's rhetoric rises to heights of moral outrage

[29] Goldie 1999, II, pp. 368–9.
[30] [Yorke?] 1794, p. 3. The author may have been Henry (alias Redhead) Yorke.
[31] [Yorke?] 1794, p. iv.

against arguments to the contrary, and its closing paragraphs invoke the dying words of Algernon Sidney, 'one of the most dignified Patriots that ever adorned the archives of human kind'.[32] After a last compliment to Locke, the writers ask: 'Will our oppressors denounce this work, too, as SEDITIOUS! — If they do, they must blush for the treason of their ancestors, and they must reprobate the Revolution of 1688, as a usurpation, and not as a benefice'. Finally, in an address to 'FELLOW CITIZENS', the writers polemicize what they take themselves to be doing in publishing such a work:

Power can never deter us from recalling from the inglorious tomb, those sages who have, in former days, enlightened and instructed our Country. — We shall rescue their works from oblivion. We shall arm ourselves with them as irresistible weapons. In the mean time, we commit to your wisdom and prudential reflection, the following Abstract from a book, difficult to be purchased, and, throughout the greatest part, uninteresting even when purchased. We have declined making any notes to the body of the work. But he who runs may read, and the Man who cannot take a broad hint from the last century, must not expect one from the *present*.[33]

The pamphlet's closing lines pinion Edmund Burke (the 'Knight Errant of Feudality') for declaring 'Locke's Treatise on Civil Government... the worst book ever written' and assert as certain 'that it needs no farther recommendation'.[34]

One would be hard put to imagine that the anonymous author of *Civil Polity* and the members of the Sheffield Constitutional Society had read the same book. While the former glossed it with Hanoverian complacencies, the latter gleaned the sense that the compiler of *Political Aphorisms* had made of the *Treatises*. The editorial decisions of the Constitutional Society, however, are themselves nothing if not interesting, for their abbreviation of the book to 'as small a compass as possible' simply lopped off the first seven chapters and turned the original's eighth chapter, 'Of the Beginning of Political Societies', into their pamphlet's first. Further, they deleted entirely the tenth, fourteenth, fifteenth and seventeenth chapters — which, respectively, in the original considered commonwealth and prerogative; compared political, paternal and despotic power; and discussed usurpation — and made various sentence-level excisions through the rest. For present purposes it might suffice to mention but one of the latter, the excision of Locke's observation,

[32] [Yorke?] 1794, p. vii.   [33] [Yorke?] 1794, p. viii.   [34] [Yorke?] 1794, p. viii.

in the final chapter on 'The Dissolution of Government', that the people are generally averse to change and that previous revolutions in England typically reverted to their old constitution of King, Lords, and Commons.[35] Thus shorn of materials that tied the book most closely to the political struggles of its original context, the 'spirit of John Locke' was assertively new-modelled to speak to late eighteenth-century British problems vis-à-vis events across the Channel. In effect, the 'change in speaking subjects' marked by the Sheffield redactions spawned a decidedly rationalist and radicalized text, one happily rid of the fabled state of nature, paternal power, the practical necessity of prerogative and all the rest that might complicate that project.

My final example of eighteenth-century readings of the *Treatise* is Thomas Elrington's 1798 publication of the *Second Treatise* as a free-standing whole. French editions of the second essay alone had began to appear soon after the original, and one American printing had appeared in 1773, but this was the only solo version of the treatise published in the British empire in the eighteenth century. Extensively annotated and footnoted as well as prefaced by a substantial introduction, Elrington's edition of *An Essay Concerning the True Original Extent and End of Civil Government*[36] took the scholarly high-ground in relation to a work that had proved itself inconveniently open to radical appropriations. That the stakes of reading Locke had become a question of the relative proximity or distance between the events of 1688 and those of a new revolutionary epoch was no small part of Elrington's concern. Here, however, we might note the scholarly form and accentuation of this variant as an element of the political life of the book. Criticisms and refutations of Locke's various arguments pepper the margins of the work, but so too do explanatory notes and other citations. That it was produced in Dublin in 1798 is also significant, for its opposition to the revolutionary edge of the *Treatise* was also an opposition not only to English friends of the French Revolution but to events brewing in Ireland as well. The choice of an edited republication rather than a separate rebuttal, however, may reflect more than the churchly calling of the editor. It might equally well signify a recognition that the relative indirection of a scholarly voice enhanced the weight and status of the criticisms for the 'better sort' among whom a volume of this kind might be thought to find its audience.

---

[35] Compare Locke 1988, II.223, with [Yorke?] 1794, p. 29.    [36] Locke 1798.

Like *Civil Polity* and *The Spirit of John Locke*, then, Elrington's critical edition itself manifested the 'active responsiveness' and 'change of speaking subjects' that, on Bakhtin's account, characterize of the chain of speech communication in time. As in the other two works as well — indeed, like the parcels of the *Treatises* braided into *Political Aphorisms* and its successors — 'Locke's' text, or what appears of it, remains embedded in the language of natural law. For the others, however, it remains akin, too, to the notions of the 'ancient constitution' and the 'ancient liberties' of the country. By contrast, and ironically since Elrington's was the only solo printing of the second *Treatise* in Britain and Ireland, here Locke's reasoning is often found deeply flawed (in ways polemicized by previous generations of critics), and far too close to the experience of recent history for comfort. All read the same text, but the diversity of the politics they drew from it is testimony to the ways in which the level of *parole* might spin off substantially different orientations to action from a single work in different times and places, even within a vernacular language that is ostensibly 'the same' as well.

## IV. THE GREAT LITERALIZATION: SATIRE, PROGRESS AND A 'VINDICATION OF NATURAL SOCIETY'

My last example of the political life of books began as a mid-eighteenth-century parody of rationalism only to be mobilized, a hundred years later, as a support for emergent social science. It has, of course, become something of a late-modern commonplace that the sense or meaning evoked by the idea of a political or social 'science' is itself a historical construct.[37] In the history of print culture, however, it might be some-thing of a surprise to find that books first pitched as criticisms of the naturalizing tendencies that culminated in such scientistic understandings could have been polemically reiterated in terms more friendly to that 'political language'. Edmund Burke's initially anonymous *Vindication of Natural Society* (1756), originally penned as a politically invested satire of Bolingbroke's ideas of natural religion might, in this context, serve as a telling instance of how the ironies of eighteenth-century rhetoric could be literalized into a practical and prospective 'science' for mid-Victorian Britain. Indeed, a recent editor of the book marks a version of this dilemma by asking whether the original should be understood 'as a satire

---

[37] See, for example, Wolin 1969; Pagden 1987a, esp. part IV; Foucault 1970; Winch 1990.

or a serious tract'.[38] The print history of the book, however, suggests that this phrasing is itself part of the historiographical, political and theoretical problem presented by the amphibolous character of the original publication.[39] But this is to get ahead of myself — so again, let me begin at the beginning.

Attributed to 'a late noble writer', the *Vindication* first launched into print in 1756. An advertisement noting its editor's regret that it had not appeared in that writer's recently published *Works* clearly implicated Bolingbroke as its author. This apparently caused quite a stir, as it extended Bolingbroke's criticisms of artificial religious institutions to political institutions as well. However this may have pleased the enemies of the recently deceased 'noble writer', the credibility of its style apparently so alarmed his friends that David Mallet, the editor of Bolingbroke's *Works*, was reported to have rushed to the shop of the *Vindication*'s publisher to deny either Bolingbroke's or his own responsibility for the book.[40] A year later, the second edition avoided that dilemma by dropping the pretense of Bolingbroke's authorship. Instead, a 'new preface' by an anonymous editorial *persona* announced the book as an imitative satire, one intended to show how the 'specious' reasoning that Bolingbroke used against the church could be similarly deployed to turn unwary readers against any artificial institutions, the state itself foremost among them.

This paratextual attempt to insulate the text from literal readings — as the modern editor has it, from the charge of 'seriousness' — was in the long run generally successful. As we have seen in previous examples, however, the mid-1790s was a perilous time for historical texts, and two reprintings of the no longer anonymous *Vindication* in 1796 seem to have shadowed Burke's *Reflections* with a renewed equivocality. Indeed, it seems to be during these years that a youthful radicalism was first ascribed to Burke by radical pamphleteers intent upon painting the *Reflections* as the mark of an inconstant and hypocritical character.

---

[38] Pagano 1982, p. xvii.
[39] The 'amphibolous' dimensions of 'classic' texts — that is, phrasings that can be understood in two (or more) ostensibly stable systems of meaning — is a core insight of Condren 1985, esp. pp. 242–50. In literary terms, of course, this is a defining feature of satire, and modern scholarship on the *Vindication* is a testimony to this dilemma. For the authenticity of Burke's ironic voice, see Prior 1824, pp. 33–5; Copeland 1949, p. 133; Weston 1958; Stanlis 1958, p. 125; Stanlis 1967; and Kirk 1967, pp. 30–1. On Burke's own ambivalence, see Kramnick 1977, pp. 88–93. For defenses of the literal sense and Burke's early 'radicalism', see Bury 1928, pp. 181–2; Halévy 1934, pp. 215–16; and Rothbard 1958, pp. 114–18.
[40] Burke 1853, I, p. 22.

One of the leading radicals of the time, however, gave a rather different account. After news of Burke's death in 1797, William Godwin added a footnote to the third edition of his *Political Justice* that recounted the statesman's central flaw not as hypocrisy, but rather as corruption.[41] In the half-century that followed, however, Burke's reputation remained largely unscathed, and the numerous editions of his *Works* issued in both Britain and the United States bore witness to his continuing stature.

Until the mid-nineteenth century there was no further solo edition of the *Vindication*. In 1858, however, an inventive reader appropriated the text of the *Vindication* from the 1854 'Bohn's British Classics' edition of Burke's *Works*. Issued by the radical publisher George Jacob Holyoake – stalwart secularist and friend of the Cooperative movement in Britain – this reprint was marked by a series of paratextual devices that again, though now more substantially, floated Burke's first book as a monument to radicalism. Newly titled *The Inherent Evils of All State Governments Demonstrated*, this was not the radicalism of the 1790s, but one of a decidedly different and more recent sort. Dropping both the 'advertise-ment' of the first edition and the 'new preface' of the second, it sub-stituted an extended preface questioning the ironic intent of the original. Beyond this, it added extensive annotations to the text as well as a lengthy appendix elaborating 'the principles' through which the *Vindication*'s 'natural society' might be realized in practice. As the editor put it, this addition supplemented 'an important deficiency' in the original by suggesting how 'Artificial Society' and its evils 'may be superseded by a "Natural Society" in which truth, peace, and happiness shall pre-dominate over error, strife, and misery'.[42] Finally, the insertion of five epigraphs on the verso of the title page associated the book both with a long-standing Biblical warning about kings and a series of European and American radicals who took a critical distance from the institution of government as such.[43]

Taken together, these paratextual changes effectively undid the ways in which the alterations of the second edition had guarded the book

[41] Godwin 1797, II, p. 546n.
[42] *The Inherent Evils of All State Governments Demonstrated* 1858, p. vi.
[43] The epigraphs are: 'Nevertheless, the people refused to obey the voice of Samuel; and they said, Nay, but we will have a King to rule over us'. – 2 SAM., viii, 9; 'Government is a necessity of undeveloped society'. S. P. ANDREWS; 'The least possible amount of governing must be the formula of the future'. VICTOR HUGO; 'Governments are the scourges of God to discipline the world; for them to create liberty would be to destroy themselves'. PROUDHON; 'I own I have little esteem for Governments. In this country, for the last few years, the Government has been the chief obstacle to the commonweal'. EMERSON.

from literalism. Indeed, they encouraged a new sort of literalism by recasting the book as a prophetic antecedent of the Equitable Society Movement, the anarcho-socialist wing of American Owenite rationalism and the European left. It is these last aspects of the newly minted *Vindication* that are particularly striking. In the appendix, for instance, Burke's 'natural society' is associated not with Bolingbroke, nor even Godwin, but with Fichte's five epochs of human development and the decidedly prospective views of 'the Science of Equitable Human Relations'. And, by a linkage to Steven Pearl Andrews' *Science of Society* (1851) and Josiah Warren's *Equitable Commerce* (1852), it was practically animated toward a new pragmatics of political action as well. Through all these editorial supplements, the *Vindication* was assertively aligned with assorted variants of social science on offer in the mid-nineteenth century, and the 'active responsive understanding' of its editor turned it more particularly toward projects of practical transformation through concerted social action.

## V.   REMAINDERS

In the discussions above I have suggested some of the ways in which generations of readers – as translators, subscribers, editors and scholars, but in any case as writers – participated in the chain of speech communication that linked a textual past to the political controversies of successive presents. Not unlike the ways in which writers, editors and publishers of fiction took up, imitated, transformed and recast earlier literatures, these readers responded to the 'utterance' of historical texts with 'utterances' of their own. In each case, their compilations, glosses and creative editorial work accord broadly with the history of the various political languages identified by Cambridge historiography. But in each case, as well, the original texts were not simply carried forward into new venues of political contestation; they were made to speak differently, or more brashly, or with calmer authority in some hands than they did in others. Further examples of this process could have been drawn from the shifting political interpretations added to dramatic works or novels, sometimes by editors and critics, sometimes by the original authors themselves: the different sense made of Shakespeare, for instance, by Johnson in the eighteenth century and Hazlitt in the nineteenth, or the migration of Felix Holt's address to working men from the pages of *Blackwood's Magazine* to the pages of George Eliot's novel. In these cases, as in those considered here, the line between fiction and political prose is anything but bright. Our conventional understandings of genre would hardly permit us to speak of Johnson, Hazlitt or Eliot as writers of political theory, but perhaps this views the enterprise far too narrowly. To the extent that political theorizing consists in offering not simply a perspective on the political world but also an orientation to action within it, its containment within conventional genre distinctions looks more like a matter of academic convenience than a characteristic of its historical expressions.

By the same token, however, perhaps attention to 'literary' works' embeddedness in political discourses, languages or ideologies is too broad to capture the ways in which specific writings might orient interested readers to political action – or what early-modern readers might have understood as opportunities for 'application'. Yet if this is the case, it may be that the nestling of 'theoretical' texts into analogously broad conceptions of political languages, compelling though it may be as *history*, also constrains our ability to grasp the sorts of 'events' that such texts can become through repetition, reiteration and adaptation. Indeed, if the 'utterance' of such texts finds an answer in the form of scholarly discourse – Elrington might well come to mind here – it becomes increasingly difficult to regard the 'active responsive understanding' of scholarship as an inherently neutral third-order analysis of second-order theoretical statements about first order political activities. Instead, generic differentia notwithstanding, all become links in a chain of speech communication that can blur the boundary between past and present and infuse all such utterances with pertinence for the political contestations of the latest time and place.

Finally, perhaps the same dynamics might operate with respect to the astonishing variety of historical and near contemporary texts now populating the internet and inviting contemporary readers to make what they will of them.[44] Admittedly, this seems far afield from my focus here on history, theory and printed books. But if the political point and theoretical edge of political literature is something persistently rearticulated in the inventive 'applications' of writing readers, the internet may well be one of the places where the reading of historical texts and the theorizing of future possibilities is likely to take shape.

---

[44] See the Online Library of Liberty, http://oll.libertyfund.org/index.html; The Constitutional Society, http://www.constitution.org; the book links at http://www.straussian.net; The Founding Fathers Party, http://www.foundingfathersparty.net; the Marxists Internet Archive, http://www.marxists.org; the Internet Classics Archive, http://classics.mit.edu/index.html; or the links at Theory.org, http://www.theory.org.uk/directory.htm

# Here and Now, There and Then, Always and Everywhere: Reflections Concerning Political Theory and the Study/Writing of Political Thought

### Richard E. Flathman

'... as it were between the games'
(Ludwig Wittgenstein)

Both political theorizing and the study/writing of the history of political thought have many and varied exemplifications. Accordingly, it is difficult to generalize confidently concerning the relationship(s) between them. Briefly, political theorizing has commonly been, and ought to be, characterized by some combination of, on the one hand, critical assessments of prevalent political and related concepts, ideas, institutions and practices and, on the other, attempts to imagine and articulate political ideals that serve both as criteria for critical assessment of extant ideas and arrangements and as proposals for a politics that is improved by normative standards. In its historical manifestations it is of course also an attempt to understand the concepts, issues and ideas to which it is addressed. This chapter then juxtaposes this conception with some leading views − which also may be regarded as idealizations − of the aims and methods appropriate to the study/writing of the history of political thought.

I

I take these to be importantly distinct activities or modes of thinking. Insofar as I advance a general view of the relationship(s) between them, it is that political theorizing provides historians of political thought with important parts (but not all) of their subject matter, while historians of political thought may provide, have sometimes provided, political theorists with an improved grasp of some of the concepts, ideas and ideals with, in and about which to think. They may also provide, have sometimes provided, an enlarged and in that respect an improved perspective on the questions they address and the answers they are inclined to give or to reject to those questions.

One way to expand somewhat on this view is to underline the idea that political theorists provide historians of political thought with part but not all of their subject matter. As regards the studies of the history of political thought that I was required to read as a graduate student,[1] we can pretty well do without the qualifier 'but not all'. These students (and many still writing) thought that there was a relatively short list of 'canonical' political theorists and the texts they produced; they devoted their efforts almost exclusively to identifying what they took to be the main concepts, ideas, ideals and arguments that formed the bodies of the texts that those canonical theorists wrote. There were (and are) minor differences among the lists with which they worked (and still work) but it would not be far wrong to say that those who made (and still make) it onto the list were understood to have a conception of political theorizing closely similar to the conception I have sketched above. Insofar as the texts in question contained elements that did or do not fit this conception they were (and in many quarters are) regarded as irrelevant to the study of the history of political theory.

A second way to expand on it is to emphasize the words 'critical assessment' and 'a politics improved by normative standards' in my earlier characterization of political theorizing. The students of the history of political thought to whom I just alluded (for convenience of reference I will call them 'students of the canon') understood the political theorists that they studied to be exposing mistaken views concerning political concepts, ideas and practices and to have the objective or purpose of replacing them with a correct, right or true account of them. They understood the canonical thinkers to be attempting to tell their readers what questions should be asked and how and what they ought to think about them and hence how and how not to act; that is, they were prescribing the form and character that politics ought to have. The students of the canon further thought that if, or to the extent that, the canonical theorists 'got it right', their theories tell *us* how and how not to think and act and how *our* politics ought to be conducted. Of course these canonical students disagreed with some of the political theorists that they studied and they disagreed with one another as to the merits of the

---

[1] For example Sabine 1955; Carlyle and Carlyle 1936; Barker 1956; Mesnard 1936.

various views that they encountered in the course of their studies. But they agreed concerning the generic objectives that political theorists should pursue and that it was their task as students of political theory to make the results of that pursuit available to their own readerships. Insofar as they thought of themselves as political theorists as well as students of the history of political thought they pursued the same generic objectives as did their canonical predecessors. It is of course a controversial question how far they or those that they studied have achieved their practical objectives.

This understanding of how to study/write the history of political thought came under heavy attack in the latter part of the twentieth century (with, of course, some earlier anticipations) and the attack on it has continued with many refinements and with steadily increasing force in the ensuing years. Both the attack and the refinements have continued into the present century. In referring to the aforementioned large and growing group of writers as 'students' of the canonical history of political thought rather than as 'historians' of political thought I am 'acknowledging' (in something like Stanley Cavell's use of 'acknowledging')[2] what is arguably the broadest objection that these twentieth- (and of course twenty-first) century critics have entered to the studies of political thought that were dominant for much of the previous century, namely that in the proper sense of the term they were not *historical*.

J. G. A. Pocock, looking back over historiographical thinking in roughly the last half of the twentieth century, has recently provided a characteristically elegant summary of this criticism. Referring to Quentin Skinner's early article 'Meaning and Understanding in the History of Ideas' (1969), 'which came to be the manifesto of an emerging method of interpreting the history of political thought', he credits Skinner with having

demonstrated that much of the received history of that activity suffered from a radical confusion between systematic theory (or philosophy) and history. The greater and lesser texts of the past were interpreted as attempts to formulate bodies of theory whose content had been determined in advance by extrahistorical understandings of what 'political theory' and 'history' should be and were. This confusion led to errors including anachronism (the attribution to a past author of concepts that could not have been available to him) and prolepsis (treating him as anticipating the formation of arguments in whose subsequent

---

[2] Cavell 1969.

formation the role of his text, if any, had yet to be historically demonstrated). After treating these fallacies with well-deserved ridicule, Skinner contended that the publication of a text and the utterance of its argument must be treated as an act performed in history, and specifically in the context of some ongoing discourse. It was necessary, Skinner said, to know what the author 'was doing'; what she or he had intended to do (had meant) and what she or he had succeeded in doing (had meant to others). The act and its effect had been performed in a historical context, supplied in the first place by the language of discourse in which the author had written and been read; though the speech act might innovate within and upon that language ... the language would set limits to what the author might say, might intend to say and be understood to say.[3]

In treating 'classical' or canonical texts' as themselves providing everything necessary to understand them, and as addressing 'perennial questions' or 'unit ideas', students of political thought produced not histories but what Skinner called 'mythologies'.[4]

In the passage quoted and some of the later pages of the same essay, Pocock is looking back at some of the key moments in the emergence of what has come to be called the 'Cambridge' or 'contextual' school of thought concerning the methods and objectives appropriate to studying and writing the history of political theory (and intellectual history generally). As he goes on to note, and as Skinner and other members of this contextualist school have emphasized, important changes, including disagreements among those who accept the basic tenets of the approach, have developed.[5] I comment on some of these later in the chapter but my purposes in the first parts of the chapter will be best served by using the distinctions I have thus far drawn, that is among an (idealized) conception of political theory, a prominent understanding of the history of political theory (the canonical conception) that brings a strongly analogous understanding of political theory to the study of its history, and the alternative approach to studying/writing the history of political theory (the contextualist approach) just sketched. As a means of doing so I make use of the main terms of my title, interpreting them in part through an overlapping but not equivalent set of distinctions proposed by the political philosopher Michael Oakeshott.

II

It is obvious, but nevertheless still worth mentioning, that all political theorizing, and all writing concerning the history of political thought,

---

[3] Pocock 2004, pp. 537–8.    [4] Skinner 1969.    [5] See esp. Skinner 2002a.

are in one or another here and now (as distinct from the everywhere and always). The thinkers that we regard as political theorists thought and wrote, think and write, in a time and place specific to them; writers concerning the history of political thought, whatever the then and there that is their focus, perform their studies and their writings in an identifiable — that is their own — times and places. All thinking and writing, however much its authors are concerned with a then and there of another specified time and place, are in the mode of the present, in the mode of the here and now. Insofar as they refer, explicitly or implicitly, to the past, that past is what Oakeshott calls the 'present past'.[6]

Oakeshott distinguishes, however, between the present 'practical past' and the present 'historical past'. If, or to the extent that, political theorists are interested in the past (as distinct from the everywhere and always), their interest is predominantly if not exclusively in the past as it bears upon the present interests and desires, objectives and purposes, of the theorist. The political theorist, *qua* political theorist, has no interest in, no use for, there's and then's that have no bearing on the here and now (though of course she or he may be influenced, knowingly or unknowingly, by there's and then's that in fact have a bearing on the here and now and it may be illuminating for historians of political thought to show that this is the case). In this respect, the interest of the political theorist in the past is, generically, the same as that of the moralist, the statesman, the businessman or the cook. For reasons already discussed, the same is true of canonical students of the history of political theory who understand it to be a search for correct answers to 'perennial questions', that is questions of present and future importance.

By contrast, contextualist historians of political thought — again as such and in what may be an idealized understanding — generally have no interest in the bearing of the concepts and ideas they study on the here and now. They seek to understand the emergence of concepts and ideas from the confluence of languages, intentions, thinkings, actings and other events that preceded and surrounded them; they seek to identify the meanings of the concepts and ideas in the then's and there's in which they, as evidenced by the texts and text analogues that come to the historian's attention, played a significant role. Mentions of the bearing of the ideas and events on the here and now of the historian (to say nothing

---

[6] Oakeshott 1933; Oakeshott 1983, chs. 1–3; Oakeshott 1991. Note that a modest version of the notion of the always and everywhere has crept in here.

of the everywhere and always) are — to up-date Stendhal — like the ringing of a cell-phone in the concert hall.

As with the distinctions drawn earlier, it is clear that those just sketched distinguish among ideal-types or, in terms that Oakeshott uses in discussing the 'Modern European States', 'ideal characters'.[7] Just as Oakeshott does not claim that all or even any modern European states have or have had, exclusively, the defining characteristics of either a *societas* (a politically organized society with no common purpose) or a *universitas* (a society held together by a common purpose), he does not claim that all instances of thinking and writing concerning the past fit neatly into the categories 'practical past', 'historical past' or 'past past'. But he does claim that the elements or components of all such instances can be parsed, can be distinguished and differentiated, by using those categories. He also claims that doing so provides the criteria relevant to evaluating the merits of the thinking and writing that one is assessing.

In the next section of my chapter, I consider the value of his distinctions and of the related distinctions introduced earlier. In particular I consider whether employing these distinctions helps to identify congruencies and complementarities as well as differences among the understandings and approaches that the distinctions differentiate. Before doing so I should say a bit more about the third pair of terms in my title, that is the always and everywhere.

Taken in full seriousness, that is as the view that there are questions pertinent not only to all known but to all possible (human?) experience, and that there are answers to those questions that not only are but must be true or valid of all human experience, this notion or view now seems to me to be little better than fantastic. If, as I think is the case, I was once attracted to it, just about everything that has transpired in the century in which I have lived most of my life, and not a little that has been recovered from earlier thinking and acting, has disabused me of it but not of the conviction that political theorizing as identified above is a possible and a valuable form of thought/action. But if we are to understand what many theorists and not a few political actors have thought they were doing, or understood themselves to be trying to do, we have to recognize that the notion of the everywhere and always, and the possibility — certainly the desirability — of giving that notion what Oakeshott and other Philosophical Idealists call 'fully coherent concreteness', has played and

---

[7] Oakeshott 1975, chs. 1, 3.

continues to play an important role in political and other modes of theorizing and (regrettably) in not a little political acting.

Leaving aside religious thinkers, it is more than merely arguable that Plato, Kant, Bradley and other Philosophical Idealists (Hegel is a difficult case) have understood their thinking about the here and now and the there and then to be also — and more importantly — thinking about the always and everywhere. Oakeshott himself saw no prospect of actually attaining to the fully coherent concrete whole, but he continued to think that the idea of such an attainment, even if only flickering in the back of the thinker's mind, was — at least for the philosopher as distinct from the theorist — a valuable, perhaps an indispensable heuristic. If Oakeshott wrote any history (which is doubtful) it was the history of historiography, that is the history of the emergence of the 'postulates' of the activity of being an historian. His writings concerning the 'Modern European State' and related essays quite clearly do not, are not intended by him, to satisfy his own criteria of historical study. In his terminology, they are reflections on the practical past. Another thinker who comes to mind in this connection is Hannah Arendt. Numerous of her writings make references and allusions to past there's and then's and her perceptions concerning the rise of what she calls 'the social' may be of interest to historians, but we will be sorely disappointed if we look to her for instruction concerning, certainly of explanations for, the there's and then's that she instances. She too is a paradigm example of history viewed from the perspective of the practical past. The same might also be said of Leo Strauss.

It is at least arguable that Thomas Hobbes thought that important aspects of his thinking, those that he pleased himself to call scientific, had a character similar to Oakeshott's heuristic conception of the always and the everywhere. He of course admitted (no, insisted) that his science of the political (and the moral) took its beginnings from stipulations that could have been otherwise. But he thought that, once accepted, what he called ratiocination (the 'adding and subtracting' of the meanings of the stipulated terms) would lead to indisputable conclusions that would hold always and everywhere unless the stipulations were changed. With an important qualification, the same can be said concerning some of those political theorists that are called utopians. Of course these theorists, perhaps most notably Karl Marx but also Jürgen Habermas, would not have said that the utopian parts of their theories were true of any actual there or then or here and now, but they held that once put into practice their theories would be true always and everywhere in the future.

As Marx sometimes put it, history, that is significant change, would end. The history of political thinking could still be investigated and recounted, but it would have no bearing on the present or the future — would be purely antiquarian. There are places in which these theorists write as if they are studying the history of political (and other modes of) thought and action, but when they do so they understand themselves to be identifying a progression that could, or should, have only one culmination. By contrast, Philosophical Idealists such as Plato and Bradley thought that their theories identified and rendered reality as it has always been and can only be, all appearances to the contrary being just that, appearances.

III

The views and understandings considered thus far emphasize the differences between political theorizing and the study/writing of the history of political thought and among contrasting and competing approaches to the latter. But they also implicitly call attention to commonalities among these modes of inquiry and reflection. If there were no commonalities, comparison among them would be, if not impossible, of little fruition. Given that there are some significant commonalities, there is the possibility of complementarities as well as differentiations among and between them.

The obvious commonality among the canonical and contextual conceptions of the study/writing of the history of political thought is two-fold: in Oakeshott's terminology, they are both concerned (but for different reasons) with the present past, with the past as it is, here and now, perceived, understood and interpreted by those who study it. In an historical perspective, however, this is also true of political theorizing, even theorizing that aims to discern and articulate the everywhere and always. Reflections with this objective are of course carried out in a specific time and place and necessarily engage with, and reflect on, concepts and ideas that have come to the theorist from present and past formulations.

This commonality between political theorizing and studies concerning the history of political thought coexists with and, I argue, creates the possibility not only of some meaningful comparisons but also of degrees of complementarity between these two forms or modes or intellectual activity. Those conventionally regarded as political theorists, say Hobbes or Mill, thought and wrote in the there and then of their own time and place, a there and then that can be fruitfully identified by students of the history of political thinking. Important aspects of their thinking may be revealed by close examination of both the there and then in which their thinking took place and of the earlier then's and there's that figured, importantly (however knowingly or self-consciously) in their reflections and articulations. Many if not all of the concepts and ideas that political theorists critique and on which they seek to improve have lengthy and complex histories; as with the rest of us, political theorists, however extrahistorical (transcendental?) their objectives may be, become familiar with parts of their histories as they learn to think in and about them. In both their critical and constructive activities political theorists often attempt to effect changes in the stock of ideas and concepts that they inherit; but neither the changes nor the continuities in their formulations can be understood, by the theorists themselves or by their audiences, apart from their histories. Thus just as political theorists provide historians of political theory with important parts of their subject matter, so historians of political theory can be valuable to political theorists by enlarging and deepening their command of the concepts and ideas in and about which they think. If political theorists aim to think constructively concerning the ideas and concepts that interest them, it is plausible to think that their theorizing will benefit from having a clear understanding of the meanings that those ideas and concepts have acquired and have become available to them. The work of John Rawls is instructive in this respect. It might be argued that the concepts and conceptions that he employs in *A Theory of Justice* (1971) can be understood without reference to the history of their uses in contractarian, utilitarian and related movements of thought and action that preceded his writing. Rawls locates his reflections in the contractarian tradition and contrasts them with utilitarianism, but he provides little of the details of either of what he recognizes as the historical antecedents of his thinking. As becomes clear from his later (including posthumuous) publications, however, his thinking was importantly inflected by the histories of these ideas.[8]

## *Interregnum I*

It is arguable that the possibility of complementarities of the kinds mentioned was significantly enhanced as the differences between political

---

[8] See especially Rawls 2000.

theorizing and among differing ways of studying/writing the history of political thought became more clearly delineated, a development that so far as I know (a 'so far as' that could easily be exaggerated) did not become clearly discernible until, at the earliest, the later years of the nineteenth century and perhaps not until the emergence of the Cambridge or contextualist school. Of course there have been histories from Herodotus and Thucydides forward and there were histories of philosophy (for example that of Diogenes Laertius), many of which recount and interpret the political ideas that their authors thought were influential in the events that were the subject matters of their histories. Many thinkers now conventionally regarded as political theorists gave those histories close attention – Machiavelli being only the most obvious example. So far as I have been able to determine, however, it was not – Vico may be a partial exception – until the late nineteenth and more likely the early parts of the twentieth century, that studies of the history of political (and philosophical) thought were distinguished from either political theorizing or general histories of politics, philosophy and related dimensions of human experience. In the early nineteenth century, William Whewell wrote a history of moral and political thought, Henry Sidgwick later did the same, while in the seventeenth, eighteenth and nineteenth centuries several histories of philosophy were written by German, French and other scholars. My impression is that these were in the 'canonical' mode. What seems clear is that in the last one hundred-plus years there have developed improved distinctions between political theorizing and the study of the history of political thought, as well as among various alternative modes of studying the latter. However one assesses the merits of inquiries and reflections in the several modes, it seems clear that the emergence of these distinctions has made possible the identification of complementarities as well as differentiations among the several modes of inquiry and reflection that are now distinguished. This is a major contribution of the contextualist school.

Whatever exact dating we assign to the emergence and clarification of the distinction between canonical and contextualist approaches with which I have been working, they are now well in place. And this enables us to ask concerning the ways they advantage and disadvantage one another. To begin with the question of the ways in which 'canonical' historians of the history of political thought may benefit from the researches of contextual historians of the subject, it is undeniable that, say, Sabine's discussions of Aristotle, Machiavelli or Hegel would have benefitted from a more detailed understanding of the contexts in which these thinkers formulated their ideas. At the same time, however, Sabine had made a close study of the texts of these writers and has provided others interested in them with detailed accounts of features prominent in those texts.[9] Of course the contextually oriented historian of political thought could acquire the same textual familiarity without any help from Sabine, but the texts in question are complex and subject to various interpretations and reading, say, Sabine's accounts of them might inform or usefully jostle the mind of the contextually oriented historians in ways that enhance their own readings. Pocock, Skinner and other contextualists recognize that the writings of canonical historians have sometimes yielded valuable results.

This brings me to a quite general question concerning the notion of context. The relationship between text and context is a variable and disputable, not an unequivocal feature of recovering and achieving an improved understanding of a text or text analogue. Consider the case of Hobbes. Pocock has located important parts of his thinking in the context of theological disputations;[10] A. E. Taylor and Howard Warrender place him in the context of natural law theories leading to Kant;[11] Skinner positions *Leviathan* in the setting of neo-classical rhetorical writings;[12] Richard Tuck treats him as continuing and developing neo-Stoical and skeptical constructions;[13] Steven Shapin and Simon Schaffer interpret him as participating in controversies concerning the appropriate methodologies of natural and mathematical sciences:[14] these students of his thought locate him in ways that can be historically validated. By contrast, Gregory Kavka and Deborah Baumgold see him as an early contributor to rational choice theory;[15] numerous students locate him in the tradition of contractarian thinking; Oakeshott characterizes him as a theorist of 'Will and Artifice' and more generally as a leading contributor to 'epic' political theory;[16] and so forth. To take but one of numerous other possible examples, J. S. Mill has sometimes been characterized as continuing but entering important modifications in Benthamite utilitarianism, as a liberal in the tradition of Constant, as an elitist individualist who is best compared with Emerson and Nietzsche and as a forerunner of twentieth and twentieth-first century feminist theory. I do not think that I am the only student of these works who, despite important disagreements with

---

[9] Sabine 1955.    [10] Pocock 1971.    [11] Taylor 1938; Warrender 1957.
[12] Skinner 1996; Skinner 2002c.    [13] Tuck 1989; Tuck 1993.    [14] Shapin and Schaffer 1985.
[15] Kavka 1986; Baumgold 1988.    [16] Oakeshott 1955.

them, has learned from all of these studies. None of these interpreters need disagree with the others.

Different as they are, these contextualizations can be viewed as complementary rather than competing or mutually exclusive. Hobbes and Mill are complex thinkers whose work can fruitfully be viewed from a variety of perspectives. Because both of them aspired to 'get it right' concerning some of the issues they addressed, they are appropriately classified and assessed as political theorists. Approached in this way, the (or at least *a*) context relevant to understanding and assessing their work is the history of other attempts, whether prior to, contemporary with, or later than their own thinking. Hobbes's blistering attacks on 'the vain philosophy of Aristotle' and 'Aristotelity', and his protracted diatribe against cardinal Bellarmine and other theologians cannot be understood or evaluated without a knowledge of what they said and especially what he took them to be saying. It is of course absurd (because both an anachronism and a prolepsis) to treat him as anticipating the thinking of Hume or Kant, but there is nothing absurd about critically comparing his skeptical nominalism with Hume's or his importantly naturalistic ethics with Kant's *Groundwork for the Metaphysics of Morals*. No one would dispute the importance of Mill's responses to Bentham and his father, but important aspects of his thinking also require attention to his critiques of Kant and Rousseau, his favourable citations of George Grote's study of Plato, the continuities and discontinuities between his and earlier writings concerning political economy. Anachronistic or proleptic as it may be, I have found it fruitful to read his *A System of Logic* with and against Wittgenstein's *Tractatus* and *Philosophical Investigations*.

At the same time, Hobbes and Mill were engaged with and vigorously responsive to intellectual and political events of the here's and now's of their own times. In this respect studies of the more immediate contexts of their thinking are not merely valuable, they are indispensable. Despite the many earlier canonical commentaries on Hobbes's thought it is only recently that we have learned more than the barest details concerning his life and his many practical involvements. Thanks to the work of Skinner, Tuck, Malcolm, and others, we now know a great deal about his activities;[17] and what they have taught us is illuminating about his thought as well as his life. Just as Peter Laslett, James Tully, John Marshall and others have transformed the study of John Locke, so the historians

---

[17] See Skinner 1996; Skinner 2000c; Tuck 1989; Tuck 1993; Malcolm 2002, among others.

just mentioned have given us insights into Hobbes' thinking that could not have been achieved in any other way.[18]

The study of important political theorists is a cooperative activity that can be done in many ways and in the pursuit of diverse objectives. That differing purposes and 'methodologies' often lead to disagreements is not only to be expected but welcomed. To borrow a figure from the Preface of Wittgenstein's *Investigations*, the same thinkers can be approached afresh from different directions, producing a picture of the 'landscape' that is their lives and thoughts. To repeat what I said above, that we now have a clearer understanding of differing conceptions of the study of political thought allows us to see the advantages and disadvantages of leading approaches and to understand ways in which their results complement as well as conflict with one another.

## IV

I now revisit the distinctions that have been introduced thus far and ask to what extent they clearly distinguish among political theorists on the one hand and, on the other, canonical students and contextualist historians of political thought. Do we in fact find thinkers and writers who, if not throughout the writings, in identifiable dimensions or aspects of their work, present clear examples of the several approaches or understandings outlined in previous sections?

I opined earlier that there are clear examples of political theorizing as I have characterized that form of thought and action. It is not merely that this is an in principle possible way or mode of thinking/acting. Rather, it is whether Plato, parts of Aristotle, parts of Hobbes and of Kant, Rousseau, Hegel and Mill exemplify it. Of course these writers thought in particular times and places and were influenced, sometimes knowingly sometimes not, by the conceptual and ideational resources that they inherited. These are aspects of their thinking that could be but seldom are investigated by canonical students of political thought and are intensively studied by the trademark methods of contextual historians of that subject. The political theorists just listed often critique, explicitly or implicitly, thinkers contemporary with them and those that preceded them (Plato critiquing the pre-Socratics; Aristotle critiquing Plato; Hobbes, Aristotle; Hegel, Kant; and so forth). But their purpose in doing so was not to

[18] See Laslett's introduction in Locke 1988; Tully 1979; Tully 1993a; Tully 1993b; Marshall 1994; Marshall 2005.

explain or understand the past, it was to arrive at right answers to the questions they addressed and to present arguments supporting those answers. In Oakeshott's terms, their concern with the past was with the practical not the historical past, but with the qualification that theory could and should govern practice, that theorizing was the most valuable kind of practicing. Oakeshott may be justified in saying that they sometimes abandoned the role of theorist and became what he scathingly calls theoreticians. He makes this charge most explicitly against Plato but he seems also to have Kant and Hegel in mind and he certainly brings the charge against all those that he designated rationalists.[19] There are admixtures of concern with the past in their texts, but their primary purpose was to arrive at demonstratively true answers to questions of continuing import. This is the most distinctive feature of their thinking. That there are major disagreements among them, and that generations of scholars who have studied them disagree with some or all of their conclusions is important; but so is the fact that those among them that came later in time found themselves obliged to engage the formulations of their predecessors, and that generations of students and historians of political thought have felt the same obligation.

## Interregnum II

What do professors of political theory teach? There is of course no single answer to this question, but the preponderance of the graduate programmes known to me (that is, those that include political theory) teach a remarkably similar selection of texts. And every such under-graduate programme also teaches a selection of those same texts. Why? It is no doubt partly because the canonical approach to the study of past political theorizing remains dominant in most universities and colleges. But while I have learned much and will surely continue to learn more from studies of that kind, I ask graduate students to read various selections of the canonical texts because doing so sharpens their thinking (and of course for the more mundane, professional, reason that when they go on to teach political theory they will be expected to be familiar with them). And I present various of those texts to undergraduates (very few of whom will go on to graduate study and academic careers) because I have found no better way to get them interested in and able to think critically about political questions. As is increasingly common in the political

[19] Oakeshott 1975, pp. 29–31.

theory programmes known to me (and it is a welcome development) I try to take account of and present the findings of contextual histories; and there are always some students who find these to be the most engaging features of the classes I teach. But these are, and I expect they will remain, a small minority. Most of the best of the students I have been privileged to teach are primarily interested in the positions and the arguments for them that they find in the political theorists they read.

My remarks in Interregnum II provide plenty of evidence (if any were needed) that there are lots of examples of studies of political theory in the canonical mode. The fact that leading contextual historians have been drawn to critique such studies, and that they have no shortage of examples of such studies to critique, makes it clear that the canonical approach is very much alive (if not necessarily in the best of health). Accordingly, I turn quickly to the contextual approach. As before, the question is less whether strict or pure versions of the contextual history of political thought are in principle possible (albeit versions of that question may again arise), but whether or to what extent there are extant examples of such histories.

Contextualist historians of political thought distinguish their approach and their objectives most persistently and most sharply from those of canonical students of that subject. They of course attend closely to the texts of the thinkers they study, but they hold that the intentions of the authors they study and the meanings of the texts they have bequeathed to us cannot be adequately understood without attending to the contexts in which they were written (enacted), in particular the issues and choices that were before their authors and the languages and styles of argument and presentation that were available to their authors. Because these contexts are constantly changing, the notion that there are timeless, perennial, questions that can be addressed, and 'unit ideas' concerning them that express, even if with some variations, answers to those questions (questions concerning the always and everywhere and timelessly correct answers to those questions) is mythological and leads not to history but to mythologies. Of course in distinguishing their approach from the (generic) approach of the canonical historians, contextualists at least appear to be denying the actuality (the possibility?) of political theorizing as characterized it here. The view that there are no timeless, perennial questions at least appears to deny the possibility of a mode of theorizing that identifies and seeks to find correct answers to such questions. I suggest below that there are some respects in which this appearance, if in fact it was ever advanced, is misleading.

Reverting to Oakeshott's distinctions, there are important respects in which contextual historians concern themselves primarily (but not, I argue, exclusively) with the historical not the practical past. They of course recognize that they work in the present past; that their historical studies are done in a here and now and are chosen and carried out in part in response to questions that previous or contemporary students of the past (and probably of political theory) have raised and attempted to answer. (An obvious example is the one already discussed: that is, the attention and energy that contextualists have devoted to critiquing the canonical approach. To mention but one prominent but more historical than historiographical example, consider the many ways in which the renaissance studies of Hans Baron figure in more recent studies of the same period.)[20] More generally, there is a personal, one might say a subjective, quality to their work as to everyone's. Why does this or that person study past political theories rather than, say, current welfare policies in Denmark or relations between the Sunnis and the Shi'ites in Iraq? Given a disposition to historical study, why does not one study the conflict between the Bolsheviks and Mensheviks or the Boer War? Given a disposition to study past political thinking, why does one study early-modern political thought rather than the history of utilitarianism or of contractualism from Locke and Kant to Rawls? However they may have developed, these dispositional preferences cannot be eliminated or entirely suppressed. But they can be explained and disciplined. In the course of their studies, contextualist historians have frequently made cogent cases for the value of their inquiries and for their claims that those of different moral, political and other sensibilities and orientations can and should endorse their historical claims.

Notwithstanding their recognition of these features of their work, contextualist historians claim that their primary objective is not to resolve, or to contribute to the resolution of, present practical political questions, but to better understand the past thinkings/actings that they study. To the limited extent that I am familiar with the studies of this school, I am convinced that numerous of them make good on this claim, this self-characterization. In my judgement especially clear cases are John Pocock's *The Ancient Constitution and the Feudal Law* (1957) and Noel Malcolm's studies of Hobbes, but there are lengthy stretches in the works of, for example, Skinner, Tully, and Tuck that do so. Present or later contextualist historians – to say nothing of Nietzschean perspectivalists

[20] Baron 1966; Hankins 2000.

and post-modernists or deconstructionists — may be able to show that the studies of Pocock, Malcolm, Skinner *et al.* are influenced by normative or other 'practical' commitments, but I see no reason to think that doing so will impugn or discredit their historical claims. The only considerations that would discredit or qualify those claims is historical evidence that goes against them.

These thoughts bring me to complexities in, and some divergencies among, the contextual historians. This school of thought has produced an exceptionally large and wide-ranging corpus of historical studies and I have neither the space nor the competence to explore these matters in a thorough-going way. Guided in part by the distinctions I have been using, I will briefly discuss a selection of the studies of Quentin Skinner and some of those of Richard Tuck.

Along with Pocock and John Dunn, Skinner has forcefully critiqued canonical studies of the history of political thought. But he has responded with equal vigour to the charge that his studies are purely antiquarian, that they provide nothing of interest or value to political theorists and/or political scientists who address issues of present importance.[21] He emphatically does not claim to be offering specific solutions to particular current political problems but he, quite rightly in my view, insists that his historical investigations can contribute in valuable ways to our think-ing about those problems. In one of several presentations of this view, and with reference to recent discussions of liberty, he writes: 'it is remarkably difficult to avoid falling under the spell of our own intellectual heritage. As we analyse and reflect on or normative concepts, it is easy to become bewitched into believing that the ways of thinking about them bequeathed to us by the mainstream of our intellectual traditions must be *the* ways of thinking about them. It seems to me that an element of such bewitchment has entered even into Berlin's justly celebrated account [of liberty or freedom]. Berlin takes himself to be pursuing the purely neutral task of showing what a philosophical analysis of our concepts requires us to say about the essence of liberty. But it is striking, to say the

---

[21] As this criticism has been mounted by Gunnell 1979; Gunnell 1982; and Tarlton 1973. Skinner 1988 correctly says that the charge has a philistine quality. I would go further: Gunnell has argued that both contextual historians and various contemporary political theorists fail to address currently pressing political questions. But rather than addressing such questions himself, he devotes himself to criticizing the writings of others. Thus even if he is correct that those he critiques are at one remove from current political questions, he himself is at two removes from the issues he claims should be the subjects of political theorizing and of the history of political thought.

least, that his analysis follows exactly the same path as the classical liberal theorists had earlier followed in their efforts to discredit the neo-Roman theory of free states'.[22]

Thus Skinner and other contextualist historians do two things at once: first, they inform the theorist of the historicity of his/her thinking; secondly, but relatedly, they inform the theorists of a historical continuity in which his/her thinking is situated. For example, Skinner argues that by 'excavating' the alternative neo-Roman conception of freedom, as with analogous recoveries of earlier conceptions of political concepts and ideas that differ from those now regnant, the 'history of philosophy, and perhaps especially of moral, social and political philosophy, is there to prevent us from becoming too readily bewitched. The intellectual historian can help us to appreciate how far the values embodied in our present way of life, and our present ways of thinking about those values, reflect a series of choices made at different times between different possible worlds. This awareness can help to liberate us from the grip of any one hegemonal account of those values and how they should be interpreted and understood. Equipped with a broader sense of possibility, we can stand back from the intellectual commitments we have inherited and ask ourselves in a new spirit of enquiry what we should think of them'.[23]

In the terms I used earlier, Skinner's position is that historical studies can widen and deepen thinking and acting in the here and now, including that mode of thinking/acting that is political theorizing. Although perhaps modest by comparison with the objectives of the canonical historians and with related but differently based views that I consider below, Skinner's defence against the charge that his studies are merely antiquarian does take it as uncontroversial that the commonalities between, say, liberal and neo-Roman conceptions of freedom are sufficient to allow us to compare and contrast them in ways not only intelligible but important to us. Once recovered, an understanding of the neo-Roman view of freedom can be brought into significant ideational and normative juxtapositions with liberal conceptions of freedom; whether effecting such juxtapositions leads us to reaffirm our commitment to the liberal view, to move our thinking in the direction of

[22] Skinner 1998, p. 116.
[23] Skinner 1998, pp. 116–17; see also Skinner 2002a, pp. viii, 5–7.

a neo-Roman understanding, or, say, to develop a hybrid view,[24] is a question that historical studies do not answer. But having the comparisons and contrasts in mind will help us to 'ruminate' in a more informed manner concerning the choices that we have made and continue to make.[25] (This is very much a Millian thought, although perhaps not one attended with the most soaring of Millian expectations or hopes.)

It is tempting to introduce at this juncture Rawls's distinction between concepts that are shared and conceptions concerning those concepts about which we are in disagreement.[26] Rawls's concern being with justice and right, his attempt to bring about reasoned agreement concerning them presupposes that we can understand and fruitfully engage with one another, do not simply and fruitlessly talk past one another, as we argue for particular conceptions of justice and right. He claims (somewhat abruptly in *A Theory of Justice*) that it is the fact that we share concepts of justice and right that makes this possible. As regards the concepts that Skinner is addressing in the work just cited, liberty or freedom, we can understand both liberal and neo-Roman conceptions, can fruitfully argue over their respective merits, because the concepts of freedom and liberty are salient features of our shared conceptual inheritance and experience.

There are, however, respects in which Skinner introduces and partly endorses positions substantially more general than Rawls's account of the particular concepts of justice and right (or, in the matter specifically at issue in the text under discussion, of liberty/freedom). In one of numerous references to the work of Donald Davidson, he says: 'There is unquestionably a deeper level of continuity underlying the dispute I have been examining over the understanding of individual liberty. The dispute revolves, in effect, around the questions of whether dependence should be recognized as a species of constraint; but both sides assume that the concept of liberty must basically be construed as absence of constraint on some interpretation of that term. The point of considering this example has not been to plead for the adoption of an alien value from a world

[24] Cf. Scheffler 1982, addressing a related issue.
[25] In a welcome invocation, Skinner 1998, p. 118, favourably cites Nietzsche's example of the cow which has a separate organ that allows it to ruminate concerning materials that it has ingested: Nietzsche 1994, p. 10.
[26] Rawls 1971, ch. 1.

we have lost; it has been to uncover a lost reading of a value common to us and to that valued world'.[27]

These are welcome and effective responses to the charge that contextualist studies are merely antiquarian, that they are studies of the past past not the historical past. What bearing do they have on the distinction between the historical past and the practical past? Certainly the largest parts of Skinner's work are in the mode of the historical not the practical past and hence show the continuing value of that distinction. Certainly his works are importantly distinct from the works of students of the canonical persuasion. As with Oakeshott's 'ideal characters', however, these distinctions sort out predominant tendencies in a large body of writing that, happily in my view, also includes elements of a 'practical' character, elements that show a concern with the relevance of then and there to here and now (and maybe to the everywhere and always).[28]

By way of further exploring complexities within the contextualist school I turn to some writings of Richard Tuck, writings that shed light on the value but also the limitations of the distinctions I am using. There are passages in Tuck's writings in which he takes a position essentially the same as the one just discussed in Skinner. For example, in *The Rights of War and Peace: Political Thought and the International Order from Grotius to Kant* (1999) he asks whether 'the long tradition of political thought which has been the subject of this book is of relevance to us any more?' His answer is as follows: 'This tradition is the richest tradition we have for thinking about human freedom. It was historically contingent, and is as a consequence precarious — it presupposes a kind of agent whom we would not now much like to encounter. But it is important that we are clear about what autonomy meant in the days when it became a central virtue, so that we can also be clear about what we may be losing in our own time'.[29] He is not *recommending* (although he gives his readers and

---

[27] Skinner 1998, pp. 117–18, n. 29, referring to Davidson 1984, pp. 125–39, 183–98. Skinner 2002a, p. 29, also endorses Davidson's view that 'unless we begin by assuming that the holding of true beliefs constitutes the norm among the peoples we study, we shall find ourselves unable to identify what they believe. If too many of their beliefs prove to be false, our capacity to give an account of the subject matter of those beliefs will begin to be undermined. Once this starts to happen, we shall find ourselves unable even to describe what we hope to explain. The implication, as Davidson himself puts it, is that "if we want to understand others, we must count them right in most matters"'. Skinner does have substantial disagreements with Davidson: see Skinner 2002a, pp. 47, 131, 139.

[28] Skinner's discussions of Reinhardt Koselleck and the *Begriffsgeschichte* school (e.g. Skinner 2002a, pp. 175–87) are also relevant here.

[29] Tuck 1999, p. 234.

conversational partners reason to think that he may be doing so) the kind of agential autonomy he has recovered but, in Skinner's terms, he thinks we can better ruminate concerning our own affairs if we have a clear understanding of it.

In partial contrast, in *Philosophy and Government, 1572–1651* (1993),[30] Tuck reports his and James Tully's thinking in the following terms: 'Tully and I have discussed our work together ever since we were graduate students together in Cambridge, and despite our many differences of opinion and emphasis, we share two beliefs about how the history of political thought should be written. One of them [generically the same as the beliefs of Skinner and Pocock but perhaps with differences concerning, say, language, meaning(s) and intentions] is that to understand the political theories of any period we need to be historians, and we have been very keen to depict as far as possible the character of the actual life which those theorists were leading, and the specific political questions which engaged their attention. But the other is that a study of the reactions to these questions should not be *purely* a piece of historical writing. It should also be a contribution to our understanding of how people might cope with broadly similar issues in our time. The point of studying the seventeenth century, for both of us, is that many of the conflicts which marked its politics are also to be found in some form in the late twentieth century; and, indeed, the better our historical sense of what those conflicts were, the more often they seem to resemble modern ones'.[31]

This is of course not to deny that historical studies may have the value claimed for them by Skinner and by Tuck himself in *The Rights of War and Peace*. Indeed recovering the tradition studied in the latter book is likely to have that and only that value for present thinking. That tradition was 'contingent' and 'as a consequence precarious'; if, as Tuck seems to be saying, it has largely disappeared, it does not 'broadly resemble' the politics of our own time and recovering it will be valuable to our present thinking and acting primarily because it helps us to see 'what we may be losing in our time'. Presumably the modes of thought and action that emerged in the seventeenth century were also contingent and could have disappeared. Also presumably, the politics of the twentieth and twenty-first centuries were contingent, and could have been different. Thus the claim that studying the seventeenth century will help people of the

---

[30] Tuck 1993.     [31] Tuck 1993, pp. xi–xii.

twentieth and twenty-first centuries to cope with their conflicts depends on a conjunction of two contingencies, both of which must be understood.

On the view Tuck advances in *Philosophy and Government*, the study of what Oakeshott terms the 'historical' past and the 'practical past' converge. Of course this is not to say that the distinction is invalidated or becomes useless. There not only can be but have been quite 'pure' examples of both modes of study and reflection. When other students assess Tuck's account of the seventeenth century they will properly do so by the criteria of the historical not the practical past. If they find the account convincing they can (if they are so disposed) ask themselves whether he also makes good on his claim that the politics of the three centuries resemble one another broadly enough to say that studying the earlier one helps us to cope with the conflicts of the later ones. As we have already seen, Tuck is confident on both counts. Here is how the book ends: 'The descriptions of modern politics we find both in the *ragion di stato* writers and in Grotius and Hobbes, with standing armies paid for out of taxation, with self-protective and potentially expansionist states, and with citizens very unsure of the moral principles they should live by, looks like an accurate description of a world still recognisable to us'.[32]

Can we also say that here, and perhaps also in those aspects of Skinner's thinking discussed above, there is a convergence between the study of the history of political thought and political theory? Of course Tuck is making empirical claims about major characteristics of twentieth- and twenty-first-century politics. These can be viewed as historical claims about recent politics (a history of recent political developments), or as political scientific claims about them. But the claims are at a high level of both conceptual and empirical generalization. Much the same is true about Skinner's analyses of beliefs and intentions, claims that are not restricted to particular here's and now's or then's and there's. Given the emphasis that both thinkers place on contingency and the constancy of change, it would clearly be going too far to treat these as claims about the always and everywhere. But both present critical assessments of prevalent political and related concepts, ideas and practices. Do they attempt to imagine political ideals that would, if accepted, lead to a politics that is improved by normative standards? This too would be going too far, at least as regards the texts here discussed. Skinner does not 'imagine' (although an element of 'imagining' may be unavoidable here)

[32] Tuck 1993, p. 348.

neo-Roman and liberal conceptions of liberty; he recovers the former and says that the latter is not only dominant but effectively without rivals in modern thinking and practicing. And Tuck recovers the sceptical, neo-Stoic configuration about which he teaches us. But Skinner effects a juxtaposition between the two conceptions of liberty and argues that we can think ('ruminate') better about both if we think about them together. Tuck effects an alignment or convergence between seventeenth- and twentieth- and twenty-first-century politics and argues that we can think better about the latter if we give informed and considered attention to the former.

It is clear that these elements of their thinking are not fully congruent with the conception of political theory that I sketched above. Skinner is not recommending either the liberal or neo-Roman conceptions, he is not arguing more than that awareness of them will help us to think better about both. Similarly Tuck is recommending attention to seventeenth-century thinking only as an aid to thinking about twentieth- and twenty-first-century politics. Thus we cannot say that either is advancing an ideal which, if adopted and acted upon, would improve our politics by normative standards. But the conception of political theory that I sketched is an idealized conception. As with the two conceptions of the study/writing of the history of political theory, and as with Oakeshott's distinctions, the conception can be useful not only in identifying 'pure' examples of political theorizing but also in distinguishing some elements in a theory that allow us to say that it is, in part, an example of political theorizing. My suggestion is no more than that the features of the texts of Skinner and Tuck discussed in this section warrant that identification.

A further, and final, identification is supplied by John Pocock. In a recent essay, he has distinguished 'history' from what he calls 'historiosophy'. 'History' is a name for events and processes that may be said to have happened and can be narrated and interpreted, possibly as still going on. By contrast, for historiosophers 'history' denotes a condition in which processes go on, and which may be (in part?) discussed independently of the narrative of what these processes have been. 'Historiosophy' is instead 'the attempt to make history a source of knowledge and wisdom'. Historororiosophy is close to what I have identified as political theory and thus we might say that the features of Skinner's and Tuck's text that I have singled out should be regarded as historiosophical.[33]

---

[33] Pocock 2004.

V

To bring this primarily taxonomic chapter to a close I borrow once more from Wittgenstein. We can think of the three main modes of inquiry and reflection I have discussed — political theorizing, the canonical study of the history of political theory and the contextual study of the history of political theory (Oakeshott's distinctions cross-cut but do not conflict with these distinctions) — as Wittgensteinian 'language games'. As Wittgenstein uses this term of art, language games are characterized by a more or less integrated web or gestalt of concepts, ideas, beliefs, intentions, rules and more or less rule-governed practices, all of these having a public as distinct from a logically private character. Language games form wholes that for many purposes can be and usually are understood and 'played' by their participants as related to but distinguishable from other games. Every language game, however, even those such as logic and mathematics, are also characterized by a greater or lesser degree of 'open texture', that is by respects in which the explicit rules as well as the less clearly formulated conventions and norms of thought and action do not entirely determine what should be thought, said or otherwise done in this or that circumstance. Practiced participants in (players of) the games are 'guided' by the rules and conventions, but at the bottom of the language games is the thoughts and actions of the participants. Moreover and particularly relevant here, along with recognizing the open texture of all games, Wittgenstein speaks of situations in which we are 'as it were between the games'.[34]

There are rules and conventions — we might call them commonly understood and frequently satisfied expectations — among those who play the three language games in question and hence we can identify clear examples of the playing of each of them; and these rules and conventions also serve as criteria for assessing plays of the games. We are, however, sometimes 'between the games' and find ourselves either drawn to more than one designation of this or that performance and more than one criterion of assessment of the performances we are considering or uncertain as to which designation is the most perspicuous. This seems to me to be the situation that obtains as regards political theory and the study of the history of political theory. For the reasons given in the course of the chapter, it is not a situation to be regretted.

[34] Wittgenstein 1958, p. 188e (ii.ix).

# Afterword

*Quentin Skinner*

One of the distinctive strengths of this book is that its contributors approach the topic of early-modern British political thought from the perspective not merely of political theory but of history and imaginative literature as well. I cannot hope to summarize their individual contributions here, but there is fortunately no need to do so, for they are all written with unfailing lucidity as well as outstanding scholarship. Instead I want to say something about the adjectives I have just employed in speaking of the volume as a whole — *early-modern*, *British* and *political*. My aim will be to tug on three corresponding threads that seem to me to run throughout the book.

First, *British*. John Morrill's principal purpose is to insist on the need to concentrate on the history specifically of British political thought. It is not perhaps surprising to find an historian of what used to be called the English revolution placing so much emphasis on what Tim Harris at the start of his chapter nicely calls the Britannic turn. One of the most valuable developments in the historiography of the civil war period during the past generation has undoubtedly been the reconsideration of the Scottish and Irish elements in the narrative. From being assigned mere walk-on parts in a basically English drama, the uprising in Scotland and the Irish rebellion have come to be discussed in such a way as to reconfigure the entire revolutionary era as a war of the three kingdoms.

One might still wonder if every important question in our chosen period needs to have a British dimension found for it. Is it necessarily 'breathtakingly blinkered', as Professor Morrill exclaims, to answer in the negative? It seems to me that the chapters by Colin Kidd, Nicholas Canny and especially Tim Harris all give grounds for suggesting that Professor Morrill's objections may be somewhat exaggerated. Professor Kidd's chapter not only addresses 'the matter of Britain' from a specifically Scottish standpoint, but acknowledges that England at all times occupied a predominant position in the debates. So too with Professor Canny's chapter, perhaps the most striking feature of which is his implicit rejection of 'Britain' as an appropriate unit of analysis. The political discourse he examines was not only exclusively Irish in provenance, but was written in part in Gaelic rather than in the English language. Furthermore, insofar as Professor Canny sees the sources of this discourse as lying outside the geographical boundaries of Ireland, he finds the main influences in a tradition rooted not in Britain but in continental Europe.

Professor Harris engages even more directly with the problems — definitional as well as historical — thrown up by the demand for a specifically British history. He illustrates the resulting difficulties from an examination of the desperately fraught period between the Exclusion crisis and the constitutional settlement of 1688. As he begins by conceding, there is certainly a case for saying that much of the political theory of those years revolved around British rather than English issues, and that the importance of this consideration remained masked until recently by traditional ways of approaching the subject. However, he is surely right to sense a danger that the privileging of the British dimension may have a procrustean effect. On the one hand, the most illuminating perspective to adopt will sometimes be a much broader one. As he rightly notes, discussions about the right of deposition generally called on natural-law arguments that not only stemmed in large part from continental sources but claimed a universal applicability. And on the other hand, some of the questions at issue — as Professor Harris shows in the case of the debate between Charles Leslie and William King — were strictly local in character. He concludes, very reasonably, that the question as to whether it makes sense to speak in purely British terms will depend on what questions we want to ask. The further moral I should want to draw is that no possible harm can inherently come from concentrating on Scottish or Irish (or indeed English) themes. If we choose to do so, we must of course ensure that no wider implications are thereby neglected; but if we respect that obvious caution, there will be no good reason to impugn our resulting studies as blinkered or (a graver accusation) as unfashionable.

Let me now turn from *British* to *political*. A number of literary scholars in the present volume express some doubts about the concept of 'political thought', interrogating the category in two contrasting ways. First of all they remind us, perhaps even warn us, that imaginative literature is seldom directly concerned with the adoption of political stances and the articulation of discursive arguments. It is true that the chapters on the role of literature concentrate exclusively on poetry and drama, saying nothing about the emergence of the art of the novel in the early-modern period. Had they considered this further genre, it is possible that their minatory tone might have been a little more muted. Nevertheless, their warnings remain highly salutary, as Jean Howard's chapter illustrates with particular force. Shakespeare's dramas, she insists, are just that: they are dramas, in which political positions are not so much adopted and defended as shown to be in collision with each other. Do not ask, she writes, whether Shakespeare is for or against Jack Cade in Act IV of *The First Part of the Contention* (2 *Henry VI*). Shakespeare should not. be thought of as announcing a commitment, but rather as inviting us to reflect on a very different world from the one in which we live.

There is a further way in which several of the literary scholars raise a doubt about the centrality of 'political thought'. The general contention they put forward strikes me as interestingly comparable to a criticism often levelled by art historians against the study of iconography. Scholars in the tradition of Erwin Panofsky, it now tends to be objected, illicitly gave priority to the written word. They treated iconographical schemes as mere illustrations of texts, whereas they ought to have recognized that paintings can equally well be works of moral or political theory in their own right. The point here is not just that artists obviously conduct their arguments in a distinctive style; it is also that paintings can act upon us with unusual power, and may even contain arguments not available elsewhere.

A strongly analogous commitment seems to me to animate, in different ways, the chapters by Andrew Hadfield, Karen O'Brien and Steven Zwicker. I have one slight doubt, I confess, about Professor Zwicker's way of setting up the case. He maintains that 'suggestion, innuendo and irony are not the familiar tools of discursive and philosophical prose', and that these techniques may constitute one of the distinctive incursions from the field of literature into the domain of political thought. Any intellectual historian who has ever tried to come to terms with Plato's numerous indirections, or Machiavelli's penchant for satire, or Hume's liking for jokes and parodies, will I think be likely to bridle at this point. Moreover, there is no reason to limit ourselves to the grandmasters by way of registering this doubt. Any work of philosophy will inescapably be a literary artifact, and if historians of philosophy neglect this Derridean insight — as they commonly do — then it is certainly to their cost.

I emphatically agree with Professor Zwicker, however, that the characteristic talents of dramatists and poets are such that they often succeed in making distinctive and challenging interventions in political debate. Professor Zwicker illustrates the claim from his reading of Dryden, who was able to state his political allegiances and to place a question-mark against them all at once, producing a fabric of reasoning that is shimmering rather than directly reflective in its effect. Dryden's irony has the consequence of introducing a subtle even-handedness into his treatment of patriarchal theories of government and political obligation, and this achievement is undoubtedly an outcome of his consummate literariness.

Professor O'Brien carries the argument still further, repudiating the usual clichés about imaginative literature as an echo-chamber and offering us a sense of how poetry can instead function as a laboratory of new ideas. *Ut philosophia poesis.* Taking the case of Enlightenment discussions about the ethics of empire, Professor O'Brien shows that one of the distinctive contributions of the poets was to foreground the comforting suggestion that imperialism can be viewed as a benevolent form of trusteeship. I would have welcomed more comment on the fascinating fact that this rhetoric appears to have reached its apogee specifically in female poets – especially Anna Seward and Hannah More – but this is hardly an objection to Professor O'Brien's general point. My only doubt is one that assailed me as soon as I started to read the works of Seward and More on which Professor O'Brien bases her case. Much of the verse turns out to be embarrassingly undistinguished, with forced and jingling rhymes and some comical aspirations to sublimity. This prompts me to wonder how far the vocation of the poet may inevitably be compromised by the ambition to write in a strongly didactic mode. And this in turn prompts me to wonder if there may not after all be a relatively limited role for poetry to play as a vehicle for effective political argument.

Professor Hadfield likewise calls in question the alleged boundary between literature and political thought. If, he persuasively maintains, we think of republicanism simply as a political theory and programme, this will not only lead us to post-date its appearance but drastically to underestimate its significance in what Castoriadis would call the social imaginary of early-modern Britain. We need to think of republicanism at the same time as an aesthetic phenomenon, and to recognize that, in the telling of stories about the nature and virtues of republican rule, we find ourselves confronting a specifically literary dimension to the debate.

I warmly endorse Professor Hadfield's contention that political historians have failed to recognize the extent to which a republican sensibility can be found in Renaissance England, especially in the closing decades of Elizabeth's reign. I would go further and add that the attempt to imagine a self-governing *civitas* in English political discourse antedates even Professor Hadfield's remarkable examples from the 1590s, since we already encounter it in Thomas More's *Utopia* of 1516.

I promised at the outset to tug on three separate threads, and I now want to turn to the category of the *early-modern* in the study of British political thought. I should like in particular to say something about the relations between early modernity and the present. Unless we wish to turn ourselves into the kind of antiquarian seemingly commended at the end of Professor Kidd's chapter, we shall want to take advantage of whatever insights we can gain from each of these historical periods in order to illuminate the other. One direction of this intellectual traffic is clearly indicated in Joanne Wright's chapter. Changes in our own social perceptions can have the effect of alerting us to neglected early-modern texts, or to new facets of familiar texts that we might not previously have been primed to recognize. Professor Wright's own example comes from her research on Margaret Cavendish. As she observes, there can be little doubt that the feminism of the 1960s, with its slogan that the personal is the political, not only served to direct scholars towards Cavendish's work, but helped them at the same time to appreciate how extraordinary and unblinking is Cavendish's understanding of marriage essentially as a power relationship. As our own world revolves, it catches light from the past in ever-changing ways.

The other direction from which we can hope, in Gadamer's phrase, to produce a fusion of horizons is powerfully illustrated in Duncan Ivison's chapter. There are at least two ways, he argues, in which the early-modern world can act as a possible resource as we grapple with our present predicament. One is that we may be fortunate enough to come upon a usable past, a set of beliefs and arguments we can hope to invoke and apply directly to our own case. Professor Ivison offers as an example the eirenic vision of the *ius naturale* presented by Grotius in his *De iure belli et pacis* (1625). Rather than helping ourselves to contentious moral premises in discussing international relations, Grotius suggests, we should seek to articulate a minimum content to the idea of natural law as a mechanism for regulating relations among states. This basic idea of a common standard is now being taken up and developed by a number of theorists of the international order. The next step will be to design the institutions needed to enforce the resulting rights, and this is the project to which Professor Ivison wants us to direct our thoughts.

As Professor Ivison also shows, however, the history of political theory can equally well provide us with a means of reflecting anew, and perhaps more critically, on some of our own most cherished assumptions and beliefs. Drawing on pathfinding work by Richard Tuck, Professor Ivison offers as an example the liberal theory of rights, considering it in relation to the imperialism of the early-modern period. The connections between liberalism and imperialism, he suggests, are not merely chronological but metaphysical, since the theory of individual rights was available to sustain as well as to criticize colonialist adventures. Suppose we equate the ownership of natural rights, as Hobbes and many of his contemporaries did, with the possession of a blameless liberty of action. Suppose we then model the rights of sovereign states on the rights of individuals thus understood, as also became usual in the early-modern period. One outcome is that imperial conquests are legitimized at a stroke: it will always be possible to affirm that conquering states are merely exercising a blameless liberty of action. To see these connections is not merely to see something that contemporary liberalism tends to overlook; it is also to acquire a new and perhaps more wary view of our current enthusiasm for the concept of human rights.

Surveying the range of topics handled in this book, no one could fail to be struck by the fact that, although a number of canonical names are duly discussed, the main emphasis falls not on major theorists but on broader 'languages' of debate. Richard Flathman, taking note of this orientation, warns us not to throw out the philosophical baby with the anachronistic bathwater. This danger will be incurred, he fears, if we wholly repudiate the more traditional and 'canonist' approach to the study of political thought. I take his point, but it does not worry me so much, if only because it seems to me that the canon has never really been given up. As many of the chapters in this book reveal, we scarcely consider it worth our while to contextualize writers whom we take to be of marginal interest or importance. As a result, we find ourselves experiencing something like a return of the repressed: the literary scholars find themselves talking about Shakespeare and Dryden, while the historians of political theory talk about Grotius and Hobbes. These canonical figures are duly contextualized, to be sure; but even if they are to some extent marginalized they remain stubbornly there.

Despite this 'canonist' survival, however, there is little doubt that the history of political theory is now being practised in a far more

historically-minded idiom than ever before. We aspire not merely to
interpret a canon of classic texts, but to listen to whole societies talking
to themselves about the values and institutions underpinning their
common life. As a result, we tend to treat the classic texts essentially as
interventions in, and contributions to, these more wide-ranging debates.
One consequence has been that, although we have not lost interest
in understanding what the classic texts say, we have become at least as
much interested in decoding the myriad speech-acts they contain. We try
to establish how far they may be endorsing and commending, or
questioning and criticizing, or satirizing and repudiating prevailing
institutions and beliefs. We are interested not only in what they *say* but
in what they are *up to*, and thus in the force of what is said.

This research programme has by now become so well-entrenched that,
as a number of contributors to this book attest, it has become more
interesting to enquire into its limitations than its strengths. Richard
Flathman cautions us against assuming that the project of recovering
speech-acts will necessarily yield more determinate interpretations than
the traditional quest for authorial meaning and intentionality. The
project, he reminds us, of identifying the intellectual traditions that seem
to offer the most illuminating contexts within which to place any given
text will always be a matter of endless scholarly dispute. Professor Zwicker
further cautions us against assuming that, if we succeed in recovering the
force of a particular utterance, this will necessarily be equivalent to
recovering the intentions with which the writer issued it. As he illustrates
with examples from Marvell, it is always possible for an utterance to bear
a certain force whether the author intended it or not. Finally, Kirstie
McClure highlights a further limitation that stems from focusing too
exclusively on texts as the encoding of speech-acts. Taking the case of the
*Vindiciae Contra Tyrannos* (among others), she underlines the fact that,
like any other contribution to political theory, the *Vindiciae* was at the
same time a material object that persisted over time. As a result, it quickly
escaped its original context to take part in arguments of which its author
was wholly unaware. To acquire an historical understanding of any text,
in other words, we need to consider its *Fortuna*, not merely the range
of speech-acts it may be said to contain.

I cannot end without confessing that I am myself a true believer in the
value of concentrating our efforts at interpretation on the recovery of
speech-acts. Because of this commitment, however, I am all the more
anxious to welcome these comments on the limitations of the approach.
No single set of hermeneutic principles can ever hope to capture more

than a fraction of what we want to know about the texts we study as intellectual historians and students of literature. We need to remain in constant dialogue with each other about the rival merits of different approaches, and no one concerned with the health of any of the three disciplines represented in this book will want this conversation to be cut off.

# Bibliography

PRIMARY MANUSCRIPT SOURCES

*British Library, London*

MS Eg. 1950


*University Library, Glasgow*

MS Gen 1213: Wodrow, Robert (1727). 'Introduction, To our Scots Biography conteaning, A Breife Account of the first setlment of Christianity in Scotland, The Kelledei or Culdees'.


*Trinity College Library, Dublin*

MS 829
MS 1688/1


PRINTED PRIMARY SOURCES

*Acts of the Parliaments of Scotland*, ed. Thomas Thomson and Cosmo Innes (1814–1875), 12 vols., Edinburgh.
Anderson, James (1705). *An Historical Essay shewing that the Crown and Kingdom of Scotland is Imperial and Independent*, Edinburgh.
(1739). *Selectus Diplomatum et Numismatum Scotiae Thesaurus*, Edinburgh.
*Anno V. Jacobi II. Regis. A Collection of Acts Passed by the Irish Parliament of the 7th May 1689* (1689), London.
Aristotle (1946). *The Politics*, ed. and trans. Ernest Barker, Oxford.
Atwood, William (1698). *The History and Reasons of the Dependency of Ireland upon the Imperial Crown of the Kingdom of England*, London.
(1704). *The Superiority and Direct Dominion of the Imperial Crown of England over the Crown and Kingdom of Scotland*, London.
(1705). *The Superiority and Direct Dominion of the Imperial Crown of England ... reasserted*, London.

Ayscough, Edward (1607). *A Historie contayning the Warres, Treaties, Marriages and other occurrents betweene England and Scotland*, London.

Baxter, Richard (1681). *A Treatise on Episcopacy*, London.

Beacon, Richard (1996). *Solon his Follie, or, A Politique Discourse Touching the Reformation of Commonweales Conquered, Declined, or Corrupted*, ed. Clare Carroll and Vincent Carey, Binghampton, N.Y.

Belhaven, John Hamilton, Baron (1705). *The Lord Belhavens Speech in Parliament the 17th of July 1705*, Edinburgh.

Bellenden, John, Lord (1821). *The History and Chronicle of Scotland*, Edinburgh.

Blackmore, Richard (1695). *Prince Arthur: An Heroick Poem*, London.

Blondel, David (1646). *Apologia pro sententia Hieronymi de episcopis et presbyteris*, Amsterdam.

Boece, Hector (1574). *Scotorum historiae a prima gentis origine*, Paris.

Bolingbroke, Henry St John, Viscount (1997). *Political Writings*, ed. David Armitage, Cambridge.

Brown, John (1845). *An Apologetical Narration* (1665), Edinburgh.

Buchanan, David (1731). Preface to John Knox, *The History of the Reformation of the Church of Scotland* (1644), Edinburgh.

Buchanan, George (1690). *The History of Scotland written in Latin by George Buchanan; Faithfully Rendered into English*, trans. J. Fraser, London.

(1715). *Opera Omnia*, 2 vols., Edinburgh.

(2003). *A Dialogue on the Law of Kingship among the Scots: A Critical Edition and Translation of George Buchanan's De Jure Regni apud Scotos Dialogus* (1570), ed. and trans. Roger A. Mason and Martin S. Smith, Aldershot.

Burke, Edmund (1756). *A Vindication of Natural Society; or, A View of the Miseries and Evils arising to Mankind from every Species of Artificial Society. In a letter to Lord **** By a late noble writer*, London.

Burnet, Gilbert (1687?). *Some Reflections On His Majesty's Proclamation of the 12th of February 1686/7 for a Toleration in Scotland*, Amsterdam?.

(1688). *An Enquiry into the Measures of Submission to the Supream Authority*, London.

Burnet, Thomas (1686). *Theses Philosophicae*, Aberdeen.

C., J. (1686). *A Net for the Fishers of Men*, London.

Calderwood, David (1842–1849). *The History of the Kirk of Scotland*, ed. Thomas Thomson, 8 vols., Edinburgh.

Caldicott, C. E. J. (ed.) (1992). 'Patrick Darcy, "An Argument"', *Camden Miscellany* 31, pp. 193–320.

Cambrensis, Giraldus [Gerald of Wales] (1978). *Expugnatio Hibernica*, ed. and trans. A. B. Scott and F. X. Martin, Dublin.

(1982). *The History and Topography of Ireland*, ed. and trans. John J. O'Meara, Harmondsworth.

Canaries, James (1685). *A Sermon Preach'd at Selkirk upon the 29th of May, 1685*, Edinburgh.

(1689). *A Sermon Preached at Edinburgh ... upon the 30th of January, 1689*, Edinburgh.

Canny, Nicholas (ed.) (1977). 'Rowland White's "Discorse Touching Ireland",
     c. 1569', *Irish Historical Studies* 20, pp. 439–63.
     (1979). 'Rowland White's "The Dysorders of the Irisshery", 1571', *Studia
     Hibernica* 19, pp. 147–60.
Cartwright, Thomas (1686). *A Sermon Preached upon the Anniversary . . . of the
     Happy Inauguration of . . . King James II*, London.
Cavendish, Margaret (1653). *Poems and Fancies*, London.
     (1655). *The World's Olio*, London.
     (1916a). *The Life of the Thrice Noble, High and Puissant Prince William
     Cavendishe* in *The Life of the 1st Duke of Newcastle and Other Writings by
     Margaret Duchess*, ed. Ernest Rhys, London and Toronto, pp. 1–178.
     (1916b). *A True Relation of My Birth, Breeding, and Life* in *The Life of the
     1st Duke of Newcastle and Other Writings by Margaret Duchess*, ed. Ernest
     Rhys, London and Toronto, pp. 179–213.
     (2000). *The Convent of Pleasure* in *Paper Bodies: A Margaret Cavendish Reader*,
     ed. Sylvia Bowerbank and Sara Mendelson, Peterborough, Ontario,
     pp. 97–135.
     (2003). *Orations of Diver Sorts, Accommodated to Divers Places* in *Political
     Writings*, ed. Susan James, Cambridge, pp. 111–292.
     (2004). *Sociable Letters*, ed. James Fitzmaurice, Peterborough, Ont.
*Of Civil Polity* (1753). London.
Clapham, John (1602). *The Historie of England*, London.
     (1606). *The Historie of Great Britannie*, London.
Claudianus, Claudius (1981). *Panegyric on the Fourth Consulate of Honorius*,
     ed. and trans. William Barr, Liverpool.
Cobbett, William (ed.) (1806–1820). *The Parliamentary History of England
     from the Earliest Period to the Year 1803*, 36 vols., London.
Collins, William (1979). *The Works of William Collins*, ed. Richard Wendorf and
     Charles Ryscamp, Oxford.
Congreve, William (1967). *The Complete Plays*, ed. Herbert Davis, Chicago.
Cowper, William (1782). *Poems*, London.
     (1980–1985). *The Poems of William Cowper*, ed. John D. Baird and Charles
     Ryscamp, 3 vols., Oxford.
Craig, Thomas (1695). *Scotland's Soveraignty Asserted*, ed. and trans. George
     Ridpath, London.
     (1934). *Ius Feudale* (1655), trans. J. A. Clyde, 2 vols., Edinburgh and
     London.
Dalrymple, James (1705). *Collections concerning the Scottish History Preceding
     the Death of King David the First, in the Year 1153*, Edinburgh.
Dalrymple, Sir John (1790). *Memoirs of Great Britain and Ireland; From the
     Dissolution of the Last Parliament of Charles II till the Capture of the French
     and Spanish Fleets at Vigo. A New Edition, in Three Volumes; With the
     Appendices Complete*, London.
Danby, Thomas Osborne, Earl of (1689). *The Thoughts of a Private Person; About
     the Justice of the Gentlemen's Undertaking at York. Nov. 1688*, London.

Davies, Sir John (1612). *A Discovery of the True Causes, why Ireland was never entirely Subdued, nor brought under Obedience of the Crowne of England, until the Beginning of his Majesties happie Raigne*, London.

Dempster, Thomas (1829). *Historia ecclesiastica gentis Scotorum: sive, de scriptoribus Scotis*, 2 vols., Edinburgh.

*Doctrine of Passive Obedience and Jure Divino Disproved, The* (1689). London.

Donne, John (1967). *The Satires, Epigrams and Verse Letters*, ed. W. Milgate, Oxford.

Drake, James (1703). *Historia Anglo-Scotica*, London.

Dryden, John (1958). *The Poems*, ed. James Kinsley, 4 vols., Oxford.

(1956–2002). *The Works of John Dryden*, ed. E. N. Hooker, H. T. Swedenberg, *et al.*, 20 vols., Berkeley and Los Angeles.

Dyer, John (1757). *The Fleece. A Poem in Four Books*, London.

Equiano, Olaudah (1995). *The Interesting Narrative and Other Writings*, ed. Vincent Carretta, Harmondsworth.

*England's Concern in the Case of His R. H.* (1680). London.

Ferguson, Robert (1687). *A Representation of the Threatning Dangers*, Edinburgh?.

(1689). *A Brief Justification of the Prince of Orange's Descent into England*, London.

Filmer, Robert (1991). *Patriarcha and Other Writings*, ed. J. P. Sommerville, Cambridge.

Fitzgerald, William (1780). *An Ode to the Memory of the Late Captain James Cook*, London.

Flecknoe, Richard (1670). *Epigrams of All Sorts, Made at Divers Times On Several Occasions*, London.

Force, Peter (ed.) (1836–1846). *Tracts and Other Papers Relating Principally to the Origin, Settlement, and Progress of the Colonies in North America*, 4 vols., Washington D.C.

Fordun, John of (1871–1872). *Chronica gentis Scotorum*, ed. W. F. Skene, Edinburgh.

Fyfe, Christopher (ed.) (1991). *'Our Children Free and Happy': Letters from Black Settlers in Africa in the 1790s*, Edinburgh.

Galloway, Bruce R. and Brian P. Levack (eds.) (1985). *The Jacobean Union: Six Tracts of 1604*, Edinburgh.

Godwin, William (1797). *Political Justice and its Influence on Morals and Happiness*, 3rd edn, London.

Goldie, Mark (ed.) (1999). *The Reception of Locke's Politics*, 6 vols., London.

Goodall, Walter (1773). *An Introduction to the History and Antiquities of Scotland* (1739), Edinburgh.

Gordon, Alexander (1726). *Itinerarium Septentrionale*, London.

Gother, John (1685). *A Papist Misrepresented and Represented*, London.

Greville, Fulke (1939). *Poems and Dramas of Fulke Greville, First Lord Brooke*, ed. Geoffrey Bullough, 2 vols., Edinburgh.

(1965). *The Remains, being Poems of Monarchy and Religion*, ed. G. A. Wilkes, Oxford.

Harrington, James (1992). *The Comonwealth of Oceana and A System of Politics*, ed. J. G. A. Pocock, Cambridge.

Herbert, Sir William (1992). *Croftus sive de Hibernia liber*, ed. Arthur Keaveney and John A. Madden, Dublin.

Heylyn, Peter (1670). *Cosmography*, London.

Hobbes, Thomas (1991). *Leviathan*, ed. Richard Tuck, Cambridge.

Holinshed, Raphael (1577). *The Firste volume of the Chronicles of England, Scotlande, and Irelande*, London.

  (1587). *The Laste volume of the Chronicles of England, Scotlande, and Irelande*, London.

  (1807–1808). *The Description of Britaine in Holinshed's Chronicles*, 6 vols., London.

Hume, David (1983). *The History of England*, ed. William B. Todd, 6 vols., Indianapolis.

*The inherent evils of all state governments demonstrated; being a reprint of Edmund Burke's celebrated essay, entitled "A vindication of natural society": With notes & an appendix, briefly enunciating the principles through which "natural society" may be gradually realized* (1858), London.

Jacob, Hildebrand (1735). *Brutus the Trojan; Founder of the British Empire. An Epic Poem*, London.

Jameson, William (1697). *Nazianzeni Querela et Votum Justum*, Glasgow.

  (1712). *The Summ of the Episcopal Controversy*, Edinburgh.

Jonson, Ben (1972). *Catiline His Conspiracy*, ed. W. F. Bolton and J. F. Gardner, London.

  (1990). *Sejanus His Fall*, ed. Philip J. Ayres, Manchester.

*Judgment of Whole Kingdoms and Nations, The* (1710). London.

Keating, Geoffrey (1902–1914). *Foras Feasa ar Éirinn*, ed. and trans. David Comyn and Patrick S. Dinneen, 4 vols., London.

Kelly, Gary (ed.) (1999). *Bluestocking Feminism: Writings of the Bluestocking Circle, 1738–1785*, 4 vols., London.

Kerrigan, John (ed.) (1991). *Motives of Woe: Shakespeare and 'Female Complaint': A Critical Anthology*, Oxford.

*King Johan*, ed. Adam Barry (1969). San Marino, CA.

King, William (1691). *The State of the Protestants of Ireland*, London.

Knox, John (1994). *On Rebellion*, ed. Roger A. Mason, Cambridge.

Lauder of Fountainhall, Sir John (1759–1761). *The Decisions of the Lords of Council and Session from June 6th, 1678, to July 30th, 1713*, 2 vols., Edinburgh.

  (1840). *Historical Observes of Memorable Occurrents in Church and State from October 1680 to April 1686*, ed. David Laing and A. Urquhart, Edinburgh.

Leslie, Charles (1692). *An Answer to a Book, Intituled, The State of the Protestants in Ireland*, London.

L'Estrange, Roger (1678). *Tyranny and Popery Lording it Over the Consciences, Lives, Liberties and Estates both of King and People*, London.

(1684–1687). *The Observator in Dialogue*, 3 vols., London.

*Life and Death of Jack Straw, The*, ed. Kenneth Muir (1957). Oxford.

Livy (1960). *The Early History of Rome*, trans. Aubrey de Sélincourt, Harmondsworth.

Lloyd, William (1684). *An Historical Account of Church-Government As it was in Great-Britain and Ireland when they first received the Christian Religion*, London.

Locke, John (1798). *An Essay Concerning the True Original Extent and End of Civil Government*, ed. Thomas Elrington, Dublin.

(1979). *An Essay Concerning Human Understanding*, ed. Peter H. Nidditch, Oxford.

(1983). *A Letter Concerning Toleration*, ed. James Tully, Indianapolis.

(1988). *Two Treatises of Government*, ed. Peter Laslett, rev. edn, Cambridge.

(1993). *Political Writings*, ed. David Wootton, Harmondsworth.

(1997). *Political Essays*, ed. Mark Goldie, Cambridge.

Lombard, Peter (1868). *De regno Hiberniae sanctorum insula commentarius* (1632), ed. P. F. Moran, Dublin.

Lord, George de F., *et al.* (eds.) (1963–1975). *Poems on Affairs of State*, 7 vols., New Haven.

Lucan (1992). *Civil War*, trans. Susanna H. Braund, Oxford.

Mackenzie of Rosehaugh, Sir George (1684). *Jus Regium*, Edinburgh and London.

(1716–1722). *Works*, 2 vols., Edinburgh.

Mackenzie, George, Dr. (1708–1722). *The Lives and Characters of the Most Eminent Writers of the Scots Nation*, 3 vols., Edinburgh.

Maitland, William (1757). *The History and Antiquities of Scotland*, London.

Major, John (1892). *A History of Greater Britain*, ed. and trans. A. Constable, Edinburgh.

*Mankind*, in *"Lost" Tudor Plays*, ed. John S. Farmer (1907). Guildford, pp. 1–40.

Marlowe, Christopher (1966). *The Jew of Malta*, ed. T. W. Craik, London.

Marvell, Andrew (1971). *Poems and Letters*, ed. H. M. Margoliouth, 3rd edn, revised by Pierre Legouis with the collaboration of E. E. Duncan Jones, Oxford.

Milton, John (1953–1982). *The Complete Prose Works*, ed. D. M. Wolfe *et al.*, 8 vols., New Haven.

(1997). *Complete Shorter Poems: Second Edition*, ed. John Carey, Harlow.

Molyneux, William (1698). *The Case of Ireland's Being Bound by Acts of Parliament in England Stated*, Dublin.

Monmouth, Geoffrey of (1718). *The British History*, trans. Aaron Thompson, London.

(1966). *The History of the Kings of Britain*, ed. and trans. L. Thorpe, Harmondsworth.

More, Hannah (1788). *Slavery, A Poem*, London.

*New Voyage to Georgia by a Young Gentleman, A* (1737). 2nd edn, London.

Nicolson, William (1705). *Leges Marchiarum*, London.
Nietzsche, Friedrich (1994). *On the Genealogy of Morality*, ed. Keith Ansell-Pearson, trans. Carol Diethe, Cambridge.
Nisbet, Alexander (1722–1742). *A System of Heraldry Speculative and Practical*, 2 vols., Edinburgh.
*Ode to the Memory of Captain James Cook . . . By a Sea Officer, An* (1780). London.
O'Flaherty, Roderic (1793). *Ogygia* (1685), trans. J. Hely, 2 vols., Dublin.
Oglethorpe, James (1732). *A New and Accurate Account of the Provinces of South-Carolina and Georgia*, London.
O'Mahony, Conor (1645). *Disputatio apologetica de iure regni Hiberniae pro Catholicis Hibernis adversos haereticos Anglos*, Lisbon.
O'Sullivan Beare, Philip (1850). *Historia catholica Ibernia compendium* (1621), ed. Matthew Kelly, Dublin.
Ovid (2000). *Fasti*, trans. A. J. Boyle and R. D. Woodard, Harmondsworth.
P., H. (1588). *A Short Apologie for Christian Souldiours*, London.
Painter, William (1890). *The Palace of Pleasure*, ed. Joseph Jacobs, 3 vols., London.
Petrie, Alexander (1662). *A Compendious History of the Catholick Church*, The Hague.
*Plea for Succession, A* (1682). London.
*Political Aphorisms: or, The True Maxims of Government Displayed* (1690). London.
Pope, Alexander (1939–1969). *The Twickenham Edition of the Works of Alexander Pope*, ed. John Butt, *et al.*, 11 vols., London.
*Popery Anatomis'd* (1686). London.
Price, Richard (1776). *Observations on the Nature of Civil Liberty, The Principles of Government, and the Justice and Policy of the War with America*, 8th edn, London.
Prynne, William (1643). *The Fourth Part of The Soveraigne Power of Parliaments and Kingdoms*, London.
    (1670). *The History of King John, King Henry III and the Most Illustrious King Edward I*, London.
Rowe, Elizabeth Singer (1739). *The Miscellaneous Works in Prose and Verse of Mrs Elizabeth Rowe . . . To which are Added Poems on Several Occasions By Thomas Rowe*, 2 vols., London.
Ruffhead, Owen (1769). *The Life of Alexander Pope, Esq.*, London.
S., J. (1681). *A New Letter from Leghorn*, London.
Sallust (1963). *Jugurthine War and Conspiracy of Catiline*, trans. S. A. Handford, Harmondsworth.
*Salus Populi Suprema Lex* (1689). Edinburgh?
Selden, John (1726). *Opera Omnia*, ed. David Wilkins, 3 vols. London.
Shakespeare, William (1960). *The Poems*, ed. F. T. Prince, London.
    (1990). *The First Part of King Henry VI*, ed. Michael Hattaway, Cambridge.
    (1995). *Antony and Cleopatra*, ed. John Wilders, London.

(1997). *The Norton Shakespeare*, ed. Stephen Greenblatt, Katherine Eisaman Maus, Jean E. Howard and Walter Cohen, New York.

(2002). *The Poems*, ed. Colin Burrow, Oxford.

Sharp, Granville (1820). *Memoirs of Granville Sharp*, ed. Prince Hoare, London.

Sheridan, William (1686). *Catholick Religion Asserted by St. Paul, and Maintained in the Church of England*, London.

Sherlock, William (1684). *The Case of Resistance*, London.

(1688). *A Letter from a Clergy-Man in the City, To his Friend in the Country, Containing his Reasons For not Reading the Declaration*, London.

*Short Historical Account Concerning the Succession to the Crown of Scotland, A* (1689). London.

Sibbald, Robert (1704a). *The Liberty and Independency of the Kingdom and Church of Scotland asserted from Antient Records*, 2nd edn, Edinburgh.

(1704b). *An Answer to the Second Letter to the Right Reverend, the Lord Bishop of Carlisle*, Edinburgh.

Sidney, Algernon (1996a). *Court Maxims*, ed. Hans W. Blum, Eco Haitsma Mulier and Ronald Janse, Cambridge.

(1996b). *Discourses Concerning Government*, ed. Thomas G. West, rev. edn, Indianapolis.

Southey, Robert (1832). *Essays Moral and Political*, 2 vols., London.

(1994). *Poetical Works, 1793–1810*, gen. ed. Lynda Pratt, 5 vols., London.

Steel, G. (1700). *Robert the III King of Scotland, His Answer to a Summonds sent Him by Henry the IV of England to do Homage for the Crown of Scotland*, Edinburgh.

Stevenson, Andrew (1753–1757). *The history of the church and state in Scotland, from the accession of King Charles I*, 3 vols., Edinburgh.

Stillingfleet, Edward (1685). *Origines Britannicae, or the Antiquities of the British Churches*, London.

Stones, E. L. G. (1970). *Anglo-Scottish Relations 1174–1328: Some Selected Documents*, 2nd edn, Oxford.

Suetonius (1957). *The Twelve Caesars*, trans. Robert Graves, Harmondsworth.

Tacitus, Cornelius (1698). *The Annals and History of C. Cornelius Tacitus made English by several hands*, 3 vols., London.

(1931). *The Annals*, trans. John Jackson, 2 vols., Cambridge, Mass.

(1956). *The Annals*, trans. Michael Grant, Harmondsworth.

(1998). *The Annals*, trans. A. J. Woodman, Indianapolis and Cambridge.

Taitt, Alexander (1741). *The Roman Account of Britain and Ireland in Answer to Father Innes*, Edinburgh.

Temple, Sir John (1646). *The Irish Rebellion; or, The History of the Beginning and First Progress of the General Rebellion Raised within the Kingdom of Ireland ... 1641*, London.

Thomson, James (1986). *Liberty, The Castle of Indolence and Other Poems*, ed. James Sambrook, Oxford.

'True Son of the Church of England' (1689). *The Letter which was Sent to the Author of The Doctrine of Passive Obedience and Jure Divino Disproved, Answered and refuted*, London.

Vattel, Emer de (1916). *Le Droit des Gens*, ed. Albert de Lapradelle, Washington, DC.

*Vindiciae Contra Tyrannos, or, Concerning the Legitimate Power of a Prince over the People, and of the People over a Prince*, ed. George Garnett (1994). Cambridge.

Vitoria, Francisco de (1991). *Political Writings*, ed. Anthony Pagden and Jeremy Lawrance, Cambridge.

*Vox Populi, Vox Dei* (1709). London.

Webster, John (1995–). *The Works of John Webster*, ed. David Gunby, David Carnegie and Antony Hammond, 2 vols. to date, Cambridge.

Wetenhall, Edward (1686). *Hexapla Jacobaea*, Dublin.

(1691). *The Case of the Irish Protestants*, London.

Williams, Nicholas (ed.) (1981). *Pairlement Chloinne Tómáis*, Dublin.

Wodrow, Robert (1721–1722). *History of the Sufferings of the Church of Scotland, from the Restauration to the Revolution*, 2 vols., Edinburgh.

(1842–1843a). *Correspondence*, ed. T. McCrie, 3 vols., Edinburgh.

(1842–1843b). *Analecta*, 4 vols., Glasgow.

Womersley, David (ed.) (1997). *Augustan Critical Writing*, Harmondsworth.

Wootton, David (ed.) (1986). *Divine Right and Democracy: An Anthology of Political Writing in Stuart England*, Harmondsworth.

Yearsley, Anne (1796). *The Rural Lyre*, London.

[Yorke, Henry?] (1794). *The Spirit of John Locke on Civil Government, Revived by the Constitutional Society of Sheffield*, Sheffield and London.

## SECONDARY SOURCES

Ackelsberg, Martha A. and Mary Lyndon Shanley (1996). 'Privacy, Publicity, and Power: A Feminist Rethinking of the Public-Private Distinction', in *Revisioning the Political: Feminist Reconstructions of Traditional Concepts in Western Political Theory*, ed. Nancy J. Hirschmann and Christine Di Stefano, Boulder, pp. 213–33.

Adair, Douglass (1974). *Fame and the Founding Fathers*, ed. H. Trevor Colbourn, New York.

Altman, Joel (1978). *The Tudor Play of Mind: Rhetorical Inquiry and the Development of Elizabethan Drama*, Berkeley.

Anghie, Antony (2004). *Imperialism, Sovereignty and the Making of International Law*, Cambridge.

Arab, Ronda Ann (2002). 'Working Masculinities in Early Modern English Drama', PhD thesis, Columbia University.

Armitage, David (2000). *The Ideological Origins of the British Empire*, Cambridge.

(2004a). *Greater Britain, 1516–1776: Essays in Atlantic History*, Aldershot.

(2004b). 'John Locke, Carolina, and the *Two Treatises of Government*', *Political Theory* 32, pp. 602–27

(2006). *The Declaration of Independence: A Global History*, Cambridge, Mass.

Armitage, David, Armand Himy and Quentin Skinner (eds.) (1995). *Milton and Republicanism*, Cambridge.

Armstrong, Robert (2005). 'Protestant Churchmen and the Confederate Wars', in *British Interventions in Early Modern Ireland*, ed. Ciaran Brady and Jane Ohlmeyer, Cambridge, pp. 230–51.

Arneil, Barbara (1996). *John Locke and America: The Defence of English Colonialism*, Oxford.

Ashcraft, Richard and M. M. Goldsmith (1983). 'Locke, Revolution Principles, and the Formation of Whig Ideology', *The Historical Journal* 26, pp. 773–800

Axton, Marie (1977). *The Queen's Two Bodies: Drama and the Elizabethan Succession*, London.

Ayers, Michael (1993). *Locke: Epistemology and Ontology*, 2 vols., London.

Aylmer, Gerald (1986). *Rebellion or Revolution? England 1640–1660*, Oxford.

Bailyn, Bernard (1967). *The Ideological Origins of the American Revolution*, Cambridge, Mass.

Baine, Rodney M. (1988). 'James Oglethorpe and the Early Promotional Literature for Georgia', *William and Mary Quarterly* 3rd ser., 45, pp. 100–6.

Baker, David J. and Willy Maley (eds.) (2002). *British Identities and English Renaissance Literature*, Cambridge.

Bakhtin, Mikhail (1986). 'The Problem of Speech Genres', in *Speech Genres and Other Late Essays*, trans. Vern W. McGee, Austin, pp. 60–102.

Bald, R. C. (1970). *John Donne: A Life*, New York.

Barber, Sarah (2005). 'Settlement, Transplantation and Expulsion: A Comparative Study of the Placement of Peoples', in *British Interventions in Early Modern Ireland*, ed. Ciaran Brady and Jane Ohlmeyer, Cambridge, pp. 280–98.

Barbour, Reid (1998). *English Epicures and Stoics: Ancient Legacies in Early Stuart Culture*, Amherst.

Barker, Ernest (1956). *From Alexander to Constantine*, Oxford.

Barnard, Toby (1993). '1641: A Bibliographic Essay', in *Ulster 1641: Aspects of the Rising*, ed. Brian Mac Cuarta, Belfast, pp. 173–86.

(2005). 'Interests in Ireland: "the fanatic zeal and irregular ambition" of Richard Lawrence', in *British Interventions in Early Modern Ireland*, ed. Ciaran Brady and Jane Ohlmeyer, Cambridge, pp. 299–304.

Baron, Hans (1966). *The Crisis of the Early Italian Renaissance: Civic Humanism and Republican Liberty in an Age of Classicism and Tyranny*, rev. edn, Princeton.

Barrell, A. D. M. (1995). 'The Background to *Cum Universi*: Scoto-Papal Relations, 1159–1192', *Innes Review* 46, pp. 116–38.

Barrow, G. W. S. (1988). *Robert the Bruce and the Community of the Realm of Scotland*, 3rd edn, Edinburgh.

Barthes, Roland (1975). *The Pleasure of the Text*, trans. Richard Miller, New York.

Barton, Anne (1994). 'Livy, Machiavelli and Shakespeare's *Coriolanus*', in *Essays, Mainly Shakespearean*, Cambridge, pp. 136–60.

Battigelli, Anna (1998). *Margaret Cavendish and the Exiles of the Mind*, Lexington, KY.

Baumgold, Deborah (1988). *Hobbes's Political Theory*, Cambridge.

Bayly, C. A. (2004). *The Birth of the Modern World, 1780–1914: Global Connections and Comparisons*, Oxford.

Beckett, J. C. (1966). *The Making of Modern Ireland*, London.

Beitz, Charles (1979). *Political Theory and International Relations*, Princeton.

  (2001). 'Human Rights as a Common Concern', *American Political Science Review* 95, pp. 269–82

Bellamy, John (1979). *The Tudor Law of Treason: An Introduction*, London.

Bevington, David (1962). *From 'Mankind' to Marlowe: Growth of Structure in the Popular Drama of Tudor England*, Cambridge, Mass.

  (1968). *Tudor Drama and Politics: A Critical Approach to Topical Meaning*, Cambridge, Mass.

Bindoff, S. T. (1945). 'The Stuarts and their Style', *English Historical Review* 60, pp. 192–216.

Boyce, D. George, Robert Eccleshall and Vincent Geoghegan (eds.) (1993). *Political Thought in Ireland since the Seventeenth Century*, London and New York.

Boys, Richard C. (1947). 'General Oglethorpe and the Muses', *Georgia Historical Quarterly* 31, pp. 19–29.

Bracken, Harry (1984). *Mind and Language: Essays on Descartes and Chomsky*, Dordrecht.

Braddick, Michael J. (2000). *State Formation in Early Modern England, c. 1550–1700*, Cambridge.

Bradshaw, Brendan (1978). 'Native Reaction to the Westward Enterprise: A Case Study of Gaelic Ideology', in *The Westward Enterprise: English Activities in Ireland, the Atlantic and America, 1480–1650*, ed. Kenneth R. Andrews, Nicholas P. Canny and P. E. H. Hair, Liverpool, pp. 65–80.

Bradshaw, Brendan, Andrew Hadfield and Willy Maley (eds.) (1993). *Representing Ireland: Literature and the Origins of Conflict*, Cambridge.

Brady, Ciaran (1981). 'Faction and the Origins of the Desmond Rebellion of 1579', *Irish Historical Studies* 22, pp. 289–312.

  (1985). '"Conservative Subversives": The Community of the Pale and the Dublin Administration', in *Radicals, Rebels and Establishments*, ed. Patrick J. Corish, Belfast, pp. 11–32.

  (1994a). *The Chief Governors: The Rise and Fall of Reform in Tudor Ireland, 1536–1588*, Cambridge.

  (ed.) (1994b). *Interpreting Irish History: The Debate on Historical Revisionism*, Dublin.

Brennan, Theresa and Carole Pateman (1979). ' "Mere Auxiliaries to the Commonwealth": Women and the Origins of Liberalism', *Political Studies* 27, pp. 183–200.

Brett, Annabel (2003). 'The Development of the Idea of Citizens' Rights', in *States and Citizens: History, Theory, Prospects*, ed. Quentin Skinner and Bo Stråth, Cambridge, pp. 97–112.

Brewer, John (1995). 'This, That and the Other: Public, Social and Private in the Seventeenth and Eighteenth Centuries', in *Shifting the Boundaries: Transformation of the Languages of Public and Private in the Eighteenth Century*, ed. Dario Castiglione and Lesley Sharpe, Exeter, pp. 1–21.

Broad, Jacqueline (2002). *Women Philosophers of the Seventeenth Century*, Cambridge.

Broun, Dauvit (2002). 'The Church and the Origins of Scottish Independence in the Twelfth Century', *Records of the Scottish Church History Society* 31, pp. 1–35.

Brown, Keith M. (1992). *Kingdom or Province? Scotland and the Regnal Union, 1603–1715*, London.

Buchanan, Allen (2004). *Justice, Legitimacy, and Self-Determination: Moral Foundations for International Law*, Oxford.

Burgess, Glenn (1990). 'On Revisionism', *Historical Journal* 33, pp. 609–27.
  (1996). *Absolute Monarchy and the Stuart Constitution*, New Haven.
  (ed.) (1999). *The New British History: Founding a Modern State 1603–1715*, London.

Burke, Peter (1853). *The Public and Domestic Life of the Right Hon. Edmund Burke*, London.

Burns, Edward (1887). *The Coinage of Scotland*, 3 vols., Edinburgh.

Burns, J. H. (1993). 'George Buchanan and the Anti-Monarchomachs', in *Political Discourse in Early Modern Britain*, ed. Nicholas Phillipson and Quentin Skinner, Cambridge, pp. 3–22.
  (1996). *The True Law of Kingship: Concepts of Monarchy in Early Modern Scotland*, Oxford.

Burns, J. H. and Mark Goldie (eds.) (1991). *The Cambridge History of Political Thought, 1450–1700*, Cambridge.

Burrell, Sidney A. (1964). 'The Apocalyptic Ideas of the Early Covenanters', *Scottish Historical Review* 43, pp. 1–24.

Bury, J. B. (1928). *The Idea of Progress*, London.

Bushnell, Rebecca (1990). *Tragedies of Tyrants: Political Thought and Theater in the English Renaissance*, Ithaca.

Caney, Simon (2005). *Justice Beyond Borders: A Global Political Theory*, Oxford.

Canny, Nicholas P. (1975). *The Formation of the Old English Elite in Ireland*, O'Donnell Lecture at the National University of Ireland, Dublin.
  (1992). Review in *Irish Economic and Social History* 19, pp. 112–15.
  (1993). 'The Attempted Anglicization of Ireland in the Seventeenth Century: An Exemplar of "British History" ', in *Three Nations – A Common History?*

*England, Scotland, Ireland and British History c. 1600–1920*, ed. Ronald Asch, Bochum, pp. 49–82.

(1995). 'Irish, Scots and Welsh Responses to Colonisation *c.* 1530–*c.* 1640', in *Grant and Stringer 1995*, pp. 147–69.

(ed.) (1998). *The Oxford History of the British Empire*, vol. 1, *The Origins of Empire*, Oxford.

(2001). *Making Ireland British, 1580–1650*, Oxford.

(2003a). 'Taking Sides in Early Modern Ireland: the Case of Hugh O'Neill, Earl of Tyrone', in *Taking Sides?: Colonial and Confessional Mentalités in Early Modern Ireland: Essays in Honour of Karl S. Bottigheimer*, ed. Vincent Carey and Ute Lotz-Heumann, Dublin, pp. 94–115.

(2003b). 'Writing Early Modern History: Ireland, Britain and the Wider World', *The Historical Journal* 46, pp. 723–47.

Carlyle, A. J. and R. W. Carlyle (1936). *A History of Medieval Political Theory in the West*, vol. 6: *Political Theory from 1300 to 1600*, London.

Carroll, Clare (2001). *Circe's Cup: Cultural Transformations in Early Modern Ireland*, Cork.

Cartelli, Thomas (1994). 'Jack Cade in the Garden: Class Consciousness and Class Conflict in *2 Henry VI*', in *Enclosure Acts: Sexuality, Property and Culture in Early Modern England*, ed. Richard Burt and John Michael Archer, Ithaca, pp. 48–67.

Castiglione, Dario and Iain Hampsher-Monk (eds.) (2001). *The History of Political Thought in National Context*, Cambridge.

Cavanagh, Dermot (2003). *Language and Politics in the Sixteenth-Century History Play*, New York.

Cavell, Stanley (1969). *Must We Mean What We Say?*, New York.

Certeau, Michel de (1984). 'Reading as Poaching', in *The Practice of Everyday Life*, Berkeley and Los Angeles, pp. 165–75.

Chalmers, Hero (1997). 'Dismantling the Myth of "Mad Madge": The Cultural Context of Margaret Cavendish's Authorial Self-presentation', *Women's Writing* 4, pp. 323–40.

Champion, J. A. I. (1992). *The Pillars of Priestcraft Shaken: The Church of England and its Enemies, 1660–1730*, Cambridge.

Chartier, Roger (1988). *The Cultural Uses of Print in Early Modern France*, Princeton.

Clare, Janet (1999). *Art Made Tongue-Tied by Authority: Elizabethan and Jacobean Dramatic Censorship*, 2nd edn, Manchester.

Clarke, Aidan (1966). *The Old English in Ireland, 1625–1642*, London.

(1978). 'Colonial Identity in Early Seventeenth-Century Ireland', in *Nationality and the Pursuit of National Independence*, ed. T. W. Moody, Belfast, pp. 57–71.

(2000). 'Patrick Darcy and the Constitutional Relationship between Ireland and England', in *Ohlmeyer 2000*, Cambridge, pp. 35–55.

Claydon, Anthony (1999). ' "British History" in the Post-Revolutionary World, 1690–1715', in Burgess 1999, pp. 115–37.

Clegg, Cyndia (1997). *Press Censorship in Elizabethan England*, Cambridge.

(2004). 'Holinshed, Raphael (*c.* 1525–1580?)', in *The Oxford Dictionary of National Biography*, ed. H. C. G. Mathew and Brian Harrison, 60 vols., Oxford, XXVII, pp. 644–7.

Coburn-Walshe, Helen (1990). 'The Rebellion of William Nugent, 1581', in *Religion, Conflict and Coexistence in Ireland: Essays Presented to Monsignor Patrick J. Corish*, ed. R. V. Comerford, Mary Cullen, Jacqueline R. Hill and Colm Lennon, Dublin, pp. 26–52.

Code, Lorraine (1995). *Rhetorical Spaces: Essays on Gendered Locations*, New York and London.

Cohen, Joshua (2004) 'Minimalism About Human Rights: The Most We Can Hope For?', *Journal of Political Philosophy* 12, pp. 190–213.

Coleman, Deidre (2005). *Romantic Colonization and British Anti-Slavery*, Cambridge.

Colie, Rosalie (1973). *Resources of Kind: Genre-Theory in the Renaissance*, Berkeley.

Collinson, Patrick (2003). *Elizabethans*, London.

Condren, Conal (1985). *The Status and Appraisal of Classic Texts*, Princeton.

Connolly, S. J. (ed.) (2000). *Political Ideas in Eighteenth-Century Ireland*, Dublin.

Copeland, Thomas (1949). *Our Eminent Friend Edmund Burke, Six Essays*, New Haven.

Cowan, Edward (1994). 'The Political Ideas of a Covenanting Leader: Archibald Campbell, Marquis of Argyll, 1670–1661', in Mason 1994a, pp. 241–62.

Crawford, Patricia (1992). 'The Challenges to Patriarchalism: How did the Revolution Affect Women?', in *Revolution and Restoration: England in the 1650s*, ed. John Morrill, London, pp. 112–28.

(1993). *Women and Religion in England 1500–1720*, London and New York.

Crawford, Patricia and Laura Gowing (eds.) (2000). *Women's Worlds in Seventeenth-Century England*, London and New York.

Cregan, Donal (1970a). 'Catholic Admissions to the English Inns of Court', *Irish Jurist* 5, pp. 95–114.

(1970b). 'Irish Recusant Lawyers in the Reign of James I', *Irish Jurist* 5, pp. 306–20.

(1995). 'The Confederate Catholics of Ireland: The Personnel of the Confederation', *Irish Historical Studies* 39, pp. 490–512.

Crick, Julia C. (1989). *The Historia Regum Brittaniae of Geoffrey of Monmouth*, vol 3: *A Summary Catalogue of the Manuscripts*, Cambridge.

(1991). *The Historia Regum Brittaniae of Geoffrey of Monmouth*, vol 4: *Dissemination and Reception in the Later Middle Ages*, Cambridge.

Crook, J. A., Andrew Lintott and Elizabeth Rawson (eds.) (1994). *The Cambridge Ancient History*, vol. 9: *The Last Age of the Roman Republic, 146–43 B.C.*, Cambridge.

Cunningham, Bernadette (2000). *The World of Geoffrey Keating: History, Myth and Religion in Seventeenth-Century Ireland*, Dublin.

Dalmiya, Vrinda and Linda Alcoff (1993). 'Are "Old Wives' Tales" Justified?', in *Feminist Epistemologies*, ed. Linda Alcoff and Elizabeth Potters, New York: Routledge, pp. 217–44.

Darnton, Robert (1985). *The Great Cat Massacre and Other Episodes in French Cultural History*, New York.

Davidson, Donald (1984). *Inquiries into Truth and Knowledge*, Oxford.

Davies, R. R. (ed.) (1988). *The British Isles, 1100–1500: Comparisons, Contrasts, and Connections*, Oxford.

(1994). 'The Peoples of Britain and Ireland: I, Identities', *Transactions of the Royal Historical Society*, 6th series, 4, pp. 1–20.

(1995). 'The Peoples of Britain and Ireland: II, Names, Boundaries and Regnal Solidarities', *Transactions of the Royal Historical Society*, 6th series, 5, pp. 1–20.

(1996a). 'The Peoples of Britain and Ireland: III, Laws and Customs', *Transactions of the Royal Historical Society*, 6th series, 6, pp. 1–24.

(1996b). *The Matter of Britain and the Matter of England: An Inaugural Lecture delivered before the University of Oxford on 29 February 1996*, Oxford.

(1997). 'The Peoples of Britain and Ireland: IV, Language and Historical Mythology', *Transactions of the Royal Historical Society*, 6th series, 7, pp. 1–24.

(2000). *The First English Empire: Power and Identities in the British Isles, 1093–1343*, Oxford.

Dawson, Jane E. A. (2002). *The Politics of Religion in the Age of Mary Queen of Scots: The Earl of Argyll and the Struggle for Britain and Ireland*, Cambridge.

Derrida, Jacques (1974). *Of Grammatology*, trans. Gayatri Spivak, Baltimore.

(1991). 'From "Difference"', in *A Derrida Reader*, ed. Peggy Kamuf, New York, pp. 59–79.

Donaldson, Ian (1982). *The Rapes of Lucrece: A Myth and its Transformations*, Oxford.

Doran, Susan and Glenn Richardson (eds.) (2005). *Tudor England and its Neighbours*, Basingstoke.

Dzelzainis, Martin (1999). 'Shakespeare and Political Thought', in *A Companion to Shakespeare*, ed. David Scott Kastan, Oxford, pp. 100–16.

Edwards, David (1992). 'The Butler Revolt of 1569', *Irish Historical Studies* 28, pp. 228–55.

(2003). *The Ormond Lordship in County Kilkenny, 1515–1642: The Rise and Fall of Butler Feudal Power*, Dublin.

Eley, Geoff and William Hunt (eds.) (1988). *Reviving the English Revolution*, New York.

Ellis, Steven G. (1995). *Tudor Power and the Making of the British State*, Oxford.

Elshtain, Jean Bethke (1993). *Public Man/Private Woman: Women in Social and Political Thought*, 2nd edn, Princeton.

Ettinger, Amos Aschbach (1936). *James Edward Oglethorpe, Imperial Idealist*, Oxford.

Erskine-Hill, Howard (1998). 'Pope and Slavery', in *Alexander Pope: World and Word*, ed. Howard Erskine-Hill, *Proceedings of the British Academy* 91, pp. 27–54.

Faulkner, Peter (1991). 'William Cowper and the Poetry of Empire', *Durham University Journal* 83, pp. 165–73.

Ferguson, William (1974). 'Imperial Crowns: A Neglected Facet of the Union of 1707', *Scottish Historical Review* 53, 22–44.

  (1977). *Scotland's Relations with England: A Survey to 1707*, Edinburgh.

  (1998). *The Identity of the Scottish Nation: An Historic Quest*, Edinburgh.

Fish, Stanley (1980). *Is There a Text in this Class? The Authority of Interpretive Communities*, Cambridge, Mass.

Fletcher, Anthony (1995). *Gender, Sex and Subordination in England, 1500–1800*, New Haven and London.

Ford, Alan (1995). *The Protestant Reformation in Ireland, 1590–1641*, Frankfurt.

Ford, Alan and John McCafferty (eds.) (2005). *The Origins of Sectarianism in Early Modern Ireland*, Cambridge.

Forkan, Kevin (2003). 'Scottish-Protestant Ulster and the Crisis of the Three Kingdoms, 1637–1652', Ph.D. thesis, National University of Ireland, Galway.

Foucault, Michel (1970). *The Order of Things: An Archaeology of the Human Sciences*, New York.

  (2003) *Society Must be Defended: Lectures at the Collége de France, 1975–1976*, trans. David Macey, New York.

Frame, Robin (1990). *The Political Development of the British Isles, 1100–1400*, London.

Franklin, Julian (1969). *Constitutionalism and Resistance in the Sixteenth Century*, New York.

Fry, Michael (1993). 'The Disruption and the Union', in *Scotland in the Age of the Disruption*, ed. Stewart J. Brown and Michael Fry, Edinburgh, pp. 31–43.

Fulford, Tim, Debbie Lee and Peter Kitson (eds.) (2004). *Literature, Science and Exploration in the Romantic Era: Bodies of Knowledge*, Cambridge.

Gallagher, Catherine and Stephen Greenblatt (2000). *Practicing New Historicism*, Chicago.

Galloway, Bruce R. (1986). *The Union of England and Scotland, 1603–1608*, Edinburgh.

Genette, Gérard (1997). *Paratexts: Thresholds of Interpretation*, trans. Jane E. Lewin, Cambridge.

Geuss, Raymond (2001). *History and Illusion in Politics*, Cambridge.

Gillespie, Raymond (2005a). *Reading Ireland: Print, Reading and Social Change in Early Modern Ireland*, Manchester.

  (2005b). 'Temple's Fate: Reading *The Irish Rebellion* in the Late Seventeenth Century', in *British Interventions in Early Modern Ireland*, ed. Ciaran Brady and Jane Ohlmeyer, Cambridge, pp. 315–33.

Gillingham, John (1993). 'The English Invasion of Ireland', in Bradshaw, Hadfield and Maley 1993, pp. 24–42.

(1995). 'Foundations of a Disunited Kingdom', in Grant and Stringer 1995, pp. 48–64.

Ginzburg, Carlo (1992). *The Cheese and the Worms: The Cosmos of a Sixteenth-Century Miller*, trans. John and Anne Tedeschi, Baltimore.

Goldie, Mark (1980). 'The Revolution of 1689 and the Structure of Political Argument', *Bulletin of Research in the Humanities* 83, pp. 473–564.

(1997). 'Restoration Political Thought', in *The Reigns of Charles II and James VII & II*, ed. Lionel K. J. Glassey, Basingstoke, pp. 12–35.

Goldstein, R. James (1993). *The Matter of Scotland*, Lincoln, Neb., and London.

Goodyear, F. R. D. (1972–1981). *The Annals of Tacitus Books 1–6*, 2 vols., Cambridge.

Gong, Gerrit W. (1984). *The Standard of Civilization in International Society*, Oxford.

Gould, Eliga (2000). *The Persistence of Empire: British Political Culture in the Age of the American Revolution*, Chapel Hill.

Gowing, Laura (1998). *Domestic Dangers: Women, Words, and Sex in Early Modern London*, New York.

Grant, Alexander and Keith J. Stringer (eds.) (1995). *Uniting the Kingdom?: The Making of British History*, London.

Grant, Ruth (1987). *John Locke's Liberalism*, Chicago.

Greenblatt, Stephen (1983). 'Murdering Peasants: Status, Genre, and the Representation of Rebellion', *Representations* 1, pp. 1–29.

Griffin, Dustin (2002). *Patriotism and Poetry in Eighteenth-Century Britain*, Cambridge.

Grote, David (2002). *The Best Actors in the World: Shakespeare and His Acting Company*, Westport, CT.

Guest, Harriet (2000). *Small Change: Women, Learning, Patriotism, 1750–1810*, Chicago.

Gunnell, John G. (1979). *Political Theory: Tradition and Interpretation*, Cambridge, Mass.

(1982). 'Interpretation and the History of Political Theory: Apology and Epistemology', *American Political Science Review* 76, pp. 317–27.

Gurr, Andrew (1996). *The Shakespearian Playing Companies*, Oxford.

Guy, John (1993). 'The Henrician Age', in Pocock, Schochet and Schwoerer 1993, pp. 13–46.

Haakonssen, Knud (1981). *The Science of a Legislator: The Natural Jurisprudence of David Hume and Adam Smith*, Cambridge.

(1996). *Natural Law and Moral Philosophy from Grotius to the Scottish Enlightenment*, Cambridge.

(2001). 'The Moral Conservatism of Natural Rights', in *Natural Law and Civil Sovereignty: Moral Right and State Authority in Early Modern Political Thought*, ed. Ian Hunter and David Saunders, New York, pp. 27–42.

Hadfield, Andrew (1998). *Literature, Travel and Colonial Writing in the English Renaissance, 1545–1625*, Oxford.

(2003). *Shakespeare and Renaissance Politics*, London.

(2005). *Shakespeare and Republicanism*, Cambridge.

Halévy, Elie (1934). *The Growth of Philosophical Radicalism*, London.

Hammond, Paul (1999). *Dryden and the Traces of Classical Rome*, Oxford.

Hanisch, Carol (2000). 'The Personal is Political', in *Radical Feminism: A Documentary Reader*, ed. Barbara Crow, New York, pp. 113–16.

Hankins, James (ed.) (2000). *Renaissance Civic Humanism*, Cambridge.

Harris, Tim (1998). 'The British Dimension, Religion, and the Shaping of Political Identities during the Reign of Charles II', in *Protestantism and National Identity: Britain and Ireland, c. 1650–c. 1850*, ed. Tony Claydon and Ian McBride, Cambridge, pp. 131–56.

(2002). 'Incompatible Revolutions? The Established Church and the Revolutions of 1688–1689 in Ireland, England and Scotland', in Macinnes and Ohlmeyer 2002, pp. 204–25.

(2005). *Restoration: Charles II and His Kingdoms, 1660–1685*, London.

(2006). *Revolution: The Great Crisis of the British Monarchy, 1685–1720*, London.

Hart, A. Tindal (1952). *William Lloyd, 1627–1717: Bishop, Politician, Author and Prophet*, London.

Hartz, Louis (1948). *Economic Policy and Democratic Thought: Pennsylvania, 1776–1860*, Cambridge, Mass.

(1955). *The Liberal Tradition in America: An Interpretation of American Political Thought since the Revolution*, New York.

Hay, Denys (1968). *Europe: The Emergence of an Idea*, rev. edn, Edinburgh.

Helgerson, Richard (1992). *Forms of Nationhood: The Elizabethan Writing of England*, Chicago.

Herzog, Don (1998). *Poisoning the Minds of the Lower Orders*, Princeton.

Hill, Christopher (1961). *The Century of Revolution, 1603–1714*, Edinburgh.

(1972). *The World Turned Upside-Down: Radical Ideas During the English Revolution*, rev. edn, London.

(1985). *The Collected Essays of Christopher Hill*, vol. 1: *Writing and Revolution in Seventeenth-Century England*, Brighton.

(1998). *England's Turning Point: Essays on 17th Century English History*, Chicago.

Hinds, Hilary (1996). *God's Englishwomen: Seventeenth-Century Radical Sectarian Writing and Feminist Criticism*, Manchester and New York.

Hobday, Charles (1979). 'Clouted Shoon and Leather Aprons: Shakespeare and the Egalitarian Tradition', *Renaissance and Modern Studies* 23, pp. 63–78.

Holland, Tom (2003). *Rubicon: The Triumph and Tragedy of the Roman Republic*, London.

Hont, Istvan (1987). 'The Language of Sociability and Commerce: Samuel Pufendorf and the Theoretical Foundations of the "Four-Stages Theory"', in Pagden 1987, pp. 253–76.

Howard, Jean E. (1984). *Shakespeare's Art of Orchestration: Stage Technique and Audience Response*, Urbana.

(1994). *The Stage and Social Struggle in Early Modern England*, London.

(2006). 'Stage Masculinities, National History, and the Making of London Theatrical Culture', in *Center or Margin: Revisions of the English Renaissance*, ed. Lena Cowan Orlin, Cranbury, NJ, pp. 201–16.

Huebert, Ronald (1997). 'Privacy: The Early Social History of a Word', *Sewanee Review* 105, pp. 21–38.

(2001). 'The Gendering of Privacy', *The Seventeenth Century* 16, pp. 37–67.

Hughes, Ann (1987). *Politics, Society and Civil War in Warwickshire, 1620–1660*, Cambridge.

Ignatieff, Michael (1999). 'Human Rights', in *Human Rights in Political Transitions: Gettysburg to Bosnia*, ed. Carla Hesse and Robert Post, New York, pp. 313–24.

Iser, Wolfgang (1974). *The Implied Reader*, Baltimore.

(1978). *The Act of Reading: A Theory of Aesthetic Response*, Baltimore.

Ivison, Duncan (1997). *The Self at Liberty: Political Argument and the Arts of Government*, Ithaca.

(2002). *Postcolonial Liberalism*, Cambridge.

(2006). 'Emergent Cosmopolitanism: Indigenous Peoples and International Law', in *Between Cosmopolitan Ideals and State Sovereignty: Studies on Global Justice*, ed. Ronald Tinnevelt and Gert Verschraegen, New York, pp. 120–31.

Jackson, Clare (2003). *Restoration Scotland, 1660–1690: Royalist Politics, Religion and Ideas*, Woodbridge.

Jagodzinski, Cecile M. (1999). *Privacy and Print: Reading and Writing in Seventeenth-Century England*, Charlottesville and London.

James, Susan (2003a). 'Introduction', in Margaret Cavendish, *Political Writings*, ed. Susan James, Cambridge, pp. ix–xxix.

(2003b). 'Rights as Enforceable Claims', *Proceedings of the Aristotelian Society* 103, pp. 133–47.

Jardine, Lisa and Anthony Grafton (1990). '"Studied for Action": How Gabriel Harvey Read his Livy', *Past and Present* 129, pp. 30–78.

Jauss, H. R. (1982). *Toward an Aesthetic of Reception*, Minneapolis.

Jay, Martin (1982). 'Should Intellectual History Take a Linguistic Turn? Reflections on the Habermas-Gadamer Debate', in *Modern European Intellectual History: Reappraisals and New Perspectives*, eds. Dominick La Capra and Steven L. Kaplan, Ithaca, pp. 86–110.

Jones, Frederick M. (1958). *Mountjoy, 1563–1606: The Last Elizabethan Deputy*, Dublin.

Jones, Howard (1981). *Master Tully: Cicero in Tudor England*, Nieuwkoop.

Jones, Peter (2001). 'Human Rights and Diverse Cultures: Continuity or Discontinuity?', in *Human Rights and Global Diversity*, ed. Simon Caney and Peter Jones, London, pp. 27–50.

Jones, Whitney R. D. (2000). *The Tree of Commonwealth, 1450–1793*, Madison.

Justice, Steven (1994). *Writing and Rebellion: England in 1381*, Berkeley.

Kahn, Coppélia (2003). 'Publishing Shame: *The Rape of Lucrece*', in *A Companion to Shakespeare's Works*, vol. 4: *The Poems, Problem Comedies, Late Plays*, ed. Richard Dutton, Oxford, pp. 259–74.

Kantorowicz, Ernst H. (1957). *The King's Two Bodies: A Study in Medieval Political Theology*, Princeton.

Karsten, Peter (2002). *Between Law and Custom: "High" and "Low" Legal Cultures in the Lands of the British Diaspora: The United States, Canada, Australia, and New Zealand, 1600—1900*, Cambridge.

Kastan, David Scott (1986). 'Proud Majesty Made a Subject: Shakespeare and the Spectacle of Rule', *Shakespeare Quarterly* 37, pp. 459—75.

(1999). *Shakespeare After Theory*, New York.

Kavka, Gregory S. (1986). *Hobbesian Moral and Political Theory*, Princeton.

Keal, Paul (2003). *European Conquest and the Rights of Indigenous Peoples: The Moral Backwardness of International Society*, Cambridge.

Keene, Edward (2002). *Beyond the Anarchical Society: Grotius, Colonialism and Order in World Politics*, Cambridge.

Kelley, Donald (1993). 'Elizabethan Political Thought', in Pocock, Schochet and Schwoerer 1993, pp. 47—79.

Kelly, Patrick (2000). 'Recasting a Tradition: William Molyneux and the Sources of *The Case of Ireland . . . Stated* (1698)', in Ohlmeyer 2000, pp. 83—106.

Kenyon, J. P. (1972). *The Popish Plot*, New York.

(1990). *Revolution Principles: The Politics of Party, 1689—1720*, 2nd edn, Cambridge.

Kidd, Colin (1993). *Subverting Scotland's Past: Scottish Whig Historians and the Creation of an Anglo-British Identity, 1689—c. 1830*, Cambridge.

(1995). 'Religious Realignment between the Restoration and Union', in Robertson 1995a, pp. 145—68.

(1999). *British Identities before Nationalism: Ethnicity and Nationhood in the Atlantic World, 1600—1800*, Cambridge.

Kirk, Russell (1967). *Edmund Burke: A Genius Reconsidered*, New York.

Kishlansky, Mark A. (1986). *Parliamentary Selection: Social and Political Choice in Early Modern England*, Cambridge.

Knights, Mark (1994). *Politics and Opinion in Crisis, 1678—1681*, Cambridge.

Knorr, Klaus E. (1968). *British Colonial Theories, 1570—1850*, Toronto.

Koebner, Richard (1961). *Empire*, Cambridge.

Kramnick, Isaac (1977). *The Rage of Edmund Burke: Portrait of an Ambivalent Conservative*, New York.

Kumar, Krishan (2003). *The Making of English National Identity*, Cambridge.

Kymlicka, Will (1995). *Multicultural Citizenship*, Oxford.

Landes, Joan B. (1998). 'Introduction', in *Feminism, the Public and the Private*, ed. Joan B. Landes, Oxford, pp. 1—17.

Laski, Harold J. (1936). *The Rise of European Liberalism*, London.

Leerssen, Joep (1986). *Mere Irish and Fíor-Ghael: Studies in the Idea of Irish Nationality, its Development and Literary Expression Prior to the Nineteenth Century*, Amsterdam and Philadelphia.

Lennon, Colm (1994). *Sixteenth-Century Ireland: The Incomplete Conquest*, Dublin.

Levack, Brian P. (1987). *The Formation of the British State, 1603—1707*, Oxford.

Lewalski, Barbara K. (1973). *Donne's Anniversaries and the Poetry of Praise: The Creation of a Symbolic Mode*, Princeton.

Lindley, Keith (1972). 'The Impact of the 1641 Rebellion upon England and Wales', *Irish Historical Studies* 70, pp. 143—76.

Little, Patrick (2004). *Lord Broghill and the Cromwellian Union with Ireland and Scotland*, Woodbridge.

Lynch, Michael (1991). *Scotland: A New History*, Edinburgh.

Lyons, Mary Ann (2003). *Franco-Irish Relations, 1500—1610*, Woodbridge.

Mac Cuarta, Brian (2004). 'Connor Maguire, Second Baron of Enniskillen (*c.* 1612—1645)', in *The Oxford Dictionary of National Biography*, ed. H. C. G. Mathew, and Brian Harrison, 60 vols., Oxford, XXXVI, pp. 143—4.

Macinnes, Allan I. (1996). *Clanship, Commerce and the House of Stuart, 1603—1788*, East Linton.

  (2004). *The British Revolution, 1629—1660*, Basingstoke.

Macinnes, Allan and Ohlmeyer, Jane (eds.) (2002). *The Stuart Kingdoms in the Seventeenth Century: Awkward Neighbours*, Dublin.

Mack, Maynard (1965). *King Lear in Our Time*, Berkeley.

  (1985). *Alexander Pope: A Life*, New Haven.

Mack, Phyllis (1992). *Visionary Women: Ecstatic Prophecy in Seventeenth-Century England*, Berkeley.

Maginn, Christopher (2005). *'Civilizing' Gaelic Leinster: The Extension of Tudor Rule in the O'Byrne and O'Toole Lordships*, Dublin.

Malcolm, Noel (2002). *Aspects of Hobbes*, Oxford.

Manheim, Michael (1973). *The Weak King Dilemma in the Shakespearean History Play*, Syracuse.

Mann, Alastair J. (2000). *The Scottish Book Trade, 1500—1720: Print Commerce and Print Control in Early Modern Scotland: An Historiographical Survey of the Early Modern Book in Scotland*, East Linton.

Manning, Brian (1976). *The English People and the English Revolution, 1640—1649*, London.

Manning, Roger A. (1988). *Village Revolts: Social Protest and Popular Disturbances in England, 1509—1640*, Oxford.

Marshall, John (1994). *John Locke: Resistance, Religion and Responsibility*, Cambridge.

  (2005). *John Locke, Toleration and Early Enlightenment Culture*, Cambridge.

Mason, Roger A. (1987). 'Scotching the Brut: Politics, History and National Myth in Sixteenth-Century Britain', in *Scotland and England, 1286—1815*, ed. Roger Mason, Edinburgh, pp. 60—84.

  (1991). 'Scotching the Brut: The Early History of Britain', in *Scotland Revisited*, ed. Jenny Wormald, London, pp. 49—60.

  (ed.) (1994a). *Scots and Britons: Political Thought and the Union of 1603*, Cambridge.

  (1994b). 'Imagining Scotland: Scottish Political Thought and the Problem of Britain, 1560—1660', in Mason 1994a, pp. 3—13.

(1994c). 'The Scottish Reformation and the Origins of Anglo-British Imperialism', in Mason 1994a, pp. 161—86.

(1998). *Kingship and Commonweal: Political Thought in Renaissance and Reformation Scotland*, East Linton.

(2004). 'Scotland, Elizabethan England and the Idea of Britain', *Transactions of the Royal Historical Society* 6th ser., 14, pp. 279—93.

McCartney, Donald (1994). *W. E. H. Lecky, Historian and Politician, 1838—1903*, Dublin.

McCavitt, John (1990). 'Lord Deputy Chichester and the English Government's "Mandates Policy" in Ireland', *Recusant History* 20, pp. 320—35.

(1998). *Sir Arthur Chichester: Lord Deputy of Ireland, 1605—1616*, Belfast.

McClure, Kirstie M. (2003). 'Cato's Retreat: *Fabula, Historia*, and the Question of Constitutionalism in Mr. Locke's *Essay on Government*', in *Reading, Society and Politics in Early Modern England*, ed. Kevin Sharpe and Steven N. Zwicker, Cambridge, pp. 317—50.

McGann, Jerome J. (1983). *A Critique of Modern Textual Criticism*, Chicago.

McIntire, C. T. (2004). *Herbert Butterfield: Historian as Dissenter*, New Haven.

McKenzie, D. F. (1986). *Bibliography and the Sociology of Texts*, London.

McLaren, Anne N. (2000). *Political Culture in the Reign of Elizabeth I: Queen and Commonwealth, 1558—1585*, Cambridge.

McNeil, Kent (1989). *Common Law Aboriginal Title*, Oxford.

Meek, Ronald (1976). *Social Science and the Ignoble Savage*, Cambridge.

Megill, Allan (2005). 'Globalization and the History of Ideas', *Journal of the History of Ideas* 66, pp. 179—87.

Mehan, Michael (1986). *Liberty and Poetics in Eighteenth-Century Britain*, London.

Mehta, Uday S. (1997). 'Liberal Strategies of Exclusion', in *Tensions of Empire: Colonial Cultures in a Bourgeois World*, ed. Frederick Cooper and Anne Laura Stoler, Berkeley, pp. 59—86.

Mendelson, Sara and Patricia Crawford (1998). *Women in Early Modern England 1550—1720*, Toronto.

Mendle, Michael J. (ed.) (2001). *The Putney Debates of 1647: The Army, the Levellers, and the English State*, Cambridge.

Mesnard, Pierre (1936). *L'Essor de la philosophie politique au XVIe siècle*, Paris.

Miller, John (1977). 'The Earl of Tyrconnel and James II's Irish Policy, 1685—1688', *Historical Journal* 20, pp. 802—23.

Miller, Peter N. (1994). *Defining the Common Good: Empire, Religion and Philosophy in Eighteenth-Century Britain*, Cambridge.

Mills, Charles (1997). *The Racial Contract*, Ithaca.

Miola, Robert S. (1983). *Shakespeare's Rome*, Cambridge.

Monahan, Arthur P. (1987). *Consent, Coercion and Limit: The Medieval Origins of Parliamentary Democracy*, Kingston and Montreal.

Moody, T. W., F. X. Martin and F. J. Byrne (eds.) (1976). *A New History of Ireland*, vol. 3: *Early Modern Ireland, 1534—1691*, Oxford.

Moore, James and Michael Silverthorne (1983). 'Gershom Carmichael and the Natural Jurisprudence Tradition in Eighteenth-Century Scotland', in

*Wealth and Virtue: The Shaping of Political Economy in the Scottish Enlightenment*, ed. Istvan Hont and Michael Ignatieff, Cambridge, pp. 73–87.

Morgan, Hiram (1993). *Tyrone's Rebellion: The Outbreak of the Nine Years' War in Tudor Ireland*, Woodbridge.

(ed.) (1999a). *Political Ideology in Ireland, 1541–1641*, Dublin.

(1999b). 'Giraldus Cambrensis and the Tudor Conquest of Ireland', in Morgan 1999a, pp. 22–44.

(ed.) (2004a). *The Battle of Kinsale*, Dublin.

(2004b). ' "Never any Realm Worse Governed": Queen Elizabeth and Ireland', *Transactions of the Royal Historical Society* 6th ser., 14, pp. 295–308.

Morrill, John (1980). *The Revolt of the Provinces: Conservatives and Radicals in the English Civil War*, London.

(1993). *The Nature of the English Revolution: Essays*, Harlow.

(1994). 'The English, the Scots and the British', in *Scotland and the Union*, ed. Patrick Hodge, Edinburgh, pp. 96–113.

(1999). 'The War(s) of the Three Kingdoms', in *The New British History: Founding a Modern State 1603–1715*, ed. Glenn Burgess, London, pp. 65–91.

(2005). *'Uneasy Lies a Head': Dynastic Crises in Tudor and Stewart Britain and Ireland, 1504–1746*, 2003 Stenton Lecture at the University of Reading, Reading.

Multamäki, Kustaa (1999). *Towards Great Britain: Commerce and Conquest in the Thought of Algernon Sidney and Charles Davenant*, Helsinki.

Muthu, Sankar (2003). *Enlightenment Against Empire*, Princeton.

Nelson, Eric (2004). *The Greek Tradition in Republican Thought*, Cambridge.

Norbrook, David (1987). '*Macbeth* and the Politics of Historiography', in *Politics of Discourse: The Literature and History of Seventeenth-Century England*, ed. Kevin Sharpe and Steven N. Zwicker, Berkeley, pp. 78–116.

(1996). 'The Emperor's New Body? *Richard II*, Ernst Kantorowicz, and the Politics of Shakespeare Criticism', *Textual Practice* 10, pp. 329–57.

(1999). *Writing the English Republic: Poetry, Rhetoric and Politics, 1627–1660*, Cambridge.

Northrop, F. S. C. (1947). 'Education for Intercultural Understanding', *The Journal of Higher Education* 18, pp. 171–81.

(1946). *The Meeting of East and West: An Inquiry Concerning World Understanding*, New York.

Nozick, Robert (1974). *Anarchy, State and Utopia*, Oxford.

Ó Buachalla, Breandán (1993). 'James our True King: the Ideology of Irish Royalism in the Seventeenth Century', in Boyce, Eccleshall and Geoghegan 1993, pp. 36–72.

(1996). *Aisling Ghéar: na Stíobhartaigh agus an tAos Léinn, 1603–1788*, Dublin.

O'Brien, Karen (1997). 'Protestantism and the Poetry of Empire', in *Culture and Society in Eighteenth-Century Britain*, ed. Jeremy Black and Jeremy Gregory, Manchester, pp. 146–62.

(1998). ' "Still at Home": Cowper's Domestic Empires', in *Early Romantics Perspectives in British Poetry from Pope to Wordsworth*, ed. Thomas Woodman, Basingstoke, pp. 134–47.

(1999). 'Imperial Georgic, 1660–1789', in *The Country and the City Revisited*, ed. Donna Landry, Joseph P. Ward and Gerald MacLean, Cambridge, pp. 160–79.

(2002). 'Poetry Against Empire: Milton to Shelley', *Proceedings of the British Academy* 117, pp. 269–96.

Ó Ciardha, Éamonn (1997). 'Tories and Moss-troopers in Scotland and Ireland in the Interregnum: A Political Dimension', in *The Celtic Dimensions of the British Civil Wars*, ed. John R. Young, Edinburgh, pp. 141–63.

(2002). *Ireland and the Jacobite Cause, 1685–1766*, Dublin.

Ó Cíosáin, Éamon (1994). 'Les Irlandais en Bretagne 1603–1780: "invasion", accueil, integration', in *Irlande et Bretagne, vingt siècles d'histoire*, ed. Catherine Laurent and Helen Davis, Rennes, pp. 152–66.

(2001). 'A Hundred Years of Irish Emigration to France, 1590–1688', in *The Irish in Europe, 1580–1815*, ed. Thomas O'Connor, Dublin, pp. 93–106.

O'Halloran, Clare (1989). 'Irish Recreations of the Gaelic Past: The Challenge of Macpherson's Ossian', *Past and Present* 124, pp. 69–95.

(2004). *Golden Ages and Barbarous Nations: Antiquarian Debate and Cultural Politics in Ireland, c. 1750–1800*, Cork.

Oakeshott, Michael (1933). *Experience and its Modes*, Cambridge.

(1955). 'Introduction', in Thomas Hobbes, *Leviathan*, ed. Michael Oakeshott, Oxford, pp. vii–lxvi.

(1975). *On Human Conduct*, Oxford.

(1983). *On History*, Totowa.

(1991). 'On The Activity of Being an Historian', in *Rationalism in Politics and other Essays*, ed. Timothy Fuller, Indianapolis, pp. 151–83.

Ohlmeyer, Jane (1993). *Civil War and Restoration in the Three Stuart Kingdoms: The Career of Randal Macdonnell, Marquis of Antrim, 1609–1683*, Cambridge.

(ed.) (2000). *Political Thought in Seventeenth-Century Ireland: Kingdom or Colony?*, Cambridge.

Ohlmeyer, Jane and Steven N. Zwicker (2006), 'John Dryden, the House of Ormond, and the Politics of Anglo-Irish Patronage', *The Historical Journal* 49(3), pp. 677–706.

Orr, D. Alan (2000). 'England, Ireland, Magna Carta and the Common Law: The Case of Connor Lord Maguire, Second Baron of Enniskillen', *Journal of British Studies* 39, pp. 389–421.

O'Scea, Ciaran (2004). 'Irish Emigration to Castile in the Opening Years of the Seventeenth Century', in *To and from Ireland: Planned Migration Schemes c. 1600–2000*, ed. Patrick J. Duffy and Gerry Moran, Dublin, pp. 17–38.

Ó Siochrú, Micheál (1999). *Confederate Ireland, 1642–1649*, Dublin.

(2005). 'Catholic Confederates and the Constitutional Relationship between Ireland and England', in *British Interventions in Early Modern Ireland*, ed. Ciaran Brady and Jane Ohlmeyer, Cambridge, pp. 207–29.

Pagano, Frank (1982). 'Introduction', in Edmund Burke, *A Vindication of Natural Society*, ed. Frank Pagano, Indianapolis, pp. xi–xxi.

Pagden, Anthony (1986). *The Fall of Natural Man: The American Indian and the Origins of Comparative Ethnology*, rev. edn, Cambridge.

(ed.) (1987a). *The Languages of Political Theory in Early-Modern Europe*, Cambridge.

(1987b). 'Introduction', in Pagden 1987a, Cambridge, pp. 1–17.

(1995). *Lords of All the World: Ideologies of Empire in Spain, Britain and France, c. 1500–c. 1800*, New Haven.

(ed.) (2002). *The Idea of Europe: From Antiquity to the European Union*, Cambridge.

(2003). 'Human Rights, Natural Rights and Europe's Imperial Legacy', *Political Theory* 31, pp. 171–99.

Palmer, Patricia (2001). *Language and Conquest in Early Modern Ireland: English Renaissance Literature and Elizabethan Imperial Expansion*, Cambridge.

Parekh, Bhikhu (1995). 'Liberalism and Colonialism: A Critique of Locke and Mill', in *The Decolonization of the Imagination*, ed. Jan Nederveen Pieterse and Bhikhu Parekh, London, pp. 81–98.

Pateman, Carole (1988). *The Sexual Contract*, Stanford.

(1989). *The Disorder of Women*, Stanford.

Patterson, Annabel (1989). *Shakespeare and the Popular Voice*, Oxford.

Pawlisch, Hans S. (1985). *Sir John Davies and the Conquest of Ireland: A Study in Legal Imperialism*, Cambridge.

Peck, Linda Levy (ed.) (1991). *The Mental World of the Jacobean Court*, Cambridge.

(1993). 'Kingship, Counsel and Law in Early Stuart Britain', in Pocock, Schochet and Schwoerer 1993, pp. 80–115.

Peltonen, Markku (1995). *Classical Humanism and Republicanism in English Political Thought, 1570–1640*, Cambridge.

Perry, Curtis (1997). *The Making of Jacobean Culture: James I and the Renegotiation of Elizabethan Literary Practice*, Cambridge.

Pettit, Philip (1997). *Republicanism: A Theory of Freedom and Government*, Oxford.

Pincus, Steven C. A. (1995). ' "Coffee Politicians Does Create": Coffeehouses and Restoration Political Culture', *Journal of Modern History* 67, pp. 807–34.

Pitts, Jennifer (2005). *A Turn to Empire: The Rise of Imperial Liberalism in Britain and France*, Princeton.

Pocock, J. G. A. (1971). *Politics, Language, and Time: Essays on Political Thought and History*, Chicago.

(1974). 'British History: A Plea for a New Subject', *New Zealand Journal of History* 8, pp. 3–21.

(1975a). 'British History: A Plea for a New Subject', *Journal of Modern History* 47, pp. 601–21.

(1975b). *The Machiavellian Moment: Florentine Political Thought and the Atlantic Republican Tradition*, Princeton.

(1982). 'The Limits and Divisions of British History: In Search of the Unknown Subject', *American Historical Review* 87, pp. 311–36.

(1985a). 'The History of British Political Thought: The Creation of a Center', *Journal of British Studies* 24, pp. 283–310.

(1985b). *Virtue, Commerce, and History: Essays on Political Thought and History, Chiefly in the Eighteenth Century*, Cambridge.

(1987a). *The Ancient Constitution and the Feudal Law: A Study of English Historical Thought in the Seventeenth Century: A Reissue with Retrospect*, rev. edn, Cambridge.

(1987b). 'Texts as Events: Reflections on the History of Political Thought', in *The Politics of Discourse: the Literature and History of Seventeenth-Century England*, ed. Kevin Sharpe and Steven N. Zwicker, Berkeley and Los Angeles, pp. 21–34.

(1992). 'Tangata Whenua and Enlightenment Anthropology', *New Zealand Journal of History* 26, pp. 28–53.

(1994). 'Two Kingdoms and Three Histories? Political Thought in British Contexts', in Mason 1994a, pp. 292–312.

(1995). 'Conclusion: Contingency, Identity, Sovereignty', in Grant and Stringer 1995, pp. 292–302.

(1999–). *Barbarism and Religion*, 4 vols. to date, Cambridge.

(2004). 'Quentin Skinner: The History of Politics and the Politics of History', *Common Knowledge* 10, pp. 532–50.

(2005). *The Discovery of Islands: Essays in British History*, Cambridge.

Pocock, J. G. A., with Gordon Schochet and Lois G. Schwoerer (eds.) (1993). *The Varieties of British Political Thought, 1500–1800*, Cambridge.

Pollock, Sir Fredrick (1903–1904). 'Locke's Theory of the State', *Proceedings of the British Academy* I, pp. 237–49.

Prior, James (1824). *Memoirs of the Life and Character of the Right Honorable Edmund Burke*, London.

Quint, David (1993). *Epic and Empire: Politics and Generic Form from Virgil to Milton*, Princeton.

Rackin, Phyllis (1990). *Stages of History: Shakespeare's English Chronicles*, Ithaca.

Rae, Thomas I. (1966). *The Administration of the Scottish Frontier, 1513–1603*, Edinburgh.

Rankin, Deana (2005). *Between Spenser and Swift: English Writing in Seventeenth-Century Ireland*, Cambridge.

Rawls, John (1971). *A Theory of Justice*, Cambridge, Mass.

(1993) *Political Liberalism*, New York.

(2000). *Lectures on the History of Moral Philosophy*, ed. Barbara Herman, Cambridge, Mass.

Raymond, Joad (2003). *Pamphlets and Pamphleteering in Early Modern Britain*, Cambridge.

Rebholz, Ronald A. (1971). *The Life of Fulke Greville, First Lord Brooke*, Oxford.

Rees, Joan (1971). *Fulke Greville, Lord Brooke, 1554–1628: A Critical Biography*, London.

Reese, Trevor R. (1963). *Colonial Georgia: A Study in British Imperial Policy in the Eighteenth-Century*, Athens, Ga.

Reynolds, Henry (1992). *The Law of the Land*, 2nd edn, Ringwood, NSW.

Reynolds, Susan (1990). *Kingdoms and Communities in Western Europe, 900–1300*, 2nd edn, Oxford.

Rhodes, Neil (2003). 'Shakespeare the Barbarian', in *Early Modern Civil Discourses*, ed. Jennifer Richards, Basingstoke, pp. 99–114.

Ricoeur, Paul (1981). 'What is a Text? Explanation and Interpretation', in *Hermeneutics and the Human Sciences: Essays on Language, Action and Interpretation*, ed. John B. Thompson, Cambridge, pp. 145–64.

(1984–1986). *Time and Narrative*, trans. Kathleen McLaughlin and David Pellauer, 3 vols., Chicago.

Riggs, David (1971). *Shakespeare's Heroical Histories: Henry VI and its Literary Tradition*, Cambridge, Mass.

Riley, P. W. J. (1978). *The Union of England and Scotland: An Episode in Anglo-Scottish Relations*, Manchester.

Robbins, Caroline (1959). *The Eighteenth Century Commonwealthman: Studies in the Transmission, Development and Circumstance of English Liberal Thought from the Restoration of Charles II until the War with the Thirteen Colonies*, Cambridge, Mass.

Robertson, John (ed.) (1995a). *A Union for Empire: Political Thought and the British Union of 1707*, Cambridge.

(1995b). 'An Elusive Sovereignty: The Course of the Union Debate in Scotland, 1698–1707', in Robertson 1995a, pp. 198–227.

Rothbard, Murray (1958). 'A Note on Burke's *Vindication of Natural Society*', *Journal of the History of Ideas* 19, pp. 114–18.

Russell, Conrad (1990). *The Causes of the English Civil War*, Oxford.

(1991). *The Fall of the British Monarchies, 1637–1642*, Oxford.

Russell, Gillian (2004). 'An "Entertainment of Oddities": Fashionable Sociability and the Pacific in the 1770s', in *A New Imperial History: Culture, Identity and Modernity in Britain, 1660–1840*, ed. Kathleen Wilson, Cambridge, pp. 48–70.

Sabine, George (1955). *A History of Political Theory*, New York.

Scanlon, Thomas (1998). *What We Owe to Each Other*, Cambridge, Mass.

Scheffler, Samuel (1982). *The Rejection of Consequentialism: A Philosophical Investigation of the Considerations Underlying Rival Moral Conceptions*, Oxford.

Schneewind, J. B. (1998). *The Invention of Autonomy: A History of Modern Moral Philosophy*, Cambridge.

(2005). 'Globalization and the History of Philosophy', *Journal of the History of Ideas* 66, pp. 169–78.

Schochet, Gordon, with Patricia Tatspaugh and Carol Brobeck (eds.) (1990–1993). *Proceedings of the Folger Institute Center for the History British Political Thought*, 6 vols., Washington, D.C.

(1999). 'Political Theory, The History of Political Thought and Intellectual History: Then and Again', Unpublished lecture delivered to the Department of Government, University of Texas, Austin.

Schwoerer, Lois G. (ed.) (1992). *The Revolution of 1688–1689: Changing Perspectives*, Cambridge.

Scott, David (2004). *Politics and War in the Three Stuart Kingdoms, 1637–49*, Basingstoke.

Scott, Joan Wallach (1996). *Only Paradoxes to Offer: French Feminists and the Rights of Man*, Cambridge, Mass.

Scott, Joan Wallach, and Debra Keates (eds.) (2001). *Schools of Thought: Twenty-Five Years of Interpretive Social Science*, Princeton.

Scott, Jonathan (1988). *Algernon Sidney and the English Republic, 1623–1677*, Cambridge.

(1991). *Algernon Sidney and the Restoration Crisis, 1677–1683*, Cambridge.

(2000). *England's Troubles: Seventeenth-Century English Political Instability in European Context*, Cambridge.

(2004). *Commonwealth Principles: Republican Writing of the English Revolution*, Cambridge.

Shapin, Steven and Simon Schaffer (1985). *Leviathan and the Air-Pump: Hobbes, Boyle, and the Experimental Life*, Princeton.

Sharpe, Kevin M. (2000). *Remapping Early Modern England: The Culture of Seventeenth-Century Politics*, Cambridge.

Sherman, William H. (1997). *John Dee: The Politics of Reading and Writing in the English Renaissance*, Amherst, Mass.

Silke, John J. (1955a). 'Later Relations between Primate Peter Lombard and Hugh O'Neill', *Irish Theological Quarterly* 22, pp. 15–30.

(1955b). 'Primate Lombard and James I', *Irish Theological Quarterly* 22, pp. 124–50.

Simmons, John (1992). *The Lockean Theory of Rights*, Princeton.

(1995). 'Historical Rights and Fair Shares', *Law and Philosophy* 14, pp. 149–84.

Simms, J. G. (1983). *William Molyneux of Dublin*, ed. Patrick H. Kelly, Dublin.

Skinner, Quentin (1969). 'Meaning and Understanding in the History of Ideas', *History and Theory* 8, pp. 3–53.

(1978a). *The Foundations of Modern Political Thought*, vol. 1: *The Renaissance*, Cambridge.

(1978b). *The Foundations of Modern Political Thought*, vol. 2: *The Age of Reformation*, Cambridge.

(1985). *The Return of Grand Theory in the Human Sciences*, Cambridge.

(1988). 'A Reply to My Critics', in *Meaning and Context: Quentin Skinner and his Critics*, ed. James Tully, Princeton, pp. 231–88.

(1996). *Reason and Rhetoric in the Philosophy of Hobbes*, Cambridge.

(1998). *Liberty Before Liberalism*, Cambridge.

(2002a). *Visions of Politics*, vol. 1: *Regarding Method*, Cambridge.

(2002b). *Visions of Politics*, vol. 2: *Renaissance Virtues*, Cambridge.

(2002c). *Visions of Politics*, vol. 3: *Hobbes and Civil Science*, Cambridge.

Slattery, Brian (1991). 'Aboriginal Sovereignty and Imperial Claims', *Osgoode Hall Law Journal* 29, pp. 681–703.

Smith, Bernard (1992). *Imagining the Pacific: In the Wake of the Cook Voyages*, New Haven.

Smith, Hilda L. (1997a). ' "A General War Amongst the Men . . . but None Amongst the Women": Political Differences Between Margaret and William Cavendish', in *Politics and the Political Imagination in Later Stuart Britain: Essays Presented to Lois Green Schwoerer*, ed. Howard Nenner, Rochester, NY, pp. 143–60.

(1997b) ' "Though it be the part of every good wife": Margaret Cavendish, Duchess of Newcastle', in *Women and History: Voices of Early Modern England*, ed. Valerie Frith, Concord, Ontario, pp. 119–44.

(ed.) (1998a). *Women Writers and the Early Modern British Political Tradition*, Cambridge.

(1998b). 'Women, Intellect, and Politics: Their Intersection in Seventeenth-Century England', in Smith 1998a, pp. 1–14.

Sommerville, J. P. (1986). *Politics and Ideology in England, 1603–1640*, London.

(1991). 'Absolutism and Royalism', in Burns and Goldie 1991, pp. 347–73.

(1996). 'English and European Political Ideas in the Early Seventeenth Century: Revision and the Case for Absolutism', *Journal of British Studies* 35, pp. 168–94.

Sommerville, Margaret (1995). *Sex and Subjection: Attitudes to Women in Early-Modern Society*, New York.

Spiller, Elizabeth (2004). *Science, Reading and Renaissance Literature: The Art of Making Knowledge, 1580–1670*, Cambridge.

Springborg, Patricia (2005). *Mary Astell: Theorist of Freedom from Domination*, Cambridge.

Stanlis, Peter (1958). *Edmund Burke and the Natural Law*, Ann Arbor.

(1967). 'Edmund Burke and the Scientific Rationalism of the Enlightenment', in *Edmund Burke: The Enlightenment and the Modern World*, ed. Peter Stanlis, Detroit, pp. 81–116.

Stevenson, David (1980). *Alasdair MacColla and the Highland Problem in the Seventeenth Century*, Edinburgh.

(1981). *Scottish Covenanters and Irish Confederates: Scottish-Irish Relations in the Mid-Seventeenth Century*, Belfast.

Stewart, Alan (1995). 'The Early Modern Closet Discovered', *Representations* 50, pp. 76–100.

Stone, Lawrence (1965). *Social Change and Revolution in England, 1540–1640*, London.
   (1972). *The Causes of the English Revolution, 1529–1642*, London.
Straznicky, Marta (2004). *Privacy, Playreading, and Women's Closet Drama, 1550–1700*, Cambridge.
Syme, Ronald (1958). *Tacitus*, 2 vols., Oxford.
Tarlton, Charles D. (1973). 'Historicity, Meaning, and Revisionism in the Study of Political Thought', *History and Theory* 12, pp. 307–28.
Taylor, A. E. (1938). 'The Ethical Doctrine of Hobbes', *Philosophy* 13, pp. 406–24.
Taylor, Barbara (2003). *Mary Wollstonecraft and the Feminist Imagination*, Cambridge.
Taylor, Barbara and Sarah Knott (eds.) (2005). *Women, Gender and the Enlightenment*, Basingstoke.
Thomas, Keith (1996). 'James Edward Oglethorpe, 1696–1785: A Lecture Given on the 5th October, 1996': http://www.cviog.uga.edu/Projects/jeo300/lecture.htm, accessed 22 October 2005.
Thomas, Richard F. (2001). *Virgil and the Augustan Reception*, Cambridge.
Tierney, Brian (1997). *The Idea of Natural Rights*, Atlanta.
Toews, John E. (1987). 'Intellectual History after the Linguistic Turn: The Autonomy of Meaning and the Irreducibility of Experience', *American Historical Review* 92, pp. 879–907.
Travers, Robert (forthcoming). *Ideology and Empire in Eighteenth Century India: The British in Bengal, 1757–1793*, Cambridge.
Trevelyan, G. M. (1904). *England Under the Stuarts*, London.
   (1939). *The English Revolution, 1688–1689*, London.
Tuck, Richard (1979). *Natural Rights Theories: Their Origin and Development*, Cambridge.
   (1987). 'The "Modern" Theory of Natural Law', in Pagden 1987a, pp. 99–119.
   (1989). *Hobbes*, Oxford.
   (1993). *Philosophy and Government, 1572–1651*, Cambridge.
   (1994). 'Rights and Pluralism', in *Philosophy in an Age of Pluralism: The Philosophy of Charles Taylor in Question*, ed. James Tully, Cambridge, pp. 159–70.
   (1999). *The Rights of War and Peace: Political Thought and the International Order from Grotius to Kant*, Oxford.
Tully, James (1979). *A Discourse of Property: John Locke and His Adversaries*, Cambridge.
   (1981). 'Current Thinking about Sixteenth and Seventeenth Century Political Theory', *The Historical Journal* 24, pp. 475–84.
   (1993a). 'Placing the *Two Treatises*', in *Political Discourse in Early Modern Britain*, ed. Nicholas Phillipson and Quentin Skinner, Cambridge, pp. 253–80.
   (1993b). 'The *Two Treatises* and Aboriginal Rights', in *An Approach to Political Philosophy: Locke in Contexts*, Cambridge, pp. 137–76.

Turberville, A. S. (1938). *A History of Welbeck Abbey and Its Owners*, vol. 1: *1539–1755*, London.

Tutino, Stefania (2005). 'Naturalized Texts and Denatured Tyrants: The Huguenot *Vindiciae Contra Tyrannos* (1579) in Seventeenth-Century England', unpublished paper presented at the William Andrews Clark Library conference, 'Naturalized Texts/Textes naturalisés: Translations, Adaptations, Influences', Los Angeles, CA, 4–5 June 2005.

Underdown, David (1985). *Revel, Riot, and Rebellion: Popular Politics and Culture in England, 1603–1660*, Oxford.

　(1996). *A Freeborn People: Politics and the Nation in Seventeenth-Century England*, Oxford.

van Gelderen, Martin and Quentin Skinner (eds.) (2002). *Republicanism: A Shared European Heritage*, 2 vols., Cambridge.

Veit, Walter (ed.) (1972). *Captain James Cook: Image and Impact*, Melbourne.

Vickery, Amanda (1993). 'Golden Age to Separate Spheres? A Review of the Categories and Chronology of English Women's History', *The Historical Journal* 36, pp. 383–414.

Waldron, Jeremy (2002). *God, Locke, and Equality: Christian Foundations of John Locke's Political Thought*, Cambridge.

　(2003). 'Indigeneity? First Peoples and Last Occupancy', *New Zealand Journal of Public and International Law*, 1, pp. 55–82.

Wallace, John (1968). *Destiny His Choice: The Loyalism of Andrew Marvell*, Cambridge.

Warrender, Howard (1957). *The Political Philosophy of Hobbes*, Oxford.

Weaver, John C. (2003). *The Great Land Rush and the Making of the Modern World, 1650–1900*, Montreal.

Webb, Stephen Saunders (1979). *The Governors-General: The English Army and the Definition of the Empire, 1569–1681*, Chapel Hill.

Weimann, Robert (1978). *Shakespeare and the Popular Tradition in the Theater*, ed. Robert Schwartz, Baltimore.

Weinbrot, Howard (1993). *Britannia's Issue: The Rise of British Literature from Dryden to Ossian*, Cambridge.

Wernham, R. B. (1984). *After the Armada: Elizabethan England and the Struggle for Western Europe, 1588–1595*, Oxford.

Weston, Corinne Comstock and Janelle Renfrow Greenberg (1981). *Subjects and Sovereigns: The Grand Controversy over Legal Sovereignty in Stuart England*, Cambridge.

Weston, John C., Jr. (1958). 'The Ironic Purpose of Burke's *Vindication* Vindicated', *Journal of the History of Ideas* 19, pp. 435–41.

Wiles, David (1987). *Shakespeare's Clown: Actor and Text in the Elizabethan Playhouse*, Cambridge.

Williams, Abigail (2005). *Poetry and the Creation of a Whig Literary Culture, 1681–1714*, Oxford.

Williams, Glyndwr (1998). 'The Pacific: Exploration and Exploitation', in *The Oxford History of the British Empire*, vol. 2: *The Eighteenth Century*, ed. P. J. Marshall, Oxford, pp. 552–75.

Williams, Gweno (2002). 'Margaret Cavendish, *A True Relation of My Birth, Breeding and Life*', in *A Companion to Early Modern Women's Writing*, ed. Anita Pacheco, Oxford, pp. 165–76.

Williams, Robert (1997). *Linking Arms Together: American Indian Treaty Visions of Law and Peace, 1600–1800*, New York.

Willman, Robert (1974). 'The Origins of "Whig" and "Tory" in English Political Language', *The Historical Journal* 17, pp. 247–64.

Wilson, Kathleen (2003). *The Island Race: Englishness, Empire, and Gender in the Eighteenth Century*, London and New York.

Winch, Peter (1990). *The Idea of a Social Science and its Relation to Philosophy*, 2nd edn, London.

Wittgenstein, Ludwig (1958). *Philosophical Investigations*, trans. G. E. M. Anscombe, 2nd edn, Oxford.

Wolin, Sheldon (1969). 'Political Theory as a Vocation', *American Political Science Review* 63, pp. 1062–82.

Wood, Tanya (2004). 'Margaret Cavendish, Duchess of Newcastle, *The Convent of Pleasure* (1668)', in *Reading Early Modern Women: An Anthology of Texts in Manuscript and Print, 1550–1700*, ed. Helen Ostovich and Elizabeth Sauer, New York and London, pp. 435–7.

Woodman, A. J. (1998). *Tacitus Reviewed*, Oxford.

Woolrych, Austin (2002). *Britain in Revolution, 1625–1660*, Oxford.

Woolf, Daniel R. (1990). *The Idea of History in Early Stuart England*, London.

Woolf, Virginia (2001). *A Room of One's Own*, ed. Shari Wattling, Peterborough, Ontario.

Wootton, David (ed.) (1996). *Republicanism, Liberty, and Commercial Society, 1649–1776*, Stanford.

Worden, Blair (1981). 'Classical Republicanism and the Puritan Revolution', in *History and Imagination: Essays in Honour of H. R. Trevor-Roper*, ed. Hugh Lloyd-Jones, Valerie Pearl and Blair Worden, London, pp. 182–200.

(1985). 'The Commonwealth Kidney of Algernon Sidney', *Journal of British Studies* 24, pp. 1–40.

(1994). 'Ben Jonson among the Historians', in *Culture and Politics in Early Stuart England*, ed. Kevin Sharpe and Peter Lake, Basingstoke, pp. 67–90.

(2002). 'Republicanism, Regicide and Republic: The English Experience', in van Gelderen and Skinner 2002, I, pp. 307–27.

Woudhuysen, Henry (1996). *Sir Philip Sidney and the Circulation of Manuscripts, 1558–1641*, Oxford.

Wright, Joanne H. (2004). *Origin Stories in Political Thought: Discourses on Gender, Power and Citizenship*, Toronto.

Zwicker, Steven N. (1984). *Politics and Language in Dryden's Poetry: The Arts of Disguise*, Princeton.

(1998). 'Reading the Margins: Politics and the Habits of Appropriation', in *Refiguring Revolutions: Aesthetics and Politics from the English Revolution to the Romantic Revolution*, ed. Kevin Sharpe and Steven N. Zwicker, Berkeley and London, pp. 101–15.

Zwicker, Steven N. and David Bywaters (1989). 'Politics and Translation: The English Tacitus of 1698', *Huntington Library Quarterly* 52, pp. 319–46.

Zwierlein, Anne-Julia (2002). 'Pandemic Panoramas: Surveying Milton's "vain empires" in the Long Eighteenth Century', in *Milton and the Terms of Liberty*, ed. Graham Parry and Joad Raymond, Cambridge, pp. 191–214.

# Index